the blue who's who

compiled by tony matthews

**officially endorsed by
birmingham city football club**

a britespot publication

First Published in Great Britain by
Britespot Publishing Solutions Limited, Chester Road, Cradley Heath, West Midlands, B64 6AB

March 2003
© Tony Matthews 2003

ISBN 1 904103 02 2

Design and layout © Britespot Publishing Solutions Limited.
All pictures © Empics Ltd

Printed and bound in Great Britain by
Cromwell Press Ltd, Aintree Avenue, White Horse Business Park, Trowbridge, Wiltshire BA14 0XB

Acknowledgments

I must say a special big 'thank you' to my good friend David Drage for once again adding to and clarifying the statistics and also confirming several of the facts & figures contained in this book. I also acknowledge the assistance afforded to me by David Barber *(of the Football Association)* and Zoe Ward *(FA Premier League)* and Roger Baker, Ivan Barnsley, Andrew Henry and Dafydd Williams for the efforts they put in initially, Karen Salt *(from Chudleigh)* and my step-daughter Cathie Smith *(from Tamworth)* for their finger-tapping work regarding players' fact-files. Thank you, too - and 'sorry' darling for the inconvenience caused - to my loving wife Margaret who once again has had to put up without me for hours upon end whilst I've been sat thrashing away on the computer keyboard, thumbing through old reference books, matchday programmes and soccer magazines, checking and re-checking the thousands of statistics and stories as well as travelling up and down the country from sunny Devon.

Last but by no means least I must give a sincere thank you to everyone who has worked on the book at Britespot Publishing Solutions Limited especially to Roger Marshall, Paul Burns, Linda Perkins and Chris Russell.

Statistical Information

The statistics for each player's profile include appearances made and goals scored in the following competitions:

- Premiership matches: 2003
- FA Cup fixtures: 1881-2003
- Inter-Cities Fairs Cup competition: 1956-61
- Football League matches: 1892-2003 (Divisions 1, 2 & 3)
- Football League Cup games: 1960-2003
- Football Alliance: 1889-92

Test Matches, Play-Offs, Texaco Cup, Anglo-Italian & Anglo-Scottish Tournaments, Full Members Cup, Simod Cup, Leyland DAF Trophy, Autoglass Trophy, Auto-Windscreen Shield, United Counties League, etc etc.

Bibliography

I have referred to several books to clarify certain relevant statistics including facts and figures, individual players' details and, indeed, stories and match reports from past seasons regarding Birmingham City FC. There is some conflicting information in these sources and we have made judgement as to which is likely to be correct, here is a list:

- Association Football & The Men Who Made It
- The Encyclopaedia of Association Football 1969
- FA Official Yearbooks: 1951-2000
- Football League Players' records: 1888-1939 (M Joyce)
- Footballers' (PFA) Factfile (B J Hugman/AFS) 1995-2002
- Where Are They Now? (A Pringler & N Fissler) 1996
- AFS Who's Who: 1902, 1903, 1907 & 1909
- English Internationals Who's Who: 1872-1972
- Football League Directory: 1985-89
- The PFA Premier & Football League Players' Records: 1946-98
- Rothmans Yearbook (Vols. 1-32) 1970-2002
- Birmingham City - Blues Heroes In Action: 1996-98

Magazines Etc...

- AFS Football Recollections & AFS Bulletins (various)
- Blues Reviews & supporters handbooks (various)
- Blues 'home' programmes (various) 1925-2003
- Blues 'home' programmes (various) 1925-2003
- Blues 'away' programmes (various) 1925-2003

I have also referred to several newspapers (especially those from the Midlands including the Birmingham Evening Mail, Sport Argus and Express & Star), also other club histories & Who's Who publications, certain autobiographies and biographies of individual players and managers and quite a number of football reference books in general for confirmation of various factual points.

CONTENTS

I am positively certain that all supporters of Birmingham City Football Club, young and old, male and female, have, at some time or another, been involved in an argument concerning a player, whether from the past or present!

I know from experience that in numerous pubs, on the work floor, at various grounds etc... discussions have taken place about certain players (and a few managers) who have been associated with Blues down the years. Some of these for sure have turned into heated arguments, with questions being asked but no definite answer given. As a result wagers have been laid as to who is right and who is wrong!

Some questions revolve round the obvious, such as...When did he join the club and where from?...How many goals did he score?...Where did go after leaving the Blues?...Did he play for England (or Wales etc)?... Was he a defender or midfielder, a left or right-winger?...Did he play in a Cup Final?

Hopefully this elaborated Who's Who can answer most, if not all of those questions, as well as offering you a lot more information besides. It will also satisfy that laudable curiosity without a shadow of doubt.

On the following pages you will find multitudinous authentic personal details of every single player who has appeared for Blues in a competitive League and Cup match from October 1881 (when the club first entered the FA Cup) up to and including the first few matches at the start of the long-awaited 2002-03 Premiership season) and there are details too on several footballers who guested for the club during the two World War periods (1915-19 and 1939-46) There is also information about the men who have managed Blues down the years and there have been a quite a few, including five during the 1990s.

For easy reference, all personnel have been listed in A-Z order, with the date and place of birth and death given, if clarified, although occasionally it has only been possible to ascertain a certain year with regards to when he was actually born and when he died. In some instances the date of death has not been included at all, although the word deceased has been added as an alternative Also included in the pen-picture portraits are details of the junior and non-League clubs that player served, any transfer fees involved (if known), honours won at club and international level, plus the respective senior appearance and goalscoring records (for Blues) which appears at the head of each individual players' write-up. An asterisk (i.e *) alongside any figures, indicates that the player was still adding to his appearance and/or goals tallies at the time the book was published.

Virtually throughout this book, the name of the club - Birmingham City (previously known as Small Heath Alliance, Small Heath and Birmingham) - is referred to as Blues. Very few abbreviations have been used, but among the more common ones are the obvious: FC (Football Club), FAC (FA Cup), FLC (Football League Cup), apps (appearances), sub (substitute).

Where a single year appears in the text (when referring to an individual player_s career), this indicates, in most cases, the second half of a season: i.e. 1975 is 1974-75. However, when the figures (dates) such as 1975-80 appear, this means seasons 1975-76 to 1979-80 inclusive and not 1974-80.

If you spot any discrepancies, errors, even omissions, I would appreciate it very much if you could contact me (via the publishers) so that all can rectified in any future publications appertaining to Birmingham City Football Club. If you have anything to add, this, too, would be welcome as people tend to reveal unknown facts from all sources when football is the topic of conversation.

NB - Several supporters have verbally stated that there were errors, omissions, discrepancies etc. in my previous Blues books - but very few have come forward with a list of what they were. I have diligently checked through several 'other' reference books (including a number of similar Who's Who publications which have been produced on other clubs) and I am now hopeful that most, if not all, the facts and figures revealed on the forthcoming pages are correct.

A

ABBOTT Walter

Inside-left: 85 Apps. 66 goals

Born: Small Heath, Birmingham, 7 December 1877.

Died: Birmingham, 1 February 1941.

Career: Rosewood Victoria, BLUES (April 1896), Everton (July 1899), Burnley (July 1908), BLUES (July 1910). Retired in May 1911.

Club honours: Everton: FA Cup winners 1906, runners-up 1907.

Representative honours: England (one full cap); Football League XI (4).

Water Abbot holds the Blues scoring record for most goals in a season - 42 in 1898-99 with 34 coming in 34 League games - and he netted on his debut against Manchester City in a Test Match. A strong-running player with a cracking shot, Abbott was converted into a wing-half at Everton, yet still hit 37 goals in a over 300 games. Following his return to Birmingham he had only one more game before retiring with a knee injury and thereafter work for some years in the motor industry at Longbridge. His son, also named Walter, played for Grimsby Town in 1920-21.

ABLETT, Gary Ian

Defender: 116+8 apps, 2 goals

Born: Liverpool, 19 November 1965.

Career: Liverpool (apprentice 1981, professional November 1983), Derby County (on loan, , January 1985), Hull City (on loan, , September 1986), Everton (£750,000, January 1992), Sheffield United (on loan, , March 1996), BLUES (£390,000, June 1996), Wycombe Wanderers (on loan, , December 1999), Scunthorpe United (on trial), Blackpool (free transfer, January 2000). Retired in May 2001.

Club honours: Liverpool: Division 1 champions 1988, 1990; FA Cup winners 1989; FA Charity Shield winners 1988. Everton: FA Cup winners 1995, Charity Shield winners 1995

Representative Honours: England (one 'B' cap, one Under-21 cap).

Composed left-sided defender, cool and calm under pressure, Gary Ablett amassed over 300 appearances in total for the two Merseyside clubs. Injuries began to interrupt his performances during the latter stages of his days at St Andrew's.

ADAMS, Richard

Inside-right: 2 apps

Born Quinton, Birmingham, 1866.

Career: Quinton Victoria, Wordsley (Stourbridge), Calthorpe, BLUES (season 1887-88), Calthorpe FC (1888-89).

Dick Adams joined Blues for one season from the Calthorpe Club from Edgbaston and had a respectable scoring record in friendly matches whilst he remained in the side.

ADEBOLA, Bamberdele

Striker: 102 + 50 apps, 41 goals

Born: Lagos, Nigeria, 23 June 1975

Career: Crewe Alexandra (trainee, July 1991, professional June 1993), BLUES (£1 million, February 1998 - June 2002), Oldham Athletic (on loan, March-April 2002), Crystal Palace (on trial, July-August 2002, signed on free transfer, September 2002).

Club honours: Blues: League Cup runners-up 2001

Dele Adebola, a powerful, forceful player, 6ft 3ins tall and 12st 9lbs in weight, was top-scorer for Crewe in 1996-97, helping them reach the Nationwide League Division One for the first time in the club's history. Scouts and managers from all over the country took note of his achievements and in February 1998, having taken his tally of goals to 46 in 152 appearances for the Gresty Road club, Adebola was snapped up by Blues boss Trevor Francis. He became an instant hit with the St Andrew's fans as he rattled in five more goals in his first five outings. His pace, power and sheer strength, his ability in the air and on the ground (he has a tremendous left foot) makes him a fearsome opponent. Indeed, most defenders know they've been in a game after facing him. A hamstring injury sidelined him for the second half of 1998-99 but he still managed 17 goals, and the following season again did the business when helping Blues reach the First Division play-offs for the second time running. Adebola, who has scored over 40 goals in more than 150 appearances for Blues was all set to leave the club for the Spanish side Las Palmas in a £1.2 million deal in July 2000, but the transfer fell through on medical grounds.

ADEY, George William

Wing-half/inside-forward: 79 apps. 2 goals

Born: Handsworth, Birmingham, 1869.

Now deceased.

Career: Nineveh Road School (Handsworth), Bournbrook FC, Stourbridge, BLUES (1898), Kettering Town (1902).

Described in the local press as a not brilliant player, George Adey was a willing worker with a reputation for being a hard nut to crack. He was very popular at Kettering after being moved into the half back line, where he was persistent in his efforts and strong in defence.

ADLINGTON, James H

Wing-forward: 6 apps. 4 goals

Born Shifnal, May 1872

Now deceased.

Career: Shifnal County School, Ironbridge FC (1892), BLUES (August 1895), Berwick Rangers of Worcester (June 1896), Stourport Swifts (1897).

A fast raiding forward with an eye for goal, Jimmy Adlington was surprisingly released after a fairly successful 1894-95 season with Blues.

AINSCOW, Alan

Midfielder: 121+4 apps. 22 goals
Born: Bolton, 15 July 1953.
Career: Blackpool (apprentice June 1969, professional
July 1971), BLUES (July 1971, Everton August 1981),
Barnsley (on loan, November 1982), Eastern FC in
Hong Kong (1983), Wolverhampton Wanderers (August
1984), Blackburn Rovers (December 1985), Rochdale
(June 1989), Horwich RMI (August 1990), Flint Town
United (July 1991), Ellesmere Town (coach, 1992-93).
Club honours: Blues: Division Two promotion 1980
Representative Honours: England (Youth caps).
Ainscow was a key figure in Blues' 1980 promotion race,
when his low, hard crosses led to many important goals.
He made 192 League appearances for Blackpool, and was
close to the 500 mark in League appearances when he
left Rochdale.

ALLEN, Frederick

Outside-right: 3 apps
Born: Hockley, Birmingham, July 1860.
Died: Birmingham circa 1926
Career: Spring Hill Methodists, BLUES (1890-92).
Fred Allen is a little known figure in the club's history, a
fragile forward whose career with Blues seemed to have
been limited to a brief spell when the team were playing
in the Football Alliance (pre-League days).

ALLEN, Gary

Forward: 1 app
Born: Hillingdon, 1955.
Career: Hillingdon Boys, BLUES (apprentice June 1971,
professional 1973), Wimbledon (July 1975), Carshalton
Athletic, Dulwich Hamlet, Boreham Wood, Hendon.
Alan was a prolific goalscorer in schools and youth
football but his career was hit by injury shortly after he
had signed professional forms for Blues. He fought back
to earn a first-team outing at Ayr United in the Texaco
Cup before he was given a free transfer in 1975.

ALLEN, George Henry

Full-back: 165 apps
Born: Small Heath, Birmingham, 23 January 1930.
Career: Coventry City (amateur), BLUES (June amateur
1952, professional November 1952), Torquay United
(January 1962), Bideford Town (1965).
George Allen was a good, solid defender, whose early
first-team chances were restricted due to the brilliance of
the Hall-Green partnership. After the tragic death of
Hall, Allen made the left-back position his own until he
suffered a fractured skull.

ANDERSON, Geoffrey Thomas

Outside-right: 1 App.
Born: Sheerness, 26 November 1944
Career: Canterbury Schools, Ramsgate (July 1960),

BLUES (December 1962), Mansfield Town (May 1964),
Lincoln City (July 1966), Brentford (August 1967).
Hastings United September 1967).
He was one of a trio of youngsters given their debuts at
Manchester United in an attempt to boost the Blues
flagging fortunes. Birmingham won that game but the
occasion proved too much for Geoff Anderson who was
never selected again

ANDERSON, George Edward

Outside-left: 80 apps. 10 goals.
Born: Sunderland, 1881. Now deceased.
Career: Sunderland Schools, Sunderland Albion (on
trial), Sunderland Royal Rovers, BLUES (August 1905),
Brentford (August 1909-May 1912), Aberdeen
(season 1912-13)
'Nosey' Anderson was a winger standing 5ft 8ins and
weighing 11st 4lb, who supported his home-town club as
a boy. Sunderland didn't sign him, however, and he
usually reserved his best performances for matches
against them. After leaving Blues he played 88 games for
Brentford, scoring six goals

ARCHER, Arthur

Full-back: 170 apps. 3 goals
Born: Ashby-de-La-Zouch, November 1877. Died: 1940
Career: Burton St Edmonds (1892-93), Tutbury
Hampton (1893-95), Swadlincote Town (January 1895),
Burton Wanderers (September 1895), BLUES (£50,
August 1897), New Brompton (£40, March 1902),
Wingfield House (April 1903), QPR (August 1903),
Tottenham Hotspur (guest, 1903-05), Norwich City
(August 1905), Brighton & Hove Albion (June 1907),
Millwall (August 1908). Retired summer 1909; Coach in
Germany (1910-12), Ghent (1912-14 & 1920-21), in
Italy (1921), in Belgium (1922-24) and with
Watford (1924-25)
Club honours: Blues: Division Two runners-up 1901.
Arthur Archer was an imposing figure, one of the
toughest defenders of his era. He drew up a fine
understanding with first Frank Lester and then William
Pratt. He had five excellent seasons with Blues and after
leaving the club he made 83 appearances for Norwich
before linking up with Brighton.

ARMSTRONG, Kenneth Charles

Centre-half: 69 Apps. one goal
Born: Bridgnorth, 31 January 1959
Career: Beith Juniors, Kilmarnock (June 1977),
Southampton (£90,000, June 1983). Notts County (on
loan, March-April 1984), BLUES (£60,000 August
1984), Walsall (£10,000, February 1986). Retired

through injury in November 1986.

Despite his English birthplace, Ken Armstrong was in every way a Scot, born whilst his father was working for the Ministry of Defence. Tall and commanding in their shared Armstrong sometimes appeared somewhat clumsy on the ground. He broken ankle in his first training session with Walsall and never played again. Holder of a Degree in marketing and mathematics, he later took employment as a prison social worker.

ASHLEY, Kevin Mark

Right-back: 65+1 apps. one goal
Born: Kings Heath, Birmingham 31 December 1968
Career: Wheelers Lane School, BLUES (YTS June 1984, apprentice July 1985, professional December 1986) so, Wolverhampton Wanderers (£500,000 September 1990). Norwich City (on loan, March 1990-94), Peterborough United (August 1994).

Kevin Ashley was another in a line of good, young full-backs brought up through the youth ranks, only to be sold on reaching maturity. He was a fast, hard-taxing player, particularly strong on the overlap.

ASHURST, Elias

Full-back: 70 apps. one goal
Born: Willington, County Durham, 28 December 1901.
Died: Winton, 7 December 1927
Career: Willington FC, Ashington, Shildon FC (1919), Stanley United (1920), BLUES (January 1922). Retired in the summer of 1926 through illness.

During his heyday Eli Ashurst, who was 5ft 11in tall and tipped the scales at 11st 6lb, was a tough full-back as one could wish to see, although he could also be used in attack with some effect. His declining health led to an early retirement, followed shortly afterwards by his untimely death. Ashurst's younger brother, William, played for West Bromwich Albion, Notts County and England, also as a full-back.

ASTALL, Gordon

Outside-right: 271 apps. 67 goals
Born: Horwich, 22 September 1927.
Career: Royal Marines, Southampton (amateur), Bolton Wanderers (trial), Plymouth Argyle (professional, November 1947), BLUES (£14,000, October 1953), Torquay United (July 1961). Retired in May 1963 and settled in the Torbay area, later coaching up Upton Vale FC while working for an insurance company.

Club honours: Plymouth Argyle: Division Three South champions 1952; Blues: Division Two champions 1955, FA Cup runners-up 1956, Fairs Cup runners-up 1958.

Representative honours: England (2 full caps, one 'B' cap); Football League XI (1).

Sturdy in build and difficult to stop when on the run, Astall could play equally well on either wing but usually preferred the right flank. He scored 42 goals in 188 League games for the Pilgrims before settling in quickly at St Andrew's and was a key figure in Blues' promotion-winning side of 1955. Astall scored in each of his two full internationals for England and during a fine career netted over 100 goals, a fine return for a winger.

ASTON, James

Inside-forward: 61 apps, 22 goals
Born: Walsall, June 1877.
Died: West Bromwich, February 1934.
Career: Walsall White Star, Fullbrook Saints, Willenhall Pickwick, Bloxwich Strollers, Wednesfield, Walsall (1896-98), Woolwich Arsenal (May 1899), BLUES (August 1900), Doncaster Rovers (July 1902), Walsall, Bilston United (season 1904-05), Walsall, Blakenhall St Luke's, Walsall Wood.

Jack 'Soldier' Aston was an efficient and plucky goalscorer who hit three goals in 11 League games for Arsenal before joining Blues. His elder brother, Jack, played centre-half for Wolves.

ATHERTON, Peter

Defender: 13 apps.
Born: Orrell, Merseyside, 6 April 1970
Career: Wigan Athletic (trainee, June 1986, professional February 1988), Coventry City (£300,000, August 1991), Sheffield Wednesday (£800,000, June 1994), Bradford City (free transfer, July 2000), BLUES (on loan, February-May 2001).

Representative honours: England (Schoolboy, one Under-21 cap)

An experienced defender, strong and solid (weighing almost 14st) whose strengths are his tackling and positional sense, Peter Atherton had already accumulated more than 550 senior appearances before he joined Blues on loan from Bradford at the end of the 2000-01 season, signed by manager Trevor Francis as the race for the play-offs gathered pace.

ATHERSMITH, William Charles

Outside-right or left: 100 apps. 13 goals
Born: Bloxwich, 10 May 1872.
Died: Shifnal, 18 September 1910
Career: Walsall Road School, Bloxwich Wanderers (1887), Bloxwich Strollers (1888), Unity Gas Depot FC (1890), Aston Villa (February 1891), BLUES (June 1901). Involved in an unsanctioned tour to Germany in 1905 for which he was suspended. Associated with Bloxwich Strollers (season 1906-07) although he was still under ban and did not play, retiring in May 1907.

Later served as Grimsby Town trainer (June 1907 to May 1909).

Club honours: Villa: Division One champions 1894, 1896, 1897, 1899, 1900; FA Cup winners 1895, 1897; runners-up 1892.

Representative honours: England (12 full caps); Football League XI (9).

Charlie Athersmith was one of the game's fastest winners during the 1890's when he was in his prime playing for Aston Villa and earning the princely sum of £6-a-week. He could centre the ball with unerring precision and could outwit full-back by sheer ball wizardry as well as pace. He was spotted by Villa playing for Unity Gas Depot FC for whom he once scored seven goals in a game from the wing. He quickly rose to the top, going on to win every honour in the game. Athersmith was a vital cog in the Villa at set-up when the League and Cup double was achieved in 1896-97 and in all he scored 86 goals in 310 appearances in the claret and blue strip. It is reported that in one game when it poured with rain, Athersmith ran down the touch-line holding up an umbrella borrowed from a spectator. He died after a short illness. He was the uncle of Ernest Victor Wright, who between the wars played in the forward-line for Liverpool.

ATKINS, Arthur Walter

Centre-half: 105 apps.

Born: Tokyo, 21 February 1925.

Died: Sutton Coldfield 7 January 1988.

Career: Erdington Boys, Paget Rangers, BLUES (August 1948, professional November 1948), Shrewsbury Town (1954). Played non-League football 1956-58.

Arthur Atkins was an old-fashioned centre-half who specialised in the goalmouth clearances and he held the number 5 spot at St Andrew's prior to the emergence of Trevor Smith. Although born in the Far East (his parents were on business there) he was educated in Erdington and was discovered by Blues playing in the Birmingham suburban youth and old boys AFA League. Walsall were keen to acquire him, but Blues got in first and he did a fine job during his stay at St Andrew's, especially in 1950-51 when Blues reached the FA Cup semi-finals.

ATKINS, Ian Leslie

Midfielder: 114+3 apps. 9 goals

Born: Sheldon, Birmingham, 16 January 1957

Career: Sheldon Heath School, Leafield Athletics (Central Warwickshire Boys League), Shrewsbury Town (apprentice June 1973), professional January 1975), Sunderland (August 1982), Everton (£70,000, November 1984), Ipswich Town (£100,000, September 1985), BLUES (on loan, March 1988, signing permanently for £50,000, April 1988), Colchester United (player-manager 1990-91), BLUES (assistant-manager 1991-92), Cambridge United (player-manager December 1992-

May 1993), Sunderland (assistant-manager July-November 1993), Doncaster Rovers (manager, January-July 1994), Solihull Borough (guest player, July 1994), Redditch United (as a player, August-December 1994), Northampton Town (manager January 1995 to May 1999), Chester City (manager July 1999 to May 2000), Carlisle United (manager season 2000-01), Oxford United (manager, November 2001). Briefly, in 2001, he was also an occasional match summariser for Sky Sport (football).

Club honours: Shrewsbury: Division Three champions & Welsh Cup winners 1979.

Ian Atkins was a competitive player with a ferocious tackle who was brought to inject some much-needed bite into a light weight Blues mid-field full stock he enjoyed 15 years in top-class football (1975-90) during which time he served with five different clubs, amassing in excess of 550 League appearances. He played in 314 senior games and scored 64 goals for Shrewsbury alone. After his return to St Andrew's, he turned out against Peterborough before his registration had been completed, an offence for which Blues were fined £10,000. He resigned as Chester boss after relegation to the Football Conference in 2000.

AULD, Robert

Outside-left: 147 apps. 31 goals

Born: Maryhill, Glasgow, 23 March 1938

Career: Springbrook School, Partick Thistle Boys Club, Panmure Thistle, Maryhill Harp, Celtic (professional March 1955), Dumbarton (on loan, October 1956 to April 1957), BLUES (£15,000, April 1961), Celtic (£12,000, summer 1965), Hibernian (May 1971, coach at Easter Road season 1973-74), Partick Thistle (manager July 1974), Hibernian (manager November 1980 to September 1981), Hamilton Academicals (manager, January 1982 to January 1983), Partick Thistle (manager July 1986), Dumbarton (manager, January 1988).

Club honours: Celtic: European Cup winners 1967, runners-up 1970, World Club Championship 1968, Scottish League Division One champions 1966-67-68 & 1970, Scottish Cup winners 1965, 1967, 1969, runners-up 1970, Scottish League Cup winners 1967-68-69-70; Blues: Football League Cup winners 1963, Fairs Cup runners-up 1961

Representative honours: Scotland (3 full caps): Scottish League XI (2).

Determined, gritty and sometimes a very fiery player, but one who always thrilled the crowd, 'Bertie' Auld starred in schoolboy and junior football in the Glasgow area before signing for Celtic. He spent a large part of the 1956-57 season on loan to Dumbarton, but after returning to Celtic he did exceedingly well and was chased by a number of clubs before finally agreeing to join Blues. Auld was a very skilful player who, after

B

returning to Celtic, became part of the great side that became the first British team to win the European Cup (1967) and swept the board by capturing all the Scottish domestic honours in the space of five years. Auld is now a publican in Glasgow.

AVEYARD, Walter
Centre-forward: 7 Apps. 3 goals
Born: Thurnscoe, near Wombwell, 11 June 1918.
Now deceased.
Career: Denaby United, Sheffield Wednesday (October 1938), BLUES (April 1947), Port Vale (June 1948), Accrington Stanley (March 1952 to May 1953).
Walter Aveyard played his early football in and around the Yorkshire coal-mining area, yet made only four appearances for Wednesday (scoring three goals). After his promising start with Blues, a troublesome thigh injury caused him a lengthy absence from action but he later recaptured his old form, scoring 26 goals in 103 games for Port Vale.

AYLOTT, Trevor Keith Charles
Striker: 31 Apps. one goal
Born: Bermondsey, 26 November 1957
Career: Scott Lidgett School, Downside Boys Club, Fisher Athletic, Chelsea (apprentice November 1975, professional July 1976), Barnsley (£60,000 November 1979), Millwall (£150,000, August 1982), Luton Town (£55,000 plus Vince Hilaire, March 1983), Crystal Palace July 1984), Barnsley (on loan, February & March 1986), AFC Bournemouth (£15,000, August 1986), BLUES (October 1990), Oxford United (on loan September 1991, signed permanently October 1991), Gillingham (1992), Wycombe Wanderers (on loan, March 1993), Bromley (July 1993).
Club honours: Bournemouth: Division Three champions 1987.
Trevor Aylott was a tall, heavily built target-man, easily recognisable by his headband. He was particularly adept at holding the ball up and then laying it off to a colleague. On his own admission he was not a prolific scorer and, in fact, during his career he netted only 90 goals in more 472 League outings.

BADHAM, John
Full-back/left-half: 190 apps. 4 goals
Born: Birmingham, 31 January 1919.
Died: Birmingham, 1 January 1992.
Career: Bordesley Green Schools, Shirley Juniors, Muntz Street Youth Club, BLUES (amateur July 1934, professional May 1946...after-service in the Army), Stourbridge (summer 1957), BLUES (junior coach), Moorlands Athletic (player-coach, 1960), Moor Green (manager May 1962-64).
Club honours: Blues: Division Two champs 1948, 1955

Jack Badham was a lion-hearted defender and a great favourite with the Blues' fans. He quickly developed into an adaptable footballer, able to kick strongly with both feet and appeared in eight different positions for the club. Badham preferred the full-back position from where he helped Blues win promotion from a Second Division on two occasions. He also played in the FA Cup semi-finals of 1951 & 1956, but was unfortunate to miss the Final against Manchester City in 1956, Johnny Newman getting the nod after Roy Warhurst had been injured.

BAILEY, Dennis Lincoln
Striker: 80+13 apps. 25 goals
Born: Lambeth, London 13 November 1965
Career: Tulse Hill Comprehensive School, Watford (Associate Schoolboy forms), Barking, Fulham (non-contract professional, November 1986), Farnborough Town (July 1987), Crystal Palace (£10,000, December 1987), Bristol Rovers (on loan, February-May 1989), BLUES (£80,000, August 1989), Bristol Rovers (on loan, March-April 1991), QPR (£150,000, June 1991), Charlton Athletic (on loan, November 1993), Watford (on loan, March 1994), Brentford (on loan, February 1995), Gillingham (August 1995), Lincoln City (non-contract, March-May 1998), Tamworth.
Club honours: Blues: Leyland DAF Cup winners 1991.
Dennis Bailey was a quick striker who failed to gain a regular place in the Palace line-up but impressed at Bristol with nine goals in 19 games. He started well at Blues (four goals coming in his first friendly outing) yet after that he found scoring much harder. He is a devout Christian.

BAILEY, Edward
Left-back: one app.
Born: Aston, Birmingham, 1860.
Died: Birmingham circa 1935
Career: Aston Shakespeare, Falling Heath Rangers, BLUES (August 1882), Aston Unity (October 1884), Lea Bank Wanderers.
Young, boyish looking reserve full-back, Ted Bailey's appearance for Blues were never more than occasional and he figured in only one competitive match.

BAILEY, Horace Peter
Goalkeeper: 53 apps
Born: Derby, 3 July 1881.
Died. Biggleswade, 1 August 1960
Career: Derby County (September 1899), Ripley Athletic (1903), Leicester Imperial (1905), Leicester Fosse (January 1907), Derby County (April 1909), BLUES (September 1910). Retired, June 1913. Later worked as a

rating officer for the Midland Railway Company
(based in Derby)
Representative honours: England (5 full caps; 8 amateur
international caps, one gold medal with Great Britain
football team in 1908 Olympics).
Although rather small for a goalkeeper - he was only 5ft
8ins tall - Horace Bailey was exceptionally agile, bold and
confident. He had a huge pair of hands and possessed a
long, accurate kick. He once conceded 12 goals in a
League game playing for Leicester against Nottingham
Forest in 1908. Bailey was a railway official
by profession.

BAK, Arkadiusz
Midfielder: 3+2 apps
Born: Poland, 6 January 1974
Career: Polonia Warsaw, BLUES (on loan, December
2001-January 2002).
Representative honours: Poland (13 full caps)
An energetic midfielder, signed by Blues' manager Steve
Bruce, 'Arek' Bak's loan contract was cancelled by
mutual consent after he had failed to come to terms with
English conditions.

BALL, William
Full-back: 165 apps.
Born: Woodside, Dudley, 9 April 1886.
Died: 30 September 1942.
Career: Dudley Welfare, Stourbridge, Leamington,
Wellington Town (1909), BLUES (May 1911),
Cannock Town (October 1921), Wellington Town.
Retired in June 1924.
Club honours: Blues: Division Two champions 1921.
Representative honours: England (one Victory cap).
'Kosher' Ball was an attacking right-back, fluent and
strong, who was a great asset to the side during the four
seasons leading up to 1915. He was one of only handful
of players to serve Blues before it during and after WW1.
He stood 5 ft 8 inches tall and weighed 11 stone.

BALLANTYNE, John
Outside right: 21 apps. 2 goals
Born: Kilmarnock, 30 June 1892.
Now deceased.
Career: Kemmuirhill Athletic, Kilmarnock (February
1912), Vale of Leven (July 1912), BLUES (April 1913),
Vale of Leven (October 1915), Glasgow Rangers (April
1916), Vale of Leven (May 1916), Dumfries (1918-19).
Jack Ballantyne was the proverbial 'diminutive winger'
with a tremendous burst of speed, who was often
criticised for a tendency to overdo the clever stuff.

BANKS, Francis
Goalkeeper: 3 apps.
Born: Aston, Birmingham February 1865.
Now deceased.

Career: All Saints, BLUES (season 1889-90), Warwick
County (1890-91).
Frank Banks, a reserve goalkeeper, was given a run out at
the end of 1899-1900 season, conceding 22 goals in his
three games. He wasn't retained!

BANKS, Frederick William
Outside-left: one app.
Born: Aston, Birmingham 9 December 1888.
Died: Nottingham, 1957
Career: Park Road FC, Myrtle Villa, BLUES (August
1909), Stourbridge (1910), Wellington Town,
Nottingham Forest (September 1911), Stalybridge Celtic
(July 1914), Nottingham Forest (1915), Worksop Town
(September 1920), Notts County (trainer 1929-31).
Fred 'Sticker' Banks was a good player on his day but
had no success with Blues, although he later proved a
capable winger with Forest, playing in 73 games and
netting five goals during his nine-year stay at the
City Ground.

BANNISTER, Keith
Half-back: 27 apps.
Born: Sheffield, 13 November 1930
Career: Rawcliffe Boys FC (Sheffield), Sheffield United
(as a professional May 1948), BLUES (August 1950),
King's Lynn (August 1954), Wrexham (July 1955),
Chesterfield (December 1955), Norwich City (July
1956), Peterborough United (July 1957), King's Lynn
(July 1958-59).
Representative honours: England
(Youth international caps).
Keith Bannister had to wait two years for his Blues'
debut due to national service. Primarily a defender, he
found it difficult to hold down a first-team place with
any of his League clubs, retiring after nine years in the
game with only 65 appearances to his credit.

BARBER Eric
Centre-forward: 5+1 apps. 2 goals
Born: Dublin 18 January 1942
Career: St Finbarr's FC, Shelbourne (1958), Grimsby
Town (on trial, January 1966), Shelbourne, BLUES
(April 1966), Chicago Spurs/NASL (June 1967) , Kansas
City Spurs/NASL (franchise charge, 1968), Shamrock
Rovers (on loan, 1969), Wiener Sportsclub/Austria (July
1970), Shelbourne (1971-75).
Club honours: Shelbourne: League of Ireland champions
1962; FA of Ireland Cup winners 1960 & 1963;
runners-up 1962, 1973 & 1975.
Representative honours: Republic of Ireland (2 full caps).
Born into a boxing family - his brother Dave was an Irish
light-heavyweight champion - Eric Barber arrived at St
Andrew's as a full international but proved to be far too
slow to make any impact on the English soccer scene,

although he did win a second cap whilst with Blues. He suffered the indignity of being sent-off in the 1973 FA of Ireland Cup Final.

BARBER, Frederick
Goalkeeper: one app.
Born: Ferryhill, 26 August 1963
Career: Darlington (apprentice, 1979, professional August 1981), Everton (£50,000, April 1986), Walsall (£100,000, October 1986), Peterborough United (on loan, October 1989), Chester City (on loan, October 1990), Blackpool (on loan, November 1990), Peterborough United (£25,000, August 1991), Chesterfield (on loan, February 1993), Colchester United (on loan, March 1993), Luton Town (£25,000, August 1994), Peterborough United (on loan, December 1994), Ipswich Town (on loan, November 1995), Blackpool (on loan, December 1995), BLUES (free transfer, January 1996). He left St Andrew's in the summer of 1996 and later became goalkeeping coach, serving with several clubs including West Bromwich Albion and Blues. Recruited by Blues following an injury scare at St Andrew's, eccentric goalkeeper Fred Barber (who has been known to wear a mask during a game) only settled down with one club - Walsall - for whom he made 189 first-class appearances during the period 1986-91.

BARKAS, Edward
Full back: 288 apps. 9 goals
Born Wardley, Northumberland 21 November, 1919.
Died: Little Bromwich, 24 April 1962
Career: St Hilda Old Boys, East Bordon Hebburn Colliery, Bedlington United, South Shields, Wardley Colliery (1919), Norwich City (amateur, October 1920), Bedlington United, Huddersfield Town (as a professional, January 1921), BLUES (£4,000 December 1928), Chelsea (May 1937), Solihull Town (player-manager, May 1939), Willmott Breedon FC (1943), Nuffield Mechanics (munitions). Worked as a charge-hand during WW2
Club honours: Huddersfield: Division One champions 1924 & 1926; FA Cup runners-up 1928; Blues: FA Cup runners-up 1931.
Representative honours: toured Canada with FA party in 1926.'Ned' Barker's started out as a centre-forward but turned into a tough-tackling, hard-working, strong-kicking full-back, never showy or spectacular. Barkas, who worked as a collier before joining Huddersfield, missed out on a third League championship medal after being ousted by Roy Goodall in 1924-25. He was manager Leslie Knighton's first signing for Blues and was then signed by Knighton when he left for Chelsea. Barkas had four footballing brothers ...Samuel who played for England, Manchester City and Bradford City, Thomas who served with Bradford City; James, who was

briefly of West Bromwich Albion, and Henry, formerly of Gateshead and Liverpool. His uncle, Thomas Geoffrey, played for Blackpool and he was also cousin to William Felton, ex-Manchester City, Sheffield Wednesday, Spurs and England.

BARLOW, Frederick
Full-back: 3 apps.
Born: Kings Heath, Birmingham, 1862.
Died Birmingham
Career: St Peter's FC (Moseley), Wednesbury Old Athletic, BLUES (seasons 1885-87), Aston Villa (briefly, in 1887), Derby Midland (1887-89).
Fred Barlow was a regular in the Blues side for two seasons, playing mostly friendly games, until work commitments took him to Derby, where he signed for the local railway company team. He was a rarity for a full-back in Victorian times because of his liking to attack.

BARLOW, Raymond John
Wing-half: 7 apps.
Born: Swindon, 17 August 1926
Career: Sanford Street School (Swindon), Swindon Town (on trial, 1942), Garrards FC of Swindon (1943), West Bromwich Albion (as an amateur, June 1944, professional from November 1944), BLUES (June 1960), Stourbridge (as cover, August 1961...although he never played for the Glassboys). Retired in May 1962. Guested for Swindon Town during season. Later played for WBA Old Stars: 1969- 81. Now lives in retirement in Pedmore, Stourbridge.
Club honours: WBA: FA Cup winners 1954, Division Two runners-up 1949, First Division runners-up 1954
Representative honours: England (one cap); Football League XI (four).
A long legged, blond haired wing half of undoubted class, Ray Barlow was a strong tackler and a master of the long 40-yard crossfield pass. He was at the veteran stage when he signed for Blues and came to the club primarily to give the benefit of his experience to the youngster players. Barlow played in almost 500 competitive games for Albion. He was a useful cricketer too, who played for local Birmingham League club, West Bromwich Dartmouth. He later ran a confectionary shop in West Bromwich and thereafter a post-office/general store near Stourbridge. He still attends games at The Hawthorns.

BARNES, Paul Lance
Forward: 15 apps, 7 goals
Born: Leicester, 16 November 1967
Career: Notts County (apprentice, 1982, professional November 1985), Stoke City (£30,000, March 1990), Chesterfield (on loan, November 1990), York City (£50,000, July 1992), BLUES (£350,000, March 1996), Burnley (£350,000+ September 1996), Huddersfield

Town (£50,000, January 1998), Bury (£40,000, March 1999), Doncaster Rovers (June 2001).

Hit the national headlines when he scored twice for York City in a sensational League Cup win at Old Trafford (v. Manchester United) striker Paul Barnes was finally snapped up by Blues' manager Barry Fry who had been tracking him for some considerable time. A natural goalscorer, he unfortunately failed to settle down at St Andrew's and left the club to become Burnley's record signing.

BARNES, Steven Leslie
Winger: 0+5 apps
Born: Harrow, Middlesex, 5 January 1976
Career: Welling United, BLUES (October 1995 to May 1996).
One of a number of players to join Blues from non-League football in the mid-1990s, Les Barnes was a small, nippy winger who failed to make an impression during his short stay at St Andrew's.

BARNETT, David Kwane
Defender: 59 apps.
Born: Birmingham, 16 April 1967
Career: Wolverhampton Wanderers (apprentice, June 1983), Alvechurch (1985-86), Windsor FC (1986), Colchester United (August 1988), Edmonton Oilers/NASL, West Bromwich Albion (October 1989), Walsall (July 1990), Kidderminster Harriers (October 1990), Barnet (£10,000, February 1992), BLUES (on loan, December 1993, signed permanently for £150,000, February 1994), Dunfermline Athletic, Port Vale (on loan, March-March 1996).
Club honours: Blues: Second Division champions 1995; Auto-Windscreens Shield winners 1995.
A strong, powerful centre-back, Dave Barnett suffered the indignity of being sent-off in his first full game for Blues, against his former club WBA on 28 December 1993. He made 30 appearances for Colchester, seven for Walsall and 72 for Barnet, yet failed to make West Brom's first team.

BARRATT, Josiah
Outside-right: 31 apps. one goal
Born: Bulkington, Warwickshire, 21 February 1895.
Died: Coventry, April 1968
Career: Nuneaton Town, Leicester City (December 1916), BLUES (February 1917), Southampton (1918-19), BLUES (February 1922, in a four-player deal), Pontypridd (June 1923), Lincoln City (June 1924), Bristol Rovers (May 1926, part-exchange for Harold Armitage), Nuneaton Town, Coventry Colliery (July 1930); appointed Coventry City youth team coach after WW2. Also had trials for Warwickshire CCC.

An experienced winger, dangerous and incisive, with a reputation for speed, Joe Barrett was signed in a deal which also featured three other players: Jack Elkes and George Getgood being exchanged for himself & Foxall. Barratt had the habit of playing with a piece of straw in his mouth. He was the father of Harry Barrett who played for Coventry City.

BARRETT, James Guy
Inside-forward: 13 apps. 5 goals
Born: West Ham, London 5 November 1930
Career: Boleyn Castle FC, West Ham United (junior 1945, professional February 1949), Nottingham Forest (December 1954), BLUES (October 1959), West Ham United (as player-manager of Hammers' A' team, August 1960), Millwall (coach, 1968-69).
A hard-working if unspectacular player, 'Young Jim' Barrett scored regularly throughout his career, retiring with a haul of 91 goals in 200 League appearances. Son of a former West Ham and England forward, his first-class career was curtailed by an injury sustained while playing for Blues in the Fairs Cup semi-final against Union St Gilloise. He later became landlord of the Napier Arms, Halstead, Essex. He played alongside his father in West Ham's 'A' team in the 1945-46 transitional season after WW2.

BARROWCLOUGH, Stewart James
Winger: 27+3 apps 2 goals
Born: Barnsley, 29 October 1951
Career: Barnsley (apprentice, March 1967, professional November 1969), Newcastle United (£33,000, August 1970), BLUES (rated at £150,000, May 1978), Bristol Rovers (£90,000, July 1979, appointed player-coach in July 1980), Barnsley (£35,000, February 1981), Mansfield Town (free transfer, August, 1983). Retired in May 1985. Local Yorkshire football between 1985-91; played briefly for Frickley Colliery (September 1991 to January 1992) and later was appointed manager of Grimethorpe Miners Welfare (July 1995-97), leading the non-League side to Wembley in the Carlsberg Pub Cup. He now runs a greengrocer's shop in Barnsley.
Club honours: Newcastle: Football League Cup runners-up 1976; Barnsley: Division Three promotion 1981
Representative honours: England (5 Under-23 caps).
An automatic first-choice with Newcastle, Stewart Barrowclough earned a reputation as a fast, direct winger who was capable of both attacking and defending. He scored 28 goals in 289 first team outings for the Magpies. Blues rated him highly enough to exchange him for Terry Hibbitt and John Connolly but, alas, he was hugely disappointing during his season at St Andrew's.

BARTON, Archibald
Right-back: one app.
Born: Moseley, Birmingham, 1862.
Now deceased.
Career: Coles Farm Unity, BLUES (season 1889-90), Kings Heath Comrades.
A tall, enthusiastic full back, Archie Barton played only one competitive game for Blues, against Birmingham St George in the Football Alliance in September 1889.

BARTON, Percival Harry
Half-back: 349 apps. 14 goals
Born: Edmonton, London, 19 August 1895.
Died: October 1961.
Career: Montague Road School, Tottenham Thursday FC, Edmonton Amateurs, Sultan FC, BLUES (January 1914), Stourbridge FC (August 1929). Retired in June 1933. Guested for Spurs during WW1.
Club honours: Blues: Division Two champions 1921.
Representative honours: England (7 full caps).
A dour, industrious player, a former butcher's boy, Percy Barton began his career at left-half before being successfully transformed into a full-back. He often fell foul of referees with his over robust play and was sent-off three times as a professional. WW1 obviously disrupted his career and he was perhaps a shade unlucky not to have appeared in more than seven internationals. He once headed a goal, against Wolves, from fully 30 yards

BASS, Jonathan David
Full-back/defender: 72+8 apps.
Born: Weston-Super-Mare, 1 January 1976
Career: BLUES (trainee, June 1992, professional June 1994), Carlisle United (on loan, October 1996), Gillingham (on loan, March 2000), Hartlepool United (free transfer, July 2001).
Representative Honours: England (Schoolboys)
A disciplined defender who reads the game well, Jon Bass had his best season with Blues in 1997-98, making 30 League appearances. He was released by the club in May 2001 after playing in only one first-class game that season.

BATES, Harry Jay
Outside-right: 3 apps.
Born: Sutton Coldfield, July 1890.
Now deceased.
Career: Ravensmoor FC (1907), Coventry City (season 1911-12), BLUES (August 1912-13), Walsall (1913-15).
Harry Bates remained an amateur throughout his career. He did not make much of an impact in any of his first team games with Blues, the bulk of his playing days being spent in Midlands non-League football.

BAYLEY, John Thomas
Full-back: 69 apps
Born: Walsall, August 1868. Now deceased.
Career: Walsall Swifts (1887-89), Walsall Town Swifts (1889-90), BLUES (1890), Walsall Town Swifts (August 1893), Gainsborough Trinity (1895), South Shields (1899-1900), Watford, Leamington.
Club honours: Blues: Division Two champions 1893.
A consistent, a sturdy defender, not noted for the power of his kicking, Tom Bayley was once a prominent member of the Blues side but was released after the Test Match failure of 1893.

BAYLEY, Samuel
Forward: one app. 1 goal
Born: Rugby, November 1878.
Now deceased.
Career: St Saviour's FC (1895), Rugby FC (August 1897), Leamington (season 1898-99), BLUES (July 1899), Leamington (December 1899 to May 1901).
Sam Bailey had a fine game on his Blues debut, scoring a goal and having a hand in two others. Surprisingly, he was never called into action again and left the club shortly afterwards

BEARD, Malcolm
Wing- half: 403+2 apps. 33 goals
Born: Cannock, 3 May 1942
Career: St Chad's School, Cannock & District and Staffordshire Schools XI football, BLUES (amateur, June 1957, professional, May 1959), Aston Villa (July 1971), Atherstone Town (1973), Saudi Arabia (coach 1974), BLUES (senior scout, 1979-81), Aston Villa (Chief scout, 1982-86), Middlesbrough (coach, 1987), Portsmouth (Youth coach, January-October 1990): Leicester City (Chief Scout, 1993), Aston Villa (Chief Scout, then reserve team manager at Villa Park from 1997).
Club honours: Blues: Football League Cup winners 1963; Fairs Cup runners-up 1961.
Representative honours: England (Youth caps), Army XI (1961-62). Former Blues wing-half Terry Hennessey once said if you had 11 men in your team like Malcolm, you couldn't go wrong. Beard was, indeed, a tremendous footballer who was held in high esteem by his fellow professionals. He spent 14 years at St Andrew's as a player, appearing in both the 1967 League Cup & 1968 F A Cup semi-finals. He was unfortunate to be sent-off in his last game for the club (against Millwall) in December 1970 after being awarded a deserved testimonial in 1969. He was in football for more than 40 years.

BEATTIE, John Murdoch
Inside-forward: 36 apps. 9 goals
Born: at New Hills, Scotland, 28 May 1912. Died: Wolverhampton, 15 January 1992
Career: Hall Russell FC, Aberdeen (as a professional, August 1931), Wolverhampton Wanderers (September 1933), Blackburn Rovers (£2,000, December 1934), BLUES (£2,000, January 1937), Huddersfield Town (£2,500, January 1938), Grimsby Town (£2,500, February 1938). Retired during WW2 after guesting for

Walsall, One of football's nomads, Jack Beattie's services were in constant demand during the 1930s. Clubs were willing to pay considerable sums for his intelligent positional play and fierce right-foot shooting. A marvellously resourceful footballer, he was always involved in the action.

BECKFORD, Jason Neil

Forward: 6+2 apps. one goal
Born: Manchester, 14 February, 1970
Career: Burnage High School, FA School of Excellence, Manchester City (YTS July 1986, professional June 1987), Blackburn Rovers (on loan, March 1991), Port Vale (on loan, September 1991), BLUES (£50,000, January 1992), Bury (on loan, April 1994), Stoke City (free transfer, August 1994 ...after a month's trial), Millwall (December 1994). Northampton Town (assistant-manager May 1995).
Representative honours: England (two Youth caps).
Brother of Darren (formerly of Port Vale & Norwich City), Jason Beckford signalled his arrival at St Andrew's with a goal on his debut, but was injured shortly afterwards. This was the first of several set-backs for the utility forward, culminating in a leg injury in 1992 which led to an operation to produce a synthetic cartilage. He was released in 1994 to give him a chance to rebuild his career.

BEEL, William John Leonard

Goalkeeper: One app.
Born: Leominster, 23 August 1945
Career Shrewsbury Town (apprentice, August 1961, professional July 1963), BLUES (January 1965), Shifnal Town (August 1965).
Billy Beel was given his chance late in the 1964-65 season, after Blues had already been relegated and a harrowing experience it must have been for the 19 year-old as Blackburn Rovers thumped five goals past him. He was released a couple of weeks later and dropped into minor football.

BEER, William John

Wing-half: 250 apps. 35 goals
Born: Poolsbrook near Chesterfield, 4 January 1879.
Died: March 1941.
Career: Staveley Town, Sheffield United (as an amateur), Chesterfield Town, Sheffield United (as a professional, August 1898), BLUES (£700, January 1902). Retired in May 1910. After football he spent many years working as a sheep farmer in Australia before returning to England to become a licensee in 1920, later taking over as manager of Blues, a position he held for almost four years, from May 1923 to March 1927.
Club honours: Sheffield United: FA Cup winner 1899.
A skilful player of explosive reflexes and subtle imagination, Billy Beer had balance and strength, a fluent body-swerve and booming shot. He joined Blues (with Charlie Field) and proved to be a great servant to the club. Beer had made over 100 appearances for Sheffield United and was a penalty-expert. Indeed, it is on record that he never missed from the spot. He was also a talented musician and it is said that he was lured south by the promise of a job as a church organist. He is possibly the only footballer to have composed a cantata.

BELL, Douglas K

Midfielder: 22 apps.
Born Paisley, 5 September 1959.
Career: Cumbernauld United, St Mirren, Aberdeen (1979), Rangers (£45,000, May 1985), Hibernian (1986), St Mirren, Shrewsbury Town (£35,000, December 1987), Hull City (on loan, March 1989), BLUES (£57,500, October 1989), Portadown (on loan, April 1990), St Mirren (on loan, January 1991). Released May 1991, joined Partick Thistle (August 1991); Portadown (August 1992), Clyde (July 1993) then a spell with Elgin City (in season 1994-95).
Club honours: Aberdeen: Scottish Premier League champions 1980, 1984 & 1985; Scottish Cup winners 1982 & 1984. Portadown: Irish Cup runners-up 1990; Budweiser & Gold Cup winners 1993.
Representative honours: Scotland (2 Under-21 caps).
Dougie Bell made his name as a ball winning midfielder in the successful Aberdeen side of the 1980s. He proved a big disappointment at Ibrox Park where he was accused of lack of consistency, a charge that was levelled at him throughout the rest of his career. He was the first Blues player to wear a pair of cycling shorts on a football pitch.

BELLAMY, Samuel Charles

Right-back: one app.
Born: Aston, Birmingham, 9 September 1913. Deceased.
Career: Jenkins Street School, St Andrews OSL, BLUES (as an amateur 1937, professional June 1937), Tamworth (1947).
Sam Bellamy, a young full back, who was born a stone's throw from St Andrew's, saw his career severely disrupted by World War 2.

BENNETT, Ian Michael

Goalkeeper. 338 apps*
Born: Worksop, 10 October 1970
Career: Queen's Park Rangers (YTS 1988), Newcastle United (as a professional, March 1989), Peterborough United (free transfer, March 1991), BLUES (£325,000 December 1993).
Club honours: Blues: Second Division champions 1995, League Cup runners-up 2001, First Division promotion 2002; Auto-Windscreen Shield winners 1995.
Over the years Ian Bennett has proved an excellent shot-

stopper, confident in all aspects of goalkeeping and in 1994 - 95 he kept ten successive clean-sheets (27 in all from 62 matches) and was the only ever-present as Blues won the Second Division title... a remarkable achievement considering that manager Barry Fry used 37 players in the League campaign alone. Bennett made 89 appearances for 'Posh' but failed to make the first team at Queen's Park Rangers or Newcastle. He was, though, rated in the £1 million class during the mid-1990s. Following a hand injury he lost his place in the Blues side to Nico Vaesen, but still made 18 League appearances as promotion was gained to the Premiership in 2002.

BENNETT, William Ambrose
Outside right: 76 apps. 13 goals
Born: Altrincham, 9 April 1872.
Now deceased.
Career: Summerfield FC, Crewe Alexandra, BLUES (summer 1896), Stafford Rangers (August 1901).
Billy Bennett was an injury-prone winger but nevertheless a very useful scorer in his heyday. In his first three seasons with Blues, his varying knocks meant that he appeared in only 14 games. Described as a 'speedy player, clever at dribbling' he could deliver crosses with fine precision and awareness.

BERESFORD, John
Full-back: one app.
Born: Sheffield, 4 September 1966
Career: Manchester City (apprentice, 1982, professional September 1983), Barnsley (free transfer, August 1986), Portsmouth (£300,000, March 1989), Newcastle United (£650,000, July 1992), Southampton (£1.5 million, February 1998), BLUES (on loan, October-November 1999). Forced to retire through injury in May 2000.
Club Honours: Newcastle Utd: Division winners 1993
Representative Honours: England
(Schoolboy, Youth & 2 'B' caps)
Prior to 1998 when he suffered a severe cruciate ligament injury, Yorkshire-born full-back John Beresford had played consistently well, making more than 475 competitive appearances. He was taken by Blues as defensive cover but was one of many players to suffer the St Andrew's injury jinx when he fell down the stairs at home and damaged his right knee. He returned to The Dell but after that was never able to play a competitive game and in the end retired at the age of 34.

BERRY, John James
Outside-right: 114 apps. 6 goals
Born: Aldershot, 1 June 1926.
Died: Farnham, Hampshire, 1995
Career: St Joseph School (Aldershot): Aldershot YMCA, BLUES (as a professional, December 1944), Manchester United (£25,000, August 1951). Forced to retire in 1958

following Munich air disaster.
Club honours: Manchester United: Division One champions 1952, 1956 & 1957.
FA Cup runners-up 1957
Representative honours: England: (4 full caps, one 'B' cap): Football League XI (1).
Manchester United had been trying to sign Johnny Berry for over a year before he finally left St Andrew's in 1951. A dashing 5ft 5in winger, skilful, with a good shot, he hit 43 goals in 273 outings for the 'Busby Babes' before his career was ended on that snowy Munich airstrip in 1958. A former cinema projectionist, and brother of Peter Berry (ex-Crystal Palace & Ipswich Town), after recovering from that tragic air crash, Berry helped run the family sports shop in Aldershot.

BERTSCHIN, Keith Edwin
Centre-forward: 134+7 apps. 41 goals
Born Enfield, 25 August 1956
Career: Mount Grace School, South Mimms FC, Barnet (August 1972), Ipswich Town (as a professional October 1973), BLUES (£135,000, July 1977), Norwich City (£200,000, August 1981), Jacksonville Tea Men (on loan, summer 1982), Stoke City (£50,000, November 1984), Sunderland (£32,500, March 1987), Walsall (£30,000, July 1988), Chester City (£5,000, November 1990), Aldershot (free transfer, August 1991), Solihull Borough (February 1992), Evesham United (October 1993), Barry Town (March 1994), Tamworth (on trial, August 1994), Worcester City (August 1994), Hednesford Town (March 1995-97), Stafford Rangers (1998-99), BLUES (coach, on four-year contract from December 2001)
Club honours: Ipswich: FA Youth Cup winner 1975; Sunderland: Division Three champions 1988; Barry: Welsh Cup winners 1994
Representative honours: England (3 Under-21 caps & Youth caps), European Youth champions 1976.
Keith Bertschin scored with his first kick in the League football, for Ipswich against Arsenal at Highbury in April 1976. He went on to register well over 150 goals in the next 15 years despite breaking the same leg twice during his four seasons as a player at St Andrew's. A keen angler and decent cricketer, he has also been a Financial Advisor, and worked for Pro-Sport, a company which provided materials (especially sand and peat) for many of the leading golf courses around the U.K. including The Belfrey, St Andrew's, Troon, Hoylake and Sunningdale, as well as the home grounds of Stoke City (when the Potters were building their Britannia Stadium), Stockport County and QPR.

BIDMEAD, William Harold
Left-back: 3 apps
Born: West Bromwich, December 1882.
Died: Bethnal Green, London 16 March 1961

Career: Elwells FC (West Bromwich), Walsall, Stourbridge, Brierley Hill Alliance (1902), BLUES (1903), Leighton (July 1906), Grimsby Town (1908), Brierley Hill Alliance (July 1909). Retired 1911.

Bill Bidmead was the man with the unenviable task of understudying the Glover-Stokes full- back partnership, regarded as one of the best at club level anywhere in the country around the turn of the 20th century. Due to their consistency Bidmead unfortunately hardly managed a first team outing and, perhaps not surprisingly, he was rather disappointing when he did play (due no doubt to lack of first team action).

BIRCH, Joseph

Right-back: one app.
Born: Cannock, 6 July 1904.
Died: Colchester, 4 December 1980
Career: Cannock Town (September 1920), Hednesford Town (August, 1926), BLUES (March 1928), Bournemouth & Boscombe Athletic (May 1929), Fulham (October 1931), Colchester United (July 1938 to April 1940).
Club honours: Fulham: Division Three champions 1932. Colchester: Southern League champions 1939

Joe Birch was a burly, but exceptionally speedy full-back with a prodigious kick who was unable to secure a regular place in Blues' first team. Later he proved a valuable servant to Fulham and played 195 times for the 'Cottagers' during his seven years with the London club. He was formerly a pit worker

BIRD, Adrian Lee

Centre-half: 32 apps one goal
Born: Bristol 8 July 1969
Career: Bristol Schools FA, Boco Juniors, BLUES (YTS, July 1985, professional July 1987), Moor Green (July 1990). Retired in May 1991

A promising youngster whose career was ruined by a knee injury, Adrian Bird spent a year at the Football Injuries and Treatment Centre, Lilleshall, before losing his battle to regain full fitness.

BIRD, John

Right-half: one app.
Born Blackheath, 1881.
Now deceased.
Career: Langley St Michael's, Rowley United, BLUES (November 1902), Walsall (1906), Kidderminster Harriers (seasons 1913-15).

One of the stalwarts of Birmingham League football before WW1, Jack Bird frequently collected rave reviews for his performances with Walsall but rather surprisingly was not snapped up by another League club. He failed to impress with Blues.

BLACK, Simon Anthony

Forward: 3+1 apps.
Born: Birmingham, 9 November 1975
Career: Kings Heath Concorde, Beeches Terriers, Baverstock School, BLES (YTS June 1991, professional June 1994), Yeovil Town (on loan, March 1995), Doncaster Rovers (July 1996).

A tall, gangling apprentice who was thrown in at the deep end in the first game of the 1993-94 season. Simon Black seemed a little overawed by the experience and was booked in the second half of his debut game

BLACKMORE, Richie

Goalkeeper: one app.
Born: Coleshill, Warwickshire, June 1954
Career: Bristol City (apprentice, June 1970), BLUES (as a professional, September 1971), Dundalk (July 1974), Galway United.
Club honours: Dundalk: Irish League champions 1975, 1976 & 1978: Cup winners 1977, 1979 & 1991.

Richie Blackmore stole the headlines after saving two spot-kicks in his only game for Blues when Stoke City were beaten in a penalty shoot-out in a 1st round, 2nd leg Texaco Cup match at St Andrew's in October 1973.

BLAKE, Anthony John

Left back: 2 apps
Born Crofton Hill, 26 February 1927
Career Rubery Owen FC, Blues (amateur, October 1948, professional January 1949), Gillingham (July 1952).

Tony Blake was a well-built player who joined Blues as a centre-forward, being converted into a defender whilst in the junior ranks.

BLAKE, Noel Lloyd George

Defender: 96 apps. 5 goals
Born: Jamaica, 12 January 1962
Career Alderlea School, Wilhemena Boys, Sutton Coldfield Town (April 1978), Walsall (non-contract), Aston Villa (as a professional, August 1979), Shrewsbury Town (on loan, March 1982), BLUES (£55,000, September 1982), Portsmouth (£150,000, August 1984), Leeds United (£175,000, July 1988), Stoke City (£160,000, February 1990), Bradford City (on loan, February-June 1992), Dundee (December 1993), Exeter City (August 1995, later player-coach, then assistant-manager and finally manager at St James' Park from May 2000 to October 2001).

Fiercely competitive player, built like a heavyweight boxer, Noel Blake proved a commanding figure at the heart of the defence, powerful in the air and strong in the tackle. He became a hero with Blues' fans and was one of the players sold by manager Ron Saunders after a series of well-publicised 'off the field' misdemeanours

BLOOMFIELD, James Henry

Inside-forward: 147 apps. 31 goals

Born: Kensington, London, 15 February 1934.

Died: Chingford, Essex 3 April 1983

Career: St Clement's School, Hayes, Brentford (October 1952), Arsenal (July, 1954), BLUES (November 1960), Brentford (June 1964), West Ham United (October 1965), Plymouth Argyle (September 1966), Leyton Orient (player-manager, March 1968), Leicester City (manager, May 1971 to 1977), Leyton Orient (manager, September 1977 to August 1981), Luton Town (Scout 1981-83).

Club honours: Blues: Football League Cup winners 1963; Fairs Cup runners-up 1961.

Representative honours: England: (2 Under-23 caps): Football League XI (1).

Jimmy Bloomfield was a member of a footballing family, his brother Bill played for Brentford and his nephew Ray was with Aston Villa. Jimmy was a potent force in the Arsenal attack and after joining Blues he became more of a playmaker and less of a goalscorer. Later on he proved to be a fine manager, leading both Leicester City and the Orient to FA Cup semi-finals.

BLOXHAM, Albert

Defender: 3 apps.

Born: Solihull, 22 November 1905.

Now deceased.

Career: Birmingham Juniors, Overton-on-Dee FC (August 1925), Oswestry Town, Torquay United (August 1926), BLUES (March 1927), Rhyl Athletic (March 1928), Chesterfield (May 1928), Raith Rovers (October 1928), Yeovil United (September 1929), Millwall (May 1931-May 1933). Later an official FA coach for Cambridgeshire. Albert Bloxham was a strong player, 5ft 10ins tall and 11 st 7lbs in weight. He was another of football's great wanderers who found it difficult to claim a first-team place with any of his clubs. Described as a 'touchline artist, director and fast as befitted a professional runner'. He was formerly an office clerk.

BLUFF, Edgar Underwood

Inside-forward: 9 apps. one goal

Born: Winchester, 19 March 1880.

Died: Northampton, May 1952

Career: High Hazels FC, Yorkshire Light Infantry, Army Corps, Reading (on trial, February 1903), Southampton (July 1904), Sheffield United (September 1905), BLUES (December 1907), St Helens Town (May 1908).

Representative honours: Sheffield & Yorkshire Select XI.

Brought out of the army, Ted Bluff enjoyed a rapid rise to fame, culminating in him been named as a reserve for England against Ireland in 1905. However, an equally dramatic loss of form led to him being released by Sheffield United, although, in truth, he never really settled in Yorkshire. He had a short and undistinguished spell which Blues. A turner by trade, his hobby was gardening.

BLYTH, James Anton

Goalkeeper: 16 apps

Born: Perth, Scotland, 2 February 1955.

Career: Perth Roselea; Preston North End (apprentice, June 1971, professional October 1972), Coventry City (October 1972), Hereford United (on loan, March 1975), BLUES (August 1982), Nuneaton Borough (August 1985), Coventry City (goalkeeping coach, 1996-97).

Representative honours: Scotland (2 full caps).

Jim Blyth was rated one of the best goalkeepers in the country during his days with Coventry when he earned his two Scottish caps. An expensive transfer to Manchester United fell through when he failed a medical on his back, and from then on he was constantly troubled by a spinal injury. During his stay with Blues Blyth was prone to making errors. His son was murdered in an incident outside a Hinckley night club in 1993.

BLYTH, William Naismith

Half-back/inside-forward. 21 apps 4 goals

Born: Dalkeith, Scotland, 17 June 1895.

Died: Worthing, 1 July 1968

Career: Wemyss Athletic, Manchester City (June 1913), Arsenal (May 1914), BLUES (May 1929). Retired May 1931. Served in the RASC during WW1

Club honours: Arsenal: FA Cup runners-up 1927; London Cup winners 1922 & 1924, runners-up 1926

Representative honours: Scotland (Junior international).

Bill Blyth gave sterling service to Arsenal, making almost 400 first-class appearances for the Gunners, and skippering the London side in the 1927 Cup Final defeat by Cardiff City. Although slight of build he was renowned for his bravery and also for the quality of his left-foot passes. He was also a pretty good golfer and ran his own business in Musselburgh, Scotland. Brother in-law of Provost Inglis of Port Seton.

BODENHAM, John

Goalkeeper: 2 apps

Born: Perry Barr, Birmingham, August 1859.

Now deceased.

Career: Aston Manor, BLUES (August 1881), Birmingham Excelsior (season 1883-84).

Jack Bodenham shared the role of goalkeeper with the ageing Will 'Pouncer' Edden for two years before joining the Perry Barr based Excelsior club. He also opened the batting for Small Heath Alliance cricket team, although he rarely scored many runs.

BODLE, Harold

Inside-forward: 110 apps. 36 goals

Born: Ardwick-le-Street, 4 October 1920

Career: Ardwick Junior School, Ridgehill Old Boys,

Doncaster Rovers (on trial), Bradford Park Avenue (on trial), Rotherham United (May, 1938), BLUES (£2,000, November 1938), Bury (March 1949), Stockport County (October 1952), Accrington Stanley (August 1953-May 1959, returning as manager June 1959 to April 1960), Burton Albion (as manager 1962-64), thereafter a local football manager in Derby. Guested for Doncaster Rovers and Rotherham United during WW2 and later ran sub-post offices in Burton and Derby
Club honours: Blues: Football League South winners 1946, Division Two champions 1948.
Representative honours: FA XI (1947-48)
A former miner, it was not until after WW2 that Harold Bodle made his name on the soccer field. A real bag of tricks, he claimed that he owed his juggling prowess to practising whilst a child by kicking a small ball against the sideboard at his home. History does not say what his mother thought of that. Bodle once got himself marooned on the cliffs whilst out walking after a Blues game at Plymouth. He was also a useful cricketer and bowls player.

BODLEY, Michael John
Defender: 3 apps
Born: Hayes, 14 September, 1967
Career: Chelsea (apprentice June 1983, professional September 1985), Northampton Town (£50,000, January 1989), Barnet (£15,000, October 1989), Southend United (free transfer July 1993), Gillingham (on loan, November 1994), BLUES (on loan January 1995). Peterborough United (July 1996), St Albans City (August 2000), Canvey Island (season 2001-02).
Club honours: Barnet: GM Vauxhall Conference champions 1991. Mick Bodley played only eight games for Chelsea and 22 for Northampton before dropping out of League football to join Barnet with whom he returned (with Barry Fry) in 1991. A strong, competent defender, sure-footed with a positive attitude, he was taken on loan by Blues during a period when injuries and suspensions were disrupting the balance of the defence.

BOND, Benjamin
Winger: 85 apps.13 goals
Born: Wolverhampton, 30 August 1919.
Died: Wolverhampton, March 1972
Career: Coseley FC, Pensnett FC, Upper Gornal FC, Wellington, Bilston United (1924), Coseley (February 1926), BLUES (as an amateur, March 1926, professional April 1926). Retired May 1932 through injury
A frail but tricky left-winger, Benny Bond seemed to be the answer to Blues' long-term left-wing problem until he was laid low with a knee injury that required three cartilage operations

BONTHRON, Robert Patrick
Right-back: 12 apps. one goal
Born: Dundee circa 1884.
Now deceased.
Career: Raith Athletic, Raith Rovers (July 1900), Dundee (May 1902), Manchester United (1905), Sunderland (May 1907), Northampton Town (June 1908), BLUES (July 1910), Leith Athletic (July 1911)
A no-nonsense defender (5ft 11ins tall & 13 stone in weight) Bob Bonthron's uncompromising attitude towards the game sometimes led to him being attacked by spectators, especially when he was with Manchester United. That apart, he was still a very capable footballer.

BOOTH, Robert
Write half: 8 apps. one goal
Born: West Hartlepool, 20 December 1890.
Now deceased.
Career: Spennymoor United, Blackpool (May 1912), BLUES (May 1920), Southend United (July 1922), Swansea Town (June 1923), Merthyr Town (March 1925), New Brighton (May 1925). Guested for Workington during WW1.
Described in a contemporary report as being 'a very quiet, hard working footballer, who never becomes ruffled' Bob Booth spent two years challenging for the right-half position at St Andrew's, but although he never let the side down, he didn't really possess the ability required in the higher divisions.

BOOTON, Harold
Right-back: 163 apps. 2 goals
Born: Annesley Colliery, 2 March 1906.
Died: Denham, Uxbridge 22 October 1976
Career Newstead Evening School FC, Annesley Colliery FC, Shirebrook FC, BLUES (April 1929), Luton Town (February 1936), Atherstone (May 1938-40)
A pre-war full-back, solid in the tackle but somewhat haphazard with his distribution, Harold Booton's powerful kicking led him to occasionally taking penalties. In later life he became the landlord of the Market Inn at Swadlincote in South Derbyshire. He was renowned in the Blues' dressing room for having a truly awful singing voice. He was a clerk in the offices at Annesley Colliery and also worked in a tea store before turning to football

BOSBURY, Charles Edwin
Outside-right: 15 apps.
Born: Newhaven, 5 November 1897.
Died: Lincoln, June 1929
Career: Pemberton Billings FC (1914), Southampton (WW1 guest, then as an amateur, August 1919), Harland and Wolf FC (1920-21), Southampton (December 1921), BLUES (August 1922), Preston North End (June 1925), Lincoln City (August 1926 to May 1929).

Charlie Bosbury struggled for several years to get regular League action, only to die shortly after achieving his goal. Tall and strongly built, he had pace and resource, being a fine sprinter on the athletics track.

BOWDEN, Frederick

Outside-left: one app.

Born: Kings Heath, Birmingham, November 1904

Career: Darwen FC (Shirebrook), Cradley Heath (August 1923), BLUES (amateur January 1925, professional December 1925), Kidderminster Harriers, Stourbridge (May 1927), West Ham United (June 1928), Coventry City (May 1929), Evesham Town (July 1931), Kidderminster Harriers (June 1933), Chesterfield (late 1933), Coventry City, West Ham United (1934), spell in French football (season 1934-35). Retired.

Fred Bowden was a fast winger but one who never really settled down in the professional ranks, dropping back into non-League football quite quickly. He gained little renown after returning to League action either.

BOWEN, Jason Peter

Forward: 44+21 apps, 11 goals

Born: Merthyr Tydfil, 24 August 1972

Career: Swansea City (trainee 1988, professional July 1990), BLUES (£350,000, July 1995), Southampton (on loan, September 1997), Reading (£200,000, December 1997), Cardiff City (free transfer, January 1999).

Club Honours: Swansea: Autoglass Trophy winners 1994

Representative Honours: Wales (2 full, one 'B' cap, 5 Under-21 caps, Youth & Schoolboy caps)

A very talented player with pace and movement, Jason Bowen enjoyed playing in any forward position earlier in his career. During his time with Blues he was most threatening when attacking down the flank but unfortunately he lacked consistency when it mattered most and was duly allowed to leave St Andrew's on a free transfer after turning down a proposed £600,000 move to Huddersfield Town. He helped Cardiff gain promotion from the Third Division in 2001.

BOWKER, Keith

Forward/full-back: 20+3 apps. 5 goals

Born: West Bromwich, 18 April 1951

Career: Staffs County FA, BLUES (apprentice 1966, professional, August 1968), Exeter City (December 1973), Cambridge United (May 1975), Northampton Town (on loan, December 1976), Exeter City (August 1977), Torquay United (August 1980), Bideford Town (August 1982), Taunton Town (player-manager, January 1987, resigned in June 1993).

Keith Bowker, a hard-working blond haired player, was overshadowed at St Andrew's by the brilliance of Trevor Francis and Bob Latchford. He finished his League career with a useful record of 81 goals in 307 appearances, 66

of them coming in 112 games for Exeter. Bowker had a few First Division outings for Blues in the right back position when he replaced the injured Ray Martin. He later worked as a postman in the Exeter area.

BOX. Arthur

Goalkeeper: 29 apps

Born: Hanley, Stoke-on-Trent, September 1884.

Died: Stoke-on-Trent.

Career: Wellington School, Hanley Villa, Northwood Mission, Stoke, Port Vale (August 1904), Stoke (August 1907), Blues (September 1909), Leek Victoria (April 1910), Croydon Common (August 1910), Crewe Alexandra (November 1911 to May 1912).

A squarely built goalkeeper, Arthur Box was unable to settle with any of his senior clubs despite a string of capable performances.

BOYD, Leonard Arthur Miller

Wing-half: 282 apps, 14 goals

Born: Plaistow, London, 11 November 1923.

Career: Ilford (amateur), Royal Navy, Plymouth Argyle (professional December 1945), BLUES (£17,500, January 1949). Retired May 1956. Attempted a delayed comeback with Hinckley Athletic (February 1959), later coach and chief scout of Redditch United (1960-65).

Club Honours: Blues: Division 2 champions 1955, FA Cup runners-up 1956.

Representative Honours: England (one 'B' cap), FA XI (1951-52)

Played in the same school team as another Blues player, Ken Green, and skippered Blues to promotion from the Second Division in 1954-55 and then led them in the 1956 FA Cup Final.

Plymouth manager Jack Tresadern spotted his undoubted talents while he was playing as an inside-forward in Malta. Boyd, tall, composed with a long stride, made rapid strides after a slow start at Home Park. He made 80 appearances for Argyle and after a splendid display for the Devon club at St Andrew's, Blues took interest! Early in 1949 Boyd wrote his name in Plymouth history books by becoming the club's first five-figure transfer when he joined Blues. The whole of the transfer negotiation, in fact, had been kept secret from the press and public until the forms were completed.

Boyd enjoyed bringing the ball out of defence into attack, driving his forwards before him with one of those imperious waves of the hand, which were to become his trademark. He took over from Fred Harris in the Blues half-back line, allowing Harris to switch to left-half in place of Frank Mitchell. He retained the number four berth, practically unchallenged until retiring in May 1956, soon after Blues had lost that season's FA Cup Final. Boyd was undoubtedly a fine player, a hard-worker who certainly endeared himself to the Blues' supporters. He now lives in Melton Mowbray, Leicestershire.

BRADBURY, Lee Michael
Striker: 7+2 apps
Born: Isle of Wight, 3 July 1975
Career: Cowes, Portsmouth (August 1995), Exeter City (on loan, December 1995), Manchester City (£3 million, August 1997), Crystal Palace (£1.5 million, October 1998), BLUES (on loan, March to May 1999), Portsmouth (£380,000, October 1999).
Representative Honours: England Under-21 (3 caps)
Lee Bradbury, a strong-running, hard-working, tireless forward, was signed on loan by Blues following an injury crisis. He later did well with Pompey before a serious knee injury disrupted his progress in December 2001. He struggled thereafter to regain full fitness.

BRADBURY, William
Inside-forward: 3 apps. 2 goals
Born: Matlock, 3 April 1933. Died: 1999.
Career: Modern Machines FC, Coventry City (as a professional May 1950), BLUES (November 1954), Hull City (October 1955), Bury (February 1960), Workington (November 1960), Southport (July 1961), Wigan Athletic (as player-coach June 1962), Prescot Cables FC (August 1963), Kirby Town (March 1964-65).
Bill Bradbury found it difficult to win a first-team place with Blues due to the form of so many other quality forwards. He had a reputation of playing to the crowd, being particularly fond of the theatrical gesture. His father George played for Clapton Orient.

BRADFORD, Joseph
Centre-forward: 445 apps. 267 goals
Born: Peggs Green, Leicestershire 22 January 1919. Died: Birmingham, 6 September 1980
Career: Coalville FC (Leicestershire), Green Victoria (August 1913), Aston Villa (on trial), Derby County (on trial), BLUES (£125, as a professional, February 1920), Bristol City (May 1935). A former cafe owner, he also became a licensee, based initially in Birmingham and then in Stourbridge, and he was a shop proprietor in Sutton Coldfield
Club honours: Blues: FA Cup runners-up 1931
Representative honours: England: (12 full caps): Football League XI ((5)
The greatest goalscorer in Blues' history, Joe Bradford could so easily have signed for rivals Aston Villa. He was scoring goals galore in Leicestershire junior football (he once netted 13 times in one game) when Villa invited him for a trial, but Blues were the only club willing to pay his travelling expenses, and consequently he signed on as a professional at St Andrew's in 1920. He was groomed in the reserves and was given an occasional

game as Blues headed for the Second Division title in 1921, but it wasn't until the following season that he gained a regular place in the side. Once in, he stayed put and was a very consistent performer for the club over the next 14 years. Indeed, he scored at least ten or more goals in 12 of those 14 seasons. He netted Blues' goal in 1931 FA Cup Final defeat by WBA and was given an emotional send-off in his last game at St Andrew's after injuries had started to affect his overall performances. His brother, William, played for Walsall and his cousin, Hugh Adcock, served both Leicester City and England.

BRAGSTAD, Bjorn Otto
Defender: 3 apps
Born: Trondheim, Norway, 15 January 1971
Career: Rosenborg, Derby County (£1.5 million, August 2000), BLUES (on loan, September 2001).
Representative Honours: Norway (15 caps)
Recruited by Blues as cover for injuries early in the 2001-02 season, 6ft 4in defender Bragstad was only at St Andrew's for a month before returning to Pride Park.

BRAZIER, Colin James
Defender/Wing-half: 16+3 apps. one goal
Born: Solihull, 6 June 1957
Career: Northfield Town, Wolverhampton Wanderers (apprentice June 1973, professional August 1975), Jacksonville Tea Men (June 1981), BLUES (October 1982), AP Leamington (March 1983), Lincoln City (April 1983), Walsall (August 1983), Kidderminster Harriers (October 1986), Tamworth (March 1995-96).
Club honours: Wolves: Football League Cup winners (as a substitute) 1980.
Representative honours: England (one semi-pro cap).
Colin Brazier was a useful squad player at Wolves, being principally a central defender or defensive midfielder, but he was never guaranteed a first-team place at Molineux. Blues bought him in to add cover to their defence, but such were the problems at the time that he had a few games at centre-forward, a position that he had an ill-concealed dislike for. After a disagreement with manager Ron Saunders he left St Andrew's and played one game for Leamington (against Blues in a friendly) before rejoining the League with Lincoln as an out and out defender. Brazier now lives in Tamworth.

BREEN, Gary Patrick
Defender: 42+3 apps. 2 goals
Born: Hendon, 12 December 1973
Career: Charlton Athletic (juniors), Maidstone United (March 1999), Gillingham (free transfer, July 1992), Peterborough United (£70,000, August 1994), BLUES

(£400,000, February 1996), Coventry City (£2.4 million, December 1997), West Ham (July 2002). Representative Honours: Republic of Ireland (51 full caps, 9 Under-21 caps).

A skilful, right-footed central defender, quick off the mark, strong in the air, Gary Breen spent 20 months at St Andrew's before moving into the Premiership. He had a superb 2002 World Cup in Japan and South Korea

BREMNER, Desmond George

Midfielder: 193 apps. 3 goals
Born: Aberchider, Kirkaldy, Scotland 7 September 1952
Career: Banks O'Dee FC, Deveronvale FC, Hibernian (July 1971, professional November 1972), Aston Villa (£250,000 plus Joe Ward, September 1979), BLUES (£25,000, September 1984), Fulham (free transfer, August 1989), Walsall (free transfer, March 1990), Stafford Rangers (August 1990), Sutton Town (March 1994).

Club honours: Hibs: Scottish League Cup runners-up 1975 & 1979; Aston Villa: Division One champions 1981, European Cup winners 1982, European Super Cup winners 1982, World Cup championship 1982.
Representative honours: Scotland (one full cap, 9 Under-23 caps).

Des Bremner first achieved fame north of the border with Hibs as a highly rated full-back. He switched successfully to right side of midfield, where he became a star in the successful Villa side of the early 1980s, scoring 10 goals in 227 appearances. A tenacious player, Bremner then served Blues in midfield supremely well, proving to be a great servant to the club for five years, sometimes occupying a defensive role. Bremner is now a Financial Advisor with the PFA, based in their Birmingham offices.

BREMNER, Kevin Johnston

Striker: 3+1 apps. one goal
Born: Banff, Scotland, 7 October 1957
Career: Deveronvale FC, Keith FC, Colchester United (£40,000, October 1980), BLUES (on loan, October 1982), Wrexham (on loan, December 1982), Plymouth Argyle (on loan, January 1983), Millwall (£25,000, February 1983, Reading (£35,000, August 1985), Brighton & Hove Albion (£45,000, July 1987, Peterborough United (July 1990), Dundee (September 1991), Shrewsbury Town (on loan, March 1992), Bora Rangers (player-manager, from July 1992), Deveronvale FC (player-manager (August 1994-Gillingham (youth team manager (1999).

Club honours: Reading: Division Three champions 1986. Peterborough: Division Four promotion 1991.
Younger brother of Des (q.v), Kevin Bremner was a fast,

lightweight striker who was one of five players tried by Blues manager Ron Saunders to combat the goal famine which had set in at St Andrew's in 1982. He set something of a record in season 1982-83 when he played for five different clubs and scored for each of them

BRENNAN, Robert Anderson

Inside/outside-left: 40 apps. 7 goals
Born: Belfast 14 March 1925.
Died: Norwich, 1 January 2002.
Career: Harland & Wolf Welders FC, Bloomfield United (1943-44), Distillery, Luton Town (October 1947), BLUES (£20,000, July 1949), Fulham (£9,500, July 1953), Yarmouth (August 1956), Norwich City (£15,000, July 1957). Retired April 1960 to become coach at King's Lynn FC.
Representative honours: Northern Ireland (5 full caps).

Bobby Brennan struck over 100 goals in more than 400 senior games during a fine career. He helped Norwich reach the 1959 F A Cup semi-finals, where they lost to his former club, Luton. A good quality footballer, he was unlucky not to have played longer in the First Division.

BRIDGES, Barry John

Utility forward: 104 apps. 46 goals
Born: Horsford near Norwich, 29 April 1941
Career: Norfolk Boys, Chelsea (juniors July 1956, professional May 1958), BLUES (£55,000, May 1966), Queen's Park Rangers (August 1968), Millwall (September 1970), Brighton & Hove Albion (September 1972), Highlands Park, South Africa (1974), St Patrick's Athletic Republic of Ireland (as player manager 1976), Sligo Rovers (manager 1978-79), Dereham Town (manager), King's Lynn (manager), Horsford FC (manager). Later ran a hotel in Brighton.
Club honours: Chelsea: FA Youth Cup winners 1958, Football League Cup winners 1965.
Representative honours: England (4 full caps, 6 Schoolboy, two Youth caps). Football League representative honour.

Barry Bridges played with great speed (he was a sprint champion at school) and was responsible for some of the most remarkable goals ever seen at St Andrew's. His over the shoulder scissor-kick which knocked Arsenal out of the 1968 FA Cup is still talked about today (by the older supporters). He became unsettled with Blues and subsequently moved south to facilitate the running of a hotel, purchased in Eastbourne. Bridges retired from major competitive football with a total of 215 League goals to his credit in 567 appearances. He appeared in both the 1967 League Cup & 1968 FA Cup semi-finals for Blues. Bridges now earns his living as a milkman.

BRIGGS, George Richard

Outside-right: 324 apps. 107 goals.

Born Wombwell, Yorkshire, 23 May 1903.

Now deceased.

Career: John Street School, Mitchell's Main Quarry FC, Ardsley Athletic, Wombwell (as a professional, 1922), Denaby United, BLUES (signed for £400 with Aubrey Scriven, December 1923), Plymouth Argyle (July 1933), St Austell FC (August 1936). Retired 1937.

Club honours: Blues: FA Cup runners-up 1931; Mitchell's Main: Nelson League champions.

After being tried in most forward births, 'Nippy' Briggs, a stocky, red-headed former miner settled down to become a firm favourite on the right wing, the position he occupied in the 1931 FA Cup Final (v. WBA). He was noted for always chasing lost causes, sometimes to good effect, most notably on the occasion when he headed his own cross into the net after the ball had been held up in the wind. Briggs, who stood almost 5ft 7ins tall and weighed a fraction over13 stone, was brother-in-law to Fred Tunstall, the Sheffield United and England player. He later worked at Moseley's in Bordesley Green.

BRIGGS, Malcolm Douglas

Forward: 0+1 app.

Born: Sunderland, 14 September, 1961

Career: Sunderland & District Schools, BLUES (apprentice 1977, professional August 1979), Durham City (August 1980).

A well-built athlete Malcolm Briggs was not even a regular reserve team player when, surprisingly, he was named as substitute at Maine Road at the end of the 1978-79 season. He made a very late entry into the action, coming on three minutes from time - giving him probably the shortest first-team career as any other Blues player mentioned in this book.

BRIGGS, Thomas Henry

Centre-forward: 52 apps. 23 goals

Born: Chesterfield, 27 November 1923. Died: Grimsby, 10 February 1984

Career: Plymouth Argyle, Grimsby Town (May 1947), Coventry City (£19,550, January 1951), BLUES (September 1951), Blackburn Rovers (£15,000, December 1952), Grimsby Town (£2,000, March 1958), Glentoran (player-manager, May 1959-June 1961).

Worked for a radio & TV company in Grimsby after quitting football. Guested for Plymouth during WW2

Representative honours: England (one 'B' cap).

A real hefty striker, Tommy Briggs claimed 286 goals in a career record of 390 League games. In one game for Blackburn (against Bristol Rovers) in February 1955, he scored seven goals. He netted a goal virtually every other game for Blues.

BROADHURST, Kevan

Defender/wing-half. 167+6 apps. 10 goals

Born: Dewsbury, 3 June 1959

Career: Woodkirk School, Morley, Bradford City (on trial), BLUES (apprentice, August 1975, professional March 1978), Walsall (on loan, November 1979).

Retired through injury, March 1986, but later insisted Knowle FC, becoming their general manager in 1991-92. Later played for Sherwood Celtic (January 1992); was caretaker-manager of Knowle (August 1993), BLUES' Youth coach (September 1993, caretaker/joint-manager December 1994; then back to Youth team coach, with the appointment of Barry Fry, combining his duties with playing for Sherwood Celtic (from March 1995). Broadhurst re-entered League football when he became manager of Northampton Town in October 2001.

A gritty, hard-tackling player who was given a destructive role, Kevan Broadhurst was good in the air for a small man and spent a season at centre-half after the departure of Joe Gallagher, but was dogged by injury throughout his career. He turned down a testimonial in 1985 because he felt that he had not played enough games for Blues to justify one when it was obvious that he was not going to recover from the knee injury. He did, however, accept a benefit match. A fine club man, he never let the side down.

BROCKEN, Budde Jan Peter Maria

Outside-right: 19 apps.

Born Tilburg, Netherlands, 12 September 1957

Career: SV Willem II (1975), BLUES (July 1981), FC Groningen (August 1982), SV Willem II (1985), BVV Den Bosch (1990-94).

Club honours: Den Bosch: Dutch Cup runners-up 1991.

Representative honours: Holland: (5 full caps, 2 'B' caps, 8 Under-21 caps, two Olympic caps).

'Bud' Brocken was already a Dutch Under-21 international and had been voted Holland's 'Young Player of the Year' in 1979 when manager Jim Smith signed him during Blues' pre-season tour. He proved to be fast and tricky but his delivery of crosses was somewhat wayward. On returning to Holland, Brocken's career blossomed and he helped Groningen battle for a place in Europe. He appeared in well over 500 League games (more than 60 goals scored) in Dutch football

BROWN, Edwin

Centre-forward: 185 apps. 90 goals

Born: Preston, 28 February 1926

Career: Preston North End (as a professional August 1948), Southampton (September 1950), Coventry City (March 1952), BLUES (October 1954), Leyton Orient (January 1959), Scarborough (1961), Stourbridge

(1962), Bedworth Town (player-manager, season 1963-64), Wigan Athletic (July 1964).
Retired in December 1964.
Club honours: Blues: Division Two champions 1955, FA Cup runners-up 1956.

Eddie Brown was almost lost to the game as a youngster when he wanted to enter the priesthood. But he was persuaded out of this by a football-mad clergyman, and developed into a marvellously gifted, orthodox centre-forward with his roaming tactics being designed to pull the centre half out of position. He played a crucial part in Blues' success in the mid-1950s, but for all his ability Brown is best remembered for his clowning antics, a favourite trick of his was to shake hands with a corner flag after scoring a goal! He also learned passages from Shakespeare to quote at press conferences. Brown - a great character off and on the pitch - later returned to his first love as a games teacher at a Roman Catholic college in Preston. He now lives at Fullwood, Preston.

BROWN, Ian O'Neill
Winger: 0+1 app.
Born: Ipswich, 11 September, 1965
Career: Luton Town (associate schoolboy), BLUES (non-contract 1984, professional, September 1985), Felixstowe Town, Sudbury Town, Stowmarket Town, Chelmsford City, Harwich & Parkeston, Chelmsford City, Bristol City (May 1993), Colchester United (on loan, March 1994), Northampton Town (on loan, December 1994-May 1995).
Ian Brown was a young winger given a run out for the last 12 minutes of a League Cup game against West Bromwich Albion in November 1985, during an injury crisis. It is believed that he never touched the ball whilst on the pitch.

BROWN, John
Outside-right: 38 apps. 7 goals
Born: Belfast, 8 November 1914.
Career: William Ewart & Son FC, Belfast Celtic (August 1933), Wolverhampton Wanderers (December 1934), Coventry City (£3,000, October 1936), BLUES (September 1938), Barry Town (January 1948), Ipswich Town (May 1948). Retired in June 1951.
Representative honours: Northern Ireland (10 full caps); Republic of Ireland (2 full caps).
Jackie Brown sprang to fame as a teenager in Ireland whilst serving his apprentice in the linen trade.
He failed to impress at Molineux, although he did gain the first of his 12 international caps, adding to his collection with Coventry. On arriving at St Andrew's his direct approach to wing play created a favourable impression but, try as he might, he was unable to inject much life into a poor attack.

BROWN, Kenneth James
Defender: 12 apps.
Born Upminster, 11 July 1967
Career: Norwich City (juniors 1983, professional July 1985), Plymouth Argyle (free transfer, August 1988), West Ham United (£175,000, August 1991), Huddersfield Town (on loan, September 1995), Reading (on loan, October 1995), Southend United (on loan, March 1996), Crystal Palace (on loan, March 1996), Reading (on loan, September 1996), BLUES (£75,000, December 1996), Millwall (£40,000, July 1997), Gillingham (free transfer March 1999), retired May 2000.
Son of the former West Ham United and England centre-half John Bond, versatile defender Kenny Bond never really settled in at St Andrew's and spent only half-a-season with Blues. During his career he amassed more than 360 senior appearances.

BROWN, Walter Ephraim
Forward: 3 apps. 2 goals
Born: Handsworth, Birmingham, 1867.
Now deceased.
Career: Key Hill School (Hockley), Grove Hill FC, Hockley Belmont, St James's, BLUES (1891), Crosswells Brewery (second half of season 1891-92)
Walter Brown was a utility forward who spent only two months with Blues, filling three different positions in four outings (one a friendly game).

BRUCE, Daniel:
Forward: 10 apps. 2 goals
Born: Bonhill, Scotland, 20 October 1870.
Died: 6 February 1921
Career: Vale of Leven, Glasgow Rangers (1891), Notts County (1892), BLUES (£100, November 1895), Perth (1896), Vale of Leven (February 1897), St Mirren (November 1897)
Club honours: Vale of Leven, Scottish Cup runners-up 1890, Notts County: FA Cup winners 1894
Representative honours: Scotland (one full cap)
A versatile performer, capable of operating in any forward position or at right half, Danny Bruce arrived in the Blues camp with a high reputation, having gained international honours. He was the club's first three-figure transfer, but failed to find his true form in Birmingham.

BRUCE, Henry
Full-back: 8 apps
Born: Coundon, County Durham, 19 May 1905.
Now deceased.
Career: Durham City, Bishop Auckland, BLUES (as an amateur, January 1925, professional February 1925), Gillingham (May 1928), Torquay United (May 1929), Colwyn Bay United (July 1930), Bankhead Albion, Rochdale (January 1931), Bankhead Albion (April

1931), Reading (May 1931).
Retired during season 1939-40.
Harry Bruce was a strong player who failed to get a Third Division (North) game with Durham City and was signed by Blues as cover for both full-back berths, staying at St Andrew's for a number of years before leaving to enjoy first-team football with the 'Gills.'

BRUCE, Stephen Roger

Defender: 82 apps. 2 goals
Born: Corbridge, 31 December 1960
Career: Gillingham (apprentice 1986, professional October 1978), Norwich City (£125,000, August 1984), Manchester United (£800,000, December 1987), BLUES (June 1996), Sheffield United (player-manager, July 1998), Huddersfield Town (manager, June 1999), Crystal Palace (manager), BLUES (manager, December 2001).
Club honours: Norwich: League Cup winners 1985, Division Two champions 1986; Manchester United: Premier League Champions 1993, 1994, 1996, runners-up 1995, Football League runners-up 1992, FA Cup winners 1990 & 1994, runners-up 1995, European Cup-winners Cup winners 1991, League Cup winners 1992, European Super Cup winners 1991, runners-up 1991 & 1994, FA Charity Shield winners 1993 & 1994. As manager he guided Blues into the Premiership in 2002.
Representative Honours: England ('B' & Youth Cups), Football League XI Centre-half Steve Bruce spent two seasons as a player with Blues, making over 80 appearances - all this after he had starred in more than 425 senior games for Manchester United, 230 for Gillingham and 180 for Norwich. A terrific competitor in every aspect of defensive play, clearly emphasised by the many scars he has on his head, Bruce returned to the club and duly guided Blues into the Premiership, bringing top-flight football to St Andrew's for the first time in 16 years.

BRUNSKILL, Norman H

Wing-half. 65 apps 2 goals
Born: Dipton, County Durham, 12 June 1912.
Died: Boston, Lincolnshire, 28 February 1988
Career: South Moor Juniors, Newcastle United (on trial), Lintz Colliery, Huddersfield Town (as an amateur, October 1930, professional May 1931), Oldham Athletic (May 1932), BLUES (£1,300, October 1936), Barnsley (£1,560, November 1938). Released in May 1946. Guested for Middlesbrough & Hartlepool United during World War 1.
Club honours: Barnsley: Division Three (North) champions 1939.
Norman Brunskill was a tall, hard-working wing half with a voracious appetite for the game and was a grafter with a fierce shot when he chose to let fly. A former coalminer and son of a well-known referee.

BRUTON, Edward Mitchell

Goalkeeper: one app.
Born: Penn, near Wolverhampton, 1871.
Now deceased.
Career: Stafford Rangers, BLUES (on trial, September 1894), Willenhall Swifts (December 1894-May 1895).
Ted Bruton was a trialist who never even tasted reserve team football with Blues. He conceded four goals in his only first team outing (in a 4-4 home draw with Preston North End).

BRYANT, Steven Paul

Left-back: 40+2 app. one goals
Born: Islington, London, 5 September 1953
Career: Middlesex County Schools, BLUES (apprentice 1970, professional July 1971), Sheffield Wednesday (on loan, August 1976), Northampton Town (December 1976), Portsmouth (March 1979), Northampton Town (March 1982). Later played in Australia for a time
Steve Bryant was originally a winger of considerable guile but was converted into a full-back by Blues. Mysteriously omitted (with Jimmy Calderwood) from the 1975 FA Cup semi-final team after putting in some promising performances in the earlier rounds, this unsettled the Londoner who was never the same player again. He reverted to midfield after leaving St Andrew's.

BUCKLEY, Alan Paul

Inside/centre-forward: 25+4 apps. 8 goals
Born: Mansfield, 20 April, 1951
Career: Nottingham Forest (apprentice June 1967, professional April 1968), Walsall (August 1973), BLUES (October 1978), Walsall (July 1979, then manager at Fellows Park from July 1979 to July 1981 and again from May 1982 to August 1986), Stourbridge (as a player, September 1986), Tamworth (October 1986), Kettering Town (manager, November 1986), Grimsby Town (manager, June 1988), West Bromwich Albion (manager October 1994), Grimsby Town (manager, May 1997), Lincoln City (manager, February 2001 to May 2002).
Club honours: (as manager): Grimsby: Division Four promotion 1990, Division Three promotion 1991 & Division Two promotion via the Play-offs, 1998; also Auto-Windscreen Shield winners, 1998
Short, stocky inside-forward with an eye for goal, Alan Buckley turned out be one of the Walsall's best-ever signings, scoring over 200 goals in some 500 games for the Saddlers during his two spells with the club. He took Walsall to the brink of promotion several times before achieving success with Grimsby. He had just one good season at St Andrew's.
Unfortunately he failed to do the business at The Hawthorns and after rejoining Grimsby, he led the Mariners to a Wembley double in 1998 when they lifted the AWS and clinched promotion by winning the Second Division Play-off final. However, after some poor

results he left Blundell Park and was out of football for a short while, before re-entering the fray as manager at Sincil Bank. His brother Steve played for Luton Town, Derby County & Lincoln City, while his two sons, Adam and Simon are both Professionals.

BUCKLEY, Major Franklin Charles
Centre-half: 56 apps. 4 goals
Born: Urmston, Manchester, 9 November 1882.
Died: Walsall, 22 December 1964
Career: Aston Villa (season 1903-04), Brighton & Hove Albion (1905), Manchester United (June 1906), Manchester City (September 1907), BLUES (July 1909), Derby County (May 191), Bradford City (May 1914).
Retired 1918, having served as a Major in the footballer's battalion of the Middlesex Regiment (1916-18); Norwich City (manager March 1919-20); worked as Commercial Traveller in London until July 1923 when he became manager of Blackpool; Wolverhampton Wanderers (manager, May 1927): Notts County (manager, March 1944); Hull City (manager, May 1946), Leeds United (manager, May 1948), Walsall (manager, April 1953). Quit football in June 1955.
Club honours: Derby: Division Two champions 1912; (as manager) Wolves. Division Two champions 1932, FA Cup runners-up 1939: League North (War) Cup winners 1942
Representative honours: England (one full cap).
Frank Buckley was a tall, heavily built defender, hard-working and forceful when attacking. He was better known for his managerial exploits, however, rather than his performances on the pitch as a player. Always open to ideas, he was a strict disciplinarian and his players were left in no doubt as to who was in charge. It was the Major who called the shots and in fact, he also suggested that shirts should carry numbers (to help spectators). He also stepped up fitness procedures, especially at Molineux. Whilst still an active player, he helped run a pig farm near Redditch with his brother, Chris, the former Villa and Arsenal defender.

BULL, Gary William
Striker: 16+6 apps. 8 goals
Born: West Bromwich, 12 June, 1966
Career: Swindon Town (Schoolboy forms, 1981), Paget Rangers (1982), Southampton (October 1986), Cambridge United (March 1988), Barnet (March 1989), Nottingham Forest (July 1993), BLUES (on loan, September 1994), Brighton & Hove Albion (on loan, August 1995), BLUES (signed on a free transfer, December 1995), York City (March 1996), Scunthorpe United (July 1998), Wolverhampton Wanderers (briefly), Grantham Town (June 2000).
Club honours: Barnet: GM Vauxhall Conference champs, 1991; Blues: Second Division champions 1995
Cousin of Wolves' Steve Bull, Gary was also an out-and-

out striker who scored 37 goals in 83 League games for Barnet before joining Forest. He had a decent loan spell at St Andrew's before returning to join Blues permanently just over a year later. During his career in the Football League Bull netted 65 goals in 253 appearances.

BULLOCK, Michael Edwin
Centre-forward: 31 apps. 11 goals
Born: Stoke-on-Trent, 2 October 1946
Career: North Staffs Schools, Stoke Boys, BLUES (apprentice, July 1962, professional, October 1963), Oxford United (June 1967), Leyton Orient (October 1968), Halifax Town (player, February 1976, retired as a player in May 1979 to become coach, then manager from July 1981 to October 1984), Goole Town manager 1986), Ossett Town (manager 1989-90).
Club honours: Oxford: Division Three champions 1968: Orient: Division Three champions 1970.
Representative honours: England (Schoolboy international).
Micky Bullock was a star of the Stoke Boys' team that won the ESFA Trophy in 1972 and his signing for Blues was obviously influenced by the fact that his brother Peter (q.v) had recently joined the club. Not particularly tall, he grafted hard and long and acquired a good scoring record during his 15 years in the game at senior level, finishing with 108 goals in 469 League appearances

BULLOCK, Peter Leonard
Inside forward: 28 apps. 3 goals
Born: Stoke-on-Trent, 17 November, 1941
Career: Stoke City (junior, July 1957, professional November 1958), BLUES (March 1962), Southend United (February 1965), Colchester United (October 1965), Exeter City (July 1968), Stafford Rangers (November-December 1968), Walsall (December 1968 to May 1970).
Representative honours: England (Schoolboy & Youth international). Peter Bullock was troubled by injuries throughout his career and found goals hard to come by in the First Division but managed a fair record in the sphere. His son, Simon, played a few games for Halifax Town when brother Micky (who also played for Blues, q.v), was in charge at The Shay. Elder brother, Brian, was an amateur with West Bromwich Albion and was also on Stoke City's books in the 1950s.

BUMPHREY, James
Wing-half: 143 apps. 6 goals
Born: Morpeth, Northumberland, 1885.
Now deceased.
Career: Ashington Alliance, BLUES (August 1908), Durham City (July 1915).
Perhaps just the right build for a footballer (5ft 8 ins tall & 13st in weight) Jim Bumphrey proved a difficult man

to meet in the tackle and he was a good header of the ball as well. He was frequently criticised for being a little wild in his challenges, however and was regularly in trouble with officialdom, yet never sent-off.

BUNCH, Walter
Left-back: 3 apps
Born: Weston-super-Mare, 1872.
Died: Somerset
Career: Compton Colts, Wolverhampton Wanderers, Bristol Rovers, Walsall (July 1899), BLUES (September 1901). Forced to retire through injury and illness in May 1902, he subsequently became licensee of the Golden Lion, Chell Street, Dudley
An experienced full-back, Walter Bunch unfortunately failed to impress during his brief spell with Blues

BURCHILL, Mark James
Striker: 7+10 apps. 5 goals
Born: Broxburn, 18 August 1980
Career: Celtic Boys Club, Celtic (June 1997), BLUES (on loan, September 2000), Ipswich Town (on loan, January 2001), Portsmouth (£600,000, August 2001).
Representative Honours: Scotland (6 full, 15 Under-21 and Schoolboy caps).
Mark Burchill, an exceptionally talented striker, made over 60 appearances for Celtic before settling in the Nationwide League with Pompey. With an excellent first touch and an eye for goal, it was a pity he couldn't agree terms with Blues!

BURKENSHAW, Laurence
Outside-right: 75 apps. 12 goals
Born: Kilnhurst, December 1893.
Died: Mexborough, spring 1969.
Career: Kilnhurst Schools, Mexborough Town, Sheffield Wednesday (April 1910), Rotherham Town (July 1914), Kilnhurst FC (August 1918), Stalybridge Celtic (1918-19), BLUES (August 1919), Halifax Town (July 1922), Mexborough Town (August 1923). Guested for Barnsley during World War 1.
Club honours: Blues: Division Two champions 1921.
'Lol' Burkenshaw was a winger who relied more on skill rather than pace who failed to gain much recognition at top-class level. His brother Jack played for Sheffield Wednesday. Burkenshaw was also a good cricketer.

BURNS, Kenneth
Defender/centre-forward: 195+9 apps. 53 goals
Born: Glasgow, 23 September, 1953
Career: Glasgow Rangers (schoolboy forms), BLUES (apprentice June 1970, professional July 1971), Nottingham Forest (£150,000, July 1977), Leeds United (£400,000, October 1981), Derby County (on loan, March 1983 and again in February 1984, signing permanently in March 1984), Notts County (on loan,

February 1985), Barnsley (August 1985), IF Elfsborg/Sweden (March 1986), Sutton Town (August 1986, then player-manager March 1987), Stafford Rangers (player, July 1987), Grantham Town (player-coach season 1988-89), Gainsborough Trinity (player-coach 1989), Ilkeston Town (player-coach 1990-93); Oakham United (player-coach), Telford United (assistant-manager July 1993-94).
Club honours: Nottingham Forest: European Cup winners 1979 & 1980; Division One champions 1978, Football League Cup winners 1978, runners-up 1980; 'Footballer of the Year' 1978; Blues: Division 2 promotion 1972
Representative honours: Scotland (20 full caps, 2 Under-23 caps). Kenny Burns was a rare talent, a player able and willing to perform in any outfield position with equal effect. Initially a central defender, he was successfully converted into an out-and-out striker after Bob Latchford had departed from St Andrew's and his aggressive, all-action style and superb heading ability made him a player feared by many. But he always wanted to get back to defend and it was here that he won most of his honours at club and international level. He helped Blues gain promotion in 1972 and was with Forest under manager Brian Clough. Burns totalled in excess of 500 senior appearances as a professional, 424 coming in the Football League, 170 of them with Blues (45 goals) and 137 for Forest. Burns is now a publican in the Stoke-on-Trent area, having previously held a similar post in Ilkeston.

BURROWS, David
Defender: 19+11 apps.
Born: Dudley, 25 October 1968
Career: St Martin's Junior & Alexander High Schools (Tipton), West Bromwich District Boys & West Midlands County Schools, West Bromwich Albion (trainee, 1984, professional November 1986), Liverpool (£550,000, October 1988), West Ham United (September 1993), Everton (September 1994), Coventry City (£1.1 million, March 1995), BLUES (free transfer, July 2000), Sheffield Wednesday (free transfer, March 2002, briefly joint caretaker-manager at Hillsborough, October 2002).
Club Honours: Liverpool: League champions 1990, FA Cup winners 1992, Charity Shield winners 1989; Blues; Division One promotion 2002.
Representative Honours: England (3 'B' & 7 U-21 caps).
Experienced full-back David Burrows had already amassed more than 420 senior appearances when he joined Blues in the summer of 2000. An asset to any club's defence, he is composed on the ball with a smashing left foot, and always gives a good account of himself, no matter what the circumstances.

BURTON, Edward George
Centre-forward: one app.
Born: Acocks Green, Birmingham, 1869.
Now deceased.
Career: Highfield Villa, BLUES (September 1891),
Springfield Villa (August 1892).
Ted Burton was given only one first team outing by
Blues (in place of the injured Harry Morris) and did
nothing to justify further inclusion in the team

BURTON, John Henry
Inside-left: 4 apps. 3 goals
Born: South Bank, 13 August 1875.
Died: Derby 13 May 1949
Career: Derby St Andrew's, Derby County (1897-98),
Chatham, Tottenham Hotspur, Grangetown FC,
Blackburn Rovers (March 1906), Preston North End
(1906-07), West Ham United (July 1908), BLUES
(September 1909), Nelson (October 1910), Cardiff City
(July 1911), Southend United (May 1914).
Jack Burton was a rangy forward with an eye for goal.
Already at the veteran stage when he joined Blues, he had
previously drawn up a pretty impressive strike-record
(mainly at reserve team level), but annoyingly he
couldn't command a regular first-team place at St
Andrew's. During his lengthy career Burton only
appeared in 17 Football League matches.

BURTON, Michael James
Winger: 0+4 apps
Born: Birmingham, 5 November, 1969
Career: Tamworth & District Schools, BLUES (YTS,
June 1986, professional July 1987), Sheffield Wednesday
(January 1991), Shrewsbury Town (March 1991), Moor
Green (February 1992), Milton Keynes Borough (May
1992), Moor Green (February 1992), Bromsgrove
Rovers, Solihull Borough (January 1994), Redditch
United (July 1994-95).
Mike Burton was a stocky, crew-cutted winger who
favoured pace to beat his opponent but tended to be a
bit wayward with his centres.

BUTLER, Herbert
Centre-half: 11 apps
Born: Eastwood, Notts, 18 November 1911.
Died: Bestwood, Notts, June 1984
Career Quarry Road Old Boys FC, Bestwood Colliery
FC (Notts), BLUES (as an amateur May 1933,
professional August 1933), Crewe Alexandra (March
1939). Guested for West Bromwich Albion during
World War 2. 'Dick' Butler was a powerfully built
defender (6ft tall & 12st 10b in weight). He was the star
of Blues' Central League side for most of the 1930s, but
his first team outings were limited due to the form and
reliability of Messrs Morrall and Fillingham. Butler was
also a fine bowls player.

BYE, James Henry
Right-half: 2 apps
Born: Aston, Birmingham, 4 March 1920
Career: St Peter's School (Harborne), Bournbrook
Alliance, Shirley Juniors, BLUES (junior May 1937,
professional August 1937). Retired in May 1944.
Guested for Nottingham Forest & West Bromwich
Albion during WW2 whilst serving in the army.
Jimmy Bye served his apprenticeship at St Andrew's but
as soon as he had gained a first-team place WW2 broke
out and unfortunately he never played again at
competitive level after the hostilities had ended.

CALDERWOOD, James
Full-back/midfielder: 147+12 apps. 5 goals
Born: Glasgow, 28 February 1955
Career: Glasgow Amateurs, BLUES (apprentice July
1971, professional July 1972), Cambridge United (on
loan, November 1979 to January 1980). Contract
cancelled by club, July 1980; went to Holland, serving in
turn with Willem II (August 1980), Roda JC (1982), SC
Heracles (1988) and FC Den Haag (July 1990), then FC
Zwolle (as assistant-manager, January 1992): SC
Cambuur Leeuwaarden (as assistant-manager, June
1993); later returned to the UK as manager of the
Scottish club Dunfermline Athletic.
Representative honours: Scotland (one Under-23 cap).
Originally a creative midfielder, Jimmy Calderwood was
converted into a fine, overlapping full-back with a good
right foot. Not the strongest in the tackle, he tended to
be made the scapegoat when things went wrong but he
did very well in Dutch football

CALLADINE, Charles Frederick
Wing-half: 127 apps. 4 goals
Born: Wessington, Derbyshire 24 January 1911. Died:
Matlock, Derbyshire, 29 October 1983
Career: Wessington FC (1927), Ivanhoe FC, Scunthorpe
United (1928), BLUES (May 1930), Blackburn Rovers
(February 1936), Guildford City (August 1938). Retired
during WW2.
Charlie Calladine was described in 1933, as being 'quick
and cunning' and he was also physically strong (at 5ft
9ins tall and 11st 2lbs in weight). He played with vigour
and power, possessing a rocket like shot. He signed for
Blues on the platform of Doncaster railway station. He
was a teetotaller and non-smoker, a keen pigeon fancier,
hiker and a former civil servant.

CAMERON, Edward S
Inside-forward: 6 apps. one goal
Born: Glasgow, 1895. Died: Stafford.
Career: Clydebank (1919), BLUES (July 1921), Walsall
(May 1922), Nelson (March 1924), Stafford Rangers
(1926), Exeter City (June 1928), Nelson (on trial, 1929),
Stafford Rangers (August 1929), Cradley Heath (1931),

Hednesford Town (1933), Stafford Rangers (July 1934). Eddie Cameron was a burly Scot who had his best spell in League football with Nelson in the Division Three (North). He was never a great goalscorer, but a player who employed direct methods.

CAMPBELL, Alan James

Midfielder: 202+7 apps. 14 goals
Born: Arbroath, 21 January, 1948
Career: Hags Head Primary & Arbroath High Schools, Arbroath Lads' Club, Charlton Athletic (apprentice, July 1964, professional February 1965), BLUES (October 1970), Cardiff City (March 1976), Carlisle United (November 1980), Redditch United (July 1982), Olton Royal FC (1986), Highgate United (assistant-manager 1989, manager, May 1982), Stratford Town (assistant-manager, June 1992, promoted to team manager June 1993-late 1993).
Cub honours: Blues: Division Two runners-up 1972
Representative honours: Scotland (one Under-23 cap, 4 Youth caps).
There were some adverse comments when Alan Campbell moved to St Andrew's rather than to one of the bigger clubs, but he proved to be a worthy signing and during his five years with Blues his displays were a barometer for the team's performances. When he played well, so too did the rest of the side. Particularly adept at finding space and a fine passer of the ball, Campbell was also a distinctive figure on the field with his long dark hair and a shirt which always looked two sizes too big for his slight frame.

CAMPBELL, Stuart Pearson

Midfielder: 0+2 apps.
Born: Corby, 9 December 1977
Career: Leicester City (trainee 1994, professional July 1996), BLUES (on loan, March 2000), Grimsby Town (£200,000, September 2000).
Club honours: Leicester: League Cup winners 1997 & 2000.
Representative Honours: Scotland: (14 Under-21 caps)
A strong and skilful midfielder, on loan at St Andrew's for a month in 2000, Campbell later made a huge contribution to the Mariners' annual battle against relegation.

CAPEL, Thomas

Inside-left: 8 apps, one goal
Born: Chorlton, Manchester, 27 June, 1922
Career: Droylsden FC, Manchester City (November 1941), Chesterfield (October 1947), BLUES (June 1949), Nottingham Forest (November 1949), Coventry City (June 1954), Halifax Town (October 1955, Heanor Town (July 1956). Served in the Marines during WW2 with Eddie Quigley (Blackburn Rovers & Preston North End) and Ken Oliver (Derby County & Exeter City). Tommy Capel was a powerful, bustling player who

scored plenty of goals elsewhere in a fine career. His brother Fred was a full-back with Chesterfield.

CARR, Derek Henry

Utility player: 4 apps
Born: Blidworth, near Mansfield, 1 September, 1927
Career: Crook, Lockheed Leamington, BLUES (amateur, December 1947, professional February 1948), Rugby Town (1950), Evesham Town, Boldmere St Michael's.
Derek Carr's appearances were split between full-back, wing half and centre-forward, and he had a spell working in the offices at St Andrew's before drifting into non-League football.

CARRIER, William

Right-back: 7 apps
Born: Ashington, 1887. Died: County Durham.
Career: Manchester United (briefly, 1904), Merthyr junior football (1905-09), BLUES (September 1909), Worcester City (August 1912-13).
A tall, muscular player noted for his heading ability, Bill Carrier was born in the North-East of England but brought up in South Wales. His spell with Manchester United was unimpressive but he was being touted for Welsh honours before it was discovered that he was an Englishman.

CARRICK, Michael

Midfielder: 1+1 apps
Born: Wallsend-on-Tyne, 28 July 1981
Career: West Ham United (trainee, July 1996, professional August 1998), Swindon Town (on loan, November 1999), BLUES (on loan, February 2000).
Representative Honours: England (2* full caps, 8 Under-21 caps, Youth).
A very competent young left-sided midfielder, Michael Carrick assisted Blues briefly in 2000 and later won full international caps for his country and is certainly a star of the future.

CARRODUS, Frank

Midfielder: 7+2 apps.
Born: Manchester, 31 May 1949
Career: Altrincham (July 1964), Manchester City (November 1969), Aston Villa (August 1974), Wrexham (December 1979), went on rebel tour to South Africa (1982), BLUES (August 1982), Bury (October 1983), Witton Albion, Runcorn, Altrincham (1988).
Club honours: Aston Villa: Football League Cup winners 1975 & 1977.
Frank Carrodus worked as a civil servant before entering League football. He broke through with Villa having been a fringe player at Maine Road. A workforce in centre midfield, he lost his place at Villa Park to Des Bremner and was later blacklisted after going to South Africa but Blues gave him another chance. A strong

pigeon fancier, he also enjoyed hiking. He now lives in Altrincham and provides corporate hospitality for sporting events while also penning a witty column in a local sports paper.

CARROLL, Thomas Roger
Right-back: 47 apps
Born: Dublin, 18 August 1942
Career: St Finbarr's FC, Shelbourne (1958), Cambridge City (August 1964), Ipswich Town (July 1966), BLUES (on loan, October 1971, signed permanently November 1971). Retired from competitive football through injury in October 1973.
Club honours: Shelbourne: Irish Cup winners 1962
Representative honours: Republic of Ireland (17 full caps). Tommy Carroll starred in both the European Cup and European Cup Winners' Cup competitions in the early 1960s with Shelbourne, for whom he appeared in every outfield position, having joined the club as a 15 year-old after he had accompanied his brother, Eddie, to a training session. He always believed in trying to play his way out of difficult situations. After returning to Ireland he served a prison sentence after being found guilty of fraud.

CARTER, Darren
Midfielder/full-back: 17+6 apps*. one goal
Born: Solihull, 18 December 1983
Career: BLUES (trainee 2000, pro, November 2001).
Club honours: Blues: Division One promotion 2002
Darren Carter was Blues' Play-off hero at Cardiff's Millennium Stadium in May 2002 when his exquisitely taken spot-kick in the shoot-out against Norwich City brought Premiership football to St Andrew's. Voted the club's 'Young Player of the Year' for his efforts, Carter is a strong box-to-box player who tackles hard but fair and has a terrific engine. He has also figured as an orthodox left-back.

CARTER, Timothy Douglas
Goalkeeper: 3 apps
Born:: Bristol 5 October, 1967.
Career: Bristol Schools, Bristol Rovers (apprentice 1983, professional October 1985), Newport County (on loan, December 1987), Sunderland (December 1987), Carlisle United (on loan, March 1988), Bristol City (on loan, September 1988), BLUES (on loan, November 1991), Hartlepool United (August 1993), Millwall (January 1994), Blackpool (free transfer August 1995), Oxford United (free, August 1995), Millwall (free, December 1995), Halifax Town (free, July 1998-June 1999).
Representative honours: England (3 Youth caps).
Tim Carter was a tall goalkeeper who played 47 League games for Bristol Rovers, 37 for Sunderland and 71 for Millwall.

CASTLE, Frederick Charles
Centre-forward: 3 apps
Born: King's Norton, Birmingham 29 January 1899.
Died Smethwick, late 1974
Career: Smethwick Highfield, BLUES (April 1925), Shrewsbury Town (August 1927).
At 5ft 7ins Fred Castle was small for a centre-forward and looked out of his depth in League football.

CASTLE, Stephen Charles
Midfielder: 31+7 apps.2 goals
Born: Barkingside, Essex 17 May 1966
Career: Leyton Orient (apprentice June 1982, professional May 1984), Plymouth Argyle (£195,000, June 1992), BLUES (£225,000, July 1995), Gillingham (on loan, February 1996), Leyton Orient (on loan, February 1997), Peterborough United (May 1997), Leyton Orient (July 2000 to May 2002).
Steve Castle's non-stop competitive work-rate showed through at each club he has served; a fine professional who appeared in almost 600 senior matches (123 goals scored) before announcing his retirement (with a knee injury) in May 2002.

CATLIN, Robert
Goalkeeper: 8 apps
Born: London 22 June 1965
Career: APIA Leichardt, Marconi Fairfield (Australia), Notts County (August 1992), BLUES (on loan, March 1993).
Born in England but brought up in Australia after his parents emigrated when he was four years old, Bob Catlin was given an early chance by Notts County but fell from grace after conceding eight goals in his first three games. He was not even a regular in County's reserve-team when Blues stepped in during an injury crisis and secured his services. He immediately kept his first clean-sheet in League football (on his debut) after which it was announced that Blues had signed him by mistake! Coach/scout Trevor Morgan had watched Magpies' reserves and raved about their goalkeeper ...who Blues agreed to sign. Unfortunately, County had fielded their youth team goalkeeper in the match Morgan was watching. Notts County had been initially fined £20,000 for irregularities when signing Catlin from Australia.

CHAPLIN, Alfred
Half back: 4 apps
Born: Foleshill, 1879.
Now deceased.
Career: Bablake School, St Paul's Bible Class FC, Folesworth St Paul's FC, Folesworth Great Heath, Coventry City (1902), BLUES (May 1903), Woolwich Arsenal (June 1905), Coventry City (season 1912-13): Longford (1913).
Representative honours: Birmingham FA (Juniors)

Alf Chaplin was signed by Blues following a promising display for Birmingham Juniors against the Scottish Juniors. He had a reputation as a quality marksman in local football, and once hit 24 goals in one match. He failed to make Arsenal's first team but later enjoyed a good spell with Coventry.

CHAPPLE, Frederick J

Inside-forward: 53 apps. 16 goals
Born: Treharris, South Wales, 1880.
Now deceased.
Career: Treharris Boys' Cub, Bristol Schools, Aston Villa (August 1906), BLUES (December 1908), Crewe Alexandra (June 1910), Brentford (July 1912), Bristol City (June 1913), Blyth Spartans (1918). Retired 1920.
Fred Chapple, a nippy footballer, elusive at times, had only nine games in two-and-a-half years with Villa. He flattered to deceive at St Andrew's where he was a regular if not a prolific scorer

CHARLERY, Kenneth Leroy

Striker: 13+11 apps. 6 goals
Born: Stepney 28 November 1964
Career: Fisher Athletic, Maidstone United (£35,000, March 1989), Peterborough United (£20,000, March 1991), Watford (£350,000, October 1992), Peterborough United (£150,000, December 1993), BLUES (£350,000, July 1995), Southend United (on loan, January 1996), Peterborough United (February 1996), Stockport County (£85,000, March 1997), Barnet (£80,000, August 1997), Boston United (September 2001), Dagenham & Redbridge (August 2001), Farnborough Town (May 2002).
Representative Honours: St Lucia (4 caps)
A very useful striker, 6ft 1in tall, almost 14st in weight, Ken Charlery followed Barry Fry around before having a decent spell with Barnet for whom he scored 38 goals in 142 League and Cup games. He had mixed fortunes at St Andrew's but still had a useful strike-record.

CHARLES, Gary Andrew

Full-back: 3 apps
Born: Newham, 13 April 1970
Career: Nottingham Forest (trainee, June 1985, professional November 1987), Leicester City (on loan, March 1989), Derby County (£750,000, July 1993), Aston Villa (January 1995), Benfica (£1.5 million, January 1999), West Ham United (£1.2 million, October 1999), BLUES (on loan, September-October 2000); forced to retire through injury, May 2002.
Club Honours: Nottingham Forest: 2DSC winners 1992; Aston Villa: League Cup winners 1996.
Representative Honours: England (2 full, 4 Under-21 caps).
A very positive right-wing-back whose strengths were his speed and crossing, Gary Charles made well over 250 senior appearances at club level before retiring.

CHARSLEY, Christopher Charles

Goalkeeper: 81 apps
Born: Leicester, 7 November 1864.
Died: Weston-super-Mare, 10 January, 1945
Career: St Patrick's Court (Stafford), Stafford Town (1881), Stafford Rangers (from 1883), Aston Villa (as a guest in 1886), BLUES (three separate spells: September 1886, December 1891 & December 1893-May 1894), West Bromwich Albion (August-December 1891).
Served in the Birmingham Police Force (from 1884) and later became Chief Constable of Coventry (August 1899). Retiring in 1918 he then moved to Weston-super-Mare and was elected to the town council, rising to Deputy Mayor in 1939-40 and remaining on the council until his death.
Club honours: Blues: Division Two champions 1893
Representative honours: England (one full cap).
Chris Charsley was an amateur goalkeeper who was signed by Blues after putting on a brilliant display for Stafford and was the first player to win a full international cap whilst a member of the club. Well over six feet tall, he had a safe pair of hands and strong kick. His brother, Walter (q.v) also played briefly for Blues

CHARSLEY, Walter Oscar

Wing-half: 3 apps.
Born: Birmingham, 1866.
Now deceased.
Career: BLUES (season 1890-91).
Walter Charsley was overshadowed by his better-known brother Chris (q.v) and made only three first-team appearances when injury took its toll of Birmingham's regular half-backs.

CHARLTON, Simon Thomas

Full-back: 75+3 apps.
Born: Huddersfield, 25 October 1971
Career: Huddersfield Town (trainee, 1988, professional July 1989), Southampton (£250,000, June 1993), BLUES (£250,000, December 1997), Bolton Wanderers (free transfer, July 2000).
Club honours: Bolton: Division One promotion 2001
Representative honours: England (Youth caps)
A solid and dependable defender, a firm favourite with the fans wherever he's played, Simon Charlton is a timely-tackler and has the ability to run all day! He made over 150 appearances for Huddersfield and 136 for Saints before moving to St Andrew's.

CHEESEWRIGHT, John Anthony

Goalkeeper: 2 apps
Born: Romford, 12 January 1973
Career: Tottenham Hotspur (YTS July1989), Southend United (March 1991), Kingsbury Town, BLUES (non-contract, October 1991), Cobh Ramblers (on loan, January 1992), Dagenham & Redbridge (September

1992), Braintree Town, Colchester United (January 1994).

John Cheesewright looked a useful prospect early in his career but he never made the grade in League football at Blues.

CHILDS, Gary Paul Colin

Midfielder: 44+18 apps. 2 goals
Born: Kings Heath, Birmingham, 19 April, 1964
Career: Maypole and Brantwood Schools (Kings Heath), South Birmingham Boys, West Bromwich Albion (apprentice June 1980, professional February 1982), Walsall (on loan, October 1983, signing permanently for £15,000, November 1983), BLUES (£21,500, July 1987), Grimsby Town (July, 1989), Grantham Town (briefly), Wisbech Town, Winterton Rangers (season 1996-97).
Club honours: Grimsby: Division Four promotion 1990, Division Three promotion 1991.
Representative honours: England (Youth caps).
Gary Childs' played over 150 games for Walsall and helped Grimsby win promotion in two successive seasons under the managership of former Blues striker Alan Buckley. A ball-playing midfielder, Childs was a firm favourite at Fellows Park but was often criticised for his unwillingness to get stuck in at St Andrew's.

CISSE, Aliou

Midfielder: 20 apps*
Born: Sedan, 24 April 1976
Career: Sedanese football, Montpellier, Paris St Germain, BLUES (£1.5 million, August 2002).
Representative honours: Senegal (12 caps*)
A strong, hard-tackling, forceful midfielder, Aliou Cisse joined Blues after a successful World Cup in South Korea and Japan. Reported to be earning £15,000-a-week, he was appointed captain by manager Steve Bruce.
Sadly, in October 2002, Cisse lost nine members of his family in a ferry sinking accident off the coast of Zambia.

CLACK, Frank Edward

Goalkeeper: 66 apps.
Born: Witney, Gloucestershire, 30 March 1912.
Died: 1995.
Career Newlands FC, Witney Town, BLUES (amateur October 1932, professional May 1933), Brentford (July 1939), Bristol City (April 1947), Guildford City (August 1949), Dover (1950); guested for Mansfield Town and Notts County in WW2
Frank Clack was a more than useful goalkeeper who spent his youth as deputy to Harry Hibbs. He did surprisingly well in non-League soccer after World War 2 and on retiring earned his living as a lawyer in his birthplace of Witney. Clack who had previously worked in a blanket factory, also enjoyed a game of cricket, tennis and bowls.

CLARIDGE, Stephen Edward

Striker: 116+4 apps 42 goals
Born: Portsmouth, 10 April 1966
Career: Portsmouth (apprentice 1982), Fareham Town (1983), AFC Bournemouth (professional November 1984) Weymouth (£10,000, October 1985), Crystal Palace (August 1988), Aldershot (£14,000, October 1988), Cambridge United (£75,000, February 1990), Luton Town (£160,000 July 1992), Cambridge United £195,000 November 1992), BLUES (£350,000, January 1994), Leicester City (£1.2 million, March 1996), Portsmouth (on loan, January 1998), Wolverhampton Wanderers (£400,000, March 1998), Portsmouth (£200,000, August 1998, briefly manager 2000-01), Millwall (on loan, March 2001, signed permanently on a free transfer, July 2002).
Club Honours: Cambridge Utd: Division 3 champions 1991, Blues: Division 2 champions 1995, Leyland DAF Trophy winners 1995; Leicester City: League Cup winners 1997.
Steve Claridge's often scruffy looking appearance, his socks seemingly always rolled down round his ankles, certainly belies the skill in his feet. Exceptionally good on the ball, and despite having 13 different striking partners in season 1994-95, he scored a goal every three games for Blues, helping them claim the Second Division title and Leyland DAF Trophy double in 1995. He scored a dramatic 120th minute play-off winning goal against his old club Crystal Palace that took Leicester into the Premiership in 1996 and a year later netted an extra-time winner for the Foxes in the Coca-Cola League Cup Final against Middlesbrough. Early in the 2002-03 season Claridge reached the personal milestone of 650 appearances at club level (over 200 goals scored).
● This is what Claridge said on leaving Cambridge United: "I knew I couldn't take anymore when, one day in training, a player shouted 'feet' meaning that's where he wanted the ball - and he was punished by being made to do 40 press-ups."
● Also during his time at The Abbey Stadium, Claridge was picked up by the police - for drunkeness! What happened is simple: One morning he went out of the house to attend a training session having eaten just a bowl of corn flakes quite quickly! Feeling somewhat peckish, he called in at a local cafe for a fry-up and a couple of chocolate bars. When he finally arrived at the ground his stomach was rumbling ten-fold, prompting him to pop into the nearest corner shop for some more chocolate. When training ended around 12.30pm - after some strenuous hill climbing - Claridge's stomach was churning over like nobody's business with eggs, bacon, beans and chocolates doing the rounds inside his body! He flaked out, totally exhausted in the back of the team's mini bus. A few hours later he got out, still feeling rather groggy, and started to walk around the Cambridge streets. A few resident s thought him unfit to continue

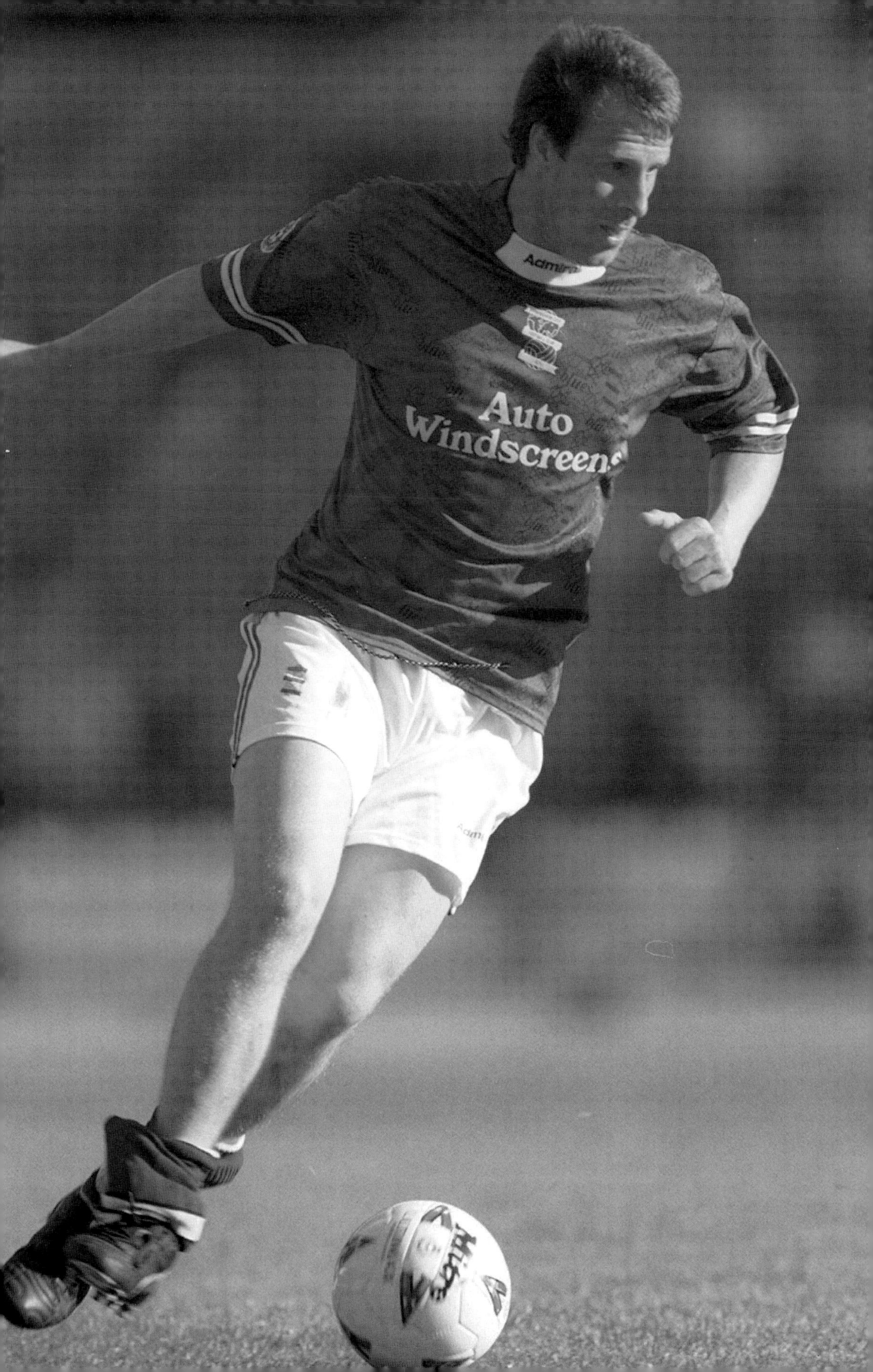
Auto
Windscreens

and called the police. They quickly arrived on the scene and duly detained a wobbly-looking Claridge for what they thought was drunkenness. But thankfully no action was taken after the truth came out in more ways than. one!

CLARKE, Wallace
Outside-left: 32 apps
Born: Jarrow, 14 July 1896.
Died: Jarrow, 20 December 1975
Career: Durham City (1914), Middlesbrough (May 1919), Leeds United (£460, May 1921), BLUES (March 1923), Coventry City (£600, October 1924), Boston Town (August 1925), Barrow (June 1926), Torquay United (1927), Connahs Quay (1929), Shotton FC (January 1930).
Wally Clarke was one of those players who simply could not settle down, although he was a regular in the Blues side until injury struck in 1924. Thereafter he began his travels around the country. He stood 5 ft 7ins tall and weighed 11 stone

CLARKE, Albert W
Inside-forward: 31 apps. 9 goals
Born: Sheffield, 25 December 1916.
Died: 1944 (killed in WW2 whilst serving with the Devonshire Regiment).
Career Mosborough Trinity, Frickley Colliery, Mexborough Town, Torquay United (September 1934), BLUES (January 1936), Blackburn Rovers (July 1938 in exchange for Walter Hassall). Guested for Torquay United during WW2.
Club honours: Blackburn: Division Two champions 1939, Wartime League Cup runners-up 1942
It is stated that Albert Clarke walked all the way from Sheffield to Devon to sign the appropriate forms which made him a Torquay player in 1934, a plausible story in those days of economic depression when men did, indeed, walk hundreds of miles around the country to find work. He was a strong, forceful player who had a powerful right-foot shot

CLARKE, Dennis
Full-back: 20+1 apps
Born: Stockton-on-Tees, 18 January 1948
Career: Newtongrange School, Stockton & Durham Boys, BLUES (on trial, 1962), West Bromwich Albion (apprentice April 1963, professional February 1965), Huddersfield Town (£25,000, January 1969), BLUES (£15,000, September 1973). Retired May 1975
Club honours: WBA: FA Cup winners 1968, Football League Cup runners-up 1967: Huddersfield: Division Two champions 1970
Dennis Clarke was a capable rather than a brilliant full-back who made history when he became the first substitute to be used in an FA Cup Final, replacing John Kaye in the 1968 showdown at Wembley. He played 26 games for Albion including two Wembley Cup Finals before he was 21, and over 175 for Huddersfield. Clarke

bravely ignored a serious leg injury to continue as a makeshift centre-forward in his last game for Blues and, alas, his courage probably ended his career. After retiring he started up a building contracting business in Huddersfield. He now lives and works in Birmingham.

CLARKE, Edward
Left-back : one app.
Born: Stechford, Birmingham, 1871.
Now deceased.
Career: Washwood Heath Council School, BLUES (season 1889-90), Ward End Unity (1890-95).
Ted Clarke was a young defender who deputised for the injured Frank Speller in his only season with the club.

CLARKE, Edward Oswald
Goalkeeper: one app.
Born: Harborne, Birmingham 1861.
Died: Birmingham
Career Harborne FC, BLUES (season 1884-85), Knowle FC (1885).
Ted Clarke was a local born 'keeper who had a poor game against Excelsior in the 1884 FA Cup and was not selected again.

CLARKE, Wayne
Striker: 105 apps. 43 goals
Born: Willenhall, 28 February, 1961
Career: Wolverhampton Wanderers (apprentice June 1977, professional March 1978), BLUES (£80,000, August 1984), Everton (March 1987), Leicester City (£500,000, July 1989), Manchester City (£500,000, January 1990), Shrewsbury Town (on loan, October 1990), Stoke City (on loan, March-May 1991), Wolverhampton Wanderers (on loan, September-October 1991), Walsall (July 1992); Shrewsbury Town (August 1993), Telford United (player-manager, August 1995-November 1996).
Club honours: Blues: Division Two promotion 1985; Everton: Division One champions 1987, FA Charity Shield winners 1987; Shrewsbury: Division Three champions 1994
Representative honours: England: (Schoolboy & Youth).
Wayne Clarke was a fine marksman and the youngest of the famous footballing family, his brothers Frank, Allan, Derek and Kelvin all having played senior League football. He was signed for Blues by manager Ron Saunders and teamed up well with David Geddis. He later returned to haunt Blues, scoring a hat-trick against them whilst on loan to Shrewsbury Town. All told Clarke, who suffered relegation with Wolves in 1984 and Blues in 1986, netted over 130 goals in more than 500 League appearances in an exceptionally fine career. He is now a postman.

CLARKSON, Ian Stewart
Defender: 159+13 apps.
Born: Solihull, 4 December 1970
Career: Chapel Fields Primary & Tudor Grange Schools,
BLUES (YTS June 1987, professional December 1988);
Stoke City (£50,000, September 1993). Northampton
Town (August 1996), Kidderminster Harriers
(free transfer, November 2000).
Club honours: Blues: Leyland DAF Trophy winners
1991, Kidderminster: Nationwide Conference
champions 2000
Ian Clarkson is a player who reads the game well. He
began as a central defender but was converted into a
determined, a hard-tackling right-back by Blues
following Kevin Ashley's departure to Wolves. In 2002
Clarkson passed the milestone of 425 senior appearances
at club level. He has supported Blues since he was ten
years of age.

CLAYTON, Harry
Inside-left: 2 apps
Born: Acocks Green, Birmingham, 1860.
Now deceased.
Career: Churchfields FC, Calthorpe, BLUES (January
1883), Birmingham CFC (1884-85).
Harry Clayton's stint with Blues was sandwiched
between two excellent spells with two of the most
prestigious amateur clubs in the city (at that time). He
was on the winning side in both his outings for Blues.

CLUTTERBUCK, Henry James
Goalkeeper: 66 apps.
Born: Wheatenhurst, June 1873.
Died: Gloucester Central Hospital, 19 December 1948
Career: Hereford Thistle, BLUES (July 1897), Queen's
Park Rangers (May 1899), Grimsby Town (May 1901),
Chesterfield (July 1902), New Brompton (1903),
Fulham (August 1904). Retired in May 1905
Harry Clutterbuck was a cool, calculated goalkeeper who
during October and November 1898 had possibly the
easiest time ever as Blues' last line of defence when his
forwards scored 35 goals without reply in only 4 games.

COCHRANE, James
Inside-right: 3 apps. one goal
Born: Brierley Hill, 26 October 1935
Career: Brierley Hill Schoolboys, BLUES (junior June
1951, professional October 1952), Walsall (June 1958,
in part exchange for Brian Taylor), Wellington Town
(May 1959), Stourbridge (October 1959).
Great things were expected of Jimmy Cochrane who was
the playmaker in the successful Brierley Hill schoolboys'
side of 1951. But after his National Service (when he
spent two years as a cook) he returned to St Andrew's a
stone overweight, out of condition, and was never the
same player again

COLE, Samuel
Centre-forward: one app.
Born: Smethwick, September 1874.
Now deceased.
Career: Stoke (amateur 1892), Smethwick Centaur
(1895), BLUES (August 1898), Harborne FC (1900).
Sammy Cole was used in the reserves as an all-purpose
forward, scoring regularly. He deputised for Bob
McRoberts in his only senior game, after being called out
of the crowd to play after Blues' 12th man (Walton) had
gone off with the reserves.

CONLIN, James
Outside-left: 23 apps. 2 goals
Born: Durham, 6 August 1881.
Died: Flanders, 23 June 1917
Career: Captain Colts Rovers, Cambuslang, Hibernian,
Falkirk (January 1900), Albion Rovers (March 1901),
Bradford City (August 1904), Broadheaath FC,
Manchester City (July 1906), BLUES (September 1911),
Airdrieonians (1912), Broxburn United (August 1913).
Killed whilst serving with the Highland Light Infantry in
Flanders in WW1.
Club honours: Man City: Division Two champions 1910
Representative honours: England (one full cap): Football
League XI (two games).
Jimmy Conlin was born in England but brought up in
Scotland. Playing the traditional Scottish dribbling game,
his skill often led to him receiving some rough treatment
and as a result he was frequently troubled by injury

CONNOLLY, John
Outside-left: 55+8 apps 9 goals
Born: Barrhead, Glasgow, 13 June 1950
Career: Barrhead High School, Glasgow United (1966),
St Johnstone (professional, January 1968), Everton
(March 1972), Blues (September 1976), Newcastle
United (May 1978), Hibernian (September 1980),
Gateshead (January 1982), Blyth Spartans (player-
manager, November 1982), Gateshead (1984), later Ayr
United (part-time coach, mid-1990s) and manager of
several non-League and minor clubs near to Scotland's
North-East coastline.
Club honours: St Johnstone: Scottish League Cup
runners-up 1970; Hibernian: Scottish Division One
champions 1981.
Representative honours: Scotland (one full cap, 2 U-23).
Clubs were lining up to sign John Connolly after he had
been in tip-top form for St Johnstone. A classy ball-
playing winger, his career was unfortunately disrupted by
injury, especially after he had moved south, although he
did have a useful first season at St Andrew's before injury
struck again. He now resides in Ayr and is working as an
advertising sales manager for a golf magazine.

COOKE, Richard Edward
Winger: 5 apps
Born: Islington, London 4 September 1965
Career: Albany Comprehensive School, Tottenham
Hotspur (apprentice, June 1982 professional March
1983), BLUES (on loan, September 1986), AFC
Bournemouth (January 1987), Luton Town (March
1989), AFC Bournemouth (March 1991,: Bashley (June
1993).Club honours: Bournemouth: Division 3 champions
1987.Representative honours: England (one Under-21
cap, 14 Youth caps). Richard Cooke, a stocky winger,
had a month on loan at St Andrew's from Spurs. There
was never a hint of him being signed on a full-term basis.

COOKE, Terence John
Forward: 1+3 apps.
Born: Birmingham, 5 August 1976.
Career: Manchester United (trainee, June 1992,
professional July 1994), Sunderland (on loan, January
1996), BLUES (on loan, November-December 1996),
Wrexham (on loan, October 1998), Manchester City (£1
million, January 1999), Wigan Athletic (on loan, March
2000), Sheffield Wednesday (on loan, September 2000
and again December 2000), Grimsby Town
(free transfer, March 2002).
Club honours: Manchester Utd: FA Youth Cup winners
1995 (scored in both legs v. Spurs).
Representative Honours: England
(4 Under-21 caps & Youth caps)
A skilful right-winger who found it tough to gain regular
first team football with any of the clubs he has served.

COOPER, Gary
Midfield/defender: 75+8 apps. 4 goals
Born: Hammersmith, 20 November 1965
Career: Stationers' Company School, Queen's Park
Rangers (apprentice 1981, professional June 1983).
Brentford (on loan, September 1985), Fisher Athletic
(1986), Maidstone United (March 1989), Peterborough
United (£20,000, March 1991) Birmingham City (free
transfer, December 1993 to April 1996); then non-
League football.
Club honours: Fisher Athletic: Southern League
Premiership champions 1987; Blues: Second Division
champions 1995, Auto-Windscreen Shield winners 1995.
Representative honours: England (11 Youth caps &
Schoolboy caps)
An adaptable footballer, enthusiastic with a superb left
foot, Gary Cooper appeared in well over 200 matches
before joining Blues, 114 of them coming for
Peterborough United.

COOPER, Mark Nicholas
Midfielder: 35+9 apps. 5 goals
Born: Wakefield, Yorkshire, 18 December 1968

Career: Bristol City (apprentice June 1986, professional
September 1987), Exeter City (June 1989), Southend
United (on loan, March and April 1990), BLUES (in
exchange for Eamonn Dolan, September 1991),
Liverpool (on trial, January 1992); Fulham (November
1992); Huddersfield Town (on loan, March 1993),
Wycombe Wanderers (on loan, January 1994), Exeter
City (February 1994), Hartlepool United (free transfer,
July 1996), Macclesfield Town (on loan, September
1997), Leyton Orient (free transfer, December 1997),
Rushden & Diamonds (January 1998).
Mark Cooper, a busy, blond haired central midfielder,
the son of former Blues manager Terry Cooper, scored a
dramatic late equaliser against Peterborough United
when making his Blues debut as a substitute in
September 1991. During his senior League and Cup
career, Cooper appeared in almost 290 games and scored
over 50 goals.

COOPER, Paul David
Goalkeeper: 26 apps.
Born: Brierley Hill, 21 December 1953
Career: Kingswood Secondary Modern School, Staffs
County Boys, Boney Hay Juniors (Cannock), Cannock
Athletic, Sutton Coldfield Town, BLUES (apprentice
June 1971, professional July 1971) Ipswich Town (on
loan, March 1974, signed permanently for £27,000, July
1974), Leicester City (July 1987), Manchester City
(March 1989), Stockport County (August 1990).
Club honours: Ipswich: FA Cup winners 1978, UEFA
Cup winners 1981: Stockport: Division 4 promotion 1991
Paul Cooper had a nightmare start to his professional
career with Blues but after leaving St Andrew's he
became a stalwart between the posts for Ipswich, for
whom he amassed more than 550 senior appearances. A
good shot-stopper he also had a magnificent record for
saving penalties. Cooper now lives in Liverpool, working
for a firm selling nuts and bolts.

CORBETT, Walter Samuel
Full-back: 48 apps.
Born: Wellington, Shropshire 26 December 1880. Died:
Birmingham 1955
Career: Vicarage Road Council School (Kings Heath),
King Edward VI Grammar Schools, Thornhill FC
(Birmingham), Astbury Richmond, Headingley FC,
Soho Villa (Handsworth), Bournbrook, Aston Villa (June
1904), BLUES (July 1907), Wellington (June 1911),
Wolverhampton Old Church (1913). Also played as a
guest for Queen's Park Rangers (September 1907) and
for Wellington Town (April 1909) whilst with Blues.
Representative honours: England (3 full caps, 18 amateur

caps); Great Britain Olympic Soccer Gold medallist 1908, Birmingham & District Juniors, Amateur & Professional XI Wally Corbett was 'one of the most gentlemanly players one could hope to meet in a long day's march' according to the Sports Argus in 1906. Corbett, who remained an amateur throughout his playing career, was indeed a terrific footballer who, it was said, never did a dirty trick on the field of play. He had a fine turn of speed and helped Villa's reserves win the Birmingham & District League three times. He skippered the Birmingham & District Juniors against Scotland in 1904-05 and was selected to represent a mixed Amateur and Professional XI on a continental tour in 1906 as partner to the great Blackburn Rovers and England full-back, Bob Crompton. Corbett, who suffered from polio as a lad, always carried a handkerchief in his withered left hand and whilst a student at grammar school (where he played rugby) he won four scholarships and became such an expert linguist that he was appointed manager of the Birmingham Export House (1922) and was also head of the wages department of Birmingham City Transport until 1945.

CORNAN, Francis
Left-half: 61 apps. one goal
Born: Sunderland, 5 May 1880,
Died: Halifax, 31 May 1971
Career: Sunderland Black Watch FC, Willington, Barnsley (professional, August 1902), BLUES (April 1905), Aston Villa (May 1908), Spennymoor United (August 1909), Barnsley (September 1909), Nelson (1910), Exeter City (July 1911). Retired May 1915 Frank Cornan was a tough-tackling, extremely hard-working player who seemed fated to be a perpetual makeweight in transfer dealings. He came to Blues as part of the Benny Green transaction and left in a complicated exchange deal with Villa. He suffered recurrences of sciatica which caused him to miss several games with each of his clubs.

CORNFORTH, John Michael
Midfielder: 8 apps.
Born: Whitley Bay, 7 October 1967
Career: Sunderland (apprentice 1984, professional October 1985), Doncaster Rovers (on loan, November 1986), Shrewsbury Town (on loan, November 1989), Lincoln City (on loan, January 1990), Swansea City (£50,000, August 1991), BLUES (£350,000, March 1996), Wycombe Wanderers (£50,000, December 1996), Peterborough United (on loan, February 1998), Cardiff City (free transfer August 1999), Scunthorpe United (free transfer November 1999), Exeter City (free transfer February 2000, appointed manager at St James' Park, October 2001, sacked October 2002).

Club Honours: Sunderland: Division Three champions 1988; Swansea City: Autoglass Trophy winners 1994.
Representative Honours: Wales (2 caps)
John Cornforth had a fine career as a mobile midfielder with excellent distribution skills and fine temperament. He never really settled down at St Andrew's and during his playing days amassed in excess of 350 senior appearances. He spent just 12 months as boss of Exeter City. He was in the same Swansea side as Jason Bowen that lifted the AGT in 1994.

COTON, Anthony Philip
Goalkeeper: 114 apps.
Born: Tamworth, 19 May 1961
Career: Mile Oak Rovers, BLUES (apprentice June 1977: professional October 1978), Watford (£330,000 September 1984), Manchester City (£1 million July 1990), Manchester United (later appointed goalkeeping coach at Old Trafford, 1999-2001).
Representative honours: England (1 'B' Cap).
Tony Coton sprang to fame when saving John Hawley's penalty with his first touch in his Football League debut game for Blues against Sunderland in Division One in season 1980-81. A tall man, with strong physique, good reflexes and a safe pair of hands, he had all the assets which combined to make him one of the country's top goalkeepers in the early 1990s. After leaving Watford for Maine Road he quickly established himself in the Manchester side after replacing Andy Dibble, and had a pretty good first season there, making 33 League appearances in all, conceding 46 goals - and saving three penalties in the process.

COTTEE, Anthony Richard
Striker: 4+1 apps. one goal
Born: West Ham, 11 July 1965
Career: West Ham United (apprentice July 1980, professional September 1982), Everton (£2.3 million, August 1988), West Ham United (September 1994), FC Selangor/Spain (March 1997), Leicester City (£500,000, August 1997), BLUES (on loan, November-December 1997), Norwich City (free transfer, September 2000), Barnet (player-manager, October 2000), Millwall (free transfer, March 2001-July 2001, retired). Now a Sky TV football reporter/summariser.
Club Honours: Leicester City: League Cup winners 2000
Representative Honours: England (7 full, 8 Under-21 caps, Youth) One of the few players to have appeared and scored in all four Divisions of English League football, Tony Cottee was a superb opportunist striker. Full of tricks with a rasping shot, he netted almost 300 goals in a little over 725 senior appearances during his 21-year career.

COX, Geoffrey

Winger: 38 apps. 5 goals
Born: Stockingford, Warwickshire, 30 November 1934
Career: Nuneaton Boys, BLUES (amateur June 1950,
professional December 1951), Torquay United
(December 1957), Plymouth Argyle (September 1967)
Geoff Cox's promising career was interrupted by national
service and after he returned to St Andrew's he found
Gordon Astall and Alex Govan firmly installed as the
club's regular wingers. Cox, who went on to make 261
League appearances for Torquay (scoring 62 goals) saw
his son Maurice, also play for Torquay United. Cox
himself, is now employed by a firm of Estate Agents in
Torbay, where he also lives.

COXFORD, John

Centre half: 16 apps.
Born: Seaton Hirst, 25 July 1901.
Died: Bury St Edmunds, mid-1978
Career: North Seaton Colliery, Stakeford United (1922)
Sunderland (May 1924), BLUES (April 1927),
Bournemouth & Boscombe Athletic (May 1930), Poole
Town (May 1934), Northfleet (August 1934)
Jack Coxford, who had a distinctive high forehead, was
signed as cover for 'Lofty' Morrall. Following the
emergence of Tom Fillingham, he found it difficult to get
a place in the first team and departed to the south coast,
where he spent four excellent seasons with Bournemouth.
Thereafter he had the briefest of spells with Poole (two
games), before rounding off his career with Northfleet

CRAVEN, Charles

Inside forward: 21 apps. 2 goals
Born: Boston, Lincolnshire, 19 December 1909.
Died: Solihull, 30 March 1972
Career: Boston's School's representative, Boston Trinity,
Boston Town, Boston United, Grimsby Town (May
1930), Manchester United (£6,000, June 1938), BLUES
(December 1938), Tamworth (June 1939), Sutton Town
(August 1951). Guested for Coventry City and BLUES
during World War 2.
Club honours: Grimsby: Division Two champions 1934
A ball-playing forward with devastating body swerve,
Charlie 'Swerver' Craven scored 99 goals in 273 League
games during an outstanding career. He had the
misfortune to join Blues at a time when the club had a
rather weak attack. A former office clerk, he was also a
stylish cricketer and useful at snooker and billiards.
He was named as reserve for England against
Holland in 1935

CRAWSHAW, Raymond

Centre-half: 4 apps
Born: Padiham, Lancashire, October 1908.
Now deceased.
Career: Great Harwood, Southport (as an amateur, July
1929), Great Harwood (1930), Burnley (July 1931),
Great Harwood (season 1932-33), Accrington Stanley
(June 1933), BLUES (£600, April 1934), Bromsgrove
Rovers (1935), Burton Town (August 1936), Droitwich
Rovers (1937).
Another good, steady defender, Ray Crawshaw's career
floundered due to the presence of a Morrall and
Fillingham. Tall and slimly built, he was useful in the air.

CRINGAN, James Anderson

Wing-half: 285 apps 12 goals
Born: Douglas Water near Lanark, 16 December 1904.
Now deceased.
Career: Douglas Water Thistle, Sunderland (on trial),
Dunfermline Athletic (on trial), Falkirk (on trial), South
Shields (on trial, August 1921), Bury (on trial, early
1922), BLUES (professional, November 1922), Boston
United (player-manager June 1934), Banbury Spencer
(manager, 1935-36)
Club honours: Blues: FA Cup runners-up 1931.
Jimmy Cringan was a described as a 'bostin' footballer
from a footballing family (his brother Willie, played for
Celtic and Scotland). He was a tenacious competitor
who enjoyed a tough battle in the centre of the park.
Essentially a defensive player, he once kept goal for Blues
in a friendly, such was his versatility.

CROSBIE, John Anderson

Inside-right: 431 apps. 72 goals
Born: Gorbals, Glasgow, Scotland, 3 June 1896.
Died: February 1982
Career; Glenbuck Cherrypickers FC (Scotland),
Muirkirk Athletic, Saltcoats Victoria, Ayr United (August
1913), BLUES (record fee of £3,700, May 1920)
Chesterfield (July 1932), Stourbridge (player-manager
November 1932); Gothenburg/Sweden (coach, February-
August 1933). A button-maker by profession, he was
coaching a works team in the Kidderminster area in
1934-35.
Club honours: Blues: Division Two champions 1921, FA
Cup runners-up 1931.
Representative honours: Scotland (2 full caps, one
Victory cap)
Scotsman Johnny Crosbie matured into an exceptionally
skilful inside forward with Blues, a craftsman of the
highest class, who provided Joe Bradford with most of
his goalscoring chances with some judicious passes. He
drew up an uncanny understanding with Bradford, and
between them they scored at a prolific rate. Crosbie was
clever at spotting openings and could send out at 40-yard
pass straight to his man.

D

CROSSTHWAITE, Herbert

Goalkeeper: 49 apps.

Born: Preston, Lancs 4 April 1887.

Now deceased.

Career: Preston Schoolboy football, Preston North End (1905), Blackpool (1906), Fulham (August 1907), Exeter City (May 1909), BLUES (December 1910), Stoke (1914). Retired May 1915 to concentrate on being a constable in the Birmingham Police Force, joining in 1910. In 1925 he was promoted to Inspector and continued to be a prominent figure in the organisation of the Birmingham Police Charity Sports.

Described as fearless and clever, Bert Crossthwaite was one of a handful of amateurs who served Blues prior to WW1. His cousin Harold played for Stockport County.

CUNNINGHAM, Kenneth Edward

Defender: 20 apps*

Born: Dublin, 28 June 1971

Career: Tolka Rovers, Millwall (September 1989), Wimbledon (£650,000, November 1994), BLUES (£500,000, August 2002).

Representative honours: Republic of Ireland (42 full caps*, 2 'B' caps, 4 Under-21 caps & Youth caps).

Signed by Blues' manager Steve Bruce after having a fine World Cup tournament with the Republic of Ireland in South Korea and Japan, Kenny Cunningham can play as an orthodox full-back, central defender or as a sweeper. Referred to as 'Captain Dependable' by the Dons' supporters, he voted their 'Player of the Year' in 2002. He made 153 appearances for Millwall and 306 for the Dons.

CURBISHLEY, Llewellyn Charles

Midfielder: 153+2 apps. 15 goals

Born: Forest Gate, London, 8 November 1957

Career: Forest Gate Boys (1972), West Ham United (apprentice July 1973, professional July 1975), BLUES (£225,000, July 1979), Aston Villa (£100,000 plus Robert Hopkins, March 1983), Charlton Athletic (£40,000, December 1984), Brighton & Hove Albion (£32,000, August 1987), Charlton Athletic (£5,000 as player-coach, July 1990, upgraded to assistant-manager October 1990, then joint-manager July 1991, taking sole charge of team affairs in June 1995).

Club honours: Blues; Division Two promotion 1980; (as manager) Charlton: Division One promotion in 1998 & 2000.

Representative honours: England (One Under-21 caps, plus Schoolboy &Youth caps). A determined, all action competitor with a lovely right foot, 'Alan' Curbishley was on the verge of full international honours when he suffered a serious injury against Brighton (his future club). He had amassed well over 600 senior appearances by the time he hung up his boots at the end of the 1990-91 season. He developed into a very successful manager.

CURRYER, Leonard

Centre-forward: 2 apps.

Born: Birmingham 1864.

Now deceased.

Career: Blues (two seasons: 1885-87)

Len Curryer was a reserve forward who was given a couple of run outs in place of the injured Harry Morris.

CURTIS, Ernest Robert

Outside-left: 180 apps. 53 goals

Born: Cardiff, 10 June 1907.

Died: Cardiff, November 1992

Career: Severn Road Old Boys FC, Cardiff Corinthians, Cardiff City (professional, November 1925), BLUES (£3,000, March 1928), Cardiff City (November 1933), Coventry City (February 1935), Hartlepool United (July 1937). Retired in September 1939, later appointed assistant coach at Cardiff City and then became a publican in the Welsh capital

Club honours: Cardiff: FA Cup winners 1927, FA Charity Shield winners 1927, Welsh Cup winners 1927; Blues: FA Cup runners-up 1931.

Representative honours: Wales (3 full caps, 2 Schoolboy caps). Switched to the left flank by Blues in order to solve a problem position, Ernie Curtis proved a difficult player to knock off the ball and scored his fair share of goals at club level. He was a Prisoner-of-War during World War 2.

DAILEY, James

Centre-forward: 42 apps. 14 goals

Born; Glenboig, Scotland, 8 September 1927

Career: Wolverhampton Wanderers (amateur 1943), Third Lanark (1945), Sheffield Wednesday (October 1946), BLUES (February 1949), Exeter City (August 1952) Workington (December 1953), Rochdale (October 1957), Weymouth (1959), Bath City, Poole Town, Bridport, Portland Town (manager) Dorchester Town (manager). Later ran sports shop in Weymouth, where he still lives.

A dynamic centre-forward whose time with Blues was hardly an unqualified success, Jimmy Dailey did, however, finish top-scorer in his one full season in the senior side and later proved a prolific marksman in the lower Divisions, netting over 100 League goals after leaving St Andrew's, including 74 in 176 games for Workington. He also scored a fivetimer for Wednesday against Barnsley in September 1947 to equal Jimmy Trotter's individual scoring record for the Owls.

DAISH, Liam Sean

Defender: 97+1 apps. 6 goals

Born: Portsmouth, 23 September 1968

Career: Portsmouth (apprentice 1984, professional September 1986), Cambridge United (free transfer July 1988), BLUES (£50,000 January 1994), Coventry City (£1.5 million, February 1996 to May 1998), Havant &

Waterlooville (August 2000).

Club honours: Cambridge: Division Three champions 1990-91. Blues: Second Division champion 1995, Auto-Windscreen Shield winners 1995.

Representative honours: Republic of Ireland (one full cap, 5 Under-21 caps, 1 'B' cap).

Liam Daish proved to be one of manager Barry Fry's best signings for Blues, being strong in the air, determined and forceful on the ground. He had an excellent 1994-95 campaign in which he skippered the team to the Second Division championship. The season also saw him booked (and ultimately suspended) for blowing a trumpet in celebration after scoring at Chester! He played in 182 senior games for Cambridge and just over 30 for Coventry before injury forced him out of the game for some two years.

• Daish and his former Blues team-mate Michael Johnson were told to plead guilty to assault following the 'Battle of Ancona' affair in the Anglo-Italian Cup competition in Italy in 1996. All was well.

DALE, Richard Armstrong

Right-half: 150 apps.

Born: Willington, County Durham, 21 March 1896. Now deceased.

Career: Walton School, Walbottle Juniors, Tow Law Town, North Walbottle FC, Stanley United, BLUES (£250, March 1922), West Bromwich Albion (£1,500, November 1928), Tranmere Rovers (£400, June 1931), Crook Town (October 1932), Tow Law Town. Retired in June 1932.

Representative honours: Staffordshire County FA (1925)

'Dicky' Dale was a chunky wing-half who was a regular member of the Blues' defence throughout the mid-1920s. Perhaps a shade uncertain at times, he was, nevertheless, always ready for a battle. .

DALY, Gerard Anthony

Midfielder: 74+2 apps. 2 goals

Born: Cabra, Dublin, 30 April 1954

Career: Dublin Schools, Bohemians (August 1971), Manchester United (£20,000, April 1973), Derby County (£175,000, March 1977), New England Teamen/NASL (two spells on loan, in the summers of 1978 & 1979), Coventry City (£310,000, August 1980), Leicester City (on loan, January 1983), BLUES (August 1984), Shrewsbury Town (October 1985), Stoke City (March 1987), Doncaster Rovers (July 1988), Telford United (as assistant/player-manager July 1989, then manager from 1990 to October 1993).

Club honours: Manchester United; Division Two champions 1975, FA Cup runners up 1976; BLUES: Division Two promotion 1985

Representative honours: Republic of Ireland; (47 full caps, one Under-23 cap)

Gerry Daly was a slim, intelligent and skilful midfield player, whose game came on in leaps and bounds after leaving Ireland. He was never suited to the long ball style used by Ron Saunders at Blues and showed an ill-concealed dislike for these tactics, although the team certainly played better when he was in the side. An ace penalty-taker, Daly was also a fine snooker player. He scored 23 goals in his 111 League games for Manchester United and 30 from the same number of starts at Derby County. In all Daly amassed 550 senior appearances at club level and netted nearly 100 goals.

DARK, Trevor Charles

Winger: 2+3 apps. one goal

Born: St Helier, Jersey 29 January 1961

Career: Arsenal (on associate schoolboy forms), Merton Boys, BLUES (apprentice July 1977, professional January 1979) Hendon (1981), Carshalton Athletic, Fisher Athletic, Tooting & Mitcham United (1986).

Trevor Dark was principally a reserve at St Andrew's, although his career was affected by him being switched from winger to full-back, a position he showed little aptitude for.

DARRELL, Michael Alan

Inside-forward: 13+ 5 apps 2 goals

Born: Bilston 14 January 1947

Career: South East Staffs Schools, BLUES (apprentice April 1962, professional January 1965), Newport County (on loan, October 1970), Gillingham (on loan, December 1970), Peterborough United (May 1971), Bilston (1973), Darlaston (season 1974-75)

A great future was predicted for this bow-legged, barrel-chested bundle of energy midfielder after he had put in a series of promising performances as an 18 year-old. Micky Darrell's career then seemed to stagnate with only nine League games in the next five seasons. His brother Brian, played for Darlaston.

DAVENPORT, Thomas

Inside-forward: 13 apps. 8 goals

Born Kingstanding, Birmingham 1860. Now deceased.

Career: Hockley Belmont, BLUES (August 1885), St Luke's FC (1886), BLUES (1888-89); Birmingham St George's (1889-90).

Tom Davenport was a dashing forward whose goals seem to be reserved for cup-ties, seven coming in the FA Cup, plus at least another five in local cup competitions

DAVIES, George

Outside-left: 29 apps. 7 goals

Born: Shropshire 19 February 1900. Now deceased.

Career: Wellington St George's FC, Ironbridge FC, BLUES (April 1918), Southend United (June 1922), Wellington Town (May 1924), Wellington Town (as a committee member from June 1934 onwards). Guested for Wrexham during WW1.

Club honours: Blues: Division Two champions 1921

A short, stubby winger (5ft 5ins tall, 10st 5lb in weight), George Davies was recommended to Blues by Jack Elkes. He joined a band of outside-lefts at St Andrew's, none of whom could be described as regular first teamers. He hit five goals in the last seven League games when Blues won the Second Division championship in 1921. Davies was replaced in the side by Ted Linley.

DAVIES, Stanley Charles
Inside/centre-forward: 17 apps. 5 goals
Born: Chirk near Oswestry 24 April 1898.
Died: Birmingham, 17 January 1972
Career: Chirk Council Schools, Chirk Schools representative, Chirk FC, Army Signals School (Dunstable), Manchester United (on trial), Rochdale (January 1919), Preston North End (April 1919), Everton (£4,000, January 1921), West Bromwich Albion (£3,300, November 1921), BLUES (May 1928), Rotherham United (player-manager, March 1929) Barnsley (August 1930), Manchester Central (October 1930), Dudley Town (1933), Chelmsford City (trainer, April 1938-May 1941), Shorts FC of Rochester (Manager during WW2). Later became a publican in West Bromwich.
Club honours: Wales (18 full caps, one 'other' cap): toured Canada with Welsh FA (June-July 1929).
Stan Davies was a big, strong, forceful player (5ft 10ins tall, 12st 12lbs in weight) who starred in six different positions for his country (including goalkeeper), an indication of his tremendous versatility. He possessed a cracking shot, could head a ball hard and true, and in his career scored well over 100 goals in some 250 appearances for his seven major clubs, including 83 in 159 games for Albion. During WW1 he distinguished himself with the Welsh Fusiliers and was awarded the Military Medal and the Croix de Guerre. His son, John, became a freelance sports writer based in Birmingham and later in Bristol.

DAWS. James
Right-half: 47 apps. one goal.
Born: Mansfield, Woodhouse, Nottinghamshire 27 May 1898. Died: Birmingham, June 1985
Career: Notts County (amateur, May-November 1919), Mansfield Town (December 1919), BLUES (January 1920), Bristol Rovers (amateur, March 1924, then professional May 1924, signed for £250), Mansfield Woodhouse (July 1925), Poole Town (player-trainer, August 1925 to May 1927)
Jimmy Daws looked a clumsy, somewhat overweight footballer with a powerful shot who was occasionally hot-tempered.

DAYKIN, Thomas
Wing-half: 94 apps. one goal
Born: Shildon, August 1882. Died: County Durham
Career: Bishop Auckland (amateur), Newcastle United

(on trial), Hobson Wanderers, Sunderland (August 1905), BLUES (December 1908), South Shields (1912). Daykin retired in 1915
The local press hailed it as quite a coup when this powerful player came to Blues. Basically a reserve at Sunderland, Tom Daykin had impressed when called into first team action but his arrival at St Andrew's coincided with a period of turmoil both on and off the field and during his spell at the club Blues dropped to the bottom of the Second Division and found themselves in severe financial difficulties.

DEACON, Henry
Inside-forward: 3 apps.
Born: Sheffield, 25 April 1900.
Died: Rotherham, 5 January 1946
Career: Sheffield Boys, Sheffield Wednesday (amateur), Hallam FC (Sheffield), BLUES (May 1920), Swansea Town July (1922), Crewe Alexandra (August 1931), Southport (June 1934), Accrington Stanley (December 1934), Rotherham United (June 1935). Retired in September 1939 (to war).
Club honours: Swansea Town: Division Three South champions 1925 Representative honours: Welsh League (v. Irish League May 1931) Harry Deacon had Johnny Crosbie to contend with for the inside-right berth in the Blues' side but after leaving St Andrew's he gave Swansea excellent service as both creator and taker of chances, netting 88 goals in 319 games, all of which made him extremely popular at Vetch Field, where 9,000 fans attended his benefit match. He was 5ft 8ins tall and tipped the scales at 11st 6lbs.

DEAKIN, John
Midfielder: 3+4 apps.
Born: Sheffield, 29 September 1966
Career: Barnsley (apprentice July 1983), Doncaster Rovers (non-contract, August 1985), Shepshed Charterhouse (August 1987), BLUES (professional, September 1989); Carlisle United (August 1991), Wycombe Wanderers (briefly), Kidderminster Harriers (August 1992).
Club honours: Kidderminster: GM Vauxhall Conference champions 1994; FA Trophy runners-up 1995
An eager, grafting player who showed no small degree of skill, John Deakin made his senior debut for Blues as a substitute against Tranmere Rovers a few days after joining the club but was later hampered by injury.

DEARDEN, Kevin Charles
Goalkeeper: 12 apps.
Born: Luton, 8 March 1970
Career: Tottenham Hotspur (apprentice June 1986,

professional August 1988), Farnborough Town (on loan, September 1988) Woking (on loan, January 1989), Cambridge United (on loan, March 1989), Hartlepool United (on loan, August 1989), Oxford United (on loan, December 1989), Swindon Town (on loan, March 19990), Peterborough United (on loan, August 1990), Hull City (January 1991), Rochdale (on loan, August 1991), BLUES (on loan, March 1992), Portsmouth (on loan, August 1992), Brentford (September 1993), Barnet (on loan, February 1999), Wrexham (June 1999), Torquay United (August 2001).

When the 2001-02 season ended - after being voted Torquay's 'Player of the Year' - Kevin Dearden's career appearance tally stood at 447 of which 254 came as a Brentford player. He was taken on loan by Blues after another loan 'keeper, Alan Miller had been recalled by Arsenal. Nurtured at White Hart Lane by both Pat Jennings and Ray Clemence, Dearden has proved to be a very competent performer between the posts.

DEARSON, Donald John
Utility player: 136 apps. 17 goals
Born: Ynysybwl, 13 May 1914.
Died: Sheldon, Birmingham, 24 December 1990.
Career: Llantwit Major Juniors, Barry (August, 1937), BLUES (professional, April 1934), Coventry City (£6,000, February 1947), Walsall (March 1950), Nuneaton Borough, Bilston United (1952). Retired during season 1953-54. Guested for Northampton Town, Nottingham Forest, Wrexham and West Bromwich Albion during WW2.
Club honours: Blues: Football League South winners 1946.
Representative honours; Wales (3 full caps, 15 wartime caps, 4 amateur caps). A youngster with an impressive physique, Don Dearson had already won amateur caps for his country before joining Blues. Initially a clever, scheming inside forward, with a powerful shot, he was moved into the half-back line and proved a great success before rounding off his Blues career at full-back. A qualified electrical engineer, Dearson was in a reserved occupation during the war and this enabled him to make a total of 166 appearances for Blues during the hostilities (25 goals scored). At one time he spent nine weeks in the Birmingham City Police Force, but resigned to work in the BSA factory, later becoming an employee of British Leyland, Coventry, while also running his own grocery business. A truly grand competitor in every sense of the word, whether involved in football or not.

DEELEY, James
Outside-left: one app.
Born: Evesham, 1871.
Now deceased.

Career: Worcester Rovers, BLUES (August 1895), Hereford Thistle (July 1896).
Jim Deeley came in for one game when the ever-reliable 'Toddy' Hands cried off with a rare injury.

DENNIS, Mark Earl
Left-back: 145 apps. one goal
Born: Streatham, London, 2 May 1961
Career: Chelsea Boys, BLUES (apprentice June 1977, professional August 1978), Southampton (£100,000, November 1983), Queen's Park Rangers (£250,000, May 1987), Crystal Palace (August 1988); Brighton & Hove Albion (on trial 1991).
Representative honours: England (3 Under-21 caps and Youth caps).
Mark Dennis was a talented player with a fiery temper who made his debut for Blues in unusual circumstances. He had travelled to Norwich with the first team to gain some experience, but when Jimmy Calderwood slipped in the dressing room, cracking his head, Dennis was called in to play as a right-back, and soon settled into the side, taking over his favourite number three shirt on a regular basis. It is impossible to talk about Dennis without reference being made to his disciplinary record (he was sent-off 14 times at various levels and booked on numerous occasions). He was also involved in tempestuous incidents both at home and away, on the training ground and once at New Street station. At his best, he was an exciting attacking full-back, capable of delivering teasing centres, and with a little more self-discipline would have surely gained more major honours than the Under-21 caps he collected whilst with Blues. Dennis now works as a sign-writer in Spain.

DE SOUZA, Juan Miguel
Forward: 8+11 apps.
Born: Canning Town, 11 February 1970.
Career: Newham Schools, Clapton (1987), Charlton Athletic (July 1989), Bristol City (free transfer, August 1990), Cheltenham Town (1991), Yeovil Town (1992), Dorchester Town, Bashley,, Dagenham & Redbridge (1993), BLUES (£25,000, February 1994), Bury (on loan, November 1994), Wycombe Wanderers (£80,000, January 1995), Peterborough United (£50,000, March 1997), Southend United (on loan, August 1998), Rochdale (on loan, October 1998), Rushden & Diamonds (player-exchange deal, December 1998), Farnborough (season 2001-02).
An enthusiastic player, Miguel De Souza seemed out of his depth in League football after spending quite some time in the lower reaches of non-League soccer. But he developed into a useful lower Divisional player after leaving St Andrew's, going on to appear in well over 150 competitive games, scoring almost 40 goals.

DEVEY, Edwin James
Left-half: 94 apps. 6 goals
Born: Small Heath, Birmingham, August 1862.
Died Birmingham, 2 September 1946.
Career: Bordesley Green Council School, Birmingham Excelsior, BLUES (April 1888), Burton Wanderers (October 1896).
Club honours: Blues: Division Two champions 1893, Division Two promotion 1894.
One of the famous set of Birmingham brothers - Jack, Henry and Bob all played for Aston Villa while Will served with both of the 'Second City' clubs - Ted Devey was a battling midfielder with a crunching tackle, possessing a powerful, if sometimes inaccurate shot.

DEVEY, Raymond
Centre-half: one app.
Born: Greet, Birmingham, 19 December 1917
Career: Forman's Road School, Shirley Juniors, Shirley Old Boys, BLUES (May 1937) Mansfield Town (August 1947). Retired in June 1950 at which point he returned to St Andrew's, serving as reserve team trainer, first team trainer, physiotherapist and then kit man before quitting football in 1983.
Ray Devey was a familiar figure to generations of Blues fans, few of whom ever saw him play. He joined the club as a teenager, learning his trade in the reserves, but WW2 put his career on hold and after serving in the Army he was forced to take a back seat behind Arthur Turner and Syd Owen. For Mansfield he made 77 League appearances in two seasons.

DEVEY, William
Centre-forward: 13 apps. 18 goals
Born: Perry Barr, Birmingham 12 April 1865.
Died: Birmingham, 10 June 1935.
Career: Clavendon Montrose, Wellington, Aston Unity (1884), BLUES (August 1885), Wolverhampton Wanderers (August 1891), Aston Villa (1892), The Swifts (May 1894), Burton Wanderers (1895), Notts County (1896), Walsall (1897), Burton Wanderers (late 1897), Walsall Darlaston, BLUES (July 1898). Retired, June 1900. Will Devey was a player who relied on skill rather than strength and was one of Blues' pre-League stars. Not a big man, he nevertheless had a powerful shot, was skilful and skippered Blues from 1888 until his departure in 1891. He was frequently criticised for a tendency to drop back to gain possession. Brother of Ted Devey (q.v).

DEVINE, Jospeh
Wing half/inside forward: 56 apps. 2 goals
Born: Motherwell, 8 September 1905.
Now deceased.
Career: Motherwell Watsonians FC, Cledale Juniors,

Bathgate, Burnley (£250, May 1925), Newcastle United (£5,575, January 1930), Sunderland (£2,599, January 1931), Queen's Park Rangers (£2,500, May 1933), BLUES (£2,000, January 1935), Chesterfield (May 1937). Later refereed in the Highland League and worked (in Scotland) as a part-time scout for Bristol City Football Club. After an early career as a goalscorer with good ball control, Joe Devine had been converted into a non-stop midfield player by the time he joined Blues, but despite some fine displays he often found himself in the second team, frequently after being made the scapegoat for the rest of the side. He usually reserved his best form for the Arsenal. Red-haired and a dog lover, he was the nephew of Joe Cassidy (Scotland) and later in life ran a successful sports outfitters shop in London.

DEVLIN, James Thomas
Inside forward: 2 apps. 1 goal
Born: Bellshill, Glasgow, October 1904. Died: Scotland
Career: Vale of Clyde, Shawfield Juniors, Kilsyth Rangers, Third Lanark (April 1922), Kings Park, BLUES (September 1924), Preston North End (£362, January 1926), Liverpool (£250, May 1927), Swindon Town (July 1928), Brooklyn Wanderers/USA (May 1929), Aberdeen (1931), Walsall (August 1932), FC Zurich/Switzerland (1933), Fleetwood Town (July 1934), Oldham Athletic (September 1934). Retired during season 1935-36.
Jim Devlin was one of the game's birds of passage, his migrations taking him to four countries. He was a ball-playing forward, direct and forceful in the traditional Scottish mould, but with Johnny Crosby holding down the inside-right purse his chances of first-team action with Blues were limited. His brother, Willie, was also a 'wanderer' appearing for 14 different clubs, most notably with Huddersfield and Liverpool.

DEVLIN, Paul John
Forward: 101+22 apps. 37 goals*
Born: Birmingham, 14 April 1972
Career: Stafford Rangers, Notts County (£40,000, February 1992), BLUES (February 1996), Sheffield United (£200,000, March 1998), Notts County (on loan, October-November 1998), BLUES (on loan, March 2001, signed permanently for £200,000 in July 2002).
Club honours: Notts County: Anglo-Italian Cup winners 1995; Blues: Division One promotion 2002
Representative honours: Scotland (two* full caps)
A tenacious, all-action player with a big heart, Paul Devlin played a massive part in helping Blues reach the Premiership in 2002. He made 180 appearances for Notts County (31 goals) and 169 for Sheffield United (29 goals). He was named in Scotland's senior squad (for the European Championships qualifiers) by manager Berti Vogts in October 2002, making his international debut in a friendly v. Canada.

DICKS, Julian Andrew
Left-back: 95+7 apps. 2 goals
Born: Bristol, 8 August 1968
Career: Washwood Heath School (Birmingham), BLUES (YTS, August 1984, professional August 1985), West Ham United (£400,000, March 1988), Liverpool (September 1993), West Ham United (November 1994), both the latter being exchanged deals. In 2000 he signed for Canvey Island, having also become a professional golfer, quickly making the grade with the smaller ball.
Club honours: West Ham United: Division Two promotion 1991
Representative honours: England (4 Under-21 caps).
Julian Dicks moved from the West Country to Birmingham whilst still at school, thinking he had a better chance of becoming a professional footballer in the Midlands. He was quickly snapped up by Blues and progressed through the ranks before making his senior debut on his 17th birthday. Dicks developed into a fiercely competitive left-back with a penchant for attack. He was, however, subject to occasional rushes of blood and had an unenviable disciplinary record, including a dismissal in his first England Under-21 appearance. He took over as skipper of West Ham and made 450 appearances during his professional career.

DILLON, Kevin Paul
Midfielder: 206+6 apps. 19 goals
Born: Sunderland, 18 December, 1959
Career: Durham Boys, Blues (apprentice June 1976, professional July 1977), Portsmouth (£200,000, March 1983), Newcastle United (July 1989), Reading (free transfer, August 1991), Newbury Town, Stevenage Borough (October 1994), Yeovil Town (as assistant to manager Graham Roberts, February 1995).
Club honours: Blues: Division Two promotion 1980
Representative honours: England (one Under-21 cap).
A player with silky skills but suspect temperament, the bulk of Kevin Dillon's career with Blues was spent as a left-winger, a position from where he scored some quite stunning goals with either a curling shot or after a mazy dribble. He had a habit of back chatting to referees. He now lives in Newcastle.

DIXON, David P
Right-back: 4 apps.
Born: North Shields, November 1898.
Now deceased.
Career: South Shields, Preston Colliery, BLUES (May 1920), Southend United (May 1925), Rhyl Athletic, Bedlington United (February 1928).
Retired, summer 1931.
Dave Dixon was a slim defender (5ft 9ins tall, 11st in weight) who was third choice at Blues behind Womack and Ashurst. He played in only another four games for Southend before they dropped out of the League.

DIXON, George
Left-back: one app.
Born: Smethwick, April 1859:
Now deceased.
Career: Oldbury FC, BLUES (August 1887-April 1888), Aston Unity (season 1888-89).
George Dixon was a capable footballer who deputised for Walter Farley in two games, one being a 6-1 win over Aston Unity, who were so impressed they signed him!

DIXON, Walter
Outside-right: 2 apps. 2 goals
Born: Perry Barr, Birmingham, 1861.
Now deceased.
Career: Brookvale FC, Aston Manor, Excelsior (1886), BLUES (July 1887), Church FC (February 1888).
Wally Dixon was a regular winger for the first part of season 1887-88 before moving to the North-West, ostensibly because he was offered a job there, although rumours abounded that Church FC had offered him a financial inducement to sign for them.

DOHERTY, Neil
Forward: 17+13 apps. 2 goals
Born: Barrow-in-Furness, 21 February 1969
Career: Watford (as a trainee, June 1985), Barrow (July 1988), Leeds United (on trial, July 1993), BLUES (£40,000, February 1994), Northampton Town (on loan, February-March 1996), Kidderminster Harriers, Barrow. Almost quit football in May 1996 to concentrate on an accountancy course - but had second thoughts!
Club honours: Barrow: FA Trophy winners 1990
Neil Doherty entered League soccer at the age of 26, when he made his debut for Blues against Peterborough United. A tricky winger who preferred the left flank, he had been marked down as a possible Premiership player before Barry Fry moved in to bring him to St Andrew's.

DOLAN, Eamonn John
Forward: 10+6 apps. one goal
Born: Chelmsford, 20 September 1967
Career: Dagenham Youth Club, West Ham United (apprentice, August 1983, professional March 1985), Bristol City (on loan, February 1989), Blues (£35,000, December 1990), Exeter City (exchange for Mark Cooper, September 1991). Forced to quit playing in 1995 with serious injury and was later 'Football in the Community' officer at St James' Park, then coach, assistant-manager and caretaker-manager in October 2002, following the sacking of another ex-Blues player John Cornforth.
Representative honours: Republic of Ireland (Youth & five Under-21 caps)
Eamonn Dolan was an energetic forward whose warming up and winding down routines earned him a place in Blues folklore. When named as a substitute he often

tended to spend most of his time jogging up and down the touchline, being escorted from the pitch by police at Exeter and getting himself arrested the Millmoor ground, Rotherham, on a charge of inciting the crowd, most of whom had left at the time. He initially signed for Blues in the summer of 1990, but a dislocated shoulder continued to cause him problems and he was sent back to West Ham. Dolan unfortunately missed the end of the 1990-91 campaign because of yet another arm injury. In May 1993 he underwent an operation for testicular cancer. His twin brother Pat played for Walsall

DOMINGEUZ, Jose Manuel Martins
Winger: 20+25 apps. 4 goals
Born: Lisbon, Portugal, 16 February, 1974
Career, Benfica (as a junior), Real Madrid (briefly), Benfica (professional, August 1992), Sport Uniao Sintrense/Portugal (on loan), AD Fafe/Portugal (on loan), BLUES (£180,000, March 1994), Sporting Lisbon (£1.8 million, August 1995), Tottenham Hotspur (£1.6 million, August 1997), FC Kaiserslautern/Germany (November 2000).
Club honours: Blues: Second Division champions 1995
Representative honours: Portugal (3 full caps, one Under-21 cap)
One of the smallest players ever to pull on a Blues shirt at 5ft 3ins, Jose Dominguez became a huge favourite with the St Andrew's fans with his tricky runs, neat body swerve and some cracking shots. He was never, in effect, a regular member of the first team, having more 'sub' outings than he actually started matches.

DONOWA, Brian Louis
Winger: 111+57 apps. 19 goals
Born: Ipswich, 24 September, 1964
Career: Ipswich Boys, Norwich City (apprentice 1980, professional September 1982), Stoke City (on loan, December 1985), Deportivo La Coruna (£40,000, February 1986), SV Willem II (1988), Ipswich Town (1989), Bristol City (£50,000, August 1990), BLUES (£50,000, August 1991), Burnley (on loan, January 1993), Crystal Palace (on loan, March 1993), Shrewsbury Town (on loan, January 1994), Walsall (on loan, October 1996), Peterborough United (free transfer, December 1996), Ayr United (December 1997), Forest Green Rovers (2000).
Club honours: Norwich: FA Youth Cup winners 1983, Milk Cup winners 1985
Blues: Second Division champions 1995, Auto-Windscreen Shield winners 1995.
Representative honours: England (3 Under-21 caps).
Louie Donowa made an early impact as a flying winger for Norwich City where he benefitted greatly from his experienced forward colleagues. He had a fairly unsuccessful spell abroad before attempting to revive his career in England. Opportunities were rather limited at

both Ipswich and Bristol City, however. He was the first Blues substitute to be substituted himself!

DORMAN, Donald
Inside-forward: 64 apps. 6 goals
Born: Hall Green, Birmingham, 18 September 1922.
Now deceased.
Career: Shirley Juniors, BLUES (initially in 1945, professional May 1946), Coventry City (September 1951), Walsall (October 1954). Retired in May 1957 and returned to Blues as a scout, rising to Chief Scout on the death of Walter Taylor. He left Blues, second time round, in 1983 and later took over as Chief Scout of Aston Villa, before quitting football in 1985 through poor health
A paratrooper, wounded and captured at Arnhem, Don Dorman's courage and his never-say-die attitude was always evident in his play. He is perhaps best remembered as the head of the scouting network at St Andrew's, which discovered such fine players as Trevor Francis, Kenny Burns, Tony Coton and many others. Dorman left the club as part of manager Ron Saunders' purge of backroom staff.

DORRINGTON, John
Goalkeeper: 111 apps.
Born: Smethwick, May 1881.
Died: Handsworth, Birmingham, 9 January, 1944
Career: Langley St Michael's, West Smethwick, West Bromwich Albion (as an amateur), Bromsgrove Rangers (August 1899), Kidderminster Harriers (1900), BLUES (July 1901). Retired in May 1913 through injury
Jack Dorrington was a grand servant to Blues, totally fearless, with a jovial temperament that did wonders for morale, even in difficult times. He was surprisingly only first choice in one of his twelve seasons at the club.

DOUGALL, Cornelius
Inside-right: 108 apps. 18 goals
Born: Falkirk, 7 November 1921
Career: Burnley (schoolboy forms 1936, professional July 1940), BLUES (£2,750, October 1945), Plymouth Argyle (March 1949). Retired in March 1959; became Plymouth's assistant-trainer, moving up to head trainer until March 1968; also acted briefly as caretaker-manager at Home Park. He guested for Coventry City in WW2
Club honours: Blues: Football League South champions 1946, Division Two champions 1948: Plymouth Argyle: Division Three (South) champions 1952, Division Three champions, 1959.
Representative honours: Scotland (1 full cap, 1 victory cap).
'Neil' Dougall came from a distinguished footballing stock - his father William played for Falkirk, Burnley and the Scottish League and his uncle James represented Preston North End and Scotland. Dougall was a powerful red-haired inside-forward with strong, accurate

shot (in both feet but mainly with his right) who made an immediate impact at St Andrew's, scoring 10 goals in his first season there. He didn't find the net too often after that but remained a vital cog in the attack mechanism. He went on to score 22 goals in 278 Football League outings for Argyle after leaving the Blues and spent more than 20 years at Home Park, becoming a very well respected gentleman in the West Country. Dougall is still living in Devon today.

DOUGHERTY, James
Left-half: 136 apps. 3 goals
Born: New Brighton, 19 November 1878.
Now deceased.
Career: New Brighton Old Wanderers, Liskeard YMCA (briefly), New Brighton Tower, Chorley, New Brighton Tower, BLUES (September 1901), Coventry City (1908), Stirchley United, Worcester City.
Jim Dougherty was originally a centre-half, but later on in years became a useful, constructive wing-half with a telling tackle. In those days before the stopper centre-half, of course, all the half-backs linked up with their attack. He was in line for international honours whilst with Blues, but was never selected for duty, although he was penned in as a reserve on two occasions. He was very proud of his magnificent waxed moustache

DOWNING, Keith Gordon
Midfielder: 2 apps
Born Oldbury, 23 July, 1965
Career: Mile Oak Rovers, Notts County (free transfer, May 1984), Wolverhampton Wanderers (free transfer, August 1987), BLUES (free transfer, July 1993), Stoke City (free transfer, August 1994), Hereford United.
Retired in 1997 and became a 'rep' for a Dudley Publishing Company, later returning to Edgar Street as player-coach as the 'Bulls' battled in vain to void relegation to the GM Conference. He completed a full circle when, in March 1999, he was appointed as youth team coach at Molineux
Club honours: Wolves: Division Three champions 1989, Division Four champions 1988, Sherpa Van Trophy winners 1988.
Keith Downing was a very competitive player, a hard tackler, whose nickname was 'Psycho'. He gave Wolves excellent service, playing for them in more than 200 games. Injury ruined his stay at St Andrew's. Under his former manager Graham Turner, he helped Hereford reach the Third Division Play-offs in 1996.

DOWNS, Gregory
Left-back: 22+1 apps. one goal
Born: Carlton, Nottingham, 13 December 1958
Career: Weaver's School, Norwich City (apprentice March 1975, professional December 1976), Connecticut Bicentennial/NASL (on loan, March-August 1977),

Torquay United (on loan, November-December 1977), Coventry City (£40,000, July 1985), BLUES (free transfer, August 1990), Hereford United (July 1991 as player coach; then manager May 1992, resigning in September 1994), Rounds Town FC (briefly), Kettering Town (November 1994), Redditch United (November 1994), Merthyr Tydfil (November 1994), Worcester City (February 1995), Forest Green Rovers (May 1995-97), Bridgnorth Town (manager). Later worked as a salesman.
Club honours: Norwich: Milk Cup winners 1985: Coventry: FA Cup winners 1987
Greg Downes made his Football League debut on the left-wing whilst on loan to Torquay but was successfully converted into a fine overlapping left-back, steady under pressure whose crosses were both precise and well-struck. He was Norwich's free-kick expert but struggled at Coventry to win over the fans and joined Blues initially as a replacement for Ian Atkins as sweeper before eventually gaining a first team slot in his accustomed role at left-back.

DRAKE, Alonzo Robson
Inside forward: 13 apps. 2 goals
Born: Parkgate, Rotherham, 16 April 1884.
Died: Hanley, Huddersfield, 14 February, 1919
Career: Parkgate FC, Rotherham Town (on trial, 1901), Doncaster Rovers, Sheffield United (professional, August 1905), BLUES (£1,000, December 1907), Queen's Park Rangers (August 1908), Huddersfield Town (1910-11).
Alonzo Drake was a hard working, dashing player said to have had bad luck with his shooting. Better known as a cricketer, he played as a professional for Yorkshire for five years (1909-14), appearing in 157 matches as a middle order left-hand batsman and slow left-arm bowler. He did the double in 1913 and followed up by taking 158 wickets in the next season (average 15.30). All told he scored 4,816 runs (average 21.69) and claimed 480 wickets at 18.00 each for the Tykes. He took 100 wickets and scored 1,000 runs in a season on two occasions, with his best run return coming in 1911 when he notched 1,487 for an average of 30.97. His best bowling figures were 10-35 for Yorkshire v. Somerset. His cricketing career was cut short through ill-health, leading to his sudden demise at the relatively early age of 34

DRAPER, Harry
Inside-left: 3 apps.
Born: Chesterfield, 1887.
Career: Rotherham Town (April 1909), BLUES (April 1910), Denaby United (September 1911).
Harry Draper was a young playmaker given a run out with the seniors as Blues struggled in Division Two. He could not settle in Birmingham and made an early return to Yorkshire

DRINKELL, Kevin Smith
Striker: 5 apps. 2 goals
Born: Grimsby, 18 June 1960.
Career: Grimsby & District Schools, Grimsby Town (apprentice June 1976, professional June 1978), Norwich City (£105,000, June 1985), Glasgow Rangers (July 1988), Coventry City (June 1990), BLUES (on loan, October 1991), Falkirk (player-coach, July 1992), Stirling Albion (player-coach, March 1994, later appointed as team manager), Montrose (manager, October 1998-2000).
Club honours: Grimsby: Division Three champions 1980: Rangers: Scottish League champions & Scottish Cup winners 1989.
Kevin Drinkell was a powerful centre-forward who was taken on loan by Blues following an injury to John Gayle. He scored 102 goals in 309 games for Grimsby before moving to Norwich and did well at Carrow Road and also at Ibrox Park. He made his Football League debut at the age of 17 and scored in his first game for Blues against Stockport in October 1991. He now lives and works in Stirling.

DRYDEN, Richard Andrew
Defender: 54 apps
Born: Stroud, Gloucestershire, 14 June 1969
Career: Bristol Rovers (trainee, June 1985, professional July 1987), Exeter City (on loan September 1988), Exeter City (March 1989), Notts County (£250,000, August 1991), Manchester City (on loan, June 1992), Plymouth Argyle (on loan, November 1992), BLUES (£165,000, March 1993), Bristol City (£140,000, December 1994), Southampton (£150,000, August 1996), Stoke City (on loan, November 1999 and again March-May 2000), Luton Town (February 2001-2002).
Club honours: Exeter: Division Four champions 1990
A versatile defender, strong and capable in every department, Richard Dryden passed the milestone of 200 senior appearances in his career during his spell with Blues. He went on to reach the 300-mark and in all played in 105 games for Exeter, scoring 15 goals (a fair return for a defender)

DUCKHOUSE, Edward
Full-back/centre-half: 127 apps. 4 goals
Born: Shelfield, Walsall, 9 April 1918.
Died: Walsall, 1980
Career: St Mark's School, Shelfield FC, Walsall Wood, Cannock Chase Colliery, Streetly Works FC, West Bromwich Albion (as an amateur, August 1937), Blues (as an amateur, July 1938, professional August 1939), Northampton Town (free transfer, August 1950), Rushden Town (July 1952). Retired in May 1955
Club honours: Blues: Football League (South) champions 1946, Division Two champions 1948
Ted Duckhouse was a solid, rock-hard defender who broke his leg in the 1946 FA Cup semi-final replay against Derby County when attempting to prevent the

first goal - an incident which had a major effect on the outcome of the game which Blues lost 4-0. He went on to make 68 League appearances with Northampton.

DUGARRY, Christophe
Striker: 2 apps. 0 goals
Born: Bordeaux France, 24th March 1972.
Career: Gironondis de Bordeaux (June 1988, professional March 1989), AC Milan (1996-97), Barcelona (June 1997), Olympique Marseille (January 1998), Bordeaux (October 1999), BLUES (on loan, January 2003).
Club honours: Barcelona (Spanish League champions 1998).
Representative honours: France: 53 full caps (8 goals). World Cup and European Championship winner: 1998 & 2000. French World Cup star Christophe Dugarry was Blues' first signing of 2003 - after the transfer window had re-opened. And manager Steve Bruce was delighted at his capture desdpuite he and the St Andrew's Board agreeing to his wage demads: £20,000-a-week. An established international with over 50 senior caps under his belt (gained between 1992-2002) Dugarry still had two-and-a-half years of his contract with Bordeaux left to run but chose to move into the Premiership with Blues, saying: "I have always wanted to play in England and now I'm going to give it my best shot."
Not a prolific scorer over the years - he had netted only 74 times in just over 400 competitive matches (64 in 387 League games) for clubs and country prior to joining Blues with his best efforts coming with Bordeaux: 43 goals in 252 League games and Marseille: eight in 52.

DUNCAN, Charles Stanley
Centre-forward: 24 apps. 9 goals
Born: Kinross, Scotland 1889. Died: Scotland
Career: Dunfermline Athletic, BLUES (April 1913), Clyde (September 1915).
Charlie Duncan was a short, bustling type of forward, very quick in the box with an eye for goal. He scored over 50 goals for Blues' Central League championship-winning side of 1914-15 but despite this form, appeared in only four senior games that season.

DUNLOP, Thomas
Right-back/right half: 62 apps. 2 goals
Born: Annbank, Scotland, 7 May 1872. Died: Scotland
Career: Port Glasgow (on trial), Annbank FC, BLUES (April 1896), Dundee Harp (August 1898-99).
A solidly built defender with a formidable kick, Tom Dunlop was originally a full-back, who developed into a defensive right-half, although when he did make the occasional foray forward, his long-range shooting was most effective.

E

EADEN, Nicholas Jeremy

Defender: 83+7 apps. 5 goals

Born: Sheffield, 12 December 1972

Career: Barnsley (trainee, June 1989, professional June 1991), BLUES (free transfer, July 2000), Wigan Athletic (September 2002).

Club honours: Barnsley: Division One promotion 1997; Blues: League Cup runners-up 2001, Division One promotion 2002

Able to play equally as well at right-back or in midfield, Nicky Eaden made 339 appearances for the 'Tykes' (helping them reach the Premiership) before moving to St Andrew's to boost Blues' squad in the summer of 2000. However, his chances became limited after Steve Bruce took over as manager and soon after the start of the 2002-03 season Eaden moved north to join Wigan.

EDGHILL, Richard Arlon

Right-back: 3 apps.

Born: Oldham, 23 September 1974

Career: Manchester City (trainee, June 1990, professional July 1992), BLUES (on loan, November to December 2000). Was released by Manchester City in June 2002.

Representative Honours: England (one 'B' cap, three Under-21).

One time captain at Maine Road, Richard Edghill tore his medial ligaments in his left leg early in the 2001-02 season and it wasn't until December that he regained fitness, having a loan spell with Blues to help him along. He made 210 appearances for City, helping them reach the Premiership in 2002, before being released by manager Kevin Keegan.

EDMUNDS, William H

Born: Bordesley Green, Birmingham 8 September 1854.

Died: Birmingham, 1925

Career: Bordesley Green Council School, BLUES (September 1875). Retired in summer of 1885

Blues' first official team captain, appointed in 1877, Billy Edmunds played in the club's first ever game in 1875 and remained with the club until the mid-1880s. An attacking player he once scored a hat-trick in five minutes - two goals for Blues, the other for the opposition. He never played in a major League or Cup game for Blues. He became a successful businessman after quitting football.

EDWARDS, Andrew David

Defender: 55+3 apps. 3 goals

Boren: Epping, 17 September 1971

Career: Southend United (trainee, June 1987, professional December 1989), BLUES (£400,000, July 1995), Peterborough United (November 1996).

Solid, well-built, reliable and commanding defender, 6ft 3ins tall and almost 13st in weight, Andy Edwards was a Barry Fry signing for Blues. He made 165 appearances for Southend and later, when he was re-united with Fry, he went on to amass more than 300 for 'Posh'

EDWARDS, Ernest Arthur

Half-back: 17 apps

Born: Stourbridge, 17 February, 1892.

Now deceased.

Career: Old Hill Unity, West Bromwich Albion (as an amateur), Kidderminster Olympic, Leamington Town, Redditch United (August 1911), BLUES (for four seasons: August 1913 to March 1919), Tipton Excelsior (albeit briefly), Merthyr Town (April-May 1919), Newport County (August 1919), Southend United (June 1923), Dudley Town (August 1926), Merthyr Town (season 1927-28). Retired in 1930. Guested for Newport County in 1915-16.

An all-purpose half-back capable of occupying any of the three positions, Ernie Edwards' chances were limited at St Andrew's but after WW1 he became a stalwart in the Newport side.

EDWARDS, George

Outside-left: 97 apps. 9 goals

Born: Kilgetty, South Wales, 2 December 1920.

Career: Narbeth Grammar School, Swansea Town (as an amateur, May 1938), Coventry City (as an amateur, August 1943), BLUES (professional, July 1944), Cardiff City (£12,000, December 1948). Retired during the 1955-56 season and later became director of Cardiff City FC, remaining in office until 1977.

Club honours: Cardiff: Welsh Cup runners-up 1951. Blues: Football League South champions 1946, Division Two champions 1948.

Representative honours: Wales: (12 full caps, one amateur cap).

George Edwards was spotted by Coventry whilst playing for RAF Wellesbourne and they switched him from inside-left to the left-wing, where he became a star performer. Fast and difficult to dispossess, he was a revelation at St Andrew's, becoming a firm favourite with the fans. He went on to make 194 League appearances for Cardiff (34 goals scored). After hanging up his boots, Edwards became a respected broadcaster and regular contributor to BBC Radio Wales while also penning a column for a Sunday newspaper. He was a qualified teacher and later held a position with a top-line oil company. He gained a MA degree at Birmingham University, his thesis being entitled 'A History of the Pembrokeshire Coalfields'.

EDWARDS, Henry Ross

Inside-forward: 5 apps. one goal

Born: Coventry, 1870.

Now deceased.

Career: Singers FC (Coventry), BLUES (May 1892), Ryton Rovers (August 1893), Leicester Fosse (October

1893), Derby County (August 1894), Wolverton LNWR (1895), Watford (December 1898), Bedford Queen's Football Club (1899-1900).

Harry Edwards was a talented youngster who was indirectly responsible for the signing of Frank Mobley, his Singers' team-mate. Alas, Edwards found it almost impossible to get a first-team game with Blues, due to the terrific form of Messrs Walton and Wheldon, and quickly moved on. He failed to settle in the East Midlands but then found quite a niche for himself in the Southern League where he was converted into an attacking centre-half.

EDWARDS, William Hague
Outside-left: 5 apps. one goal
Born: Coventry, February 1874.
Now deceased.
Career: Singers FC (Coventry), BLUES (September 1896), Rugby (season 1897-98).
The defection of 'Toddy Hands' left a considerable gap in the Blues attack and the inexperienced Bill Edwards was given the first chance to plug it. Enthusiastic, he also proved the rather limited although it is on record that he had a habit of stroking the ball with the sole of his foot whenever he received a pass. He was the younger brother of Henry Edwards (q.v) and played with him for Singers in season 1891-92.

ELKES, Albert John
Inside-right: 35 apps. 15 goals
Born: Woodhouse Row, Shropshire 31 December 1894.
Died: Rayleigh, Essex 22 January 1972
Career: St George's Amateurs, Wellington Town (1911), Stalybridge Celtic (1914), Shifnal Town, BLUES (January 1918), Southampton (March 1922), Tottenham Hotspur (£1,050, May 1923), Middlesbrough (August 1929), Watford (August 1933), Stafford Rangers (August 1934), Oakengates Town (1935). Retired in May 1937, when he became coach to the Ford Motor Works football team based at Dagenham, Essex.
Representative honours: Football League XI, FA tour to Australia 1925; England trialist.
Former miner Jack Elkes was a tall, long-striding inside-forward with surprisingly good, close control for such a big man. Very much a playmaker in his wartime appearances, he found it difficult to get a first team game once the regular players came back. He appeared in three England trials after impressive displays for both Southampton and Spurs (for whom he made over 200 appearances). In later years he switched to centre-half, a more suitable position for one who was 6ft 2ins tall.

ELLIMAN, Richard
Left-back: 4 apps.
Born: Carters Green, West Bromwich, 1859.
Now deceased.
Career: Christ Church FC, Sandwell FC (1880), BLUES (August 1882), Smethwick Highfield (Sep 1886-87).
Dick Elliman was a steady performer who was first choice for three years, and occasionally appearing as a stand in forward.

ELLIOTT, Anthony Robert
Goalkeeper: one app.
Born: Nuneaton, 30 November 1969
Career: Park Hall School, FA School of Excellence, BLUES (YTS June 1986, professional December 1986), Hereford United (December 1988), Huddersfield Town (July 1992), Carlisle United (June 1993), Cardiff City (July 1996), Scarborough (February 1998).
Club honours: Carlisle: Auto-Windscreen Shield runners-up 1995
Although highly thought of by the staff at the School of Excellence, Tony Elliott had to wait for his Blues debut - and when it came, it turned out to be a nightmare. On a wet, slippery surface, Blues crashed 5-0 to rivals Aston Villa in a League Cup-tie at Villa Park. Two months later he was released by the club, yet went on to make around 200 senior appearances at senior level.

ELLIS, William Thomas
Outside-left: 36 apps. 8 goals
Born: Wolverhampton, 5 November 1895.
Died: Nottingham, October 1971
Career: Willenhall Swifts, Hickman's Steel Works FC, Bilston Juniors, Highfield Villa, Bilston Juniors, Sunderland (May 1919), BLUES (November 1927), Lincoln City (August 1929), York City (November 1930 to January 1931). Retired in May 1932
Bill Ellis was Sunderland's regular left-winger for five years before his transfer back to the Midlands. He earned a reputation as a fine provider of chances in the North-East, but failed to capture his best form at St Andrew's. He scored 31 goals in 200 League & FA Cup games for Sunderland.

EMMANUEL, John Gary
Midfielder: 67+11 apps. 6 goals
Born, Swansea, 1 February 1954
Career: Swansea Schools, BLUES (apprentice June 1970, professional July 1971), Bristol Rovers (December 1978), Swindon Town (July 1981), Newport County (July 1984), Bristol City (non-contract, July 1985), Swansea

City (August 1985), Barry Town, Llanelli, Haverfordwest. Retired in June 1993.
Representative honours: Wales (one Under-23 cap).
Son of Len Emmanuel, formerly of Swansea Town, Gary was a willing worker, always striving to be in the thick of the action. Perhaps a shade too slow for the top flight, he later carved out a reasonable career in the lower Divisions, making well over 300 League appearances after leaving St Andrew's.

ESTEVES, Rui Manuel Guereiro Nobre
Midfielder: one app.
Born: Lisbon, Portugal, 30 January 1967
Career: Real Benfica, SC Othanense, Louletano DC, SC Farense (July 1990), SCU Torriense, Vitoria Setubal, SL Benfica (on loan), BLUES (on loan, March-April 1995), Benfica (1996). All his foreign clubs were in Portugal.
A blond, relatively slim midfielder who had little experience of top-flight Portuguese soccer, having spent most of his career in Division Two, Rui Esteves was thrown in at the deep-end for his Blues debut in the Auto-Windscreen Shield Area Final at Orient. He showed a nice touch on the ball, but was perhaps lacking a bit in physical strength. He quickly returned to his homeland of Portugal.

EVANS, Anthony
Inside-forward: 71+5 apps. 33 goals
Born: Liverpool, 11 January, 1954
Career: Formby FC (1971), Blackpool (professional, June 1973), Cardiff City (June 1975), BLUES (June 1979), Crystal Palace (August 1983), Wolverhampton Wanderers (April 1984), Bolton Wanderers (on loan, February 1985), Exeter City (on loan, March-April 1985), Swindon Town (August 1985), Walsall (non-contract, September 1986), Stafford Rangers (November 1986). Later appointed Wolves' Community Officer, appointed in 1993.
Club honours: Cardiff City: Welsh Cup winners 1976
Tony Evans worked as an electrician in Lancashire before joining Blackpool. He never made his mark at Bloomfield Road but after teaming up with Cardiff he became a useful striker. Lack of control let him down at times but generally speaking he did well, finishing up with a League career of 254 games and 87 goals

EVANS, Gwilym Hugh
Inside-forward: 14 apps.
Born: Ynysybwl, Wales, 12 December 1919
Career: St Stephen's School (Luton), Bedford Town (on trial), Redditch United, BLUES (December 1947), Bournemouth & Boscombe Athletic (June 1950), Walsall (August 1951), Watford (August 1952), Bedford Town (1954-56).
Hugh Evans was brought up in Luton and spotted while

serving in the army, Blues signing him only minutes before a scout from Wolves turned up. He was an out-and-out trier but certainly not good enough to keep a poor Blues side in the First Division. During his career he scored 22 goals in a total of 73 League games, 12 of them coming in 33 games for Walsall.

EVANS, Robert Owen
Goalkeeper, 3 apps.
Born: Wrexham, August 1881.
Died: Coventry 8 March 1962
Career: Olympic Juniors (1895), Stansty Villa, Wrexham (August 1898), Blackburn Rovers (£150, April 1903), Croydon Common (May 1908), Coventry City (April 1909), BLUES (June 1913), Nuneaton Town (season 1914-15).
Club honours: Wrexham: Welsh Cup winners 1902, runners-up 1903
Representative honours: Wales (10 full caps)
A star of the Edwardian Era, 'R.O' (Bob) Evans brought fulsome praise from one contemporary reporter who described him as '...skilful to the degree, quite this personified and rarely indeed does he misjudge the flight of the ball.' His courage led to sundry injuries throughout his career, most notably a dislocated knee early in one Welsh international match. Despite being in obvious pain he bravely saw the game out. Evans was in the twilight of his career with Blues. He played cricket for Derbyshire and his younger brother, Brad Evans, was a footballer with Plymouth Argyle

EVANS, Sidney John Vivian Leonard
Goalkeeper: 2 apps.
Born: Cardiff, 20 May 1919.
Died: Bournemouth, 26 December 1977
Career: Cardiff Corinthians (1922), Aberdare Athletic (October 1926), Merthyr Town (July 1927), Cardiff Corinthians (October 1927), Lovell's Athletic, Barry Town (1928), Cardiff City (as an amateur, April 1930), BLUES (as an amateur, September 1933, professional October 1933, then assistant-trainer at St Andrew's, May 1934), Svenborg/Sweden (1935), Blackburn Rovers (first XI trainer, June 1937 to September 1939).
Club honours: Lovell's Athletic: Welsh Cup winners 1928
Representative honours: Wales (4 full caps, 12 amateur caps, Schoolboy caps).
A Barry policeman, Len Evans followed Chris Charsley, Tom Watson and Bert Crossthwaite in the line of constable's to have kept goal for Blues. He was something of a risk-taker but nonetheless was a classy and reliable 'custodian', his only weakness was that he tended at times to be a bit haphazard when clearing the ball. Evans was capped whilst in Cardiff's reserve team when understudying the tall Irishman, Tom Farquharson. The situation was mirrored at Blues where he spent his

time as deputy to Harry Hibbs. He later worked as a PT Instructor and athletics coach, and was also good at swimming, boxing, cricket, baseball and gymnastics - a real sportsman. He sang in a choir and had ambitions to become a clergyman but in the end chose to wear a goalkeepers' jersey instead of a dog collar.

EVANS, Thomas Eli
Right-half: 6 apps
Born: Dudley, February 1896.
Now deceased.
Career: Pensnett Schools, Great Bridge Celtic, Tipton Parish Church FC, Bradley United, Cradley St Luke's, BLUES (December 1917), Brighton & Hove Albion (July 1921), Cradley Heath (June 1922 to May 1927). One of a host of players to make their debut for Blues during WW1, Tom Evans was a solid Black Countryman who was unable to hold down a first-team place in peacetime football. He stood 5ft 7ins tall and weighed 10st 7lbs.

EVERS, Albert
Half-back: 2 apps.
Born: Winson Green, Birmingham, 1868.
Now deceased.
Career: Summerfield Tavern FC, Royal Oak Rangers, BLUES (January 1891), Yardley Victoria (Oct 1891). A sturdy defender, Bert Evers played in most of Blues' friendly games towards the end of the 1890-91 season whilst Cesar Jenkins was under suspension

EVETTS, Robert
Full-back: 8 apps one goal
Born: Kings Heath, Birmingham, 1864.
Now deceased.
Career: Stirchley Rangers, St Stephen's Church FC, BLUES (April 1884), Warwick County (1887-88). Bob Evetts demonstrated an ability to play on either flank and appeared in Blues 1886 FA Cup semi-final side, beaten 4-0 by West Bromwich Albion.

EYRE, Edmund
Outside-left: 82 apps. 16 goals
Born: Worksop, December 1882.
Now deceased.
Career: Worksop West End, Worksop Town, Rotherham Town, BLUES (March 1907), Aston Villa (December 1908), Middlesbrough (April 1911), BLUES (April 1914). Retired May 1919
A speedy winger and prolific goalscorer during his spells with both Worksop clubs and Rotherham, Edmund 'Ninty' Eyre favoured the fast and whipping low cross and was said to have possessed a fiery temper. WW1 severely interrupted his spell at St Andrew's.

FAIRMAN, Robert
Full-back/half back: 39 apps. one goal
Born: Southampton, July 1885.
Now deceased.
Career: Southampton, BLUES (May 1907), West Ham United (August 1909), BLUES (June 1912). Retired in April 1920.
A tall, well-built defender who had two spells with Blues, Bob Fairman was a great favourite with the supporters each time. A local reporter claimed that he covered his position well and kicked strongly from all angles - ample qualifications for any full-back of his era.

FALL, John Walter
Goalkeeper: 2 apps
Born: Southampton, December 1867
Career: Leigh Street FC, Middlesbrough Ironopolis (albeit briefly), Newton Heath (1893), Kettering Town (1894), BLUES (May 1895), Altrincham (August 1896). Jack (John) Fall had literally 'fallen' on hard times when Blues signed him, initially as third choice goalkeeper behind Partridge and Roach. He failed to impress when given his chance, although he had been a regular with Newton Heath for a season

FARLEY, Walter
Wing-half: one app.
Born: Selly Oak, Birmingham, 1859.
Now deceased.
Career: Harborne, Excelsior, BLUES (July 1885), Stourbridge (season 1887-89).
An experienced player by the time he made his bow for Blues, Walter Farley held down a place in the first team for just three months, playing well in friendly and local cup-ties but then his form deteriorated

FARMER, Frederick Brian
Full-back: 145 apps.
Born Wordsley, Stourbridge, 29 July 1933
Career: Stourbridge (season 1949-50), BLUES (as an amateur, July 1950, professional May 1954), Bournemouth & Boscombe Athletic (January 1962), retired May 1965. Fred Later worked as a Midlands-based scout.
Club honours: Blues: Fairs Cup runners-up 1960 & 1961
A reliable if unspectacular performer, capable of filling either full-back berth, Brian Farmer got his chance following the tragic death of Jeff Hall and he held his place in the first team for two years before the emergence of Winston Foster, coupled with the signing of Stan Lynn. This led to him being relegated to the reserves and his ultimate departure from St Andrew's. Farmer played in almost 250 games in the Football League (117 for Blues).

FARMER, Michael Chester
Wing-half: one app. one goal
Born: Leicester, 22 November 1944
Career: Leicester Schools, BLUES (apprentice, August 1961, professional April 1962), Lincoln City (May 1965): Skegness Town (1966), Arnold Town, Skegness Town, Arnold, Skegness Town, Grantham Town (1970), Oadby Town (1973), Grantham Town (February 1974).
Mick Farmer was a tall, well-built midfielder with a powerful shot who scored on his only outing for Blues, but was surprisingly never chosen again despite the team's persistent relegation battles

FARNALL, Thomas
Wing-half: 53 apps. 2 goals.
Born: Gloucester, 1871.
Now deceased.
Career: Eastville Rovers (Bristol), BLUES (April 1895 to May 1897), Eastville Rovers, BLUES (season 1899-1900), Watford (August 1900), Bristol Rovers (July 1901), Bradford City (July 1903), Barrow (1906), Gloucester (1907-08).
'Tot' Farnall was a West countryman with a fancy for returning to his old clubs. He was a strong tackler who enjoyed a long-range shot at goal

FARRAGE, Thomas Oliver
Outside-left: 7 apps. 2 goals
Born: Chopwell, November 1917.
Died: killed in action in 1944 whilst a pilot in the Army Air Corps
Career: Walker Celtic, BLUES (November 1937). Guested for Leeds United, Luton Town and Middlesbrough during WW2.
Tom Farrage, a promising young player with an eye for goal, was a casualty of WW2.

FARRELL, Gregory James Philip
Outside-right: 5 apps
Born: Motherwell, 19 March, 1944
Career: St Vincent's School, Saltley Boys, Small Heath Unity, BLUES (as an amateur, June 1969, apprentice January 1960, professional March 1961), Cardiff City (March 1964), Bury (March 1967). Retired in May 1970, later assisted Homecare FC in the Birmingham mid-week League
Club honours: Cardiff: Welsh Cup winners 1964
Greg Farrell was a clever ball player whose chances were few and far between at St Andrew's owing to the form of Mike Hellawell and Bertie Auld.In later years he always played well against Blues. His brother, Joe, was also on Blues' books as an amateur

FAULKNER, Kenneth Gordon
Forward: 2 apps
Born: Smethwick, 10 September 1923

Career: Smethwick Schoolboy football, Smethwick Highfield, BLUES (on trial, 1943, amateur August 1946), Oldbury United (August 1947).
Representative honours: England (Schoolboy caps).
Ken Faulkner made fifteen WW2 appearances for Blues, but failed to make a name for himself after the hostilities.

FELTON, Walter Oscar
Half-back: 7 apps. one goal
Born: Coventry, 1861.
Now deceased.
Career: The Grove FC, BLUES (September 1884), Walsall Swifts (1886-88).
Walter Felton occupied all three half-back positions during his three years with Blues and was a very adaptable player.

FENTON, Ronald
Inside-forward: 31+9 apps. 8 goals
Born: South Shields, County Durham, 2 September 1940
Career: South Shields & District Schools, Durham Boys, West Bromwich Albion (on trial, 1955), South Shields, Burnley (junior April 1956, professional September 1957), West Bromwich Albion (£15,000, November 1962), BLUES (£7,500, January 1965), Brentford (January 1968), Notts County (July 1970). Retired in May 1971 to become coach at Meadow Lane, later Magpies' manager 1975-77. Thereafter assistant-trainer, then coach at Nottingham Forest (October 1977) before being promoted to assistant-manager (under Brian Clough) in 1987 after ten years' service at The City Ground. He resigned in May 1993, when Clough also left. Later became an England scout
Ronnie Fenton was a battler, a player who gave his all. He grafted hard and long and never really repeated his Albion performances whilst with Blues. He netted a total of 52 goals in 212 senior appearances as a professional, 18 of them in 66 outings for Albion. Remarkably, half of his goals for Blues came as a substitute.

FENWICK, Paul Joseph
Defender: 13+11 apps.
Born: Camden, London 25 August 1969
Career: NASL with Edmonton Oilers, Hamilton Steelers, Toronto Blizzard and Winnipeg Fury (the latter from 1991), then BLUES (as a professional, November 1992 to December 1994), Dunfermline Athletic (March 1995), St Mirren (July 1996), Raith Rovers (March 2000), Hibernian.
Club honours: Winnipeg Fury: Canadian League Champions 1992
Representative honours: Canada (one full cap, 8 appearances in Olympic Games)
Paul Fenwick was a solid defender who was introduced to first team football only a month after joining Blues from soccer in the NASL where he had met with a fair degree of success. After leaving St Andrew's he went on

to amass more than 100 League appearances North of the Border.

FERGUSON, Michael John
Centre-forward: 25 apps. 9 goals
Born: Newcastle-upon-Tyne, 3 October 1954
Career: Coventry City (apprentice June 1970, professional December 1971), Everton (£280,000, August 1981), BLUES (on loan, November 1982, signed permanently for £60,000 June 1983), Coventry City (on loan, March 1984), Brighton & Hove Albion (£40,000, in deal involving Mark Jones, September 1984), Wealdstone United (1987), Sunderland (Youth team coach and later appointed as 'Football In Community' Officer at Roker Park: 1995-96).
Mike Ferguson was a powerfully built striker, good in the air, who netted a combined total of 54 goals in 128 League games for Coventry. He top-scored in his first season with Blues but a series of injuries kept him out of the side for long periods the following year. However, during his loan spell at Highfield Road he netted some vital goals that helped keep the Sky Blues in the old First Division, paradoxically at Blues' expense.

FERRARI, Carlos Eduado
Striker: 0+4 apps.
Born: Londrina, Brazil, 19 February 1979
Career: FC Mirassol (Sao Paulo, Brazil), BLUES (on loan, August 2001 to May 2002).
Signed on loan by Blues for a season, the young physically strong Brazilian unfortunately broke his foot shortly before Christmas and consequently took no further part in the action.

FERRIS, Raymond Osborn
Half-back: 106 apps. 4 goals
Born: Newry, County Down, 22 September 1920.
Now deceased.
Career: Distillery (on trial), Glentoran (on trial), Newry Town (on trial), Brentford (as an amateur 1938), Cambridge Town (July 1939), Tottenham Hotspur & West Ham United (WW2 guest), Crewe Alexandra (professional, March 1945), BLUES (March 1949), Worcester City (September 1953). Retired through injury in April 1954.
Representative honours: Northern Ireland (3 full caps); toured Canada with Irish FA (prior to joining Worcester City Football Club).
An industrious, strong tackling red head, son of Jack Ferris, the former Belfast Celtic and Irish International, Ray Ferris made over 100 appearances for the 'Alex' before transferring to Blues. A serious leg injury, suffered whilst on tour in Canada, effectively ended his senior playing career.

FIELD, Charles William Franklin
Outside-left: 89 apps 15 goals
Born: Hanwell, Yorkshire, December 1879.
Now deceased.
Career: Hanwell, Royal Ordnance (Southern League), Brentford (August 1896), Sheffield United (1898), BLUES (January 1902). Retired in May 1906
Club honours: Sheffield Utd: FA Cup runners-up 1901.
Representative honours: Sheffield XI (v Glasgow)
On the slight side, but a player who could hold his own, Charlie 'Oakey' Field was a prolific scorer in junior football, a record he maintained with Brentford, opening his senior career with a hat-trick from the inside-left position. He registered four hat-tricks and a six-timer in season 1897-98, and such was his marksmanship that the bigger clubs flocked to see him in action. It was no surprise when he joined Sheffield United, for whom he starred as an inside-right. He was subsequently transferred to Blues with team-mate Billy Beer, and later fought a lengthy battle against injury. He impressed observers with his pace and dribbling skills as well as his shooting.

FIGURES, William Horace
Inside-left: 9 apps. 2 goals
Born: Small Heath, Birmingham, 1862.
Now deceased.
Career: St John's United, St Andrew's Rovers, BLUES (April 1885), Great Bridge Unity (December 1887), Cradley Heath Welfare.
Bill Figures joined the club from a Sparkbrook church side and became a fixture in the team at inside-left as Blues raced through the 1886 FA Cup semi-final. He struck up a find understanding with Teddy Hill but after Hill departed (through injury in 1887) Figures' form slumped and he went off to try his luck in the Black Country.

FILLINGHAM, Thomas
Centre-half: 192 apps. 9 goals
Born: Bulwell, Nottinghamshire, 6 September 1904.
Died: Bulwell, 1 May 1960.
Career: Bulwell Wesleyan Mission, Butlers Hill Primitives, Daybrook Baptists, Hucknall Colliery FC, Bromley United, BLUES (professional August 1928), Ipswich Town (June 1938). Guested for Mansfield Town & Nottingham Forest in WW2, retired in April 1945.
Given his early chance as a forward (he scored twice on his debut) 'Tosher' Fillingham later developed into a linchpin of the Blues' defence. Tall, long-legged and strong in the tackle, he was a versatile performer, particularly good in the air, and was seen as the ideal replacement for 'Lofty' Morrall. He retained his forward's instincts throughout his career and could frequently be seen unleashing shots on the opposition goal. Fillingham became Ipswich Town's captain and

starred in their first season of League football. Unfortunately he lost an eye in 1950, as a result of an injury sustained playing for Blues against Spurs in April 1934. A one-time dye-house worker, he had previously been employed at Hucknall Colliery. He was an excellent cricketer, especially stylish with the bat, and a pretty useful golfer, teeing off with a handicap of 14.

FINNAN, Stephen
Full-back: 13+9 apps. one goal
Born: Limerick, 20 April 1976
Career: Welling United, BLUES (£100,000, June 1996), Notts County (on loan, March 1996, signed permanently for £300,000, October 1996), Fulham (£600,000, November 1998).
Club honours: Notts County: Division 3 champions 1998; Fulham: Division 2 champions 1999, Division One champions 2001.
Representative honours: Republic of Ireland (21* full, one 'B', 8 Under-21 caps).
An ever-present in Fulham's first-ever season in the Premiership (2001-02), Steve Finnan was subsequently chosen in the PFA team of the year and he also had a fine World Cup in the Far East. A player who has done superbly well since leaving St Andrew's, Finnan loves to attack and delivers a quality crosses when given the chance.

FINNEY, Charles William Thomas
Inside-forward: 17 apps. one goal
Born: Stoke-on-Trent, 5 September 1931
Career: Stoke-on-Trent Schoolboy football, Edensor Youth Club, Crewe Alexandra (as an amateur 1947), Stoke City (professional, May 1949), BLUES (November 1955), Queen's Park Rangers (May 1957), Crewe Alexandra (July 1958), Rochdale (September 1959), Cheltenham Town (November 1959)
Bill Finney was a capable schemer who was signed to provide cover for the three inside forward positions.

FIRTH, Jack
Wing-half/inside-forward: 98 apps. 8 goals
Born: Doncaster, 8 August 1907.
Died: Doncaster, 8 December 1987
Career: Brodsworth Main Colliery, Doncaster Rovers (as an amateur), BLUES (as an amateur March 1926, professional, August 1926), Swansea Town (August 1933), Bury (May 1936).
Jack Firth was a burly ex-miner who provided excellent cover for both wing-half and two inside-forward positions during his seven seasons with Blues, being first choice for one campaign when Leslie was injured. He played over 100 games for Swansea and was also a useful cricketer with Brodsworth Main CC. He stood 5ft 9in tall and weighed just over 11 stones.

FIRTH, Robert Edwin
Outside-right: 26 apps. 2 goals
Born: Sheldon, Birmingham, 20 February 1887.
Now deceased.
Career: Gower Street School (Aston), 6th Battery Royal Field Artillery, Birmingham Corporation Trams FC, Golder's Green FC (Birmingham), BLUES (professional, April 1909), Wellington Town (May (1911), Nottingham Forest (September 1911), Port Vale (June 1921), Southend United (July 1922). Retired in May 1923
Bob Firth was working as a tram conductor when Blues signed him full-time in 1909. Mainly a provider of chances, able to centre accurately on the run, his play was little appreciated at St Andrew's and he left with his pal, Fred Banks, for pastures new. The pair remained together, on opposite wings, for nine years before Banks retired. Firth called it a day at the age of 36.

FITZPATRICK, Paul James
Midfielder: 7 apps
Born: Liverpool, 5 October 1965
Career: Liverpool (apprentice 1981), Tranmere Rovers (apprentice, 1982), Preston North End (on trial), Bolton Wanderers (professional, March 1985), Bristol City (August 1986), Carlisle United (October 1988), Preston North End (on loan, December 1988), Leicester City (July (1991), BLUES (January 1993), Bury (on loan, March 1993), Northampton Town (February 1994), football in Hong Kong, then Rushden & Diamonds (briefly), Leicester United (until May 1995), Telford United (August 1995 to May 1997).
Paul Fitzpatrick had already made over 200 appearances during his career (109 in the League for Carlisle) before joining Blues. An enterprising player who always gave nothing less than 100 per-cent every time he took the field.

FLEMING, Curtis
Full-back: 6 apps.
Born: Manchester, 8 October 1968
Career: St Patrick's FC (Dublin), Middlesbrough (£50,000, August 1991), BLUES (on loan, November-December 2001), Crystal Palace (£100,000, Dec 2001).
Club honours: Middlesbrough: Division 1 Title 1995
Representative honours: Republic of Ireland (10* full, two Under-23, 5 Under-21 & Youth caps).
A hard-tackling, resourceful right full-back, signed on loan from Middlesbrough in November 2001, Curtis Fleming was quickly recruited by manager Francis again when he left St Andrew's to take charge of Palace.

FLETCHER, Thomas Wilberforce
Inside-left: 2 apps.
Born: Wednesfield, July 1878.
Now deceased.
Career: Willenhall, BLUES (season 1900-01), Cradley St Luke's (September 1901), Bellswood

Rangers/Wolverhampton (season 1903-04).
Tom Fletcher partnered Bob McRoberts in Blues' attack but failed to impress the selection committee.

FORINTON, Howard Lee
Striker: 2+8 apps. one goal
Born: Boston, Lincolnshire, 18 September 1975
Career: Yeovil Town, BLUES (July 1997), Plymouth Argyle (on loan, December 1998), Peterborough United (£250,000, September 1999), Yeovil Town (July 2002).
Howard Forinton - quick, strong and brave - had very little opportunity to show what he could do at St Andrew's but after linking up again with his ex-manager Barry Fry he did reasonably well with 'Posh', scoring 10 goals in 60 appearances before his departure to Yeovil in May 2002.

FORSTER, Nicholas Michael
Striker: 29+47 apps. 12 goals
Born: Caterham, 8 September 1973
Career: Horley Town, Gillingham (May 1992), Brentford (£100,000, June 1994), BLUES (£700,000, November 1997), Reading (£650,000, June 1999).
Club honours: Reading: Division Two promotion 2002
Representative honours: England (4 Under-21 caps)
A very efficient striker, especially at a lower level, two-thirds of Nicky Forster's appearances for Blues were as a substitute. He was selected in the Second Division PFA team for 2001-02 when he helped Reading gain promotion with 19 goals. He netted 47 times in 136 outings for Brentford.

FORSYTH, Richard Michael
Midfielder: 24+17 apps. 2 goals
Born: Dudley, 3 October 1970
Career: Kidderminster Harriers, BLUES (£50,000, July 1995), Stoke City (£200,000, July 1996), Blackpool (free transfer, July 1999), Peterborough United (July 2000).
Club honours: Kidderminster Harriers: GM Vauxhall Cheltenham Town (2002) Conference champions 1994
Representative honours: England (semi-pro, 3 caps)
A very enthusiastic, hard-working midfielder, Richard Forsyth gave Blues good value during one season at St Andrew's. He reached the milestone of 250 League and Cup games at senior level in 2002.

FOSTER, Arthur Webster
Inside-left: 2 apps. one goal
Born Deritend, Birmingham, 12 November 1894.
Died: Acocks Green, Birmingham, 9 January 1954
Career: Repton School, Cambridge University, Old Reptonians, Corinthians (Birmingham), BLUES (as an amateur, September 1913), Acocks Green FC (April 1914), Army football, Old Reptonians (1919-20).
Arthur Foster was one of the lesser-known members of the famous Birmingham sporting family - his brother FR

'Bob' Foster played cricket for Warwickshire and England. Arthur was associated with Blues between coming down from university and signing for the army. He was described as being 'not used to heavy football' although he did score often for the reserves. He played one match for Warwickshire as a wicketkeeper, taking two catches and scoring one run.

FOSTER, Winston Arthur
Full-back/centre-half: 169+1 apps. 2 goals
Born: South Yardley, Birmingham, 1 November, 1941
Career: Church Road Junior & Cockshutt Secondary Modern Schools, Birmingham County FA, BLUES (as a junior, June 1955, professional November 1958), Crewe Alexandra (on loan, March 1969), Plymouth Argyle (June 1969), Chelmsford City (July 1971), Bromsgrove Rovers (as a player, 1972-73, then assistant-manager 1973-74).
Club honours: Blues: Fairs Cup runners-up 1961
Born during the war, hence his patriotic Christian name, Winston Foster began as a long-legged, awkward looking full-back until an injury to Trevor Smith led to switching over to the centre-half position where he looked far more at ease. He performed credibly in this role until laid up with cartilage trouble.

FOUNTAIN, Edwin Jospeh
Inside-forward: 3 apps.
Born: Aston, Birmingham, 1871
Career: Calthorpe FC, Small Heath Langley, BLUES (August 1894), Birmingham St George's (November 1895), Worcester Rovers (1896), Hereford Town (October 1897-98).
Ted Fountain was an all-action left-sided player who had to bide his time owing to the form and consistency of Wheldon and Hands. He moved to St George's to help boost the flagging fortunes of the Cape Hill club.

FOX, Matthew Christopher
Centre-back: 13+2 apps.
Born: Sheldon, Birmingham, 13 July 1971
Career: Heathlands & Byng Kendrick Schools, Birmingham Boys, Hurley Colts, Blues (YTS June 1987, professional July 1989), Cheltenham Town (on loan, October 1991), Northampton Town (March 1993), Shrewsbury Town (on trial, September-October 1993), Bridgnorth Town (November 1993-95).
Dogged defender, hard in the tackle and quick to cover, Matthew Fox was forced to miss the entire 1989-90 season through injury. He now works in a city-centre sports shop.

FOX, Stephen Douglas
Outside-right: 26+3 apps. one goal
Born: Tamworth, 17 February, 1958
Career: Aston Villa (associate schoolboy), Tamworth,

BLUES (apprentice June 1975, professional February 1976), Wrexham (December 1978), Port Vale (October 1982), Chester City (July 1984), Llangollen, Tamworth, Rhyl Athletic, Tamworth (1989-90).

Club honour: Wrexham: Welsh Cup runners-up 1979

Steve Fox was a highly combative winger with plenty of flair but seemingly lacking ambition and consequently most of his career was spent in the lower Divisions of the Football League. He became a lorry driver, and also worked as a debt collector and occasional gardener (for old people). He now lives in Tamworth.

FOXALL, Frank

Inside-forward: 22 apps. 3 goals
Born: Sheffield, 1884.
Career: All Saints Sunday School, Roundel FC, Wombwell Town (1901), Doncaster Rovers (1902), Gainsborough Trinity (1903), Sheffield Wednesday (April 1907), BLUES (April 1910), Shrewsbury Town (August 1911-13).

Club honours: Roundel: Chard Cup winners 1900.

Frank Foxall did well with Wednesday, scoring nine goals in 45 games, but after the Hillsborough club had signed Scottish international George Robertson he was allowed to move to Blues, who at that time, were at their lowest ebb, having had to apply for re-election the previous season. He had spent most of his time on the wing but Blues tried him as an inside-forward, an experiment that failed to succeed, and he was quickly switched back to the wing, before changing clubs again.

FOXALL, Frederick Howard

Outside-left: 28 apps. 4 goals
Born: Stourbridge, 2 April 1898.
Died: Smethwick, 17 June 1926
Career: Saltwells FC, Aston Villa (as a professional, April 1915), Blackheath Town (1916), Southampton (May 1919), Aston Villa (May 1921), BLUES (March 1922), Watford (July 1923). Retired in May 1924 through poor health.

Fred Foxall's transfer to Villa Park in 1921 was annulled by the FA as Southampton had not been consulted about the deal. This did not upset the player, however, and he continued to render sterling service to the Saints as an out-and-out left-winger. His fifteen months at St Andrew's (when he teamed up with his old colleague Joe Barrett) were fraught with injury and illness, and he was grateful to move to Watford. Younger brother to Arthur Foxall, Fred was forced to quit the professional scene in 1924 and he sadly died two years later, aged only 28.

FOY, David Lee

Midfielder: 3+1 apps.
Born: Coventry, 20 October, 1972
Career: Allesley Primary & Coundon Court Secondary

Schools, BLUES (as a trainee 1989, professional, July 1991), Cobh Ramblers (on loan, January 1992), Scunthorpe United (March 1993), Weymouth, Stafford Rangers (October 1993), Tamworth (on loan, January 1994, full transfer October 1994).

David Foy was a strong player, determined and courageous, but alas wasn't quite up to League standard.

FRAIN, John William

Midfielder/left-back: 327+10 apps. 26 goals
Born: Yardley, Birmingham, 8 October, 1968
Career: Holy Souls Primary & Archbishop Tyseley Schools, Birmingham Boys, BLUES (apprentice June 1984, non-contract forms July 1985, professional October 1986), Northampton Town (January 1997)

Club honours: Blues: Leyland DAF Cup winners 1991. Northampton: Third Division Play-off winners 1997.

John Frain formed an effective Youth team full-back partnership with Julian Dicks but failed to impress in that position when playing in the full League side. Lacking in pace he was then put into midfield where his distribution skills made him a natural, but eventually he settled in again at left-back. Frain - a penalty expert - made his Blues debut away at Newcastle in April 1986, scoring a goal to celebrate the occasion, and he was the club's longest-serving player when he moved to Northampton in 1997. At the end of that season he re-visited the Empire Stadium - this time helping the Cobblers beat Swansea City in the Third Division Play-off Final. In April 2000 Frain took his career appearance up to 500 (first-class matches).

FRANCIS, Carlos Everton

Wing-forward: 2+3 apps.
Born: West Ham, London, 21 August 1962
Career: BLUES (apprentice June 1979, professional August 1980), Hereford United (on loan, December 1983), Enfield (season 1984-85).

The first coloured footballer to play for the club, Carlos Francis was very quick but inconsistent and most of his career with Blues was spent in the reserves. He could not cope with his rejection and Blues were forced to place a restraining order on him after he refused to stay away from the club's training ground. After this sad time he had an unsuccessful spell with Enfield.

FRANCIS, Kevin Derek Michael

Striker: 44+49 apps. 21 goals
Born: Moseley, Birmingham, 6 December, 1967
Career: Holy Family & Waverley Schools, Emerald Social FC, Redditch United, Mile Oak Rovers, Derby County (free transfer, February 1989), Stockport County (£60,000, February 1991), BLUES (£800,000, January 1995), Oxford United (£100,000, February 1998), Stockport County (March 2000), Hull City (December 2000), Hednesford Town (July 2001).

Club honours: Stockport: Division Four promotion 1991, Autoglass Trophy runners-up 1992 & 1993; Blues: Second Division champions 1995, Auto-Windscreen Shield winners 1995.

At 6 ft 7ins, the tallest player ever to appear in the Football League (at that time), Kevin Francis equalled Blues' record signing when he joined the club early in 1995 after an on-off transfer with Stockport which lasted a month owing to a medical report on an injury to Francis's right knee. Nicknamed the 'Inchman', he scored over 120 goals in some 200 senior games for Stockport before arriving at St Andrew's. He was a Blues supporter as a lad and had no hesitation in moving to the club, once he was given a clean medical report. Earlier, Everton had shown an interest in taking him into the FA Premiership but that move came to nothing. He quickly helped Blues win the Second Division and Auto-Windscreen Shield double (1995) and scored roughly a goal every four games before moving to Oxford in 1998. Two years later Francis returned to his former home at Edgeley Park.

FRANCIS, Sean Robert

Forward: 0+6 apps.
Born: Birmingham, 1 August, 1972
Career: Oratory Roman Catholic School, BLUES (YTS, June 1988, professional July 1990), Cobh Ramblers (on loan, August 1991); Telford United (July 1992), Worcester City (on loan, January 1992), Northampton Town (August 1993), Cobb Ramblers (Oct 1993-94).
A pale looking youngster, Sean Francis was one of the stars of Blues' Youth team in 1990-91 with his intelligent off-the-ball runs, thus creating space for his colleagues.

FRANCIS, Trevor John

Inside-forward: 327+2 apps. 133 goals
Born: Plymouth, 19 April, 1954
Career: Ernesettle Youth Club, Plymouth Boys, BLUES (apprentice, June 1969, professional May 1971), Detroit Express/NASL (on loan, May-August 1978), Nottingham Forest (£975,000 + VAT & levy charges, February 1979), Detroit Express, again (on loan, June-August 1979), Manchester City (£1.2 million, September 1981), Sampdoria/Italy (£800,000, July 1982), Atalanta/Italy (£900,000, July 1986), Glasgow Rangers (free transfer, September 1987), Queen's Park Rangers (March 1988, appointed player-manager in December 1988), Sheffield Wednesday (free transfer, February 1990, manager from June 1991 to May 1995), BLUES (manager, May 1996 to October 2001), Crystal Palace (manager, from November 2001).
Club honours: Blues: Division Two promotion 1972; Nottingham Forest: European Cup winners 1979 (scored the winning goal), League Cup runners-up 1980; Sampdoria: Italian Cup winners 1985; Rangers: Scottish League Cup winners 1988; Sheffield Wednesday: League

Cup winners & Division Two promotion 1991; (as manager) Sheffield Wed: FA Cup runners-up 1993, Football League Cup runners-up 1993; Blues: League Cup runners-up 2001.

Representative honours: England (52 full caps, 5 U-23). With the VAT & 10% levy charges included, Trevor Francis became Britain's first £1 million footballer when he moved to Forest in 1979. He had exploded onto the League scene with 15 goals in his first 21 games for Blues, including four in one match against Bolton in February 1971 when he was still only 16 years of age. He displayed electrifying speed off the mark, intricate dribbling skills, a powerful shot and amazing self-confidence that were to be his trademarks during a long and successful playing career. His impressive total of goals for Blues would have been even better but for two serious injuries. A further lengthy spell on the treatment table whilst with Forest earned him the quite unjustified accusation of being injury-prone, but he made his critics eat their words as he continued to play until he was 39. Throughout the 1970s it seemed as though Francis alone was keeping Blues in the First Division, but with the team destined for the drop in 1979 he was whisked away by Brian Clough after asking to leave St Andrew's. From there he changed clubs regularly, yet always played at top level, going on to amass a terrific record of more than 750 appearances (with all clubs) and scoring over 220 goals. He did not have too good a time in his first spell as manager, with QPR, but with Wednesday he did rather better and to a certain extent he did quite well with Blues having the ill-luck to miss out in the Play-offs three seasons running: 1999, 2000 & 2001, and they lost in the Final of the Worthington Cup, albeit on penalties to Liverpool, also in 2001.

When he returned 'home' to take charge of Blues in 1996, Francis said: "People will think I'm crackers. I'm voluntarily going back to the madhouse."

● On 14 February 1979, just 24 hours after moving to Forest, Francis played in an 'A' team game v. Notts County (away) in front of 40 spectators. Afterwards the FA stated that 'He wasn't properly registered, and that the Football League had not received the player's registration papers.'

● In August 1998, it was reported that Francis had signed a new one-year deal worth £4,000-a-week, making him the highest-paid person in the club's history. He saw that through but stayed only until the autumn of 2001 before losing his job - being eventually replaced by Steve Bruce, the man he took over from at Crystal Palace.

FRASER, Adam

Left-back: 24 apps
Born: Paisley, Scotland, 1871.
Now deceased.
Career: Glasgow Nomads, Glasgow Northern, BLUES (November 1895), Heart of Midlothian

G

(season 1896-97).

Adam Fraser was much hyped on his arrival when it was claimed that he had been a regular player with Celtic. Alas, he proved to be something of a let down when it was found that he had actually appeared in only 16 games in the Scottish Second Division for the little-known Glasgow Northern side. He had a reasonable season with Blues but was unable to get into the Hearts side after leaving the club.

FRASER, John Cameron

Full-back: 41+1 apps.

Born: Blackford, Perthshire, Scotland, 24 May 1941

Career: Larbert Schools, Gairloch United, Dunfermline Athletic (August 1958), Aston Villa (October 1962), BLUES (February 1965), Falkirk (June 1966).

Club honours: Dunfermline: Scottish Cup winners 1961; Aston Villa: League Cup runners-up 1963

Representative honours: Scotland (2 Under-23 caps).

'Cammie' Fraser was highly-rated in Scotland but seemed little more than an average footballer after moving south. After making 40 appearances in the claret and blue strip he walked out of Villa Park following a contract dispute and joined his wife in a hairdressing business in London before Blues tempted him back into League action. His initial games came as part of Joe Mallett's defensively minded 'M' formation that failed to keep Blues in the First Division. Fraser was the son of William Fraser, a former Aldershot & Northampton Town player.

FREEMAN, Neil

Goalkeeper: 33 apps

Born Northampton, 14 February, 1955

Career: Northampton Town (apprentice June 1971), Arsenal (professional, June 1972), Grimsby Town (March 1974), Southend United (July 1976), BLUES (July 1978), Walsall (on loan, August 1980), Huddersfield Town (on loan, January 1981), Peterborough United (September 1981), Northampton Town (non-contract, August 1982). Retired in February 1983 to become a policeman - like a few other Blues' keepers before him! Neil Freeman was nicknamed 'The Hulk' in the Blues dressing room for he stood 6ft 2ins tall and weighed around 14st - precisely the necessary physical attributes for a goalkeeper. However, several lapses in concentration tended to cost the team dearly. As a police officer he later patrolled the perimeter of the Northampton pitch he once played on.

FREEMAN, Walter Douglas

Inside-forward: 37 apps. 11 goals

Born: Handsworth, Birmingham, June 1887.

Now deceased.

Career: Lowestoft FC, Aston Villa, Fulham (February 1906), BLUES (September 1909), Walsall (April 1911), Wellington (November 1914), Walsall (January 1915).

Retired after WW1.

Club honours: Fulham: Southern League Title 1907.

The lesser-known brother of Bert Freeman, the former Everton, Burnley & England centre forward who guested for Blues during WW1, Walter Freeman was an electrician by trade who proved to be a good all-round forward, able to dribble and shoot with equal effect.

FURLONG, Paul Anthony

Striker: 124+29 apps. 56 goals

Born: Wood Green, London, 1 October 1968.

Career: Enfield, Coventry City (£130,000, July 1991), Watford (£250,000, July 1992), Chelsea (£2.3 million, May 1994), BLUES (£1.5 million, July 1996), Queen's Park Rangers (on loan, August 2000), Sheffield United (on loan, February-March 2002), Queen's Park Rangers (on loan, July-August 2002, signed in September 2002)

Club honours: Enfield: FA Trophy winners 1988

Representative honours: England (semi-pro, 5 caps).

After scoring twice (one from the penalty spot) for Enfield against Telford United in the FA Trophy Final replay at The Hawthorns in 1988, striker Paul Furlong did very well over the next 12 years before losing his way with Blues. He netted 41 goals in 92 appearances for the Hornets, grabbed 17 goals in 84 outings as a Chelsea player and for two seasons was excellent in the Blues attack, helping the team twice reach the First Division play-offs. Despite suffering a few injury problems, his career record at the end of the 2001-02 season was very good - over 120 goals in some 280 senior appearances.

GABBIADINI, Marco

Striker: 0+2 apps.

Born: Nottingham, 20 January 1968

Career: York City (trainee, June 1994, professional May 1995), Sunderland (£80,000, September 1987), Crystal Palace (£1.8 million, October 1991), Derby County (£1 million, January 1992), BLUES (on loan, October 1996), Panionios/Greece (July 1997), Stoke City (free transfer, December 1997), York City (free, February 1998), Darlington (free, July 1998), Northampton Town (free, June 2000).

Club honours: Crystal Palace (Division 3 Title 1988)

Representative honours: England (one 'B' and 2 Under-21 caps). A nomadic scorer of the highest quality, Marco Gabbiadini spent only a short while with Blues, but overall his scoring record speaks for itself! Up to December 2002 he had netted more than 250 goals in 700 first-class matches.

GADSBY, Walter

Inside-right: 4 apps. 3 goals

Born: Bromsgrove, 1872.

Now deceased.

Career: Astwood Bank, Redditch Excelsior, BLUES

(April 1896), Watford (August 1898), Redditch Excelsior (season 1899-1900).

The press hardly went overboard about this hard shooting forward. After a match during which he scored twice, had one goal disallowed and made another for his partner, the Birmingham Gazette announced that he had made 'a promising debut.'

A stalwart of the reserves, unfortunately Gadsby found it difficult to get first-team football and subsequently dropped down into the Southern League.

GALLAGHER, Joseph Anthony

Centre-half: 330+5 apps. 23 goals
Born: Liverpool, 11 January, 1955
Career: Lancashire & Merseyside Schools, BLUES (apprentice June 1970, professional January 1972), Wolverhampton Wanderers (£350,000, August 1981), West Ham United (December 1982), Burnley (August 1983), Halifax Town (on loan, October 1983), Padiham (on loan, 1984), Coleshill Town (manager 1989-90). Retired and became Community Liaison Officer at St Andrew's (November 1990); later Atherstone United (manager June 1991 to February 1992); Kings Heath (manager June 1994), making a comeback as player in September 1994. He resigned in February 1995.
Representative honours: England (one 'B' cap).

Joe Gallagher's first outings for Blues were at full-back, but a lack of manoeuvrability led to him being switched to centre-half. Commanding in the air but a little awkward on the ground, he retained the number five shirt until 1977 when a broken leg, sustained in a car crash, led to his absence from the game for the first four months of the 1977-78 season. He returned to action with a goal and duly retained his place in the side until moving to Molineux in a deal which triggered off some rancour between the clubs as talks were suddenly wound up with most of the transfer money involved still being owed to Blues. His England 'B' cap came in 1980 v. Australia at St Andrew's. For a brief spell in the early '90s Gallagher enjoyed a working as Blues' Community Liaison Officer.

GALLIMORE, George Arthur

Outside-left; 18 apps. one goal
Born: East Vale, Longton, Stoke-on-Trent, August 1886.
Died: Stoke-on-Trent, 1949
Career: Ashwood Villa, East Vale FC, Hanley Swifts, Stoke (1903), Sheffield United (1908), BLUES (April 1910), Leek Town (September 1911-12), East Vale (to World War 1).

George Gallimore was a dribbling winger who was among those players brought in to help drag Blues up from the bottom of the table in 1910. He lost his first-team place soon after Christmas 1910 and rarely looked like regaining it.

GARD, Alfred

Outside-right: 3 apps.
Born: Reading, 1876.
Career: Trowbridge Town (1898), BLUES (July 1900), Maidenhead FC (August 1901).

Alf Gard was a useful winger whose only season with Blues coincided with one of Billy Bennett's relatively injury-free years. He deputised for Bennett when needed but unfortunately did not impress at a higher level

GARDNER, Albert Edward

Wing-half: 120 apps. 4 goals
Born: Kings Heath, Birmingham, April 1887.
Died: Birmingham, April 1923.
Career: BSA Sports, BLUES (August 1908), Kings Heath (on loan, 1914). Retired in 1920.

Albert Gardner, who was profoundly deaf, was discovered playing in the Birmingham Works League. He was a real battler, long on work-rate but short on subtlety. He also had a hard shot but, alas, was rarely on target. He was known as 'The Silent Knight.'

GARRETT, Archibald Campbell Elson

Inside-forward: 18 apps. 6 goals
Born: Lesmahagow, Scotland, 17 June 1919.
Died: Bristol,1994.
Career: Larkhall Saints, Airdrieonians (1935), Preston North End (July 1936), Heart of Midlothian (December 1938), Northampton Town (September 1946) BLUES (November 1947), Northampton Town (December 1948), Wisbech Town (May 1951), Holbeach United (1953). Guested for Northampton & Bristol City in World War 2.

A highly talented and beautifully built goalscorer, Archie Garrett, played a useful part in Blues' post-war promotion winning side, his appearances being limited by manager Harry Storer who believed in fielding a settled side. Garrett later worked for the GPO in Bristol in the 1960s.

GARTON, William Francis

Centre-half: 5 apps.
Born: Salford, 15 March 1965.
Career: Salford Schools, Manchester United (apprentice June 1981, professional March 1983), BLUES (on loan, March 1986). Retired in May 1990, but made comeback with Salford City (as player-manager, July 1993); Witton Albion (1993), Hyde United (1994-95).
Club honour: Manchester United: FA Youth Cup winner 1982

Billy Garton came to St Andrew's to gain League experience, but when Blues asked to sign him permanently, Manchester United were not interested. Injuries and illness led to an early retirement from top-class football.

GAYLE, Howard Anthony

Outside-right: 58+1 apps. 11 goals

Born: Liverpool, 18 May 1958

Career: Liverpool (apprentice June 1974, professional November 1977), Fulham (on loan, January 1980), Newcastle United (on loan, November 1982), BLUES (on loan, January 1983, signed permanently June 1983), Sunderland (£5,000, August 1984), Dallas Sidekicks/NASL (during the summer of 1986), Stoke City (£125,000, March 1987), Blackburn Rovers (£5,000, August 1987); Carlisle United (on trial, early 1992), Halifax Town (July 1992), Accrington Stanley (September 1993).

Club honours: Sunderland: Milk Cup runners-up 1985

Representative honours: England (3 Under-21 caps).

Howard Gayle was ready to sign for Newcastle when Blues stepped in, but he proved something of an enigma at St Andrew's. On his day he was fast, aggressive and a potential match winner, but sometimes he looked sluggish and disinterested. He was transferred to Sunderland after off-field misdemeanours. He went on to top 200 League appearances before dropping into non-League football.

GAYLE, John

Striker: 49+6 apps 14 goals

Born: Turves Green, Birmingham, 30 July, 1964

Career: Turves Green Boys School, Highgate United, Mile Oak Rovers, Tamworth, Bromsgrove Rovers, Burton Albion (1987), Wimbledon (March 1989), BLUES (November 1990); Walsall (on loan, August 1993), Coventry City (September 1993), Burnley (September 1994), Stoke City (£70,000 January 1995), Gillingham (on loan, March 1996), Northampton Town (£25,000, February 1997), Scunthorpe United (free transfer, July 1998), Shrewsbury Town (free, November 1999), Torquay United (free, December 2000), Moor Green (July 2001).

Club honours: Blues: Leyland DAF Cup winners 1991.

John Gayle was a powerfully built striker who had been around the Midlands non-League scene before surprisingly linking up with Wimbledon. His time at Plough Lane was acrimonious, culminating in a club suspension following a training-ground confrontation with skipper Keith Curle. He struggled to win over the fans at St Andrew's but his two goals at Wembley earned him the 'Man of the Match' award as Blues carried off the 1991 Leyland DAF Cup. During his spell with the 'Iron' he was sent-off twice in three weeks and served four separate suspensions in 1998-99 but he kept battling on and passed the milestone of 250 senior appearances as a professional footballer (50 goals scored). Gayle, a former Kings Heath printer, is 6ft 4ins tall and weighs in at more than 15 stones.

GEDDIS, David

Striker: 53+ 3 apps. 21 goals

Born: Carlisle, 12 March, 1958

Career Ipswich Town (apprentice June 1973, professional August 1975), Luton Town (on loan, February 1977), Aston Villa (£300,000, September 1979), Luton Town (on loan, December 1982), Barnsley (£50,000, September 1983), BLUES (£50,000, December 1984), Brentford (on loan, November 1986), Shrewsbury Town (£25,000, February 1987), Swindon Town (£25,000, October 1988), Darlington (free transfer, March 1990); then Football in the Community Officer at Middlesbrough (1993-2000).

Club honours: Ipswich: FA Cup winners 1978, FA Youth Cup winners 1975. Darlington: GM Vauxhall Conference winners 1990.

Representative honours: England (one 'B' & Youth caps).

David Geddis sprang to prominence after a fine display in the 1978 FA Cup Final (v. Arsenal) but the predicted rosy future never materialised as he spent most of the 1978-79 season on the 'subs' bench. He did not really hit it off with Villa yet did well with both Barnsley (24 goals in 50 games) and to a certain extent with Blues. After leaving St Andrew's, however, his career went down hill somewhat, although he did help Darlington regain their Football League status by scoring three goals in nine games during the latter stages of the 1989-90 Conference campaign. Geddis was a strong, determined player with good shot.

GEMMILL, Archibald

Midfielder: 115 apps. 14 goals

Born: Paisley, Scotland, 24 March 1947

Career: Drumchapel Amateurs, St Mirren (1964), Preston North End (£13,000, May 1967), Derby County (£66,000, September 1970), Nottingham Forest (September 1977), BLUES (£150,000, August 1979), Jacksonville Teamen/NASL (March-August 1982), Wigan Athletic (September 1982), Derby County (November 1982 to May 1984), Nottingham Forest (June 1984, initially as coach, then as reserve team manager), Rotherham United (as joint-manager with John McGovern, September 1994 to 1996).

Club honours: Derby Co: Division One champions 1972 & 1975; Nottingham Forest: Division One champions 1978, League Cup winners 1979, European Cup winners 1979; Blues: Division Two promotion 1980.

Representative honours: Scotland (43 full caps, one U-23).

Despite standing only 5ft 5ins tall, Archie Gemmill was an all-action, dynamic, aggressive midfielder who amassed more than 650 League appearances (324 in two spells with Derby) in a marvellous career, spanning some 20 years. He did a terrific job with Blues, helping the club regain its First Division status. Gemmill was the first substitute to be used in the Scottish League (by St Mirren v Clyde in August 1966). After nine years on the

'staff' at Forest (mainly as a coach) he managed Rotherham United (with ex team-mate McGovern) and his first game in charge was against Blues!

GEORGE, William

Goalkeeper: one app.
Born: Shrewsbury, 29 June 1874. Died: Birmingham, 4 December 1933.
Career: Woolwich Ramblers (August 1894), Royal Ordnance & Royal Artillery Plumstead (February 1895), Trowbridge Town (during service with a Army), Aston Villa (£50, professional October 1897). Retired and became BLUES' trainer (July 1911). After leaving game he worked at the Austin Rover plant at Longbridge, Birmingham. He had three spells playing cricket for Warwickshire (in 1901 & 1902 and again in 1907). He also served with the Wiltshire and Shropshire County cricket clubs.
Club honours: Aston Villa: Division One champions 1899 & 1900, FA Cup winners 1905.
Representative honours: England (3 full caps); Football League XI.
Billy George was a grand servant to Aston Villa whom he served for 14 seasons, accumulating a total of 399 senior appearances. A real heavyweight between the posts, he was rather out of condition when called up by Blues during an injury crisis for his only game for the club. He stood almost 6ft 2ins tall and tipped the scales at around 16 stones...a really big guy.

GESSEY, Samuel

Full-back/centre half: 4 apps
Born: Fordhouses, Wolverhampton, 10 February 1858. Now deceased.
Career: Wighwick School, Wolverhampton St Luke's, BLUES (September 1877), Willenhall FC (August 1884). In later years served as a Director of the Small Heath Athletics Club.
Sam Gessey (affectionately known as 'Father Sam') joined Blues on their move to Muntz Street - he owned the land on which the ground was built. He formed a solid full-back partnership with George Edden, Larry Summers and eventually his brother George. He moved to centre-half which he took as a licence to roam - and could often be seen chasing the ball all over the pitch. He became part of Small Heath folklore, so much so, that a local newspaper referred to him by his nickname in its team sheets. Gessey was a tailend batsman and occasional bowler for the Small Heath Alliance cricket team.

GETGOOD, George

Wing-half: 10 apps.
Born: Colyton, Ayrshire, 15 November 1892.
Died: Kidderminster, 22 July 1970
Career: Ayr United (season 1911-12), Reading (July 1914), BLUES (August 1921), Southampton (February 1922), Wolverhampton Wanderers (January 1923),

Kidderminster Harriers (March 1925), Aberdare Athletic (July 1926), Shrewsbury Town (November 1926), Bathgate (1927), Bo'ness FC (1928), Nuneaton Town (February 1929). Midland Red Sports FC (August 1931); Guested for Ayr United (August 1915)
Club Honours: Wolves: Division Three (North) champions 1924. George Getgood was a burly, balding, strong tackling player who was signed to strengthen the team after promotion to Division One, but failed to settle. He made 59 appearances for Wolves whom he skippered during their Third Division championship-winning season of 1923-24. Later he became a bus conductor and also worked as a porter in Worcester. He stood a shade over 5ft 8in tall and weighted 11st 2 lb. Getgood changed his name from Goodman.

GIBSON, Richard Samuel

Outside-right: 120 apps. 19 goals
Born: Holborn, London, February 1889. Now deceased.
Career: Sultan FC, BLUES (September 1911), Manchester United (June 1921 to May 1922). Guested for Leicester Fosse during WW1.
Dick Gibson was a diminutive flying winger with the tendency to overdo the fancy stuff. He played initially as an inside-forward but after switching to the wing he showed great ability, although he had a fiery temper. His final contribution to the club was to recommend his former junior club colleague, Percy Barton, to St Andrew's.

GILDEA, William Franklyn

Centre-half: 20 apps. one goal
Born: Broxborn, Scotland, 1885.
Now deceased.
Career: Falkirk (1909) Bradford City (February 1911), BLUES (September 1911), Belfast Celtic (January 1912).
Club Honours: Bradford City: FA Cup runners-up 1911 (first game)
A swarthy Scot, Bill Gildea made a rapid rise to fame, appearing in an FA Cup Final after only nine games for Bradford. He was not a success and was dropped for the replay when City lost to Newcastle United. He never played for the Yorkshire club again and, in fact, he was not a success with Blues either.

GILL, Jeremy Morley

Defender: 58+18 apps.
Born: Clevedon, 8 September 1970
Career: Trowbridge Town (1986), Leyton Orient (free transfer, December 1988), Weston-Super-Mare FC (free, July 1990), Clevedon Town, Yeovil Town (free), BLUES (£30,000, July 1997), Northampton Town (August 2002).
Club honours: Blues: Division One promotion 2002.
Representative honours: England (one semi-pro cap).
After establishing himself as Blues' regular right-back, performing with dedication and commitment, the hard-working Jerry Gill always offered a professional approach

to the game. Unfortunately he found himself out of favour once Steve Bruce moved into St Andrew's as manager - and when Jeff Kenna arrived from Blackburn Rovers, Gill's days were numbered!

GITTINS, Walter

Full-back: 5 apps.
Born: Aston, Birmingham, 1865. Died: Birmingham
Career: Lozells Sports Club, BLUES (August 1889), Stafford Rangers (September 1890)
Walter Gittins was a chunky defender with a powerful kick who joined Blues for their first season in the Football Alliance.

GIVENS, Daniel Joseph

Utility forward: 53+11 apps. 10 goals
Born: Limerick, 9 August 1949
Career: Dublin Rangers (season 1964-65), Manchester United (apprentice, June 1965 professional December 1966), Luton Town (April 1970), Queen's Park Rangers (£40,000, July 1972), BLUES (£165,000, August 1978), AFC Bournemouth (on loan, March-April 1980). Sheffield United (March 1981), Neuchatel Xamax/Switzerland (June 1981). Retired in May 1987; later returned as Youth team coach at the Swiss club in June 1993, taking over as team manager in November 1993, before acting as assistant-manager. On moving back to Ireland he was subsequently appointed manager of the Eire Under-21 side and later Caretaker-boss of the Senior team(2002).
Club honours: Neuchatel Xamax: Swiss League champions 1987.
Representative honours: Republic of Ireland (56 full caps)
'Don' Givens, the son of a champion hurdler, followed the well-trodden path from Ireland to Old Trafford. He suffered badly from homesickness early on in his career but decided to stay in England where he developed into a fine goalscorer, going on to partner Malcolm Macdonald at Luton Town. He won his first cap for the Republic of Ireland against Denmark in May 1969, whilst still a member of Manchester United's reserve side and did not make his League debut until three months later. It was the first of 408 in the competition, 113 goals scored, 76 of them coming in 242 games for QPR. With his very last kick in the Football League - for Sheffield United against Walsall in May 1981 - he missed a penalty that sent the Blades down to the Fourth Division. He was plagued by hip injuries whilst with Blues and it was an arthritic hip that eventually led to his retirement. He scored 19 goals in his 56 full internationals. Givens stayed in Switzerland for eight years, coaching at various levels as well as acting as assistant-manager, before returning to Southern Ireland.

GLEGHORN, Nigel William

Midfielder: 176 apps. 42 goals
Born: Seaham, 12 August 1962
Career: Deneside Junior & Northlea Senior Schools, Seaham Red Star (1978), Ipswich Town (£5,000, as a professional, August 1985), Manchester City (£47,500, August 1988), BLUES (£175,000, September 1989); Stoke City (October 1992), Burnley (July 1997), Brentford (on loan, November-December 1997), Northampton Town (on loan, February-March 1998), Altrincham (June 1998), Witton Albion, Nantwich Town (player-manager, 2002). He has also worked as England's Under-14 & Under-21 scout and was employed as a sports lecturer at South Trafford College.
Club Honours: Blues: Leyland DAF Cup winners 1991. Stoke: Division Two champions 1993.
A former fireman, Nigel Gleghorn entered League football late, not signing professional forms until he was 23 years of age. Having a surprisingly delicate touch for such a big man, he possessed a powerful left-foot shot and his unusual surname has led to him being one of the most mis-spelt of all League players (Gleghorn being the most common). He made 208 appearances for the Potters. Gleghorn is no mean cricketer. He represented Durham Under-18s and Under-21s and once held the record in the Durham Coast League with a highest score of 135. He also had an unsuccessful trial as a wicket-keeper-batsman at Lords (for Middlesex CCC).

GLOVER, John William

Right-back: 124 apps 2 goals.
Born: West Bromwich, 28 October 1876.
Died: Dudley, 20 April 1955
Career: Christ Church School, West Bromwich Unity, Great Bridge Unity, Halesowen, Rudge-Whitworth FC, West Bromwich Albion (reserves 1896), Blackburn Rovers (May 1897), New Brompton (£100, July 1899), Liverpool (£350, October 1900), BLUES (£250, January 1904), Brierley Hill Alliance (August 1908). Retired in May 1910.
Club Honours: Liverpool: Division One Champions 1901 Representative honours: Football League XI; England international trialist.
John Glover was on the small side for a full-back of his era, and in his younger days was frequently brushed aside by bigger opponents. However, later on he developed into a strong tackler and appeared in international trials for England. He formed a wonderful partnership at Blues with Frank Stokes. On retiring Glover kept a pub in Brierley Hill and he also represented Shropshire at bowls.

GODDEN, Anthony Leonard

Goalkeeper: 37 apps.
Born: Gillingham, Kent, 2 August 1955
Career: Napier Secondary Modern School (Gillingham), Leonard Star FC, Eastcourt United, Gillingham & District Schools, Gillingham (as an amateur, August 1969), Ashford Town (September 1971),

Wolverhampton Wanderers (on trial, July 1974), West Bromwich Albion (£5,000, August 1975), Preston North End (on loan, September 1976), Walsall (two loan spells in season 1983-84: October-December & March-April), Chelsea (on loan, March 1986, signing permanently, May 1986), BLUES (£35,000, August 1987), Bury (on loan, December 1988), Sheffield Wednesday (on loan, March-April 1989), Peterborough United (August 1989), Wivenhoe Town (July 1990), Colchester United (on loan, March 1991), Warboys Town (manager, August 1991), March Town (manager, July 1993), Kings Lynn (coach, December 1993, then team manager, February 1994), Bury Town (manager/coach, May 1996), Wisbech Town (manager/coach, 1997-98), Rushden & Diamonds (coach), Notts County (coach), Northampton Town (coach), Peterborough United (coach: season 2001-02). Tony Godden was an experienced goalkeeper when he joined Blues, having played 329 games for West Brom. Although he had good reflexes and was a superb shot-stopper he was perhaps a shade suspect when going for high crosses, and during his spell with Blues his performances were sprinkled with errors. He holds Albion's record of 228 consecutive first-team appearances (to October 1981). He had an indifferent time at Stamford Bridge. After retiring he managed several non-League teams and following that was a successful goalkeeping coach at various League clubs

GODFREY, Joseph
Centre-forward: 3 apps. one goal
Born: Walesford, Sheffield, September 1894.
Now deceased.
Career: Kiveton Park, Brighton FC (Sheffield), Nottingham Forest (1916), BLUES (April 1918), Coventry City (October 1919), Manchester United (November 1919), Merthyr Town (May 1920), Rotherham Town (August 1921), Denaby United (March 1922) Beighton Recreationalists, Mexborough Town, Denaby United (April 1925).
'Joby' Godfrey was a former miner who leapt to prominence during WW1 when he scored a hatful of goals (26 coming in 1918-19). With the return of first-class football he found things much more difficult, flitting from club to club with alarming speed before returning to a Yorkshire coal mine. His brother Bruce, a goalkeeper, played several games for Blues during the period from 1915 to 1919.

GOLDIE, Archibald
Right-back: 79 apps.
Born: Hurlford, 5 January 1874.
Died: Bordesley Green, 2 April 1953
Career: Clyde, Liverpool (June 1895), Bootle, New Brighton Tower (August 1900), BLUES (April 1901), Crewe Alexandra (September 1904).
Club honours: Liverpool: Division Two champions 1896.

Unusual amongst Edwardian defenders in that Archie Goldie preferred to pass the ball to his half-backs rather than hoof it down field. He was a regular in the Liverpool side for five seasons, making 125 League appearances and after a year with 'Tower' he teamed up well with the more strong-kicking, hard-tackling figure of Arthur Archer for two campaigns with Blues. After retiring he settled in Birmingham to work at the BSA factory. Two of his brothers, William and John, were also professional footballers.

GOOCH, Percival George
Centre-forward: 4 apps. one goal
Born: Lowestoft, 1 September 1882.
Died: Lothingland, 22 June 1956
Career: Leiston Road School, Lowestoft Fearnought FC (1896), Kirkley Juniors, Lowestoft Harriers, Lowestoft IOGT, Lowestoft Town (November 1901), Norwich City (as an amateur, July 1903, professional September 1905), BLUES (March 1907), Notts County (March 1908), Norwich City (Aug 1909) Lowestoft (trainer to 1914).
Representative honours: Norfolk County
Percy 'Putt' Gooch was a tall, impressive-looking, moustachio'd forward who was a huge favourite in East Anglia football circles before his transfer to Blues. Unfortunately he found it difficult to adjust to the higher grade and quickly returned home. His nickname came about from his habit of telling his team mates to put(t) the ball in front of him when he wanted a pass.

GOODE, Terence Joseph
Winger: 0+2 apps.
Born: Islington, London, 29 October 1961.
Career: Islington & North London Schools, BLUES (apprentice June 1977, professional September 1979), Kettering Town (August 1982)
Blues were already doomed to relegation when Terry Goode, a speedy winger, was given his League baptism. The signing of the two Dutchmen - Van Mierlo & Bud Brocken – resulted in Goode leaving St Andrew's. He is a nephew of Charlie George, the former Arsenal, Derby & Southampton striker.

GOODWIN, John William
Outside-right: 33 apps. 8 goals
Born: Worcester, 29 September 1920.
Died: Worcester, 7 May 1995
Career: Worcester City (1935), BLUES (May 1946), Brentford (April 1949), Worcester City (May 1954), Dartford (August 1955). Later back at Brentford as trainer-coach for six years: 1957-63; then in the USA (as a coach)
Jack Goodwin joined Blues on demob from the Army. A sturdily built player, he was a bustler rather than being tricky and after leaving St Andrew's he scored 22 goals in 131 League games for Brentford before returning to his

former club. He represented the Army during WW2. In 1967 he became chief organiser for the Police Sports Department and toured the USA, coaching soccer. He later worked for Thames Gas.

GORDON, Colin Kenneth

Striker: 22+8 apps. 3 goals
Born: Stourbridge, 17 January 1963
Career: Lye Town, Oldbury United, Swindon Town (professional, October 1984), Wimbledon (£80,000, July 1986), Gillingham (on loan, February 1987), Reading (£80,000, July 1987), Bristol City (on loan, March 1983), Fulham (£90,000, October 1988), BLUES (£80,000, June 1989), Hereford United (on loan, September-October 1990), Walsall (on loan, December-January 1990-91), Bristol Rovers (on loan, February-March 1991), Leicester City (£100,000, July 1991), Sixes Sports Club (manager 1992-94)
Colin Gordon was a well-travelled forward who was recruited to provide some much needed height to the Blues attack. He struggled with a series of injuries in his first season at St Andrew's and then fell out of favour with the manager Dave Mackay when he missed training to take his wife for a medical check up. Despite both parties declaring that the player would never turn out for Blues again, he was soon to return to the first team. He was the recipient of one of the most unusual injuries ever to strike a Blues player when, in 1989, he missed several matches due to blood poisoning, contracted when a Swansea City player accidentally bit into his arm.

GORDON, John Duncan Sinclair

Inside-forward: 115 apps. 40 goals
Born: Portsmouth, 11 September 1931.
Died: Hampshire, 27 May 2001.
Career: Portsmouth Civil Service, Hillside Youth Club, Portsmouth (as a junior, July 1947, professional January 1949), BLUES (£10,000, September 1958), Portsmouth (£7,500 March 1961). Retired in May 1967. Was later co-owner of Little's Wine Bar in Southsea.
Club honours: Blues: Fairs Cup runners-up 1960: Portsmouth: Division Three champions 1962.
Johnny Gordon was an all-action forward who was very much the Pompey fans' favourite son, scoring 105 goals in 443 League games in two excellent spells at Fratton Park. He netted on his debut for Blues and continued to be a regular marksman for the club, but the lure of his hometown team proved too strong and he duly returned to Portsmouth.

GORMAN, Paul Anthony

Midfield: 7 apps
Born: Dublin, Ireland, 6 August 1963
Career: Crumlin Road Secondary School, Arsenal (apprentice, June 1979, professional October 1980), BLUES (June 1984), Carlisle United (£10,000, March 1985), Shrewsbury Town (on loan, November 1989, signing permanently for £20,000, December 1989), Carlisle United (December 1991), Peterborough United (on trial, March 1992), Gretna Green FC (1992-93).
Representative honours: Republic of Ireland (one Under-21 cap, Schoolboy & Youth caps)
Paul Gorman was a successful junior player in Ireland and was spotted by an Arsenal scout in Dublin. His appearances for the Gunners were few and far between and it was little surprise when he was released. Although highly-rated by his Blues colleagues, he found it difficult to fit into the team pattern, chiefly because his play was not suited to the long ball game employed at the time.

GOSNEY, Andrew Robert

Goalkeeper: 24 apps.
Born: Southampton, 8 November 1963
Career: Portsmouth (apprentice 1979, professional November 1981), York City (on loan, October 1991), BLUES (£35,000, August 1992). Exeter City (September 1993 to May 1994).
Representative honours: England (5 youth caps)
Due to the consistency of Alan Knight, Andy Gosney made only 60 appearances in 13 years at Fratton Park. A competent goalkeeper, he would have surely held down a regular first team place with another club, had he chosen to leave Pompey earlier. He spent just over a year at St Andrew's.

GOVAN, Alexander

Outside-left: 187 apps. 60 goals
Born: Glasgow, 16 June 1929
Career: Bridgeton Boys Club, Plymouth Argyle (juniors, June 1944, professional September 1946), BLUES (£6,500, June 1953), Portsmouth (March 1958). Retired in May 1960
Club honours: Plymouth: Division Three South Champions 1952, Division Three champions 1959; Blues: Division Two champions 1955, FA Cup runners-up 1956.
Alex Govan was a rattling good left-winger, industrious, fast and tricky, and a consistent scorer especially during his first spell with Argyle (30 goals in 117 appearances). His scoring prowess blossomed at St Andrew's, particularly in 1956-57 when he claimed 30 goals in all competitions, the only Blues winger ever to reach this feat in a season. In fact, it was not until 1972 that the 30-goal barrier was reached again (this time by Bob Latchford). Govan's haul in 1956-57 included five hat-tricks, three in four games, which is still a club record for a wing-forward. His play out wide on the left was based upon speed and his preferred manner of taking on an opponent was to push the ball past him and then beat him by sheer speed. Govan is credited with bringing the

club's anthem 'Keep Right On To The End Of The Road' to St Andrew's during the club's excellent FA Cup run of 1956. He now lives in Plymouth.

GRAHAM, Harry

Inside-forward: 12 apps. 4 goals
Born: Edinburgh, 16 December 1887.
Now deceased.
Career: Granton Oak Vale FC, St Bernard's FC (November 1908), Bradford City (April 1910), BLUES (October 1911), Raith Rovers (September 1912), Heart of Midlothian (June 1913), Leicester City (December 1920), St Bernard's (Nov 1924), Reading (July 1925)
Club honours: Raith : Scottish FA Cup runners-up 1913
Representative honours: Scottish League XI
A qualified dentist whose pre-WW1 stay in English soccer was far from successful, Harry Graham was principally a schemer, one of many forwards tried out in the dreadful Blues team of season 1911-12. His transfer back to Scotland was held up when St Bernard's claimed that Raith Rovers should pay them a fee as they held his Scottish registration. The situation was eventually resolved in Rovers' favour. He came back to England later and had four excellent years with Leicester, for whom he scored 16 goals in more than 100 games.

GRAINGER, Martin Robert

Full-back: 239+23* apps. 27* goals
Born: Enfield, 23 August 1972
Career: Colchester United (trainee, July 1989, professional July 1992), Brentford (£60,000, October 1993), BLUES (£400,000, March 1996).
Club honours: Blues: League Cup runners-up 2001, Division One promotion 2002.
Signed from Brentford in a deal that took George Parris to Griffin Park, left-back (or left-sided midfielder) Martin Grainger, an uncompromising, strong tackling performer, stood out like a beacon as Blues reached the play-offs in three successive seasons from 1998-99, and then he starred again when promotion to the Premiership was finally gained at the fourth attempt in 2001-02. He made 57 appearances for Colchester and 124 for the Bees.

GREEN, Arthur

Right-back; one app.
Born: Grantham, Lincolnshire, 1885.
Now deceased.
Career: Seaton Main FC, Mansfield Town (1910), BLUES (July 1911), Lincoln City (1912), Grantham Town (seasons 1913-15).
Arthur Green was a reserve defender whose only appearance for Blues was against Gainsborough Trinity in October 1911. His performance drew the comment that he was not strong or fast enough for League football.

GREEN, Benjamin Haigh

Inside-forward: 198 apps. 46 goals
Born: Penistone, 23 February 1883.
Died: Yorkshire, 1945
Career: Oxspring Board School, Penistone Rising Star, Penistone FC, Barnsley (August 1901), BLUES (October 1903), Burnley (May 1909), Preston North End (August 1911), Blackpool (December 1913).
Retired during WW1.
A chunky little bag of tricks, Benny Green had the distinction of scoring the first goal at St Andrew's, a feat for which he was awarded a piano. In netting that goal (against Preston in December 1905), Green threw himself headlong at the ball and ended up in a pile of snow behind the goal. He was a consistent marksman throughout his career but had the reputation of being a trouble-maker.

GREEN, Colin Robert

Full-back: 217 apps. one goal
Born: Brynteg, near Wrexham, 10 February 1943.
Career: Wrexham Boys, Everton (amateur July 1957, professional February 1959), BLUES (£12,000, December 1962), Wrexham (on loan, January 1971), Tamworth (May 1971), Rhyl FC.
On retiring in May 1976 he went into a garage business, and later became a sales representative for a veterinary medicine company in Wrexham.
Club honours: Blues: Football League Cup winners 1963
Representative honours: Wales (15 full caps, 7 U-23)
Colin Green made his Football League debut as a teenager facing Stanley Matthews. He was a barrel-chested defender, speedy on the overlap and particularly quick to recover. His career was unfortunately hampered after breaking a leg while playing against Bristol City in November 1965. He regained fitness quite quickly and immediately won back his international place. Carroll suffered a mysterious chest virus that kept him out of top-class football for two years before his eventual departure from the game after he had clocked up more than 200 League appearances. He now lives in Wrexham.

GREEN, Kenneth

Full-back; 443 apps. 2 goals
Born: West Ham, London 27 April 1924.
Died: Sutton Coldfield, June 2001.
Career: Millwall (amateur, August 1940), BLUES (professional, November 1943). Retired in April 1959, later ran a sub-post office in Handsworth (Birmingham).
Club honours: Blues: Division Two champions 1948, 1955, FA Cup runners-up 1956.
Representative honours: England (2 'B' caps): Football

League XI (2), FA XI (1)

One of the most durable of all Blues players, Ken 'Slasher' Green was a canny full back who shared in most of the club's triumphs of the post WW2 period. He joined the St Andrew's staff whilst stationed at Droitwich in the Army, having written in for a trial. He impressed the club's officials so much that he was signed immediately in, of all places, the dressing room at Villa Park. He was then posted overseas, not returning until 1947 when he was drafted into the Blues team at right back. Green held that position for five years until the emergence of Jeff Hall led to him switching over the left flank, a position he filled to equal effect. He scored for the FA XI in a 4-1 win over the Army in season 1952-53.

GREEN, Walter Maurice

Forward: 2 apps.

Born: Bordesley Green, Birmingham 1860.

Died: Birmingham

Career: Coventry Road Congregational Church, BLUES (September 1882), Nechells FC (November 1883 to April 1885).

Captain of Blues' reserve team, Walter Green had a three-month spell in the first team during the 1882-83 season. He made his debut for the club in an 18-1 win over Elwells of Wednesbury, a match in which Blues had only ten men for all but the first 30 minutes.

GREENHOFF, James

Inside-forward: 36 apps. 15 goals

Born: Barnsley, 19 June 1946

Career: Barnsley Schools (English Schools Trophy Winners 1961), Yorkshire Boys, Leeds United (apprentice, June 1961, professional August 1963), BLUES (£70,000, August 1968), Stoke City (£100,000, August 1969), Manchester United (£120,000, November 1976), Crewe Alexandra (December 1980, first as a player then as player-manager), Toronto Blizzard/NASL (as player-coach, May 1981), Port Vale (August 1981), Rochdale (player-manager, March 1983), Port Vale (player-manager, March 1984, later coach at Vale Park). Retired in May 1985 to concentrate on coaching youngsters at holiday camps, which he combined with insurance-broking. He later developed his own insurance business, Greenhoff Peutz & Co, based in Audley, Staffs and also worked for a Staffordshire paint company.

Club honours: Leeds: Fairs Cup runners-up 1967, winners 1968, Football League Cup winners 1968; Stoke: Football League Cup winners 1972; Manchester United: FA Cup winners 1977, runners-up in 1979. Representative honours: England (5 Under-23 caps); Football League XI

Jimmy Greenhoff could not command a regular first-team place with Leeds and was signed by Blues manager Stan Cullis in the middle of the two-legged Fairs Cup Final against Ferencvaros, having appeared in the first game. A high quality forward, he scored on his debut for Blues and went on to claim eleven goals in his first ten outings for the club, including a four-timer against Fulham in October 1968, when he also missed a penalty. Very fast, and surprisingly good in the air, Greenhoff soon made it apparent that Blues would be unable to retain his services and after joining Stoke he became one of the most consistent forwards in the Football League. He scored the winning goal for Manchester United in 1977 F A Cup Final when Lou Macari's shot deflected off him into the net. Greenhoff hit 97 goals in 338 games for Stoke and claimed 36 in his 122 outings for United. Brother of Brian (they played together at Leeds and Old Trafford), Jimmy scored the 'Goal of the Season' for Stoke City against Blues at St Andrew's shortly after he left for The Victoria Ground. He also netted in two FA Cup semi-finals for different clubs on the same ground - firstly for Stoke in 1972 and then for Manchester United in 1979, both games at Goodison Park. He also scored in another semi-final at Villa Park.

GREER, Thomas Gershom

Centre-forward: 2 apps

Born: Bathgate, Scotland, 1889. Died: Scotland

Career: Coatbridge Rob Roy FC, BLUES (December 1910), Reading (August 1912), Swansea Town (August 1913). Tommy Greer was regarded by the local press as rather too lightweight to lead the attack, and after an undistinguished season at Reading he moved to Wales where he achieved the distinction of scoring Swansea Town's first ever hat-trick.

GREGG, Robert Edmond

Inside-forward: 75 apps. 15 goals

Born: Ferryhill, County Durham, 19 February 1904. Died: 1991

Career: Ferryhill Athletic, Comford Juniors, Winlaton Juniors, Spennymoor United, Charlton Colliery, Durham City, Ferryhill Athletic (July 1926), Darlington (September 1926), Sheffield Wednesday (May 1928), BLUES (£2,200, January 1931), Chelsea (£1,500, September 1933), Boston United (May 1938), Sligo Rovers (September 1940). Retired in May 1944.

Club honours: Sheffield Wed: Division One champions 1929; Blues: FA Cup runners-up 1931.

After four seasons in the lower reaches, Bob Gregg was signed by Sheffield Wednesday in time to play a significant part in helping the Owls win the League title in 1929. However, the following year Wednesday bought in the prolific Harry Burgess and Gregg found himself on the side-lines. He stayed at Hillsborough for another few months before joining Blues just prior to their FA Cup run. Best remembered by all Blues fans as the man who scored that controversial 'offside goal' at Wembley in 1931, he struggled quite a lot with injuries whilst at St Andrew's, and was described as being a tricky forward but with the tendency to overdo the clever stuff.

GRIEMINK, Bart
Goalkeeper: 25+1 apps.
Born: Holland, 29 March 1972
Career: WK Emmen (Netherlands), BLUES (November 1995), Peterborough United (£25,000, October 1996), Swindon Town (initially on loan, February-March 2000, signed permanently on a free transfer, July 2000).
A fine shot-stopper, Bart Griemink's chances were limited at St Andrew's but after leaving Blues he went from strength to strength and when the 2001-02 season ended his career appearance record stood at more than 180 (152 in the Football League).

GROSVENOR, Arthur Thomas
Inside-right/wing-half: 115 apps. 18 goals
Born: Netherton, near Dudley, 22 November 1908.
Died: 31 October 1972.
Career: Northfield Road School, Tippity Green Victoria, Vono Works FC, Stourbridge, BLUES (amateur, March 1928, professional September 1928), Sheffield Wednesday (February 1936), Bolton Wanderers (May 1937), Dudley Town. Retired in May 1943.
Representative honours: England (3 full caps); Football League X I (1).
Tom Grosvenor was a lanky Black Country man who was likened to Charlie Buchan. He was a brilliant ball player, being more of a creator of chances than an out and out goalscorer. His career was hampered by a series of injuries including two broken legs but he was particularly adept at controlling high balls with either foot. He played only 75 more games after leaving Blues and later worked as a sheet metal-worker in Smethwick. He also kept racing pigeons and grew prize-winning tomatoes in his spare time. His brother, Percy, played for West Bromwich Albion and Leicester City and another brother, Cliff, was also associated with Leicester.

GUEST, William Francis
Outside-left: 84 apps. 17 goals
Born: Brierley Hill, 8 February 1914.
Died: Darwen 15 November 1994
Career: Brierley Hill Juniors, Bromley Juniors (Kingswinford), Blues (juniors, August, 1928, professional February 1932), Blackburn Rovers (January 1937, in exchange for Jack Beattie), Walsall (August 1947), Peterborough United (August 1948), Kidderminster Harriers (July 1949), Lovell's Athletic, Hinckley United, Bilston United, Brandwood Rovers (as coach). Guested for West Bromwich Albion & BLUES during WW2. Later became a storeman at GEC in Witton.
Club honours: Blackburn: War Cup runners-up 1940.
Billy Guest was an enterprising winger, good on the ball, with a powerful kick. A Black Country man through and through, after the hostilities he came back to the Midlands to sign for Walsall. He was also a good cricketer with Moseley CC (in the Birmingham League)

and Warwickshire Club and Ground. He joined Blues at the age of 14 and developed rapidly, making his debut whilst still in his 'teens'. His speed and fast low centres soon gained him accolades from the press. Although not the most prolific of goalscorers, he could be relied upon to notch a few each season. He did very well with Blackburn.

HAARHOFF, James Phiri
Striker: 0+1 app.
Born: Lusaka, Zambia, 27 May 1981
Career: BLUES (trainee, June 1997, professional June 1998), Chester City (July 2000).
Did well at reserve team level with Blues but was never given a chance in the first XI, his only outing coming as a late second-half substitute (for Dele Adebola) against Crystal Palace in October 1999.

HADDON, Harry
Centre-forward: 8 apps. 2 goals
Born: Pelsall, near Walsall, 1871.
Now deceased.
Career: Pelsall Villa, Lichfield Barracks/38th Regiment (1894), BLUES (January 1896), Walsall Wood FC (September 1897-99).
Here was a local player who lost out to the more prolific Jack Jones in the battle to replace Frank Mobley in the Blues attack. Something of a bustler, Haddon was criticised for not being clever enough to be a centre-forward!

HAGAN, James
Defender: 150+17 apps.
Born: Monkstown, Northern Ireland, 10 August, 1956
Career: Larne Town (August 1974), Coventry City (part-time professional, January 1977, full-time, November 1977), Torquay United (on loan, September-October 1979), Detroit Express/NASL (on loan, March 1980), Seiko FC/Hong Kong (on loan, 1980), BLUES (free transfer, June 1982), Real Celta Vigo/Spain (August 1987), Larne (August 1989), Colchester United (October 1989), Larne (January 1990), IFK Oddevold (May 1990), Ballymena United (player-manager, June 1991), Carrick Rangers (October 1993), Larne (player-manager, March 1994).
Representative honours: Northern Ireland (6 Youth caps): Ulster 'Young footballer of the Year' 1976
Jim Hagan was a booking clerk on the Larne-Stranraer ferries when Coventry City enticed him over to England. He failed to settle at Highfield Road and was loaned out several times before joining Blues on a free transfer. He proved a reliable player but was prone to the occasional lapse in concentration. After leaving St Andrew's he did well in Europe and all told played League football in six different countries.

HAINES, Wilfred Henry
Outside-right: 3 apps.
Born: Stone, Staffs, June 1882.
Career: Mount Pleasant Alliance, Newcastle Swifts (1903-04), Stoke (1905-06), Hanley Swifts (1906-07), Stafford Rangers (1907-08), BLUES (£250, July 1908), Leek United (August 1909), Stafford Rangers (1911-12).
After relegation in 1908, Wilf Haines was one of a group of players signed by Blues to boost the expected promotion run. He failed to establish himself in the side and with the introduction into the ranks of Jack Wilcox it was obvious that his Blues days were numbered. He was released at the end of the season.

HALL, Frederick
Centre-forward: 5 apps. 2 goals
Born: Worksop, 24 November 1924.
Career: Whitewell Old Boys FC, BLUES (March 1947), Bedford Town (July 1949).
Fred Hall was a miner in Nottinghamshire when he came to Blues' attention. He was given an early chance to prove his worth as a centre-forward and although he scored on his debut, his short comings were evident and consequently his appearances were limited.

HALL, Jeffrey James
Right-back; 264 apps. one goal
Born: Scunthorpe, 7 September 1929.
Died: Birmingham, 4 April 1959
Career: Bingley & District Schoolboy football, St Anne's FC (Keighley), Wilsden FC, Bank Top FC (1947), Bradford (amateur, August 1949), REME (during National Service), BLUES (professional, May 1950 until his untimely death as a result of polio in 1959)
Club Honours: Blues: Division Two Champions 1955, FA Cup runners-up 1956. Representative honours: England (17 full caps, 1 'B' cap); Football League XI (4), FA XI (2).
Jeff Hall had been tried in most positions during the early part of his career before eventually developing into an international-class right back. He earned the reputation throughout the game as a difficult defender to oppose and would have won many more caps but for his tragic early death. A memorial clock and score board were erected at the City End of St Andrews in Jeff Hall's honour.

HALL, John Henry
Inside/centre-forward: 102 apps. 48 goals
Born: Hucknall, Nottinghamshire, 3 July 1883.
Died: Nottingham, 1938
Career: Hucknall Boys' Club, Newark, Nottingham Forest (on trial), Mansfield Town (on trial), Stoke (professional, October 1904), Brighton & Hove Albion (June 1906), Middlesborough (April 1908), Leicester Fosse (May 1910), BLUES (December 1910), Hucknall

Town (1915), Retired in May 1918.
Jack Hall was a terrific marksman who had four-and-a-half excellent seasons at St Andrew's leading up to WW1 and in fact he topped the scoring charts for each of his clubs from 1906 to 1913. Signed by Blues for what was said to be a 'substantial fee', he immediately set about repaying that money by scoring in each of his first seven games. He was very good in the air despite being only 5ft 9ins tall.

HALLAM, John
Outside-right: 151 Apps. 62 goals
Born: Oswestry, February 1869,
Died: Swindon, 7 March 1949
Career: Oswestry Town (1885), Oswestry Crescent (season 1887-88), Oswestry Town (August 1888), BLUES (September 1890), Swindon Town (August 1896 to May 1901).
Club Honours: Blues: Division Two champions 1893, runners-up 1894.
Representative honours: Wales (one full cap)
Jack Hallam was a pint-sized winger with a devastating burst of speed who was an integral part of the prolific Blues attack of the Victorian era. He later worked for the Great Western Railway based in Swindon.

HALLWORTH, John
Left-half: one app.
Born: Stoke-on-Trent, 1884. Now deceased.
Career: Twyford Youth Club, BLUES (September 1906), Leek Alexandra (August 1907), Barlaston Manor Football Club (1910).
Jack Hallworth was used as cover for all three half-back positions during his one season with Blues but got only one outing, replacing the injured Jim Dougherty. He had a relatively poor game and despite Dougherty's continuing absence, Hallworth was not given a second chance.

HALSALL, Michael
Midfield: 44+2 apps. 3 goals
Born: Bootle, Merseyside 21 July 1961
Career: Liverpool (apprentice June 1977, professional May 1979), BLUES (March 1983), Carlisle United (£5,000, October 1984), Grimsby Town (£10,000, February 1987) Peterborough United (£25,000, July 1987, coach August 1993), Barnet (coach, mid-1990s), Walsall (reserve team manager from 2001)
Club honours: Peterborough United: Division Four promotion 1991.
Representative honours: England (Youth Caps).
Micky Halsall never made the first team during his six-year stay at Anfield but he proved to be a willing worker and could never be faulted for his enthusiasm, although he lacked a little skill to shine in the top flight. He was sent-off in his last game for Blues. He skippered Peterborough in their promotion campaign of 1990-91.

HALSALL, Walter George
Half-back: 24 apps.
Born: Liverpool, 29 March 1912.
Now deceased.
Career: Bootle Celtic, Liverpool (amateur), Marine FC, Burscough Rangers, Bolton Wanderers (amateur, December 1931), Blackburn Rovers (amateur, November 1932, professional February 1933), BLUES (July 1938), Chesterfield (May 1939). Retired during WW2.
Club Honours: Marine: FA Amateur Cup runners-up in 1932.
After a brief but distinguished amateur career, Wally 'Salty' Halsall made his name as an elegant wing half at Blackburn. But when Rovers signed Charlie Calladine from Blues, the two players, being similar in style, had to contest a first team place for the best part of three years before both were released, Halsall moving to Blues. He made an immediate impact with the local newspaper critics who described him as a 'tall stylish player with the heart to do two men's work.' Unfortunately his sterling qualities were not enough to save Blues from relegation and he was released in the summer of 1939. He later became a commercial traveller.

HAMPTON, Joseph Henry
Centre-forward: 59 apps. 31 goals
Born: Wellington, Salop 21 April 1885.
Died: Rhyl, 15 March 1963
Career: Wellington Council School, Shifnal Juniors, Wellington Town (1902), Aston Villa (professional April 1904), BLUES (February 1920), Newport County (September 1922 to May 1923, when he prematurely retired), Wellington Town (January 1924), Preston North End (coach from June-December 1925), BLUES (colts coach, October 1934 to April 1936). Guested for Derby County & Nottingham Forest during WW1.
Club honours: Aston Villa: Division One champions 1910, runners-up 1913; FA Cup winners 1905, 1913 and 1920; Blues: Division Two champions 1921.
Representative honours: England (4 full caps): Football League XI (3)
'Appy' 'Arry' Hampton was a fine, thrustful forward with an all-action style; sometimes he used to run at full speed into the penalty area before throwing himself headlong at the goalkeeper.
This method was obviously effective as he once managed to charge over the line the legendary 20 stone giant, Willie Foulke, who was left tangled up in the netting. Known as the 'Wellington Whirlwind' Hampton had scored 242 goals in 376 games for Aston Villa before signing for Blues in the twilight of his career. He still turned on the heat, however, and fired home 16 vital goals to help Blues win the Second Division title. After pulling out of football he ran a successful catering business in Rhyl. He discovered that his first name was Joseph, quite late in life when there was a query about

his birthday and he unearthed his own birth certificate at Somerset House.

HANDLEY, Thomas Henry
Centre-half: 13 apps
Born: Cotteridge, Birmingham, 1882. Now deceased.
Career: Cotteridge County School, Kings Norton Metal Works FC, BLUES (August 1907), Bradford Park Avenue (September 1909).
A tall, muscular defender who looked a useful replacement when called in to substitute for the injured Wigmore, Tommy Handley was surprisingly allowed to leave St Andrew's after finishing the 1908-09 campaign as a first team regular.

HANDS, Thomas
Outside-left: 149 apps. 43 goals
Born: Small Heath, 4 January 1870. Now deceased.
Career: Green Lane School, Small Heath Langley, Small Heath Unitary Road Methodists, Coventry FC, Small Heath Unity, BLUES (December 1890), Kings Heath FC (August 1896)
Club honours: Blues: Division Two champions 1893.
'Toddy' Hands did the rounds of the Small Heath clubs and having lived in Langley Road, he is arguably the most local player Blues have ever had, being born within 100 yards of the club's former Muntz Street ground. First choice on the wing for some six years, in keeping with the rest of the 1893 forward line, he was small, fast with a great heart, and a Blues man through and through. Surprisingly, he walked out on the club in 1896 because of a dispute about his wages and he never played League football again.

HANDYSIDES, Ian Robert
Midfielder: 111+22 apps. 12 goals
Born: Jarrow, 14 December 1962.
Died: Solihull, 17 August 1990
Career: Durham Boys, BLUES (apprentice June 1978, professional January 1980), Walsall (£17,000, January 1984), BLUES (March 1986), Wolverhampton Wanderers (on loan, September-October 1986). Retired through ill health in October 1988.
Club honours: Blues: Division Two promotion 1980
Representative honours: England (Youth caps)
Hailed as the new 'Trevor Francis' on his arrival at St Andrew's, the high expectations proved to be a millstone around Ian Handysides' neck. In fairness he was a different style of player to Francis, being a 'buzzing' midfielder rather than a striker. He found it hard to cope with First Division football and few people were surprised when Walsall stepped in to sign him. He matured somewhat at Fellows Park but it came as a shock when John Bond brought him back to St Andrew's in 1986. He showed far more consistency in his second spell and finally succeeded in gaining a regular first team

spot. In August 1988 he scored a hat-trick in a friendly win over Willenhall. Following that game, however, Handysides complained of a severe headache and shortly afterwards Blues' fans were stunned to hear that a brain tumour had been diagnosed. Ian underwent surgery and seemed to be recovering, but further tumours developed on his spinal chord, resulting in his tragically early death at the age of 27.

HANSBURY, Roger
Goalkeeper: 68 apps
Born: Barnsley, 26 January, 1955
Career: Wesborough High School, Yorkshire Youths, Norwich City (apprentice August 1971, professional, January 1973), Bolton Wanderers (on loan, March 1977), Cambridge United (on loan, November 1977), Leyton Orient (on loan, December 1978), Eastern Athletic/Hong Kong (December 1981), Burnley (August 1983), Cambridge United (July 1985), BLUES (March 1986), Sheffield United (on loan, October November 1987), Wolverhampton Wanderers (on loan, March-April 1989), Colchester United (on loan, August 1989), Cardiff City (on loan, October 1989, signed permanently for £20,000, December 1989). Retired in May 1990.
Club honours: Cardiff City: Welsh Cup winners 1992.
Roger Hansbury took a long time to establish himself as a Football League player due to the consistency of Kevin Keelan at Norwich, and even when Keelan retired, he was sidelined with a broken leg. The Canaries then signed Chris Woods and, on recovery, the injured goalkeeper found himself out in the cold again. He arrived at St Andrew's as cover for David Seaman after many travels, covering two continents - and when Seaman left, Hansbury once more claimed a regular place in League action. Basically a line goalkeeper, he was at his best as a shot-stopper but sometimes was found wanting when asked to deal with crosses.

HARDING, Paul Jay
Midfielder: 23+3 apps. one goal
Born: Mitcham, 6 March, 1964
Career: Chelsea (apprentice, season 1980-81), Wimbledon, Sutton United, Whyteleafe, Epson & Ewell Carshalton Athletic, Dulwich Hamlet, Enfield, Barnet (February 1990), Notts County (September 1990), Southend United (on loan, August 1993), Watford (on loan, November 1993), BLUES (on loan, December 1993, signed permanently for £50,000, January 1994), Cardiff City (free transfer, August 1995 to May 1997). Thereafter it was back to non-League football.
Club honours: Enfield: FA Trophy winners 1988.
A hard-tackling midfielder, Paul Harding was 26 years of age when he made his Football League debut for Notts County in 1990. He was the only signing by Blues' joint caretaker-managers Trevor Morgan and Kevin Broadhurst. Harding played with Paul Furlong in the

1988 FA Trophy win.

HARDS, Walter Oscar
Outside-left: 5 apps. 2 goals
Born: Edgbaston, Birmingham, August 1859.
Now deceased.
Career: Warwick County, Summerhill Works FC, BLUES (August 1881), Stourbridge (1884).
The stylish Walter Hards was a stalwart of the Blues during the club's early days, being first choice for five seasons. He slowed down a little later on and was switched to an inside-forward berth where he proved to be a talented performer although not much of a marksman. He probably played in 100 'other' games for Blues.

HARE, Charles Boyd
Inside-forward: 45 apps. 14 goals
Born: Yardley, Birmingham, June 1871.
Died: February 1934.
Career: Warwick County, Birmingham United, Aston Villa (April 1891), Woolwich Arsenal (August 1895), BLUES (November 1896), Watford (July 1898), Plymouth Argyle (1903). Retired in June 1904.
Club honours: Aston Villa: Division One champions 1894. Charlie Hare was one of the host of fine players produced by Warwick County. At his best he was a clever, incisive footballer whose early career was plagued by injury. He was a great favourite with the Blues' fans and it was rather a surprise when he left for Watford. Hare, who scored 13 goals in 26 games for Villa, served with the Warwickshire Yeomanry in the Boer War. On returning from South Africa he attempted to resume his career in Devon but with limited success.

HARE, Jeremiah
Right-back: 8 apps.
Born: Edgbaston, Birmingham 1860. Now deceased.
Career: Pershore Saints FC, BLUES (August 1884), Kings Heath (September 1888)
As Blues reputation increased locally they were able to attract players from some of the better clubs in the area, and Jerry Hare, an old-fashioned big kicker, was duly recruited to add stability to the defence. A solid, somewhat limited performer, he faded badly after the 1886 FA Cup semi-final defeat when he was given a roasting by Albion's tricky winger George 'Spry' Woodhall. Hare remained with the club for another couple of years, playing in the reserves.

HARFORD, Michael Gordon
Striker: 109 apps. 33 goals
Warned: Sunderland, 12 February 1959.
Career: Sunderland Schools, Wearside & District Boys, Lambton Star Boys Club, Lincoln City (as a professional, July 1977), Newcastle United (£216,000, December 1980), Bristol City (£160,000, August 1981), Newcastle

United (£100,000, March 1982), BLUES (£100,000, March 1982), Luton Town (£250,000, December 1984), Derby County (£480,000, January 1990), Luton Town (£325,000, September 1991), Chelsea (August 1992), Sunderland (March 1993), Coventry City (July 1993), Wimbledon (£70,000, August 1994). From 1997 Harford coached and acted as assistant-manager, even caretaker-boss at Wimbledon before becoming Luton Town coach in 2001. He was with the Dons when they lost their Premiership status in May 2000

Club honours: Luton: Milk Cup winners 1988, runners-up 1989, Simod Cup runners-up 1988. Representative honours: England (one full cap, one 'B' cap).

Mick Harford, a tall target man, powerful in the air and possessing a nice touch on the ground, scored regularly throughout his career and each transfer commanded a six-figure fee with his move from Lincoln to Newcastle setting a new Fourth Division record. Whilst he was at Bristol, the club was on the verge of folding up and he was transferred back to Newcastle to pay off the club's debts; this must surely be rated as one of the shortest days a player has ever spent with one club as he signed for Blues just one hour later! Harford started off with a debut goal for Blues and maintained a reasonable strike-rate that would have been far better had he had more support. He turned out to be one of the best strikers in the First Division while with Luton, although during the latter stages of the 1980s he was hampered by injury. His transfer fees totalled around £2.25 million.

HARLAND, Stanley Clarence
Wing-half: 51+1 apps.
Born: Liverpool, 19 June 1940.
Died: Yeovil, 2 September 2001.
Career: Liverpool & District Schools, Burnley (as an amateur in July 1955), New Brighton (1956), Everton (as a professional, December 1959), Bradford City (July 1961), Carlisle United (June 1964), Swindon Town (August 1966), BLUES (December 1971), Yeovil Town (player-manager, May 1973), Portsmouth (assistant-manager 1978), Gravesend & Northfleet (manager), Portsmouth (coach), Yeovil Town (Commercial Manager). Later he ran a delicatessen and after that managed a supermarket in Yeovil.
Club honours: Swindon: Division Three champions 1969, League Cup winners 1969, Anglo-Italian Cup winners 1970.
Stan Harland was an efficient, hard-working player who had an excellent five-year stint with Swindon for whom he amassed in excess of 250 senior appearances, this after failing to make the breakthrough at Goodison Park. He skippered Swindon in their double-winning season of 1968-69. Sadly, his lack of pace was cruelly exposed after promotion. Throughout his career Harland continued to reside in Liverpool and covered literally thousands of miles while commuting to his various clubs. In all he

accumulated a League record of 471 appearances and scored 33 goals.

HARLEY, Alexander.
Centre-forward: 29 apps. 9 goals
Born: Glasgow, 28 April 1936.
Died: Birmingham, winter 1969.
Career: Third Lanark, Manchester City (August 1962), BLUES (£42,500, August 1963), Dundee (November 1964), Leicester City (briefly in May 1965), Toronto City, Newton Unity (Birmingham Works League, 1967-69).
A prolific scorer in both Scotland & Manchester, Alex Harley was the subject of a Blues record transfer fee when he moved to St Andrew's from Maine Road in 1963. Although he finished well up in the scoring list he found the going tough in one of Blues' perennial relegation struggles and was soon on his way to Dundee. At the time of his sudden death he was a croupier in a Birmingham Casino, playing local non-League soccer at weekends.

HARPER, Dennis
Inside-right: one app
Born: Wednesbury, 12 October 1936.
Career: Darlaston, BLUES (amateur, July 1955, professional August 1956), Romford (April 1959), Burton Albion (May 1961), Nuneaton Borough (July 1961 to May 1962).
Dennis Harper, a nicely built youngster, was plucked out of Midland junior football, and received a surprise debut despite not being a reserve team regular when Noel Kinsey, Bryan Orritt, Bill Finney and Albert Linnecor were all injured at the same time.
He seemed overawed by the occasion and did not get another chance.

HARPER, Rowland Richard G
Outside right: 29 apps. 2 goals
Born: Lichfield, April 1881.
Died: August 1949
Career: Walsall Wood, BLUES (April 1904), Burton United (April 1907), Aston Villa (August 1907), Notts County (March 1908), Mansfield Invicta (1910-12).
Described as a smart footballer, Roly Harper opened his first-class career with a debut goal in Blues' 5-0 thrashing of hapless Nottingham Forest in December 1905, and by the end of the season had established himself as the regular right-winger. But when Charlie Tickle shrugged off his injury problems Harper was relegated to the reserves.

HARRIS Andrew
Utility: 0+2 apps.
Born: Birmingham, 17 November 1972
Career: BLUES (YTS 1988, professional June 1990), Oxford United (on loan, October 1991), Exeter City

(November 1991), Nuneaton Borough (April 1994 to May 1996).

Andy Harris was an injury-prone youngster who demonstrated a liking for most positions although he looked most comfortable in attack.

HARRIS, Frederick
Inside-forward/wing-half: 312 apps. 68 goals
Born Solihull, 2 July 1912.
Died: South Warwickshire, October 1998.
Career: Forman's Road School, Sparkbrook FC, Birmingham City Transport FC, Osborne Athletic, BLUES (professional, March 1933).
Retired in May 1950.
Club honours: Blues: Division Two champions 1948, Football League South champions 1946.
Representative honours: Football League XI (1).
Fred Harris' career fitted neatly into two sections around WW2. At the time of his debut, in front of a Villa Park crowd of more than 54,000 in August 1934, he was a sharp-shooting inside forward, and he admitted that when he saw the vast audience that day he wanted to disappear. But it didn't stop him from scoring the opening goal and he continued to find the net regularly, right up to the outbreak of WW2. The demands of wartime football, however, led to him being converted into a wing-half and it was from this position that he found his true metier. His style of hard tackling and clever distribution impressed manager Harry Storer so much that he was made club captain. Harris was almost 38 years of age and still a regular in the Blues side when he retired from football to set up in business as a chiropodist/physiotherapist in Acocks Green.

HARRIS, James
Forward: 115 apps. 53 goals
Born: Birkenhead, 18 August 1933.
Career: Birkenhead Schools, Everton (juniors 1948, professional September 1951), BLUES (£20,000, December 1960), Oldham Athletic (July 1964), Tranmere Rovers (August 1966), Rhyl Athletic (October 1966). Retired in May 1967 and later became senior steward of the Prenton golf club (Birkenhead).
Club honours: Blues: Fairs Cup runners-up 1962, Football League Cup winners 1963.
Representative honours: England (one Under-23 cap): Football League XI (1).
A speedy two-footed striker who was a most difficult player to contain, Jimmy Harris was an individualist who netted over 100 goals in first-class soccer, having by far his best spell as a professional with the Goodison Park club for whom he served 12 years.

HARRIS, Wallace Norman
Outside-right: 94 apps. 15 goals
Born: Hockley, Birmingham, 22 February 1900.
Died: Davos, Switzerland, 7 September 1933.
Career: Ada Road School, Dudley St James, Burton All Saints, BLUES (November 1922), Walsall (September 1929).
Representative honours: England trialist.
Wally Harris, a frail-looking winger, had a deceptive change of pace which often confused even the most experienced defenders. He replaced Billy Harvey and made an immediate impression leading to an England international trial the following year. He kept his place in the first team for three seasons before increasing health problems led to his release. After a short spell with Walsall, his declining health forced him to retire and he died in a sanatorium in Switzerland, aged 33. He was the son-in-law of Mr J T Harris, a Blues Director.

HARRISON, Arthur
Outside-right: 4 apps. 3 goals
Born: Stirchley, Birmingham, September 1878.
Now deceased.
Career: Cotteridge Council School, Linton FC, BLUES (1902), Brownhills Athletic (for two seasons: August 1903-May 1905).
As deputy to the great Charlie Athersmith, Arthur Harrison had very few opportunities to show his worth. A sprightly winger of considerable goalscoring prowess, he scored twice on his League debut for Blues against Lincoln City in December 1902 (won 3-1).

HARRISON, Michael
Central-defender: 3 apps.
Born: Leicester, 21 February 1952.
Career: Leicester Schools, BLUES (apprentice June 1968, professional October 1970), Southend United (July 1972), Yeovil Town (June 1973).
Mick Harrison was a fine defender who skippered Blues' Youth team. His senior debut (in his home town) coincided with a remarkable performance by Blues - a 4-1 win over the eventual Second Division champions Leicester City at Filbert Street in January 1971. Harrison always looked capable of producing the goods, but perhaps his lack of height went against him and he dropped out of League football with only 19 games to his credit.

HARRISON, Wilbert
Centre-forward: one app. 2 goals
Born: Bordesley Green, Birmingham, 1867. Now deceased.
Career: Coventry Road FC, Birmingham Excelsior, Birmingham St George's (1886), BLUES (August 1891), Summerfield Saints (season 1892-93).
One of the many stars unloaded at by the threatened St George's club in 1891, 'Fay' Harrison had been the fulcrum of the 'Dragon's attack for some time and was

tipped to do great things for Blues, but sadly his career faded after his move. He did, though, score twice in his only senior game for the club (a 2-2 draw at Ardwick in the Football Alliance in January 1892).

HART, Paul Anthony
Central-defender: one app.
Born: Golborne, near Manchester, 4 May 1953.
Career: Stockport County (apprentice June 1969, professional September 1970), Blackpool (June 1973), Leeds United (March 1978), Nottingham Forest (May 1983), Sheffield Wednesday (August 1985), BLUES (December 1986), Notts County (player-coach, June 1987), Chesterfield (manager, November 1988 to January 1991), Grantham Town (as a player), Nottingham Forest (coach, June 1991), Sheffield Wednesday (coach, 1994), Leeds United (Director of Youth Coaching and also acted as caretaker-manager for a brief spell when Howard Wilkinson left Elland Road in September 1996), Nottingham Forest (club coach, Youth Academy Director, then manager, July 2001).
Paul Hart had the terrible misfortune to suffer a broken leg in his debut game for Blues, against Plymouth Argyle in December 1986 when he collided with team-mate Tommy Williams. This turned out to be his only appearance for the club. A solid, uncompromising stopper, generally recognised as one of the hard men of League football, Hart was signed to bolster up a leaky Blues defence but that freak accident brought to an end to his career at St Andrew's. He moved to Notts County before fully-fit but Blues could hardly be blamed for selling the 34 year old. He is the brother of Nigel Hart, a former Wigan Athletic, Leicester City, Blackburn Rovers, Crewe and Bury defender, and the son of Johnny Hart, who starred for Manchester City as an inside forward.

HARTWELL, Ambrose Walter
Full-back/centre half: 51 apps one goal
Born: Exeter, Devon, 28 June 1883. Now deceased
Career: Budleigh Town schools team, Erdington, Feltham FC, Redditch Excelsior, Erdington, BLUES (August 1901), Bradford (June 1908), Queen's Park Rangers (August 1909), Kidderminster Harriers, Shrewsbury Town.
A 'thorough trier' seems to be a fair description from Walter Hartwell's contemporaries. In seven seasons with Blues he played in only 51 first team games but was always regarded as a good man to have in reserve. The only player in the club's history so far to choose a reserve match as his benefit game, he was renowned for his prodigious kicking, and it was said that he once fired a penalty clean out of the ground (the ball flying over the bar - not through the net).

HARVEY, Charles
Outside-right: 2 apps.
Born: Small Heath, Birmingham, 1879.
Now deceased
Career: Dixon Road Council School, St Phillip's YMCA, BLUES (July 1904), Leek (September 1907), Shrewsbury Town (1909-11).
Charlie 'Soldier' Harvey was an army sergeant stationed at Whittington Barracks near Lichfield when Blues signed him, primarily as a reserve. He failed to make an impact when called into the first team, one critic saying he has some notions of football but they are crude as yet.

HARVEY, Edmond
Outside right: 14 apps.
Born: Kiveton Park, Sheffield, 8 September 1900.
Career: Kiveton Park FC, Huddersfield Town (amateur), BLUES (January 1924), Bradford City (June 1927). Retired through injury in February 1930.
'Martin' Harvey started his career with Blues by alternating with namesake Billy Harvey on the right-wing. After a promising opening season a combination of injuries and loss of form took its toll and he was transferred to Bradford City where he showed a goalscoring talent that was never obvious in his Blues' days, scoring 16 times in his 47 games for the Valley Parade club before injury struck again.

HARVEY, William Henry Tompkins
Outside-right: 79 apps. 2 goals
Born: Freemantle, Hampshire, 12 April 1896.
Died: South Africa, July 1970.
Career: Yorkshire Amateurs, 2nd Battalion West Riding Regiment, Sheffield Wednesday (October 1919), BLUES (as an amateur July 1921, professional November 1921), Southend United (August 1925), BLUES (assistant-secretary, August 1926, then team manager March 1927 to May 1928), Chesterfield (manager from June 1932 to June 1938), Gillingham (manager, June 1938 to September 1939).
Club honours (as manager): Chesterfield: Division Three North champions 1936.
Representative honours: England (one amateur cap v. Ireland): FA tour to South Africa 1920.
Speedy right-winger Billy Harvey - with his heavy moustache - was a regular in the Blues side before being superseded by his namesake. He was also a very useful cricketer, playing for Warwickshire and also for Border Province in South Africa.

HASTIE, Ian Scott
Outside-right: one app.
Born: London, 1887. Now deceased
Career: Edmonton Royal, BLUES (May 1911), High

Wycombe FC (April 1912).

The least successful of the trio of players signed from North London junior football prior to WW1 (Barton and Gibson were the others), Ian Hastie was a dribbler with a tendency to keep the ball to himself.

HASTINGS, Walter Jesse

Outside-left: 44 apps. 7 goals
Born West Hartlepool, 1889. Now deceased
Career: Spennymoor United, West Hartlepool, Brighton & Hove Albion (August 1908-May 1909), BLUES (February 1912), Watford (August 1914), Hartlepool United (1919-21).
Club honours: Brighton: Southern League title 1910.
Walter Hastings was a hard-working winger who liked to cut inside to have a shot at goal. He had to fight off several challengers to retain his position before finally losing out to 'Ninty' Eyre. He later became a football referee.

HATELEY, Anthony

Striker: 29+1 apps 6 goals
Born: Derby, 13 June 1941.
Career: Normanton Sports Club (April 1954), Derby County (schoolboy forms, July 1955), Notts County (as an amateur, March 1956, professional June 1958), Aston Villa (£20,000, August 1963), Chelsea (£100,000, October 1966), Liverpool (£100,000, July 1967), Coventry City (£80,000, September 1968), BLUES (£72,000, August 1969), Notts County (£20,000, November 1970), Oldham Athletic (£5,000, July 1972), Bromsgrove Rovers (May 1974), Prescot Town (July 1975), Keyworth United (December 1978). Retired in August 1979 and later worked in the Everton lottery office before becoming a free trade representative for a Nottingham-based brewery.
Club honours: Notts Co: Division Three promotion 1960, Division Four champions 1971: Chelsea: FA Cup runners-up 1967.
Tony Hateley was one of the great post-war travellers of League football. A fine header of the ball and coached by Tommy Lawton at Notts County, he scored 211 goals in a total of 434 League games during a splendid career although, in truth, he never really fulfilled the promise he had shown as a youngster. Subject of one of the early six-figure transfers, he was a tall, muscular player, who probably could have done a lot better with Blues if the team had fielded a quality winger to provide him with the centres which he thrived on. Hateley netted four goals for Villa in an away First Division match at Spurs in 1966, which ended in a 5-5 draw before finishing with a tally of 86 goals in 148 outings for Blues' arch rivals. His son Mark Hateley played as a striker for Coventry City, Rangers and England.

HATTON, Robert John.

Inside / centre-forward: 212+6 apps. 73 goals
Born: Hull, 10 April, 1947
Career: Wath Wanderers (June 1962), Wolverhampton Wanderers (apprentice, June 1963, professional November 1964), Bolton Wanderers (March 1967), Northampton Town (October 1968), Carlisle United (July 1969), BLUES (October 1971), Blackpool (July 1976), Luton Town (July 1978), Sheffield United (July 1980), Cardiff City (December 1982). Retired from League football in May 1983. Later assisted Lodge Cotterill FC (Birmingham Sunday club).
Like Tony Hateley, Bob Hatton was another terrific nomadic striker who could score goals from any angle, with either foot and with his head, in all Divisions, from almost any distance. He netted 217 times in 620 League appearances, including 58 in 175 First and Second Division outings for Blues. A well-built player who preferred to occupy a slot on the left side of the field, Hatton became the final cog in Blues' 1971-72 promotion attack. Lacking the glamour of Messrs Francis and Latchford, he was often the unsung hero but his unselfish work and clinical finishing made him a vital member of the side. He later worked for an insurance company and regularly attends St Andrew's. He has also worked occasionally on local radio (as a matchday summariser).

HAUSER, Stanley

Goalkeeper: 34 apps
Born: Handsworth, Sheffield, 20 July 1890.
Died: Handsworth, Birmingham, 10 June 1958
Career: Handsworth Grammar School Old Boys, Stockton FC, BLUES (on trial, 1911), Handsworth Oakhill, BLUES (November 1913), Stourbridge (December 1922), Shrewsbury Town (1923), Netherton FC (1924), Cradley St Luke's (1925).
Retired in May 1927.
Club honours: Blues: Division Two champions 1921.
Representative honours: England (2 amateur caps in 1914).
Stan Hauser was a capable amateur goalkeeper and dressing room comedian who served Blues before, during and after WW1. He combined his football with working in the family shop and was spotted by Blues playing in the local 'Early Close' League, this after failing a trial with the club two years earlier. He was then given a rapid promotion to the first-team, making his debut only four weeks after signing. However, with so many capable 'keepers on the books at time, he found it nigh on impossible to hold down a first-team place. Like so many goalies he had his personal eccentricities, and one particular habit of his was to hang his wristwatch on the netting behind him during a game.

HAVENGA, William Stephen

Outside-right: one app.

Born: Bloemfontein, South Africa, 6 November 1924

Career: Bremner Old Boys/South Africa, BLUES (July 1948), Luton Town (May 1950), Ipswich Town (January 1952), Kettering Town (June 1953), Worcester City (1954-55), Hinckley Athletic, Halesowen Town. Retired in June 1962.

During the late 1940s and early 'fifties, a string of trialists arrived in Birmingham from South Africa. Willie Havenga was one of the earliest and also one of the few to make a Football League appearance. He remained in this country for several years, performing mainly in non-League circles. Havenga hit six goals in 18 League games for Luton and three in 19 for Ipswich.

HAWKER, Philip Nigel

Left-back; 36+1 apps. one goal

Born: Solihull, 7 December 1962

Career: Langley Secondary School, BLUES (apprentice June 1978, professional June 1980), Walsall (on loan, December 1982, signed permanently March 1983), West Bromwich Albion (on loan, September-October 1990), Kidderminster Harriers (December 1990), Solihull Borough (1991). Retired in October 1993 through injury.

Representative honours: England (2 Youth caps).

Phil Hawker was a tall, long-striding defender whose regular appearances were made during the period when Mark Dennis was absent through suspension. He was thought by many to have a potential as a central-defender but rarely was he tried in that role at St Andrew's. He proved a very useful competitor in the lower Divisions with Walsall, making 175 League appearances for the Saddlers.

HAWLEY, Frederick

Centre-half: 3 apps.

Born: Derby, 28 July 1894. Now deceased

Career: Derby Midland, Shelton United, Leys Recreationalists, Ripley Town, Sheffield United (January 1913), Coventry City (1919), BLUES (January 1920), Swindon Town (May 1920), Bristol City (March 1923), Brighton & Hove Albion (June 1925), Queen's Park Rangers (May 1926), Loughborough Corinthians (April 1928). Retired in May 1929. Guested for Derby County, Notts County, BLUES & Nottingham Forest during World War 1.

Before the 1914-18 conflict Fred Hawley, a powerfully-built defender, was a First Division regular but he took some time to settle down after the hostilities were over. Neither of his Midlands clubs received much service from him but he did give a good account of himself with each of his Southern League clubs until the end of his long career.

HAYNES, Harry

Centre-half: 10 apps.

Born: Walsall, 21 April 1873.

Died: Southampton, 29 March 1902.

Career: Walsall (1890), Walsall Unity (1891), Wolverhampton Wanderers (February 1893), BLUES (July 1895), Southampton St Mary's (July 1896). Retired in 1900 through injury. Was later the landlord of the Turks Head and Edinburgh Castle pubs in Southampton.

Harry Haynes signed for Southampton St Mary's (the present-day Southampton FC) on a Birmingham railway station with a pen borrowed from the booking office, Blues retaining his League registration. A big, bruising moustached defender, solidly built with legs like tree trunks, he could withstand the fiercest of challenges and was utterly fearless. His career with Blues coincided with that of Alec Leake, but he became a regular left-back with the Saints, doubling-up with a life as a pub landlord.

HAYWOOD, George

Centre-forward: 46 apps. 18 goals.

Born: Coleorton, 11 December 1906.

Died: circa 1975

Career: Coleorton Bible Class FC, Whitwick Imperial (September 1927), Southend United (on trial), Chesterfield (November 1927), Gresley Rovers, BLUES (November 1928), Chesterfield (June 1934), Cradley Heath, Southport (December 1935), Cradley Heath (August 1936). Retired in September 1939.

George 'Abie' Haywood, only 5ft 7ins tall, was a swarthy ex-miner who demonstrated exceptional jumping ability, frequently beating much taller men to a high ball. Allied to his splendid aerial skills, he had good ball control and proved an efficient deputy to Joe Bradford. He hit two goals on his Blues debut against Manchester City in December 1929 (won 3-0). He later worked as an office clerk at the New Lount Colliery.

HEATH, Frederick Sydney

Forward/half-back: 5 apps. one goal

Born: Smethwick, 1865. .

Career: Smethwick Hall School, Bearwood White Star, Bearwood FC, Cookham FC, BLUES (August 1889), Stourbridge (July 1890), Hockley Rose (season 1891-92).

Signed for the princely sum of £1, Fred Heath was a versatile performer who understudied six different roles throughout his short career. Later he became a prominent referee.

HEDGES, Thomas

Goalkeeper: 8 apps.

Born Winson Green, Birmingham 1858.

Died: Birmingham, 1941.

Career: Birmingham Heath, Walsall Phoenix, Walsall

Swifts, BLUES (September 1883), Darlaston (July 1887). Later became Director of West Bromwich Albion.

Tom Hedges was a competent, squarely built goalkeeper who had four fine seasons with Blues before losing his place to Chris Charsley. When he became a Director of West Brom, he formed a link with the club against whom he had played in the 1886 FA Cup semi-final when Blues lost 4-0 in a snowstorm.

HELLAWELL, Michael Stephen

Outside-right: 213 apps 33 goals
Born: Keighley, Yorkshire, 30 June 1938.
Career: Salts FC, Huddersfield Town (amateur July 1954), Queen's Park Rangers (professional August 1955), BLUES (May 1957), Sunderland (January 1965), Huddersfield Town (September 1966), Peterborough United (December 1968), Bromsgrove Rovers (August 1969). Retired in May 1971.
Club honours: Blues: Fairs Cup runners-up 1961, Football League Cup winners 1963.
Representative honours: England (2 full caps); Division Three South XI (1957).
A red-haired winger with an astonishing turn of speed over 25 yards, Mike Hellawell was exchanged for Bill Finney. After scoring on his Blues debut, he then had to wait three seasons before gaining a regular place in the side. However, he impressed sufficiently to win his first England cap two years later (versus France in October 1962). As well as creating chances he also hit his fair share of goals but after leaving Blues he found scoring much more difficult. On retiring he set up in business, running a shop in his hometown of Keighley. His brother John, played for each of the two Bradford clubs as well as Darlington and Rotherham. Mike himself was also an exceptionally fine cricketer and played in one county match for Warwickshire.

HENDERSON, Crosbie Gray

Left-back: 6 apps.
Born: Hylton, 12 May 1885.
Died: 27 April 1970.
Career: Hylton Rangers, Hylton Star, Newcastle United (May 1906), Grimsby Town (May 1908), BLUES (August 1910), Brighton & Hove Albion (May 1911), Luton Town (July 1912).
Henderson came to Blues with a reputation of being a good, solid full-back but fell from favour after a short run in the first team at the opening of the 1910-11 season. The consistency of Frank Womack ensured that Crosbie Henderson did not break back into the side and at the end of the campaign he was glad to get away to pastures new.

HENDERSON, John Neil

Inside-forward: 4 apps.
Born: Dumfries, Scotland 1874.
Died: Maxwelltown, Scotland, 30 August 1930.
Career: 5th Kings Rifle Volunteers, Dumfries FC (1894); Celtic (1895) Victoria United (May 1897), Lincoln City (May 1898), Leicester Fosse (December 1900) BLUES (March 1901), Maxwelltown Volunteers (September 1902); Carlisle United (August 1905), Maxwelltown Volunteers (1906); Annan United (September 1910), Nithsdale Wanderers (November 1910).
John Henderson had just finished an unsuccessful spell at Leicester when Blues signed him to strengthen their promotion bid, but alas he proved disappointing and quickly disappeared back to the junior ranks.

HENDON, Ian Michael

Defender: 4 apps.
Born Hornchurch, Essex, 5 December 1971.
Career: Havering Schools, Essex Schools, London Schools, Tottenham Hotspur (YTS 1988, professional December 1989), Portsmouth (on loan, January 1992), Leyton Orient (on loan, March 1992), Barnsley (on loan, March 1993), Leyton Orient (August 1993), BLUES (on loan, March 1995), Notts County (£50,000, February 1997), Northampton Town (£30,000, March 1999), Sheffield Wednesday (£40,000+ October 2000).
Club honours: Spurs: FA Youth Cup winners 1990, FA Charity Shield finalists 1991; Notts Co: Division Three champions 1998
Representative honours: England (Schoolboy international, 19 Youth caps, 7 Under-21 caps).
Ian Hendon, a powerfully built defender, captained England's Youth side whilst at Spurs. Never given a chance to settle in Tottenham's first team, he was loaned out several times to gain experience before eventually moving on to Orient. There he found himself in a struggling side and was grateful for a chance to St Andrew's where he was picked immediately following an injury to Dave Barnett. In 2002 he was in sight of his 400th senior appearance at club level.

HENDRIE, Paul

Inside-right: 29+3 apps. one goal
Born: Lennoxtown near Glasgow, 27 March 1954.
Career: St Patrick's High School, Kilsyth Rangers, Celtic (apprentice), Kirkintilloch Rob Roy, BLUES (professional, March 1972), Portland Timbers/NASL (April 1976), Bristol Rovers (September 1977), Halifax Town (July 1979), Stockport County (August 1984), Chelmsley Town (player-coach, July 1991), Redditch United (manager, March 1992), Tamworth (manager, February 1995 to 1999).
Paul Hendrie was a diminutive of long-haired winger who was often confused at first glance with Steve Phillips. Possessing plenty of skill and pace, he also had a

suspect temperament. After being converted into a midfielder, he went on to chalk up an impressive set of statistics in the lower Divisions with Halifax Town and Stockport County despite being suspended many times. His nephew John played for several clubs including Coventry City, Newcastle United, Middlesbrough and Leeds United while his son Lee is now an established and senior professional with Blues' rivals Aston Villa.

HENNESEY, William Terrence
Wing-half: 203 apps. 3 goals
Born: Llay, Mid-Wales, 1 September 1942.
Career: BLUES (juniors, June 1958, professional September 1959), Nottingham Forest (November 1965), Derby County (£100,000, February 1970), Tamworth (manager, April 1974), Kimberley Town (manager, 1977), Tulsa Roughnecks/NASL (assistant-coach 1978), Shepshed Charterhouse (coach 1978 to October 1980), Tulsa Roughnecks/NASL (assistant-coach, November 1980, then chief coach 1981-83), Vancouver Whitecaps/NASL (assistant-coach mid-1980s to Alan Hinton, ex-Wolves, Derby and Forest winger), Heidelberg FC/Australia (manager, 1987-88).
Later moved to Melbourne where he now manages a cling-film company.
Club honours: Blues: Inter Cities Fairs Cup runners-up 1961, Football League Cup winners 1963: Derby Co: Division One champions 1972, Texaco Cup winners 1972. Representative honours: Wales (39 full caps, 6 Under-23 caps, Schoolboy caps).
One of the finest products to come through the club's Youth scheme, Terry Hennessey first sprang to fame in April 1961 when, with only a handful of first-team games under his belt, he played a major part in Blues' Fairs Cup semi-final win over the Italian giants, Inter Milan. A strong tackler, he was able to bring the ball out of defence and then distribute it with telling effect. Throughout the 1960s he was the leading light in Blues' regular battles against relegation. He finally left St Andrew's after the club had been demoted to Division Two. Hennessey spent four good seasons with Forest and became Derby's first six-figure signing when he left The City Ground in 1970, but sadly a spate of injuries ruined his stay with the Rams. He made 160 League appearances for Forest and 63 for Derby.

HERRIOT, James
Goalkeeper: 212 apps.
Born: Chapelhall, Airdrie, 20 December 1939
Career: Douglasdale, Dunfermline Athletic (August 1958), BLUES (May 1965), Mansfield Town (on loan, November 1970), Hibernian (August 1971), St Mirren (July 1973), Partick Thistle (February 1975), Morton (on loan, October 1975), Dunfermline Athletic (1976), Morton (late 1976). Later worked as a bricklayer in Strathclyde.

Club honours: Dunfermline: Scottish FA Cup runners-up 1972; Scottish League Cup Winners 1973. Representative honours; Scotland (8 full caps): Scottish League XI (2).
Jim Herriot was a distinctive figure on the field owing to his habit of smearing boot polish under his eyes, American football style, in the belief that this reduced glare from the floodlights etc. He was an infuriating goalkeeper, occasionally brilliant but prone to some spectacular errors of judgement letting a ball go past him and then turning to see it buried in the back of the net. He enjoyed lasting fame when his name was chosen as a pen-name by the well-known veterinary author who liked the sound of it.

HEY, Antoine
Midfielder: 10+1 apps. one goal
Born: Berlin, Germany 19 September 1970
Career: Fortuna Cologne/Germany, BLUES (£300,000, July 1997, released in May 1999), FC Wuppertoi/Germany (August 1999 onwards).
After signing for Blues in 1997, Tony Hey was hoping to establish himself in English League football but unfortunately niggling calf and Achilles problems resulted in him losing his place on the right side of midfield, replaced by another new recruit, Jon McCarthy (from Port Vale). He was never in the running after that and returned to German football in 1999.

HIBBITT, Terrence Arthur
Midfielder: 122 apps. 11 goals
Born: Bradford, 1 December 1947. Died: Ponteland, Newcastle-upon-Tyne, 5 August 1994.
Career: Leeds United (apprentice, June 1963, professional December 1964), Newcastle United (£30,000, August 1971), BLUES (£100,000, August 1975), Newcastle United (May 1978 to May 1981), Gateshead (July 1982 as player, then player-coach January 1983, and thereafter as manager from August 1986, dismissed in October 1986).
Club honours: Leeds Utd: Fairs Cup runners-up 1968: Newcastle Utd FA Cup runners-up 1974, Texaco Cup winners 1974.
Terry Hibbitt made a dramatic entry into League football when he scored with his first touch on his debut for Leeds. Most of his time at Elland Road was spent in the 'shadow squad' but there is no doubt he was a highly skilful schemer with a magic left foot who sadly during his three-year spell at St Andrew's failed to win over the vociferous elements of Blues fans - this after four excellent seasons with Newcastle where he laid on scores of goals for hot-shot Malcolm Macdonald. Brother of Kenny, formerly with Wolves and later Walsall and Cardiff City manager, Hibbitt teamed up with Howard Kendall and Alan Campbell in the Blues' midfield and it was a niggling knee injury which eventually forced him

out of the big-time in 1981, after he had amassed close on 430 senior appearances for his three major clubs. On quitting football he went into the newsagent's business in Newcastle before taking over a pub in Ponteland on the outskirts of his adopted city. He cruelly died of stomach cancer at the age of 46.

HIBBS, Henry Edward

Goalkeeper: 389 apps.
Born: Wilnecote near Tamworth, 27 May 1906.
Died: Hatfield, Herts, 23 May 1984.
Career: Wilnecote Holy Trinity FC, Tamworth Castle, BLUES (amateur April 1924, professional May 1924). Retired in May 1940 (soon after appearing in a wartime game against Aston Villa in front of a 15,000 crowd at St Andrew's); Walsall (manager from August 1944 to June 1951), permit player for de Havillands FC (February 1953 to May 1954), then Ware Town (manager, August 1960), Welwyn Garden City (manager 1962 to 1964).
Club honours; Blues: FA Cup runners-up 1931.
Representative honours: England (25 full caps); Football League XI (3); FA tour to South Africa 1929.
Although born into a goalkeeping family (his uncle Hubert Pearson and cousin Harold Pearson both kept goal for West Bromwich Albion, and a further cousin, Horace Pearson for Coventry City), Harry Hibbs was originally an inside-forward. However, Tamworth Castle had a huge reputation for producing fine goalkeepers and whilst there he was subsequently converted from a goalscorer into a goal-stopper - and he never looked back! Quite short, pale and relatively lightweight, Hibbs did not really look the ideal build to be a goalkeeper, but his ability was so obvious that Blues quickly signed him up. After a lengthy apprenticeship under the tutorship of big Dan Tremelling, Hibbs finally gained a regular spot in the side in 1929, and so good was he that he did not lose it until his retirement. His style of keeping was the exact opposite to Tremelling, Hibbs preferring to rely upon anticipation rather than athleticism to make his saves. That is not to say that he wasn't capable of spectacular efforts when the need arose. A totally unflappable temperament was also part of his make-up, resulting in him being arguably the greatest of all the fine goalkeepers enlisted by Blues over the years. Hibbs, in fact, was the first footballer to be granted a wartime benefit match.

HICKS, George Wolstenholme

Outside-left: 80 apps. 18 goals
Born: Weaste near Salford, 30 April 1902
Career: Salford Lads' Club, Droylesden, Manchester Central, Manchester City (November 1923), BLUES (October 1928), Manchester United (January 1932), Bristol Rovers (September 1932), Swindon Town (August 1933), Rotherham United (November 1933), Manchester North End (September 1934 to May 1936)
Club honours: Manchester City: FA Cup runners-up 1926, Division Two champions 1928.
Blues finally seemed to have ended their long search for a left-winger when they signed George Hicks, a relatively slim player, in 1928. He had scored over 40 goals in his five years at Maine Road and continued in this vein with 12 more in his first season at St Andrew's. Goals proved harder to come by during the next year as his game was modified to become a provider of chances rather than a taker. Hopes were high as Blues got off to a good start in 1930-31 but after seven games Hicks suffered a severe knee injury. He later took his appearance tally in League football to 231.

HICKS, Martin

Central-defender: 69+4 apps. 2 goals
Born: Stratford-upon-Avon, 27 February 1957
Career: Stratford Town, Charlton Athletic (professional, February 1977), Reading (£20,000, February 1978), BLUES (free transfer, August 1991, acting reserve team manager April-June 1993); Newbury Town (player-manager, July 1993), Stratford Town, Worcester City (February 1995-96). Became a postman in 1995.
Club honours: Reading: Division Four champions, 1979, Division Three champions 1986, Simod Cup winners 1988.
Martin Hicks was a vastly experienced professional when he arrived at St Andrew's, having been the linchpin of the Reading defence for many years. He appeared in well over 500 senior games for the Royals and with his career coming to an end, he chose Blues to be nearer to his place of birth.

HIGGINS, James

Centre-forward: 6 apps. 3 goals
Born: Cradley Heath, March 1874. Now deceased
Career: Colley Gate FC, Stourbridge, BLUES (August 1897), Netherton (September 1898), Halesowen Town (1900).
Jimmy Higgins, a Black Country youngster, was given a run out in the absence of Hare and Lewis at the end of his only season with Blues. He repaid the club's faith in him handsomely but with the signing of Bob McRoberts he chose to return to his native surroundings.

HIGGINS, James

Centre-forward: 54 apps. 14 goals
Born: Dublin, 3 February 1926
Career: Dundalk, BLUES (November 1949), Hereford United (July 1953), Dundalk (1955).
Representative honours: Republic of Ireland (one full cap)

Jimmy Higgins was signed along with team-mate Eddie O'Hara and was rushed into the first team. A bit of a tearaway with a bustling style he will always be remembered by the older fans for his dynamic goal after just 45 seconds play against Manchester United in 1951 which took Blues into the semi-finals of the FA Cup.

HIGGINS, John Bernard
Inside-left: one app.
Born: Harborne, Birmingham, 31 December 1885.
Died: Malvern, 3 January 1970.
Career: King Edward VI School (Birmingham), Bournville Excelsior, Bournville Youth, Aston Villa (1906), BLUES (August 1907), Brierley Hill Alliance (September 1908).
Jack Higgins was a true Corinthian, remaining an amateur throughout a long sporting career. He was never particularly prominent on the soccer field, being much better known as a middle order batsman and slow left arm spinner in his days with Worcestershire from 1912 to 1930, during which time he amassed 4,149 runs (average 19.57) in 121 matches (223 innings), with a seasonal best of 1,041 coming in 1928 (average 30.61). His best bowling return was 5-72 and in all he took 30 wickets at an average of 53.46, claiming 59 catches in the process. He also represented Staffordshire CCC and after retiring from active sport, he was employed at Rugby School as their cricket professional.

HIGGINSON, Jack
Forward: 14 apps. 4 goals
Born: Dudley 1876. Now deceased
Career: Gornal Wood FC, Dudley Town, BLUES (August 1900), Stourbridge (1902)
Jack Higginson was a useful utility forward, principally left-sided who had a good run as a stop gap inside left in 1900-01. The arrival of Johnny McMillan ended his regular spell and from then on in he was rarely selected.

HILEY, Scott Patrick
Right-back: 58 apps.
Born: Plymouth, 27 September 1968
Career: Exeter City (apprentice 1984, professional August 1986), BLUES (£100,000, March 1993), Manchester City (£250,000, February 1996), Southampton (free transfer, August 1998), Portsmouth (£200,000, December 1999) Exeter City (2002-03).
Club honours: Exeter City: Division Four champions 1989-90
Scott Hiley, a competent full back, enjoyed over-lapping. He appeared in 259 League and Cup games for Exeter before joining his former manager, Terry Cooper, at St Andrew's. He suffered with injury in 1994-95 and never really recovered full fitness, leaving Blues for Maine Road after spending almost three years at the club.

HILL, Daniel Ronald
Midfielder: 7 apps
Born: Enfield, Middlesex 1 October 1974
Career: Tottenham Hotspur (trainee, 1990, professional September 1992), BLUES (on loan, November 1995 to January 1996), Watford (on loan, February 1996), Cardiff City (on loan, February 1998), Oxford United (free transfer, July 1998), Cardiff City (free, November 1998), Dagenham & Redbridge (July 2001).
Representative honours: England (4 Under-21 caps & Youth caps).
Unable to make his mark at White Hart Lane, Danny Hill was signed on loan by Blues and although impressing with some quality passing, using both feet, and looking a cut above the rest of the players around him, he was forced to return to Spurs.

HILL, Dennis
Outside-left; 4 apps 0 goals.
Born: Willenhall, 16 August 1929.
Career: Wolverhampton Technical College, Willenhall St Stephen's FC, Willenhall Pickwick, Darlaston, Leicester City (briefly as an amateur), BLUES (professional, June 1951), Burton Albion (February 1957-59).
Pacy winger Dennis Hill had a wait of two-and-a-half years before getting a run out in the first team at St Andrew's. Although he proved capable at his job, he lacked the goalscoring touch of Alex Govan and hence opportunities were always going to be limited. He showed commendable loyalty to the club before eventually abandoning the full time game to concentrate on working as a draughtsman.

HILL, Edward Sebastian
Outside-left: 10 apps. 5 goals
Born: Willenhall, July 1860. Now deceased
Career: Walsall Phoenix, BLUES (August 1885), Darlaston (September 1889 to May 1891).
So highly-rated was Ted Hill, a goalscoring winger, that Blues completely reshuffled their attack to accommodate him. The reshuffle obviously worked as Blues reached the first FA Cup semi-final that year only to lose heavily to West Bromwich Albion. Hill continued to hold down a place until the formation of the Football Alliance when he decided that regular competitive football was not for him.

HIRONS, John Walter
Outside-left: 5 apps.
Born: Erdington, October 1876. Now deceased
Career: Witton Shell Depot FC, Erdington FC, Pleck Ramblers, Walsall (1901), BLUES (February 1903), Walsall (April 1906).
Jack Hirons was an out-and-out trier of limited ability, chiefly used as understudy to Field, although he did have a run in the left-half position from time to time.

HOCKEY, Trevor
Winger/midfield: 231+1 apps. 13 goals
Born: Keighley, 1 May 1943.
Died: Keighley, 2 April 1987
Career: Eastwood School (Keighley), West Riding
Under-19's, Keighley Central Youth Club (1957-58); also
played Rugby Union for Abertillery & Rugby League for
Keighley as youngster; Bradford City (amateur June
1958, professional May 1960), Nottingham Forest
(£15,000, November 1961), Newcastle United (£25,000
November 1963), BLUES (£22,500 November 1965),
Sheffield United (£35,000 January 1971), Norwich City
(February 1973), Aston Villa (£38,000, June 1973),
Bradford City (June 1974), Athlone Town (player-
manager, March 1976), San Diego Jaws/NASL (April
1976), Las Vegas Quicksilver/NASL (March 1977), San
Jose Earthquakes/NASL (June 1977), Stalybridge Celtic
(manager, August 1977). Later attempted to start a
soccer section at Keighley Rugby League Club; coached
the British Army on the Rhine children's team and also
coached soccer at Pontins Holiday camp in Filey.
Club honours; Newcastle United; Division Two
champions 1965
Representative honours: Wales (9 full caps).
Trevor Hockey was yet another footballing nomad whose
professional career spanned close on 16 years, during
which time he accumulated well over 600 senior
appearances whilst playing on all 92 League club grounds
in that time, and having by far his best times with Blues.
Initially a winger, Hockey developed into a hard
working, sometimes fiery but very effective midfielder, a
player full of Yorkshire grit who always gave 100 per-
cent. His job was to man mark an opponent and he
often came into conflict with the authorities for his over
robust play. Off the field he was a larger than life
personality, the proud owner of a pink piano and he
made a record entitled 'Happy 'Cos I'm Blue' appearing
on stage in a concert at Birmingham Town Hall. He was
one of the first players to appear for Wales on a parental
qualification. He died of a heart attack after playing in a
five-a-side tournament in his native Keighley.

HODGES, Frank Charles
Inside-right: 32 apps. 5 goals
Born: Nechells Green, Birmingham, 26 January 1891.
Died: Southport, 5 June 1985
Career: Alum Rock All Souls, Birmingham Gas FC,
BLUES (amateur 1911, professional May 1912),
Manchester United (August 1919), Wigan Borough
(June 1921), Crewe Alexandra (August 1922), Winsford
United (August 1926), Guested for St Mirren during
World War 1.
Frank Hodges was a local junior who was so impressive
partnering Charlie Duncan in the reserves where he
notched three hat-tricks, that he was given a prolonged
spell in Blues' first team during 1914-15. With Jimmy

Windridge playing his normal striking role, Hodges was
able to give vent to his normal creative urges. Wounded
in the leg during WW1, he decided not to re-join Blues
after the conflict.

HODGETTS, Dennis
Inside-left: 23 apps. 9 goals
Born: Hockley, Birmingham, 28 November 1863. Died:
Aston, Birmingham 26 March 1945.
Career: Birmingham St George's FC (1878), Great Lever
FC (1879), Birmingham St George's (1882), Aston Villa
(February (1886), BLUES (October 1896). Retired in
May 1898 when he returned to Villa Park as coach to the
younger players. Later became a publican in Birmingham
(June 1910), initially taking charge of the Salutation Inn
in Summer Lane, Aston. He was elected vice-President of
Aston Villa in June 1930, a position he held with pride
until his death at the age of 81.
Club honours: Aston Villa: Division One champions
1894 & 1896, FA Cup winners 1887 & 1895,
runners-up 1892.
Representative honours: England (6 full caps); Football
League XI (1)
'Denny' Hodges with his immaculately waxed moustache
and smartly greased and parted hair, was a born-
footballer, a player who was admired by everyone,
spectators and fellow professionals alike. He was a clever
player, with many ideas. He used both feet with equal
effect, was difficult to dispossess (because of his
tremendous size and build) and his skilful distribution
was so effective, at home and away. He was an
uncommonly fine inside-forward (or sometimes outside-
left) who in later years turned out to be an admirable
coach. In his ten years with Villa he scored 91 goals in
215 appearances.

HOGAN, Thomas Eric
Forward: 0+2 apps.
Born: Cork, 17 December 1971
Career: FAI School of Excellence (Dublin), Rockmount
FC, Cobh Ramblers (1990), BLUES (on trial, then
signed for £30,000, August 1991) Cobh Ramblers (on
loan, February 1992), Shamrock Rovers (September
1992), Cobh Ramblers (July 1993), College Corinthians
(1994-95).
Eric Hogan was a slim, red-haired forward who
impressed during his trial with Blues on their Irish tour
in the summer of 1991. He left his job in an aluminium
factory to become a full-time professional at St Andrew's.

HOLDSWORTH, David
Defender: 93+8 apps. 8 goals
Born: Walthamstow, 8 November 1968
Career: Watford (apprentice June 1985, professional
November 1986), Sheffield United (£450,000, October
1996), BLUES (£1.2 million, March 1999), Walsall (on

loan, January-March 2002), Bolton Wanderers (free transfer, September 2002).
Representative honours: England (one Under-21 cap & Youth caps)
As a Watford player David Holdsworth made almost 300 appearances and followed up with 118 for the Blades. Impressive during his first two years at St Andrew's, always giving 100 per-cent on the field, a change of manager spelt the end for the dogged defender and following his release by Blues, Holdsworth teamed up with his twin brother, Dean, at The Reebok Stadium.

HOLLAND, Christopher James
Midfielder: 50+37 apps.
Born: Clitheroe, Lancs 11 September 1975
Career: Preston North End (trainee, June 1992, professional 1993), Newcastle United (£100,000 January 1994), BLUES (on loan, September 1996, signed permanently for £600,000, October 1996), Huddersfield Town (£150,000, February 2002).
Representative honours: England (10 Under-21 and Youth caps)
A totally committed midfielder who was always willing to assist the defence when required, Chris Holland was very impressive at times. Prior to the start of the 2002-03 season his tally of senior appearances stood at 190.

HOLLIS, George
Goalkeeper: 32 apps.
Born: Kenilworth, Warwickshire, 1869.
Died: circa 1940.
Career: Warwick County, BLUES (August 1891); reinstated as an amateur and joined Bournbrook (September 1894). Retired in May 1897.
Club honours: Blues: Division Two champions 1893.
A swarthy goalkeeper with prominent sideburns, George Hollis deputised regularly when Chris Charsley was away on other duties. He kept his shorts up with a decorative cummerbund rather than using a traditional belt.

HOLMES, Ezra
Centre-forward: 2 apps.
Born: West Bromwich, 1882. Now deceased
Career: South Staffordshire Regiment, Gainsborough Trinity, BLUES (£400, November 1907), Stamford FC (March 1908).
Blues made a grave error in judgement when they paid a large fee for this pint sized forward who failed to impress on his two appearances. Ezra Holmes did not even have time to move home to Birmingham before he found himself on his way back to Lincolnshire.

HOLMES, Paul
Defender: 13 apps.
Born: Stocksbridge, 18 February 1968
Career: Doncaster Rovers (apprentice June 1984,

professional February 1986), Torquay United (£8,000, August 1988), BLUES (June 1992), Everton (£100,000, March 1993), West Bromwich Albion (£80,000, January 1996), Torquay United (free transfer, November 1999).
Paul Holmes, a speedy defender, able to occupy the right-back berth as well as that of centre half, was cool and collected, always assured who might well have become a Liverpool player before joining Blues. He had a good spell at The Hawthorns (115 games) and later took his overall tally to senior appearances with Torquay to past the 260 mark (up to May 2002). He is the son of Albert Holmes, a former Chesterfield defender.

HOLMES, William
Outside-right: one app.
Born: Ambergate, Derbyshire, 10 August 1908
Career: Milford Ivanhoe, Coventry City (November 1931), Heanor Town (November 1933), Notts County (December 1933), BLUES (November 1934), Heanor Town (August 1935).
'Harry' Holmes was a capable amateur winger, very popular with the fans during his spell at Coventry. Reluctant to give up his job as a constructional draughtsman for a career in football, he was the last amateur to play first team football for Blues, lining up in a League game v. Leicester City (home) in November 1934.

HOOPER, Harold
Winger: 119 apps. 42 goals
Born: Pittington, County Durham, 14 June 1933,
Career: Hylton Colliery Juniors, West Ham United (junior, June 1949, professional November 1950), Wolverhampton Wanderers (£25,000, March 1956), BLUES (£20,000, December 1957), Sunderland (£18,000 September 1960), Kettering Town (May 1963), Dunstable Town (1965), Heanor Town (1967).
Club honours: Blues: Fairs Cup runners-up 1960.
Representative honours: England (6 'B' caps, 2 Under-23 caps); Football League XI (1)
Harry Hooper came from a footballing family - his father played for Sheffield United and his brother Alf, for Halifax Town. Harry junior was the Durham sprint champion before turning to football and throughout his career used his speed to good effect. He signed for the Hammers whilst his father was trainer at Upton Park, and was given an early chance to show his ability, soon making the right wing position his own and impressing sufficiently to earn a call up for the full England squad. Wolves were impressed enough to pay a record fee for his services, but despite turning in some fine displays, he did not stay too long at Molineux. On moving to St Andrew's he was switched to the left flank where he continued to perform well and became a firm favourite

with the fans. After a few years, when it became obvious that Blues were going nowhere, Hooper moved back to his native North-East. He now lives in Kettering.

HOOPER, Lyndon

Midfielder: 2+4 apps
Born: Guyana, 30 May 1966
Career: (in Canada) Eastern Ontario All Stars, Ottawa Pioneers (1987), Montreal Supra (1988), & Toronto Blizzard (1989); BLUES (£50,000, October 1993). Released in July 1994.
Representative honours: Canada (49 full caps, one Olympic Games appearance, plus Under-21 & Youth). Regarded as the best player in Canada, Lyndon Hooper was the last of the three Canadians brought over by coach Tony Taylor to join Blues. After a trial in the reserves he made an early debut at Villa Park in the League Cup-tie in front of 35,000 spectators. Unfortunately, his arrival coincided with a period of instability at the club and he was unable to convince Barry Fry of his worth. At the end of the season his work permit was not renewed as he had made insufficient appearances. His sister, Charmaine, was regarded as the star player of Canada's women's soccer team whilst younger brother Ian played in the North Carolina State University's side. His most famous relation, however, is cousin Carl Hooper, the West Indies Test cricketer.

HOPE, Robert

Inside-forward: 42+4 apps. 5 goals
Born: Bridge of Allan, Scotland, 28 September 1943.
Career: Clydebank High & Dunbartonshire West Schools, Drumchapel Amateurs, Sunderland (on trial), Scotland Boys, West Bromwich Albion (amateur August 1959, professional September 1960), BLUES (£66,666, May 1972), Philadelphia Atoms/NASL (April 1975), Dallas Tornados/NASL (May-August 1976), Sheffield Wednesday (September 1976), Dallas Tornados (on loan, April-August 1977 & again, April-August 1978), Bromsgrove Rovers (player-coach, August 1978, appointed manager May 1983), Burton Albion (manager, August-October 1988), Bromsgrove Rovers (manager June 1989 to September 1994). Played in over 150 charity games for WBA Old Stars (1979-95) and in 1989 was a part-time scout for Wolverhampton Wanderers. He returned to The Hawthorns as Albion's Youth Development Officer in July 1998, taking over as the club's Chief Scout in 2001.
Club honours: WBA: FA Cup winners 1968, Football League Cup winners 1966, runners-up 1967 & 1970.
Representative honours: Scotland (2 full caps, one Under-23 cap, 2 Schoolboy caps).
Bobby Hope was a wonderfully creative midfielder who scored 42 goals in 403 games for Albion, laying on

chances galore for Tony Brown and Jeff Astle. A diminutive performer and by far one of the best passers of a ball in the game.

HOPKINS, Robert Arthur

Forward/midfield: 195+10 apps. 33 goals
Born: Hall Green, Birmingham, 25 October 1961
Career: Pitmaston School, South Birmingham Schools (playing in English Schools Trophy), West Midlands County Boys, Aston Villa (apprentice July 1977, professional July 1979), BLUES (March 1983, in exchange for Alan Curbishley), Manchester City (£130,000, September 1986), West Bromwich Albion (£60,000, March 1989 in exchange deal involving Imre Varadi), BLUES (£25,000, March 1989); Shrewsbury Town (free transfer, July 1991), Instant Dictionary FC/Hong Kong (May 1992), Solihull Borough (September 1992), Colchester United (February 1993), Solihull Borough (season 1994-95), WBA Old Stars.
Club honours: Aston Villa: FA Youth Cup & Southern Junior Floodlit Cup winners 1980; Blues: Division Two promotion 1985, Leyland DAF Cup winners 1991 (as a non-playing substitute).
A Blues fanatic all his life, the early career of Robert 'Hoppy' Hopkins' was liberally punctured by disciplinary problems before he settled down to become a good professional, turning out at centre-forward, on the right-wing, in central-midfield and from time to time at full-back. It was unfortunate that the happiest day of his footballing life - when his beloved Birmingham City finally won something at Wembley - turned out to be the last time he was selected for a Blues squad.

HORNE, Barry

Midfielder: 40 apps.
Born: Rhyl, 18 May 1962
Career: Rhyl, Wrexham (June 1984), Portsmouth (£60,000, July 1987), Southampton (£700,000, March 1989), Everton (£675,000, July 1992), BLUES (£250,000, June 1996), Huddersfield Town (free transfer, October 1997), Sheffield Wednesday (free, March 2000), Kidderminster Harriers (free, August 2000), Walsall (free, March 2001), Belper Town (July 2001).
Club honours: Wrexham: Welsh Cup winners 1986; Everton: FA Cup & Charity Shield winners 1995
Representative honours: Wales (59 full caps)
Barry Horne had well over 500 club games under his belt when he joined Blues. A very effective, hard-working midfielder he was never found wanting and when he dropped out of senior football in 2001 he had amassed in excess of 760 competitive appearances at club and international level.

HORSFIELD, Geoffrey Malcolm
Striker: 81+30* apps. 26* goals
Born: Barnsley, 1 November 1973
Career: Scarborough (as a junior, June 1990, professional July 1992), Halifax Town, (March 1994), Witton Albion, Halifax Town (May 1997), Fulham (£325,000, October 1998), BLUES (£2 million+ July 2000).
Club honours: Halifax: Conference champions 1998; Fulham: Division 2 champions 1999; Blues: League Cup runners-up 2001, Division One promotion 2002.
A hard-working, aggressive striker, a battler to the last, Geoff Horsfield put in his fair share of graft as Blues climbed into the Premiership in 2002. Prior to joining the club from Fulham, he had scored 40 League and Cup goals at senior level. He lost his place in the side to the new strike-force of Stern John and Clinton Morrison at the start of the 2002-03 campaign but was always there on the bench when required.

HORSMAN, William
Winger: 83 apps. 3 goals
Born: Doncaster, 1902. Now deceased
Career: Selby Town, BLUES (1928), Chester (1935). Retired during World War 2.
A useful winger who was perpetually on the verge of a breakthrough but never quite made it in Division One, Bill Horsman proved to be a valuable acquisition for Chester, exhibiting goalscoring flair that had never been obvious during his lengthy spell with Blues.

HOUGHTON, Henry Brian
Centre-forward: 4 apps. one goal
Born: Madras, India, 1 September 1936
Career: St Wilfred's Youth Club, Bradford (as an amateur, July 1954, professional October 1955), BLUES (£5,250, October 1957), Southend United (October 1958), Oxford United (£2,000, March 1961), Lincoln City (£6,000, October 1963), Chelmsford City (July 1965), Cambridge United, Wellington Town, Cheltenham Town, Morris Motors.
Club honours: Oxford: Southern League champions 1961 & 1962.
A burly, bustling forward who was always a great favourite with the crowd wherever he went, 'Bud' Houghton was a prolific scorer in the lower Divisions, but his style did not suit Blues' game at the time which was built around a more mobile centre forward.

HOWARD, Henry
Wing-half: 51 apps. one goal
Born: Rotherham 1871. Now deceased
Career: Yorkshire local football, Rotherham Town (on trial, 1893), Sheffield Wednesday (on trial, 1894), Sheffield United (1895), BLUES (April 1902), Wisbech Town (August 1906 to May 1907).
Harry Howard was a solidly built, defensively minded

player who always seemed to promise more than he achieved. He made 48 League appearances for the Blades.

HOWARD, Patrick
Central-defender: 43 apps.
Born: Dodworth, Yorkshire, 7 October 1947
Career: Barnsley Boys, Barnsley (apprentice April 1963, professional October 1965), Newcastle United (£21,000, September 1971), Arsenal (£50,000, September 1976), BLUES (£40,000, August 1978), Portland Timbers/NASL (on loan, April-August 1978), Bury (July 1979). Retired in May 1982 to concentrate on running a snooker centre and sports shop in Bury.
Club honours: Newcastle: FA Cup runners-up 1974, Football League Cup runners-up 1976.
An experienced defender who was signed as an emergency replacement for Joe Gallagher after his car crash, Pat Howard gave Blues good service in his first season, helping to hold together a rather leaky defence. Injuries suffered during his spell in the NASL in the summer of 1978 restricted his appearances the following season and he was eventually given a free transfer.

HOWELL, David Christopher
Defender: 2 apps.
Born: Hammersmith, London, 10 October 1956
Career: Fulham (apprentice, 1972-73), Enfield, Hillingdon Borough, Hounslow, Enfield, Barnet (October 1990), Southend United, (player-coach July 1993), BLUES (coach, December 1993, registered as a player-coach, September 1994 to 1996).
Club honours: Barnet: Conference winners 1991: Enfield: Conference winners 1986, FA Trophy winners 1988.
Representative honours: England (15 semi-pro caps).
David Howell made his debut for Blues in December 1994 at the age of 38, as a replacement for the suspended Liam Daish. A big pal of Barry Fry since his Hillingdon days, a true professional, totally committed, Howell actually came to Blues, not as a player but as a coach.

HOWITT, David John
Right-back: 3 apps.
Born: Birmingham, 4 August 1952
Career: Hodge Hill School, BLUES (apprentice June 1968, professional March 1970), Bury (August 1973), Workington (July 1974), Aldershot (June 1975), Milton Keynes City (player-manager, August 1981), Milton Keynes Borough (as a player, season 1983-84), Newport Pagnall Town (1985).
David Howitt made close on 200 League appearances during his senior career, 137 for Aldershot. He was a successful schoolboy midfielder before joining Blues and was converted into a full-back whilst in the reserves. He made his first team debut after Blues had made a poor

start to the 1972-73 campaign, but failed to impress and was released at the end of the season. Howitt later acted as player-manager of Milton Keynes City, staying with that club until it folded having failed to record a single win in its last season.

HOYLAND, Wilfred

Outside-right. 6 apps

Born: Pontefract, Yorkshire, March 1898. Now deceased
Career: Swansea Town (February 1921), Bury (1922), Glossop, BLUES (September 1923), Brighton & Hove Albion (May 1924 to June 1926).
Fred Hoyland was a well-built winger who had a brief spell in the team in place of the injured Billy Harvey. He remained a reserve during his time with Brighton in the Third Division South.

HUBBARD, Arthur A

Left-back: 5 apps.
Born: Erdington, Birmingham, 10 May 1911.
Career: Chester Road School, Moor Green, Wright & Eagle Range Company FC, BLUES (amateur, August 1932, professional February 1933), Luton Town (August 1935), Dunstable Town (1939-40). Did not play after World War 2.
Representative honour: FA Amateur XI
A solid full-back, Arthur Hubbard was signed from a local works League team. Basically a reserve, his first team outings were restricted to only five owing to the impressive form of Ned Barkas.

HUGHES, Bryan

Midfielder: 203+52* apps. 34 goals*
Born: Liverpool 19 June 1976
Career: Wrexham (trainee, June 1992, professional July 1994), BLUES (£750,000+ March 1997).
Club honours: Wrexham: Welsh Cup winners 1995; Blues: League Cup runners-up 2001, Division One promotion 2002.
A very talented player, happy with the ball at his feet, Bryan Hughes enjoys a role on the left from where he does most damage. His presence in the engine-room went a long way in helping Blues reach the Premiership in 2002 but found it difficult to get into the side the next season following the arrival of Messrs Cisse and Savage. He made 127 appearances for Wrexham before moving to St Andrew's.

HUGHES, Jack

Centre-half: one app.
Born: Birmingham, 1866. Now deceased
Career: Birmingham Unity, BLUES (August 1890), Lea Hall Constitutionals FC (September 1891).
Caesar Jenkyns' deputy in one game for Blues (a 5-2 defeat away to Walsall Town Swifts in September 1890), Jack Hughes was never given another chance.

HUGHES, John Norman

Outside-left: 7 apps.
Born: Tamworth, 10 July 1921
Career: Tamworth Castle, BLUES (June 1947), Tamworth (August 1949), Atherstone Town (1952). Was later assistant-manager of Tamworth for two seasons (from August 1955).
Jack Hughes rose to prominence in non-League circles during WW2 when he impressed with his versatility. Blues used him principally as a winger, a role for which he was not ideally suited and his League chances were restricted accordingly.

HUGHES, William Marshall

Left-back: 110 apps.
Born: Carmarthen, 6 March 1918.
Died: Birmingham, 16 June 1981
Career: Llanelli Boys' School, Swansea Grammar School, Carmarthen, Archer Corinthians, Llanelli, Watchers Celtic, Llanelli Town (1934), Swansea Town (on loan, March 1935), BLUES (professional, May 1935), Luton Town (July 1947), Chelsea (£12,000, March 1948), Hereford United (August 1951), Flint Town (January 1954). Retired in May 1955 and later scouted for Chester. Guested for Arsenal, Queen's Park Rangers, Tottenham Hotspur & West Ham United during WW2.
Club honours: Flint Town: Welsh Cup winners 1954.
Representative honours: Wales: (10 full caps, 14 Wartime/Victory caps); played for Great Britain v Rest of Europe in 1947.
Billy Hughes matured quickly into a highly-skilled full-back, an effective ball-winner who always tried to be constructive, forever looking to play his way out of difficulty rather than kicking in hope of finding a colleague. He appeared in over 60 games for Blues during the wartime period, having been a teenager when he made his senior debut.

HUME, William Sanderson

Wing-half/inside-forward: 10 apps. 2 goals
Born: Armadale, Scotland, 18 December 1935
Career: Dunfermline Athletic, BLUES (February 1958), St Mirren (1960), Berwick Rangers, Bangor City, Hakoah/Melbourne (Australian State League).
A strong man and good ball player, Billy Hume made his first-team debut for Blues in a friendly against Valencia. It was a problem where to play him, but he eventually settled down at inside-left and had one reasonable run in the first team but met with limited success overall.

HUNT, Jonathan Richard

Midfielder: 86+16 apps. 25 goals
Born: Camden Town 2 November 1971
Career: Woking, Barnet (juniors, June 1987, professional November 1989), Southend United (free transfer, July 1993), BLUES (£50,000, September 1994), Derby County (£500,000, May 1997), Sheffield United (on loan, August-September 1998), Ipswich Town (on loan,

October 1998), Sheffield United (free transfer, March 1999), Cambridge United (on loan, March-April 2000), Wimbledon (free transfer, September 2000 to July 2001).
Club honours: Blues: Second Division champions 1995, Auto-Windscreen Shield winners 1995.
A very skilful right-sided player, Jon Hunt made a big impact at St Andrew's before injury forced him out of the action early in the 1994-5 season...after he had scored hat-tricks in the Auto-Windscreen Shield game against Peterborough in the September and in Blues' 5-0 League win over Crewe Alexandra the following month (the one he netted against 'Posh' was, in fact, the first treble by a Blues player for over nine years). He recovered full-fitness and went on to play in over 100 first-class games for the club before transferring to Derby. He reached the milestone 300 senior appearances at club level before leaving the 'Dons' in July 2001 to enter non-League football.

HUNTER, William
Centre-half; 42 apps.
Born: Cardenden, Scotland 16 August 1900.
Died: circa 1970
Career: Brownhill Juniors, BLUES (April 1921), Grimsby Town (January 1927), Coventry City (September 1927), Walsall (1928), Torquay United (December 1929). Retired in May 1930.
Rather on the small side for a centre half at 5ft 8in and 10st 12lb, Billy 'Sailor' Hunter was nevertheless one of the mainstays of Blues' reserve side throughout the early 1920s. He could always be relied upon to turn in a solid performance when given a first team chance. He gained his nickname from his Naval service during WW1.

HUTCHINSON, Jonathan
Defender: 4+3* apps.
Born: Middlesbrough, 2 April 1982
Career: BLUES (trainee, June 1998, July 2000).
A very promising central defender, good in the air and on the ground, Jon Hutchinson reads a situation well.

HUXFORD, Richard John
Full-back: 5 apps.
Born: Scunthorpe, 25 July 1969
Career: Scunthorpe United (apprentice), Matlock Town (1987), Burton Albion (1989), Gainsborough Trinity (season 1989-90), Kettering Town, Barnet (August 1992), Millwall (free transfer July 1993), BLUES (on loan, February 1994), Bradford City (October 1994), Peterborough United (on loan, October 1996), Burnley (January 1997), Dunfermline Athletic (on loan, February 1998, signed permanently, March 1998).
Richard Huxford, a no-nonsense full-back, was taken on a month's loan by Blues after Scott Hiley was injured, ironically at Millwall whence Huxford then came.

HYDE, Graham
Midfielder: 37+22 apps. 2 goals
Born: Doncaster, 10 November 1970
Career: Sheffield Wednesday (trainee, 1986, professional May 1988), BLUES (free transfer, February 1999), Chesterfield (on loan, August 2001), Peterborough United (on loan, August 2002).
An aggressive midfielder, Graham Hyde had injury problems during the latter stages of his St Andrew's career and after a promising start drifted out of the spotlight. He made 218 appearances for Wednesday.

HYND, John Roger Shankly
Central-defender: 197+8 apps. 5 goals
Born: Falkirk: 2 February 1942.
Career: Lanark Grammar School, Glasgow Rangers (1961), Crystal Palace (£12,000, July 1969), BLUES (£25,000, July 1970) Oxford United (on loan, October 1975), Walsall (December 1975), Motherwell (manager, June 1978).
Club honours: Rangers: European Cup-winners Cup runners-up 1967; Blues: Division Two promotion 1972.
Nephew of the great Bill Shankly, Roger Hynd was a defender with the physique of a weightlifter who became a huge favourite with the fans with his refusal to give less than one hundred per-cent. Although principally a centre half, he lined up at centre-forward for Rangers in the 1967 European Cup-winners Cup Final. Disgusted with the result and his own display, he threw his medal into the crowd after the match. Palace signed him to boost their newly promoted side but he met with only limited success at Selhurst Park. Freddie Goodwin then enticed him to be the pivot of the Blues defence, and he proved to be a very popular signing, his strong heading, firm tackling and distinctive running style, which involved a very high knee lift, signalling him out above the rest of the team. Hynd, who is probably the only Blues player ever to perform with a trombone, later worked as a P.E teacher in Wishaw.

INGLIS, James Allen
Outside-right: 62 apps. 28 goals
Born: Kirkland, Scotland, 1872. Now deceased
Career: Airdrieonians, BLUES (£40, September 1896), Luton Town (August 1899).
Jimmy Inglis was a fast, direct winger with terrific goalscoring record and he seemed to be the long-term replacement for Jack Hallam until suffering a loss of form, prompting Blues to sign Billy Bennett. Inglis' move to the ailing Luton club was disastrous, for he had only three games before that club dropped out to the Football League.

ISHERWOOD, Dennis
Right-back: 5 apps. one goal

Born: Brierley Hill, 20 January 1947
Career: Brierley Hill Schools, BLUES (junior June 1962, professional January 1964), Bromsgrove Rovers (August 1968), Kidderminster Harriers.
Dennis Isherwood was a neat, compact full-back who had an eventful first team career with Blues. He scored on his home debut for Blues with a 25-yarder against Hull City in March 1967 and then put through his own-goal the following week at home to Bolton (2-2). He now resides in Kingswinford where he is a prominent figure in junior tennis circles.

ISHERWOOD, Harold

Left-back: one app.
Born: Darwen, Lancashire, 12 May 1905
Career: Fleetwood, Sunderland (May 1926), BLUES (May 1927), Bournemouth & Boscombe Athletic (June 1928), Worcester City (August 1929 to 1931)
Harry Isherwood, a stocky defender, failed to make the first team with Sunderland. His only game for Blues came in the last match of the 1926-27 season, and after spending the next term in the reserves he went on to play in 18 matches for Bournemouth before dropping out of the Football League.

ISLIP, Ernest

Inside-forward: 89 apps. 24 goals
Born: Parkwood Springs, Sheffield, 31 October 1892.
Died: Huddersfield, August 1941.
Career: Sheffield Douglas FC (1910) Huddersfield Tow (professional June 1911), BLUES (£1,500, November 1923), Bradford City (£400, May 1927), Kidderminster Harriers (£20, August 1928), Ashton National FC (September 1928), Wrexham (November 1928). Retired in February 1929. Guested for Rotherham County, Sheffield Wednesday & West Ham United during WW1.
Club honours: Huddersfield: FA Cup winners 1922, runners-up 1920, Division Two runners-up 1920.
An aggressive and wholehearted player, Ernie Islip hit 26 goals in 98 League games in four seasons as a centre-forward with Huddersfield before joining Blues.
He had been a prolific marksman in local Yorkshire junior football prior to turning professional with the Terriers. He was left in the cold at St Andrew's following the emergence of George Briggs.

IVEY, Paul Henry Winspeare

Forward: 4+ 3 apps
Born: Westminster, London, 1 April 1961.
Career: London & District Schools, BLUES (apprentice June 1977, professional January 1979), Chesterfield (free transfer, June 1982), FC Karlskrona/Sweden (late 1982), Alvechurch, Kalmar AIK/Sweden, Vasalund/Sweden.
As a lad Paul Ivey was described as having a lot of skill, a nice touch on the ball and the right potential. The potential went unfulfilled in England, but he made a

name for himself in the Swedish Second Division where he became a regular goalscorer.

IZON, Charles John

Forward: 26 apps. 8 goals
Born: Stourbridge, 1870. Now deceased
Career: Old Hill Wanderers, Halesowen, BLUES (September 1893), Walsall (seasons 1897-99).
Charlie Izon was highly-rated in local football and as a result Blues, keen to obtain his services, beat several other West Midlands clubs to land his signature. He announced his arrival at St Andrew's with a hat-tick on his debut (against Walsall Town Swifts) but scored only one more goal that season and thereafter struggled to gain a place in the side, although he also netted in his last game for the club.

JACKSON, Alec

Utility-forward: 84+1 apps. 12 goals
Born: Tipton, 29 May 1937
Career: Park Lane Secondary Modern School (Tipton), Tipton St John's FC, WG Allen's FC, West Bromwich Albion (amateur, May 1954, professional September 1954), BLUES (£12,500, June 1964), Walsall (February 1967), Nuneaton Borough (August 1968), Kidderminster Harriers (1970), Warley (1971), Oldbury Town (1972), Warley Borough (February, 1973), Darlaston (August 1973), Blakenhall (1974-76), Lower Gornal (1976-77), Rushall Olympic (1977-78), Bush Rangers (1978-79). Retired in May 1979. Appeared in over 100 charity matches for West Bromwich Albion All Stars (1968-85). Was coach to Coseley Rovers Youth Club (1980-82).
Club honours: WBA: FA Youth Cup runners-up 1955.
Representative honours: Football League XI (1)
A true Black Country yokel, Alec Jackson could play - and play well - in any forward position and he did just that during his ten-year stay at The Hawthorns. He scored on his senior debut at Charlton in 1954 and went on to net 52 goals in 208 games for the Baggies. A player with neat footwork, speed over 20-30 yards, a big heart and willpower, he pulled out of League football with 325 appearances to his name (60 goals scored). He still lives in his beloved Tipton.

JACKSON, Alexander James

Centre-forward: 10 apps. 7 goals
Born: Glasgow, 28 November 1935
Career: Shettleston Juniors, BLUES (signed for £2,000 as a full-time professional, April 1958), Plymouth Argyle (March 1960), Weymouth (1964-65); later lottery manager of Exeter City.
Alex Jackson was not the tallest of centre-forwards but he was certainly a hard worker and a very useful goalscorer who was surprisingly sold by Blues despite an impressive record. Plymouth Argyle used him in both of the inside-

forward berths as well as at number '9' and he proceeded to score 27 times for the 'Pilgrims' in 75 games. He was badly affected by a broken leg in 1963 and never quite regained his form.

JACKSON, Matthew Alan
Defender: 10 apps.
Born: Leeds, 19 October 1971
Career: Luton Town (trainee, June 1988, professional July 1990), Preston North End (on loan, March 1991), Everton (£600,000, October 1991), Charlton Athletic (on loan, March 1996), Queen's Park Rangers (on loan, August 1996), BLUES (on loan, October-November 1996), Norwich City (£450,000, December 1996), Wigan Athletic (free transfer, October 2001).
Club honours: Everton: FA Cup winners 1995
Representative honours: England (10 U-21 & Youth caps).
An experienced defender, sound and reliable, Matt Jackson was drafted into the Blues' squad during an injury crisis. He reached the milestone of 400 club and international appearances in 2002

JACKSON, Walter S
Outside-right: 4 apps. one goal
Born: Northfield, Birmingham 1870. Now deceased
Career: Selly Park Nomads, Harborne, BLUES (September 1893), Berwick Rangers/Worcester (May 1894-95).
Given his chance due to an injury to Jack Hallam, Walter Jackson was criticised for having the tendency to dally far too long on the ball, and was generally regarded as not being in Hallam's class. He followed the well-trodden road of Blues' rejects to the Worcestershire non-League side, Berwick Rangers.

JAMES, Arthur
Outside-right: 5 apps. 3 goals
Born: Longbridge, Birmingham, January 1855.
Died: Birmingham, June 1911
Career: Birmingham Carriage Works FC (season 1874-75), BLUES (September 1875). Retired through injury and illness in the summer of 1887.
Representative honours: Birmingham County FA
The middle of the three James brothers who were involved in the founding of the Blues, Arthur was unusual in being the only forward amongst the trio, and a very fine one at that. Fast and tricky, with a hard shot, he was a first choice for the Birmingham County FA side in several representative matches.

JAMES, Frederick
Left-back/centre-half: 12 apps.
Born: Bartley Green, Birmingham February 1853.
Now deceased.
Career: Northfield Prims, Birmingham Carriage Works FC, BLUES (August 1875). Retired in April 1886.

Oldest of the James brothers, Fred was left-back in Blues' first ever match against Holte Wanderers in 1875. A big-hearted player, with little finesse, he later took over captaincy of the team when Billy Edmunds set up his legal practice in Nottingham. He was still a first team player when he decided to retire.

JAMES, John Edward
Inside-forward: 7 apps. 2 goals
Born: Harborne, Birmingham 19 February 1934
Career: Brighton & Hove Albion (as an amateur, September 1949), Paget Rangers, BLUES (junior, June 1950, professional March 1951), Torquay United (June 1955), Minehead (August 1960).
'Jimmy' James was combining work in a local brass factory with that of cleaning the boots of the Paget Rangers players when Blues signed him in 1950. After some careful grooming he made his senior debut against Spurs in an FA Cup-tie in 1953 in place of the injured Peter Murphy. At the time the side was being built up for a push for promotion and his outings after that were rather limited. He did well after leaving St Andrew's, scoring 11 goals in 123 Football League games for Torquay United whom he served for five years.

JAMES, Thomas
Wing-half: 7 apps. one goal
Born: Bartley Green, Birmingham, April 1857.
Died: Birmingham, 31 October 1928.
Career: Birmingham Carriage Works FC, BLUES (August 1875), Retired in May 1885.
The youngest of the James brothers and the one who had the shortest career, Tom was an efficient right-half in Blues' inaugural fixture and remained in the side until the start of the 1884-5 season when injuries began to take their toll. More adventurous than Fred, he could frequently be found in the attack.
* It is interesting to know that all three James brothers were sufficiently well-known to be referred to by just their first names in newspaper reports of the day.

JENKINS, James Lindley
Midfielder: 3 apps.
Born: West Bromwich, 6 April 1954
Career: South Staffs Boys, BLUES (apprentice June 19870, professional July 1971), Walsall (free transfer July 1974), Tividale FC (1975-77).
Former England schoolboy trialist, Lindley Jenkins was the workhorse of the Blues' Youth team in the Francis-Burns era. He made his senior bow during a bad patch for the club and was perhaps a little too sluggish for football at the highest level.

JENKINS, Lee Robert
Midfielder: one app.
Born: West Bromwich, 17 March 1961
Career: Barr Beacon School, Aston Villa Boys, Aston

Villa (apprentice June 1977, professional January 1979), Port Vale (free transfer, November 1980), FC Rovaniemi Palloseura/Finland (August 1981), BLUES (October 1985), FC Finnairin Palloilijat/Finland (1986-90).
Club honours: Aston Villa: FA Youth Cup runners-up 1978.
Representative honours: England (Youth caps).
After an unsuccessful spell in England, Lee Jenkins came good in Finland. He returned briefly for a spell with Blues (under Ron Saunders' managership) but broke his ankle in his first game, against West Bromwich Albion. He never played for Blues again, returning to continue his successful career in Finland.

JENKINS, Stephen Robert
Full-back: 4 apps.
Born: Merthyr Tydfil, 16 July 1972
Career: Swansea City (trainee, June 1988, professional July 1990), Huddersfield Town (£275,000, November 1995), BLUES (on loan, December 2000).
Club honours: Swansea: Autoglass Trophy winners 1994
Representative honours: Wales (16 full, two Under-21 and Youth caps).
Experienced and reliable full-back, Steve Jenkins joined Blues on loan having already amassed around of 500 appearances at club and international level.

JENKINSON, Leigh
Utility-forward: 2+1 apps.
Born: Thorne, 9 July 1969
Career: Hull City (apprentice July 1985, professional June 1987), Rotherham United (on loan, September 1990), Coventry City (£300,000, March 1993), BLUES (on loan, November 1993). Played non-League football from 1994.
A strong running wide player, 6ft tall with good close control, Leigh Jenkinson managed 14 goals in over 150 games whilst at Boothferry Park.

JENKYNS, Caesar Augustus Llewellyn
Centre-half: 99 apps. 13 goals
Born: Builth, Wales, 24 August 1866.
Died: Birmingham, 23 July 1941.
Career: Southfield, St Andrew's Sunday School, BLUES (August 1884), Unity Gas, BLUES (July 1888), Newton Heath (May 1896), Walsall (November 1897), Coventry City (coach 1902), Saltley Wednesday FC (guest player in 1904). Retired in May 1905 to take over the George Inn, Moxley, later serving in the Birmingham police force.
Club honours: Blues: Division Two champions 1893, Division Two promotion 1894.
Representative honours: Wales (8 full caps)
A burly player with a fierce shoulder charge and shuddering tackle, 'The Mighty Caesar' was the back-bone of the Blues' defence. A born leader, he skippered all the clubs he played for and even his country, and was an inspiration to the rest of the team. He could head a

ball half the length of the field and once won a competition by sending a dead ball kick fully 100 yards first bounce. He took great pleasure in thwarting Blues' forwards during later meetings. Controversial to the last, his one game for Saltley led to him receiving a suspension, as he had not been reinstated as an amateur. He was certainly a tough character and was sent-off several times during his career. He left Blues in 1895 under a cloud, being sacked for brawling with a Derby player whom he alleged had spat at him. His son, Octavius, (classical names ran through the family) had trials with Blues shortly before WW1 but was never signed on.

JENNINGS, Dennis Bernard
Outside-right/left-back: 212 apps. 14 goals
Born: Habberley Valley, Kidderminster, 20 July 1910.
Died: Cornwall, March 1996.
Career: Franche FC (Kidderminster), St Barnabas FC, Foley Park, Stourport Swifts, Romsley Village, West Bromwich Albion (as an amateur, early 1928), Kidderminster Harriers (July 1929), Huddersfield Town (October 1930), Grimsby Town (September 1932), BLUES (£1,200, January 1936), Kidderminster Harriers (player-coach, March 1951 to May 1953), Lockheed Leamington (June 1953). Later retired to live in the village of Little Dinham near Wadebridge, Cornwall. Guested for Nottingham Forest during WW2.
Club honours: Grimsby: Division Two champions 1934, Blues: Football League South champions 1946 & Division Two champions 1948.
He played in every position for Blues except centre-half during his lengthy stay at St Andrew's, making 174 wartime appearances as well as those at senior level (amassing 386 all told). He produced many calm, unflustered performances in each of his many roles, having started off as an out-and-out winger. Dennis Jennings relied on skill rather than speed and he was almost 41 years of age when he finally left St Andrew's (the club's oldest player).
His speciality was the bicycle-kick, used more often than not when clearing his own lines.
After football he ran a successful caravan park with his brother and was 85 when he died.

JOHN, Stern
Striker: 37+1* apps. 15* goals
Born: Trinidad, 30 October 1976.
Career: Columbus Crew (USA), Nottingham Forest (£1.5 million+, November 1999), BLUES (February 2002).
Club honours: Blues: Division One promotion 2002
Representative honours: Trinidad & Tobago (4* full caps)
Stern John was, to a certain extent, a victim of the small print written into his contract when he moved from America in 1999. It was revealed that Forest (his buyers)

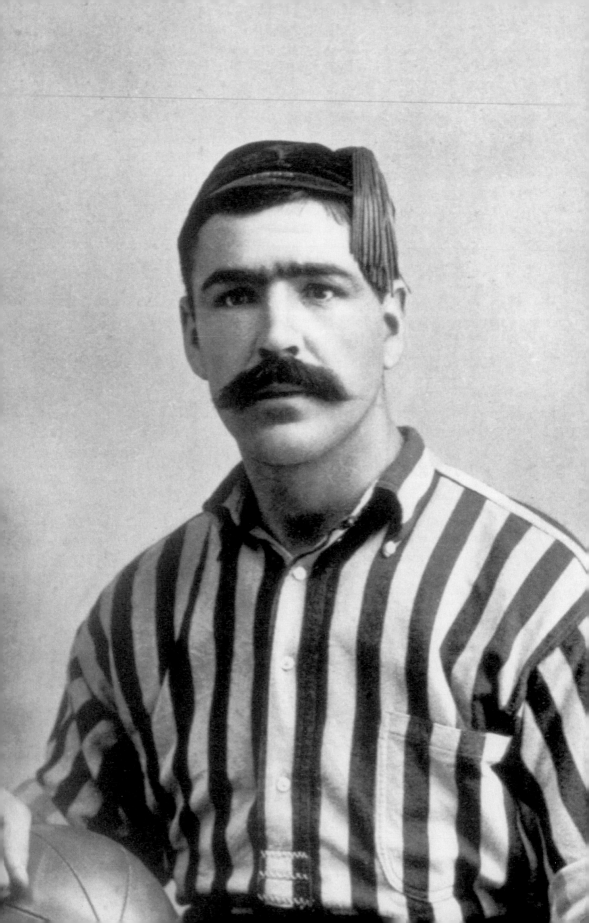

would have to pay £90,000 a goal once he had netted 15 times...that wasn't on and he was allowed to move to St Andrew's for a 'cut down price.' And what a signing he has turned out to be! He scored eight important 'promotion' goals at the end of the 2001-02 season when his poise, pace, close control and, indeed, his overall ability added something special to the Blues' attack at a crucial stage of the proceedings! He grabbed a hat-trick when Blues beat Leyton Orient 3-2 in a 2nd round Worthington Cup-tie in October 2002, having earlier netted 20 goals in his 80 games for Forest.

JOHNSON, Andrew

Midfielder/striker: 52+51 apps. 13 goals
Born: Bedford 10 February 1981
Career: BLUES (trainee June 1996, professional March 1998), Crystal Palace (£750,000, August 2002).
Club honours: Blues: League Cup runners-up 2001, Division One promotion 2002.
Representative honours: England (youth caps)
Speedy, young striker or midfielder, direct in style with a strong tackle and an eye for goal, Andy Johnson left St Andrew's for Selhurst Park as part of the deal that brought Clinton Morrison to Blues. He had the misfortune to miss the vital last penalty in the 2001 Worthington Cup Final shoot-out v. Liverpool at the Millennium Stadium, and as a result Blues lost out the Merseysiders.

JOHNSON, Arthur

Outside-left: 9 apps.
Born: Atherstone, July 1904
Career: Atherstone Town, Huddersfield Town (November 1924), Barnsley (October 1925), BLUES (August 1927), Bristol City (May 1928), Coventry City (July 1931 to 1933).
A tall winger who returned home after an unhappy spell in Yorkshire, Arthur Johnson impressed in practice matches and was given the chance of filling one of Blues' problem positions but had little success.

JOHNSON, Damien Michael

Midfielder: 22+6* apps. 2* goals
Born: Lisburn, Northern Ireland, 18 November 1978
Career: Blackburn Rovers (trainee June 1995, professional February 1996), Nottingham Forest (on loan, January 1998), BLUES (March 2002).
Club honours: Blackburn: League Cup winners 2002
Representative honours: Northern Ireland (16 full, 11 Under-21 & Youth caps)
Talented central midfield player, committed to the game, Damien Johnson is combative, never shirks a tackle and surprisingly left Ewood Park for St Andrew's soon after Rovers and lifted the League Cup, helping Blues clinch promotion.

JOHNSON, Michael Owen

Defender: 267+44* apps. 17* goals
Born: Nottingham, 4 July 1973
Career: Notts County (trainee, June 1989, professional July 1991), BLUES (£300,000, September 1995).
Club honours: Notts County (Anglo-Italian Cup winners 1995); Blues: League Cup runners-up 2001, Division One promotion 2002
Representative honours: Jamaica (7* caps)
Michael Johnson, who made almost 140 appearances for Notts County, is a resilient performer who had to contest a first team place with the likes of Gary Ablett, Gary Breen and current manager Steve Bruce when he first joined Blues. But he stuck in there and is now a key member of the squad. Nicknamed 'Magic' for obvious reasons, Johnson is a very consistent performer and a firm favourite with the supporters. He was first capped by Jamaica in season 1999-2000
* Johnson received a death threat in February 2000 from the neo-Nazi group Combat 18. The tone of the letter advised him to leave the country or be killed. Thankfully, nothing materialised after the police had been informed.

JOHNSTON, Allan

Winger: 8+2 apps.
Born: Glasgow, 14 December 1973
Career: Tynecastle Boys Club, Heart of Midlothian (professional, June 1990), Stade Rennais FC/France (July 1996), Sunderland (£550,000, March 1997), BLUES (on loan, October-November 1999), Bolton Wanderers (free transfer, January 2000), Rangers (free, June 2000), Middlesbrough (£1 million, September 2001).
Club honours: Sunderland: Division 1 champions 1999
Representative honours: Scotland (15 full, 2 'B', 3 U-21)
Tricky winger, loaned to Blues for a period during the 1999-2000 season, Allan Johnston has never really settled down since leaving Sunderland.

JOHNSTON, George

Inside-forward: 7+3 apps. one goal
Born: Glasgow, 21 March, 1947
Career: St George Road Youth Club, Maryhill Boys, Cardiff City (juniors, June 1962, professional May 1964), Arsenal (£20,000, March 1967), BLUES (£30,000, may 1969) Walsall (on loan, September-October 1970), Fulham (£6,000, October 1970), Hereford United (£2,500, August 1972), Newport County (£1,500, September 1973), Caerau/Welsh League (seasons 1974-76)
Club honours: Cardiff: Welsh Cup winners 1965
George Johnson, a former Glasgow Corporation tea-boy, first caught the eye by scoring regularly for Cardiff whilst sill a teenager. Two goals against Arsenal in a charity match led to the Londoners signing him. From there, though, his career took a downward turn and he was never a first-team regular at Highbury. He moved to Blues as replacement for Fred Pickering but found it difficult to hold down a first team place and eventually set off on a tour of the lower Divisions.

JOHNSTON, William McClure
Outside-left: 18 apps.
Born: Maryhill, Glasgow, 19 December 1946
Career: Fife County Schools, Bowhill Strollers, Lochore
Welfare (1961), Manchester United (on trial), Glasgow
Rangers (as an amateur July 1962, professional, February
1964), West Bromwich Albion (club record fee of
£138,000, December 1972), Vancouver
Whitecaps/NASL (£190,000, March 1979), BLUES (on
loan, October 1979 to February 1980), Vancouver
Whitecaps (February, 1980), Glasgow Rangers (£40,000,
August 1980), Vancouver Whitecaps (May, 1982), South
China/Hong Kong (summer 1983), Heart of Midlothian
(as head coach, September 1983), East Fife (coach,
1985), Raith Rovers (coach, March-June 1986). Quit
football to become a publican in Glasgow, but returned
to the game in July 1987 as coach to Falkirk. He now
runs a pub in Kirkaldy.
Club honours: Rangers: European Cup-winners' Cup
winners 1972, runners-up 1967, Scottish FA Cup
winners 1966, runners-up 1969, 1971 & 1981, Scottish
League Cup winners 1965, 1971runners-up 1966 &
1967; WBA: Division 2 promotion 1976; Vancouver
Whitecaps: NASL Super Bowl winners 1979; Blues:
Division Two promotion 1980.
Representative honours: Scotland (22 full caps, 2 Under-
23 caps, Youth caps); Scottish League XI (2).
A marvellous, dashing winger, skilful and entertaining,
but a player who had a fiery temper, Willie 'Bud'
Johnston was sent-off no fewer than 17 times during his
career (which is probably an all-time record) and was
once suspended for 67 days by the SFA prior to joining
West Bromwich Albion in 1972 (after falling foul of his
Ibrox boss, Jock Wallace, a former Albion goalkeeper.)
Nevertheless he was a fine winger, although Blues saw
him towards the end of his playing days. He scored over
160 goals in more than 400 games as a professional, and
once netted a hat-trick of penalties for Rangers against St
Johnstone after coming on as a substitute. He also scored
two crucial goals to help Rangers win the European Cup-
winners Cup in 1972 against Dinamo Moscow. Johnston
was sensationally sent home from the Scottish World
Cup party on a drugs charge in 1978.

JOLLY, Edwin
Utility: 21 apps. 2 goals
Born: Lozells, Birmingham, June 1871. Now deceased
Career: Lozells FC, BLUES (August 1893), Berwick
Rangers/Worcester (September 1896)
Jolly by name, Jolly by nature, Teddy was the life and
soul of the Blues' dressing room, and always willing to
try his hand in any position. His two goals came when
he made a surprise appearance on the wing. He scored a
hat-trick of own-goals in a Birmingham League match in
March 1895 - but that apart he was a pretty useful footballer.

JONES, Aaron
Forward: 5 apps.
Born: Rotherham, 1884. Died: Yorkshire, 1950.
Career: Newstead Byron FC, Barnsley, BLUES (£170,
May 1905), Notts County (August 1907).
A versatile forward described as able and energetic, Aaron
Jones' five appearances came in three different roles.

JONES, Abraham
Centre-forward: 3 apps. 2 goals
Born: Tantany Estate, West Bromwich, April 1889.
Now deceased.
Career: Walsall Street & Bratt Street Schools, West
Bromwich Sandwell, BLUES (September 1919), Reading
(August 1921), Brighton & Hove Albion (June 1922),
Merthyr Town (August 1923), Stoke City (1924). Also
engaged as a pro boxer during the 1916-18 period.
An enthusiastic, dashing forward 'Abe' Jones started his
League career with two goals on his Blues debut, but was
then kept in the background by Harry Hampton. He
remained a reserve for most of his playing days. He was
the son of 'Abe' Jones, the former West Bromwich
Albion and Middlesbrough centre half, and nephew of
ex-Blues star, William Henry 'Bullit' Jones (q.v).

JONES, Charles Thomson
Outside-left: one app.
Born: Moseley; Birmingham July 1888. Now deceased
Career: Verity's Works FC, BLUES (August 1908),
Bristol Rovers (season 1909-10).
An amateur winger, speedy but not particularly accurate
with his crosses, Charlie Jones made only spasmodic
appearances for Bristol Rovers, mainly as deputy for ex-
Blues man, Willie Peplow.

JONES, Charles Wilson
Centre-forward: 150 apps 69 goals
Born: Pentre near Broughton, Wrexham, 29 April 1914.
Died: Birmingham, 9 January 1986.
Career: Brymbo Green FC (1930), Blackburn Rovers (on
trial), Bolton Wanderers (on trial), Wrexham
(professional, August 1932), BLUES (£1,500, September
1934) Nottingham Forest (September 1947), Redditch
United, Kidderminster Harriers (August 1948). Retired
in June 1950 to go into licensing trade where he stayed
until 1978. Guested for Blackpool, Huddersfield Town,
West Bromwich Albion and Wrexham during WW2
Club honours: Blues: Football League South
Champions 1946.
Representative honours: Wales (2 full caps).
A pale, red-haired, deceptively frail-looking forward,
Charlie Wilson Jones (he was always referred to as
Wilson Jones) had a sterling rise to fame. After two years

in Wrexham's reserves, Blues signed him and within six months he was leading his country's attack. He had two excellent years as Blues' main striker before injuries and loss of form affected his overall play. He lost popularity with the fans and was possibly the first Blues player to receive concerted barracking, but despite this he continued to give several years of stalwart service. He scored 45 goals in 75 wartime games for Blues.

JONES, David Wilmott Llewellyn
Inside-forward: 9 apps.
Born: Kingsley, 9 April 1940
Career: Crewe Alexandra (juniors 1955, amateur May 1956), BLUES (professional April 1957), Millwall (December 1959 to May 1964); then non-League football to 1972.
Club honours: Millwall: Division Four champions 1962
Representative honours: England (one Youth cap)
David Jones was a talented young forward who played in 26 League games for Crewe whilst still an amateur (he actually made his League debut at the age of 16). Nurtured carefully for a year at St Andrews, he was coming along nicely until a major leg injury halted his progress. He did splendidly with Millwall, however, for whom he scored 75 goals in 179 competitive games in five years at The Den.

JONES, Frederick R
Inside-left: one app.
Born: Halesowen, 1910. Deceased
Career: Old Hill White Star, Halesowen, Huddersfield Town (on trial), Leeds United, BLUES (August 1934), Cheltenham Town (September 1935 to May 1936).
One of the few mystery men in Blues' history, Fred Jones' only appearance came as a late replacement for Joe Bradford and, in fact, it was an appearance credited in some sources to Wilson Jones, who had not signed for Blues at that time! He later played an important part in Cheltenham Town's FA Cup run in 1935-36 when they reached the third round of the competition.

JONES, Frederick William
Left-back; 9 apps
Born: Llandudno, January 1867.
Died: Llandudno, 27 December 1910 of a seizure.
Career: Gloddath Athletic (1886-90), Llandudno Swifts, Bolton Wanderers (on trial), West Manchester, Burslem Port Vale (September 1890), Newton Heath, BLUES (August 1892), Lincoln City (season 1893-94), Reading, Ellesmere Port, Chirk, Llandudno Swifts (four seasons: 1896 to1900), Caernarfon Ironopolis, Llanrwst Major

(1903-04).Representative honours: Wales (one full cap).
Fred Jones was a lumbering full-back and the first Blues player to be capped for Wales, an honour which crowned a rapid rise to the top. His descent was equally rapid and he was latterly called upon as an emergency goalkeeper rather than as a defender. He was found dead in a street in Llandudno. His brother, Arnold, played briefly for Blues' reserves during the 1892-93 season.

JONES, Gary Kenneth
Outside-right: 36+2 apps. one goal
Born: Whiston, Liverpool, 5 January 1951.
Career: Everton (apprentice, June 1966, professional October 1968), BLUES (£110,000, July 1976), Fort Lauderdale Strikers/NASL (April 1978).
An aggressive winger, never afraid to run at defences, Gary Jones was, nevertheless, plagued by inconsistency throughout his Blues career. His goal-tally was a poor return for a player whose primary function was that of an attacker. On returning from America he became a landlord of The Albert, one of the trendiest pubs in Liverpool.

JONES, John
Inside-forward: 39 apps.18 goals
Born: Swan Village, West Bromwich, October 1874.
Died: Edmonton, London 13 September 1904
Career: Gunns Lane School, Tantany Rovers, Shaftsbury White Rose, Sandwell Albion, Dudley, Halesowen, BLUES (December 1894), Eastville Rovers (August 1897), Tottenham Hotspur (July 1902, until his death).
Jack Jones was a skilful, two-footed player who maintained a respectable strike-rate throughout his career and who still holds the Bristol (Eastville) Rovers record for most goals in a match (six against Weymouth in a 1900-01 FA Cup-tie). He was known as 'Bristol Jones' during his days with Spurs, to distinguish him from another John Jones - and was reported to be 'The deadliest forward in the South' during his time with the London club for whom he scored 40 goals in 67 games. He died of typhoid, aged 29 and Spurs' marked Jones' untimely death with a memorial benefit match in December 1904, to raise funds for his dependants.

JONES, John William
Left-back: 237 apps. one goal
Born: Rotherham, 8 February 1891.
Died: Rotherham, 20 July 1948
Career: Alma Road School, Allerton Bywater Colliery, Industry FC, Bird-in-Hand FC, Maltby Main Colliery, Army football (RAF), Sunderland (November 1914), BLUES (£2,000, May 1930), Nelson (May 1927), Crewe Alexandra (March 1928), Scarborough (September 1930). Retired in May 1931.
Club honours: Blues: Division Two champions 1921
Representative honours: Football League XI (1)

A formidable full-back, well-built with a biting tackle, Jack 'Cracker' Jones was something special in the 1920's, being as rough as his partner Frank Womack was fair. Wingers rarely relished a confrontation with this muscular former miner and it was perhaps surprising that he was seldom involved in disciplinary action. He played in dentures until one notable occasion, on a close season tour to Spain, when they were smashed as he took a full blooded shot in the face, only to have a penalty for handball awarded against him!

JONES, Mark Anthony William

Full-back/utility: 38+2 apps.
Born: Warley, West Midlands, 22 October 1961
Career: Warley Schools, Aston Villa (apprentice June 1977, professional July 1979), Brighton & Hove Albion (£50,000, March 1984), BLUES (player-exchange for Mick Ferguson, October 1984), Shrewsbury Town (on loan, February 1987, signed permanently, March 1987), Hereford United (June 1987), Worcester City (free transfer, July 1991), Redditch United (on loan, October 1992), Merthyr Tydfil (season 1993-94).
Club honours: Aston Villa: European Super Cup winners 1982, World Club Championship 1983, FA Youth Cup & Southern Junior Floodlit Cup winners 1980.
Mark Jones was a talented full-back at Villa Park and was signed by his former manager, Ron Saunders, for Blues after a short spell with Brighton. His career at St Andrew's was hampered by injury and he was frequently asked to play in positions where he was not suited.

JONES, Paul Tony

Winger: 0+2 apps.
Born: Solihull 6 February 1974
Career: Knowle Juniors, St Peter's School, BLUES (YTS June 1990, professional February 1992), Moor Green (July 1993).
Paul Jones was mainly a reserve at St Andrew's, making just two appearances as a substitute, coming on both times because of injury to another player.

JONES, Roger

Goalkeeper: 4 apps.
Born Upton-on-Severn, 8 November 1946
Career: Portsmouth (apprentice, June 1963, professional November 1964), Bournemouth & Boscombe Athletic (May 1965), Blackburn Rovers (£30,000, January 1970), Newcastle United (March 1976 for a valuation of £20,000, but fee not paid), Stoke City (February 1977), Derby County (£25,000, July 1980), BLUES (on loan, February-March 1982), York City (£5,000, August 1982). Retired as a player in May 1985 when he was appointed assistant-coach at Bootham Crescent, later taking a similar position with Sunderland from November 1988 until May 1993.
Club honours: Blackburn: Division Three Champions 1984.

Representative honours: England (one Under-23 cap). Released by Portsmouth when they scrapped their reserve team, Roger Jones developed into a most consistent goalkeeper whilst with Bournemouth and if it had not been for a series of knee injuries he would have surely gone on to greater things. He was nearing the veteran stage when he joined Blues on loan, helping the club out in a crisis after becoming manager Jim Smith's last signing. Jones, a very safe handler of the ball, spent more than 20 years in the game and made over 750 appearances - 242 in the League for Blackburn.

JONES, Thomas

Inside-forward: 31 apps. 12 goals
Born: Prescot, Merseyside, 1885. Now deceased
Career: Bootle, Everton (1905), BLUES (September 1910), Southport Central (1912).
Tommy 'Prescot' Jones was a classy forward who found his career hampered by Scottish international 'Sandy' Young although he rarely let Everton down. After 15 games and five goals, he left Goodison Park for St Andrew's and proved to be the ideal replacement for Wally Freeman before striking up a fine understanding with Jack Hall. Injury curtailed his appearances during the 1911-12 season and he eventually joined the ambitious Southport club.

JONES, Thomas Trevellyan

Outside-left: 3 apps.
Born: Shrewsbury, December 1879. Now deceased
Career: Wolverhampton Wanderers (as an amateur 1898-99), Shrewsbury Town, BLUES (April 1904), Shifnal Town (season 1905-06)
An amateur winger, Tom Jones found League football too much for him. It was said of his debut (against Derby County, away in December 1904) that he lacked confidence and committed a sad error of judgement in persisting to be offside.

JONES, Walter

Centre-forward: 4 apps
Born: Coventry, 1859. Now deceased
Career: The Grove, BLUES (September 1881), Blackheath (1884)
After a season in the reserves, Wally Jones - described as a 'dashing forward' - got his chance in the first team in 1882 and turned out to be one of the most consistent players in the side, the high spot of his career being his four goals in as many minutes against Darlaston All Saints, a game which was called off after an hour's play with Blues winning 16-0, eight of the goals having arrived in the first 15 minutes of the second-half. He did not do too well in 1883-4 however, and was allowed to move to Blackheath.

JONES, William Henry

Centre-forward: 253 apps. 102 goals

Born: Tipton, 12 April 1880.
Died: Sussex, 1957
Career: Princes End, Smethwick Town, Halesowen
(September 1899), BLUES (professional August 1901),
Brighton & Hove Albion (June 1909), BLUES (re-signed
for £225, April 1912), Brighton & Hove Albion
(November 1913). Retired after WW1 and was later
employed as Brighton's trainer for 19 years, from
1920 until 1939.
Club honours: Blues; Division Two promotion 1903;
Brighton & Hove Albion: Southern League
champions 1910.
Representative honours: England (International trialist);
Football League XI (1).
Billy 'Bullit' Jones (known also as 'The Tipton Slasher')
was a rip-roaring, all-purpose centre-forward who simply
loved to have a crack at goal, with any foot, from almost
any distance (hence his nickname). He stood only 5ft
6ins tall but weighed 13 st 8lb and was all-action and
feared no-one. He spearheaded the Blues' attack with
great menace and it was noticeable that the decline of the
team in the late Edwardian era coincided with a series of
injuries to Jones. Blues eventually released him, thinking
he was past his best, but the team struggled badly
without him and he was re-signed two years later. For a
further twelve months or so, he held the front-line
together before age and injury caught up with him.
Upon the outbreak of WW1, he was one of the first
players to sign up with the Footballers' Battalion of the
Middlesex Regiment.

JONES, William T
Right-back; one app.
Born: Bournbrook, Birmingham, 1862. Now deceased
Career: Calthorpe, BLUES (September 1881), West
Bromwich Standard (1883)
Little known full-back Bill Jones' only first team
game for Blues was in the FA Cup-tie against Burton
Wanderers in 1885 when he stood in for the 'missing'
Jerry Hare.

JORDAN, John William
Forward: 25 apps. 3 goals
Born: Romford, Essex, 8 November 1921
Career: Bromley, Gray's Athletic, West Ham United (as
an amateur 1946), Juventus/Italy (August 1948), BLUES
(March 1949), Sheffield Wednesday (September 1950),
Tonbridge (June 1951), Bedford Town (July 1953
to 1954).
An energetic footballer, Johnny Jordan had one good
season with Spurs before throwing in his lot with the
Italy's Serie 'A' giants, Juventus. Unfortunately he had an
unhappy time in Turin, and after three weeks of
negotiations returned to England to sign for Blues, who
at the time were going through a bad patch. They needed
Jordan to score goals, but these never materialised in any

great number and shortly after the club had suffered
relegation he moved on to Wednesday. He was the
cousin of 'Clarrie' Jordan, the former Doncaster Rovers
and Sheffield Wednesday centre-forward.

KEARNS, John H
Left-back: 64 apps. one goal
Born: Nuneaton, April 1880
Died: Walsall, January 1949
Career: Brownhills Albion (August 1898), Hartshill
Unity, Coventry City (September 1903), BLUES (£100,
April 1906), Aston Villa (in a player-exchange deal,
February 1909), Bristol City (April 1912). Retired in
May 1915.
Jack Kearns was a wonderful positional player who allied
a biting tackle with some exciting kicking, having learned
his trade as understudy to Messrs Stokes and Glover,
both acknowledged masters of the full-back art. He also
understudied a fine pair of full-backs at Villa Park
(Lyons and Miles) but eventually became first-choice
with Bristol City, for whom he made almost 100
senior appearances.

KEATING, Reginald Edward
Inside-forward: 5 apps. one goal
Born: Halton near Leeds, 14 May 1904.
Died: Northumberland South, 13 October 1961.
Career: Halton Grange, Annfield Plain (August 1925),
Scotswood (April 1926), Newcastle United (October
1926), Lincoln City (season 1927-28), Gainsborough
(June 1928), Scarborough (May 1929), Stockport
County (May 1930), BLUES (June 1931), Norwich City
(June 1932), Cardiff City (June 1933), North Shields
(on trial, August 1933), Bath City (October 1933),
Cardiff City (January 1934), Doncaster Rovers (June
1936), Bournemouth & Boscombe Athletic
(November 1936), Carlisle United (1937).
Retired in September 1939.
Reg Keating was a pacy footballer, brother of the well-
travelled forward Albert Keating who was principally
with Bristol City and Blackburn Rovers. He lacked his
brother's consistency but still managed to score over 50
goals in his League career despite rarely settling in any
one place. A contemporary report claimed that 'he works
hard and puts across a lot of centres'.

KELLY, Alan Thomas
Goalkeeper: 6 apps.
Born: Preston, 11 August 1968
Career: Preston North End (apprentice June 1983,
professional September 1985), Sheffield United
(£200,000, July 1992), Blackburn Rovers (£675,000,
July 1999), Stockport County (on loan, April 2001),
BLUES (on loan, August-September 2001).
International honours: Republic of Ireland (34 full, one
Under-23 and Youth caps)

Blues recruited the vastly experienced and ageing Alan Kelly on loan as cover for Nico Vaesen and Ian Bennett. He had already accumulated well over 450 senior appearances before setting foot inside St Andrew's.

KELLY, John

Inside/centre-forward: 12 apps. one goal
Born: Hetton-le-Hole, 2 March 1913
Career: Hetton Juniors, Burnley (as an amateur, October 1930, professional November 1930), Newcastle United (in a player-exchange deal, April 1933), Leeds United (£1,150, February 1935), BLUES (January 1938), Bury (May 1939). Retired during WW2.
A highly individualistic player, often to the detriment of the team's efforts, Jack Kelly's career suffered accordingly and he was a regular first choice in only one of his nine League seasons. He was a butcher by trade and also worked as a part time magician.

KELLY, Michael John

Goalkeeper: 72+2 apps.
Born: Northampton 18 October 1942
Career: Islington Boys, Wimbledon (as an amateur 1958), Queen's Park Rangers (professional March 1966), BLUES (£18,000, August 1970), Minnesota Kicks/NASL (player-coach, 1976), Plymouth Argyle (reserve team manager 1976, manager May 1977 to February 1978), Fulham (assistant-manager, February 1978 to 1981), Crystal Palace (assistant-manager, 1981), Portsmouth (chief coach), West Bromwich Albion (assistant-manager/coach, September 1982 to February 1984), FA School of Excellence (as Chief coach) England goalkeeping coach (1987 to 1990), Liverpool (goalkeeping coach 1991), Coventry City (reserve team coach 1992-93), Switzerland (coach 1993-94), Middlesbrough (coach, November 1994); China (as coach, 1995 to 1997), thereafter continued coaching the England goalkeepers (at various levels) until 2000.
Club honours: Wimbledon; FA Amateur Cup winners 1963: Blues: Division Two promotion 1972.
Representative honours: England (3 Amateur caps)
Mike Kelly was a competent goalkeeper with a loud voice, who always commanded his penalty area with authority. He had an unusual pre-match ritual that involved kicking the base of both goal posts and touching the crossbar in the centre. He later developed into an exceptionally fine and well respected 'goalkeeping' coach who served overseas for a number of years.

KENDALL, Howard

Midfield: 134 apps. 18 goals
Born: Ryton-on-Tyne, 22 May 1946
Career: Ryton & District Schools, Preston North End (apprentice, June 1961, professional May 1963), Everton (£80,000, March 1967), BLUES (£350,000, February 1974 in a deal involving Bob Latchford), Stoke City (£40,000, August 1977), Blackburn Rovers (player-manager, June 1979 to May 1981), Everton (manager, May 1981 to June 1987), Athletic Bilbao/Spain (manager, June 1987 to November 1989), Manchester City (manager, December 1989 to November 1990), Everton Manager (November 1990 to December 1993), Xanthi/Greece (manager, May-November 1994), Notts County (manager, January-April 1995), Sheffield United (manager: 1995 to 1997).
Club honours: PNE: FA Cup runners-up 1964, Everton: FA Cup runners-up 1968, Division One champions 1970; (as manager) Blackburn: Division Three champions 1980; Everton; Division One champions 1985 & 1987, FA Cup winners 1984, runners up 1985, European Cup-winners Cup winners 1985, FA Charity Shield winners 1984, 1985 & 1986 (shared)
Representative honours: England (6 Under-23 caps, Youth & Schoolboy caps), Football League XI (1).
Howard Kendall rose to prominence when he was the youngest player ever to appear in an FA Cup Final, lining up for Preston against West Ham United in 1964, aged 17 years 345 days, a record he lost to Paul Allen of West Ham in 1980. On 8 May 1981 he became the youngest manager ever appointed by Everton (aged 34 years, 351 days) and he also played a few games in his first season back at Goodison Park. Kendall was voted 'Manager of the Year' for 1984-85 after steering the Merseysiders to the First Division title, the FA Cup Final and success in the European Cup-winners Cup. The 'complete midfielder', he teamed up exceedingly well with Colin Harvey and Alan Ball at Everton, where he became a firm favourite with the fans, who also took to him later as a manager. He skippered Blues and helped the club retain its First Division status. During his League career Kendall, always battling away tigerishly in the engine-room, amassed a total of 613 appearances and scored 65 goals.

KENDALL, Mark Ivan

Goalkeeper: one app.
Born: Nuneaton, 10 December 1961
Career: Aston Villa (apprentice 1979, professional November 1981), Northampton Town (July 1982), BLUES (March 1984), Tamworth (1986), Mile Oak Rovers, Hitchin Town, Worcester City, Atherstone Town, Bedworth United, Willenhall, Polesworth North Warwick FC.
Representative honours: England (Youth caps).
No relation to his namesake, formerly of Tottenham Hotspur, Newport County, Wolves and Swansea City, goalkeeper Mark Kendall understudied Tony Coton at St Andrew's and after leaving Blues drew up quite an impressive record on the non-League scene. He played on until he was 40.

KENDRICK, Kenneth
Centre-forward: 10 apps. 3 goals
Born: Bartley Green, Birmingham, May 1913.
Career: Bromsgrove Rovers, Halesowen Town, BLUES
(September 1936). Retired in June 1944 through injury.
A familiar figure in local non-League circles, Kenny
Kendrick was quite mature by the time he joined Blues
where he linked up with his father, Billy, the club's long
serving trainer. Rather on the small side for a centre
forward (5ft 8ins tall & barely 10st in weight) he was
not ideally suited for the rough and tumble aspects of
that position.

KENNA, Jeffrey Jude
Full-back: 46+1* apps one*goal.
Born: Dublin, 27 August 1970.
Career: Southampton (trainee, July 1986, professional
April 1989), Blackburn Rovers (£1.5 million, March
1995), Tranmere Rovers (on loan, March 2001), Wigan
Athletic (on loan, November 2001), BLUES (free
transfer, December 2001).
Club honours: Blues: Division One promotion 2002
International honours: Republic of Ireland (28* full, one
'B', 8 Under-21, Youth & Schoolboy caps).
Having lost his place at Blackburn and following loan
spells elsewhere, experienced right-back Jeff Kenna was
snapped up by Blues' manager Steve Bruce halfway
through the 2001-02 season - and he certainly gave some
sterling performances as the Premiership race hotted up.
Kenna made 132 appearances for Saints and 194 for
Rovers. He was recalled to the Irish squad for the
European Championship qualifiers in October 2002.
He scored his first goal for the Blues in the 1-1 draw
with Spurs in November 2002.

KENNEDY, Andrew John
Centre-forward: 62+25 apps. 21 goals
Born: Stirling, 8 October 1964
Career: Sauchie Athletic, Glasgow Rangers, Seiko
FC/Hong Kong (on loan), BLUES (£50,000, March
1985), Sheffield United (on loan, March 1987),
Blackburn Rovers (£50,000, June 1988), Watford
(£60,000, August 1990), Bolton Wanderers (on loan,
October 1991), Brighton & Hove Albion (September
1992), Gillingham (non-contract, September 1994 to
March 1995).
Club honours: Blues: Division Two promotion 1983
Representative honours: Scotland (Youth caps)
A hard-working player, always willing to take on
defenders, Andy Kennedy achieved instant popularity
with the fans at St Andrew's following several important
goals in Blues' 1982-83 promotion campaign. In the
long term, however, the faults in his technique (a poor
first-touch and tendency to lie too wide) became obvious

and he was latterly utilised mainly as substitute in the
hope that his pace would unsettle tiring defences.

KERNS, Frederick
Inside-right: one app.
Born: Paddington, London 1883. Now deceased
Career: Aston Villa (1906), BLUES (December 1908),
Bristol Rovers (July 1909).
A forward of limited experience, Fred Kerns arrived at
St Andrew's with no League games behind him, being
a makeweight in a player-exchange deal. A series of
lacklustre reserve appearances did nothing to enhance
his reputation and it took an injury crisis to push him
into the first team. He failed to make the senior side
at Bristol.

KIDD, Jack Walter
Inside-forward: 44 apps. 8 goals
Born: Glasgow 1884. Now deceased
Career: Glasgow Royal, St Johnstone, BLUES
(November 1910), Brierley Hill Alliance (August 1912
to May 1913)
An agile Scottish ball player who preferred the right side
but could turn out on the left if required, Jack Kidd later
became one of a group of former Blues players who took
pubs in the Brierley Hill area, being landlord of the Star
Inn, just down the road from the establishments run by
Jack Glover and Walter Wigmore.

KING, Henry Edward
Centre-forward: 30 apps. 7 goals
Born: Northampton, February 1886. Now deceased
Career: Evesham Star, Worcester City, BLUES (£150,
November 1907), Crewe Alexandra (July 1910),
Northampton Town (June 1913), Arsenal (April 1914),
Leicester City (October 1919, Brentford (September
1920, released in May 1921)
Ted King was a well-built forward, signed by Blues whilst
still learning his trade. The Blues' team of that era was
not much of a schooling establishment, but he developed
into a marksman of considerable talent, going on to score
67 goals in 99 games for Northampton and 26 in 37
outings for Arsenal, including a four-timer in the
Gunners' last game in Division Two to date. He also
netted Brentford's first-ever Football League hat trick.
One who got away? Possibly so.

KING, Sidney Harvey
Goalkeeper: 2 apps.
Born: Bordesley Green, Birmingham, 1914
Career: Coventry Road Methodists FC, Cradley Heath,
BLUES (October 1936), Hereford United
(season 1946-47)
Sid King came to Blues as first-choice goalkeeper before
WW2 but never looked like earning a first team place in
peacetime football. He had very few opportunities during

the hostilities and his two games for the club were both in the FA Cup competition as Gil Merrick's deputy.

KINGSTON, Ezekiel
Outside-right: one app.
Born: Walsall, 1858. Now deceased
Career: Wednesbury Old Athletic, BLUES (April 1881), Bloxwich Strollers (1883).
Ezekiel Kingston had only a brief flurry in Blues' first team, playing in the FA Cup-tie against Stafford Road and in three friendly matches, including an 18-1 win over Elwell's of Wednesbury.

KINSEY, Noel
Inside-right: 173 apps. 56 goals
Born: Treorchy; 24 December 1925
Career: Treorchy Amateurs (1938), Cardiff City (as an amateur 1941), Norwich City (professional, May 1947), BLUES (June 1953), Port Vale (February 1958), King's Lynn (1961), Lowestoft Town (player-coach, June 1962 to August 1966). Afterwards he worked for a firm of Solicitors in the Norwich Union Insurance offices before retiring to live in the village of Thorpe, near Norwich.
Club honours: Blues: Division Two Champions 1955, FA Cup runners-up 1956. Lowestoft: Eastern Counties League runners-up & Cup winners.
Representative honours: Wales (7 full caps).
Noel Kinsey was a scheming inside forward or occasional wing-half, who earned a great reputation at Norwich before becoming the brains of the Blues' attack during the mid-1950s. As well as making goals, he showed a fair ability to take chances himself, particularly in his first three seasons at St Andrew's when he found the net no fewer than 42 times. He had the pleasure of scoring for Blues in the 1956 FA Cup Final at Wembley.

KIRBY, Conyers
Outside-right: one app.
Born: Bordesley Green, Birmingham, 1884,
Died: Spain, 1945.
Career: Royal Army Medical Corps, Fulham (1905), BLUES (August 1906), Blackpool (July 1907), Kidderminster Harriers (1908), Willenhall Pickwick (1911), Fulham (1913). Retired in the summer of 1918; he later emigrated to Spain where he took up referring.
A sprint champion in the Army, 'Con' Kirby never gained a regular first team place with either of his major clubs, totalling a mere six games in his League career.
He refereed Blues' friendly against Real Madrid in May 1923 when he sent-off Alex McClure for arguing at a penalty decision.

KIROVSKI, Jovan
Midfielder: 7+8*app. 2 goals
Born: Escondido, California, USA, 18 March 1976.

Career: La Jolla Nomads (California), Manchester United (July 1995), Borussia Dortmund/Germany, Sporting Lisbon/Portugal, Crystal Palace (£350,000, August 2001), BLUES (August 2002).
Representative honours: USA (54* full caps)
Steve Bruce's first signing for Crystal Palace was right-sided midfielder Jovan Kirovski, 6ft 1ins tall and almost 12st 5lbs in weight. The American then followed his manager to St Andrew's after failing to agree a new contract at Selhurst Park. A very competitive player, he was released from Old Trafford without ever making the first team, but is hoping to make his mark in the Premiership - his lifetime ambition.

KLONER, Hymie
Right-half: 1 apps. 0 goals
Born: Johannesburg, South Africa, 23 May 1929
Career: Marist Brothers FC (Transvaal, South Africa), BLUES (November 1950). Returned to South Africa in December 1950.
Hymie Kloner was another of the string of South African trialists who were recruited by Blues boss Bob Brocklebank in the early 1950s. Unfortunately he failed to impress but did get one League outing, more than a lot of his colleagues managed. His parents were Polish.

KNIGHT, Richard
Goalkeeper: 0+1 app.
Born: Burton-on-Trent, 3 August 1979
Career: Burton Albion, Derby County (professional, June 1997), Carlisle United (on loan, March 1999), BLUES (on loan, August 1999), Hull City (on loan, October 1999), Macclesfield Town (on loan, December 1999), Oxford United (on loan, January 2000, signed permanently on a free transfer, March 2000), Colchester United (on loan March 2002).
Representative Honours: England (Youth caps)
Standing an inch over six foot and weighing 14 stones, Richard Knight has all the assets required to be a League goalkeeper. He finally made his mark with Oxford, winning the club's 'Player of the Season' award in 2000-01.

KUHL, Martin
Midfielder/defender: 123+9 apps. 6 goals
Born; Finchley, 10 January 1965
Career: Schools, BLUES (apprentice, June 1981, professional January 1983), Sheffield United (player-exchange deal involving Steve Wigley, March 1987), Watford (rated at £300,000 in player-exchange deal with Tony Agana, February 1988), Portsmouth (£125,000, September 1988), Derby County (£650,000, September

1992), Notts County (on loan, September 1994), Bristol City (£300,000 December 1994), Farnborough Town (late 1990s), Weymouth (August 2002)

Club honours: Blues: Division Two promotion 1985

Martin Kuhl was an enthusiastic, hard-working player who took time to settle before becoming a regular first teamer with Blues, but his adaptability led him to appearing in all outfield positions for the club in his first two seasons as a professional before he eventually chose to play as a midfield workhorse. He scored the goal against Leeds United that led to the infamous riot at St Andrew's. He was set to sign permanently for Notts County but they shipped him back to Derby after he was sent-off, eventually departing to Bristol City.

LAING, Robert Smith
Outside-left: 19 apps. 2 goals
Born: Glasgow, 1 February 1925.
Died Birmingham, September 1985
Career: Falkirk, BLUES (January 1946), Watford (June 1950 to May 1952), Worcester City, Halesowen Town, Brierley Hill Alliance, Brush Sports.
Retired in May 1957.
At under 5ft 5ins tall and 9st 7lb in weight, Bobby Laing was one of the smallest players ever to pull on a Blues shirt. His first appearance for the club came during WW2 when he was stationed at Hednesford, and he made an explosive start to his League career, netting within five minutes of his debut. He remained as second choice winger for some time before his eventual transfer to Watford, for whom he scored eight goals in 60 League games prior to rounding off his playing days in West Midlands non-League football.

LANE, Henry
Outside/inside-right: 2 apps.
Born: Hednesford, 21 March 1909.
Died: Cannock, March 1977
Career: Hednesford Town, Rugeley Villa, Bloxwich Strollers, BLUES, (December 1930), Southend United (May 1933), Plymouth Argyle (March 1938), Southend United (May 1946). Retired in May 1949, aged 40. Guested for Port Vale during WW2.
Harry Lane occupied most forward positions during his career, at barely 5ft 6ins tall he was a little short for the role as leader of the attack, and with Johnny Crosbie and George Briggs already well established, he did not get much of a look in. He proved a durable performer in the lower Divisions.

LANE, James Charles
Centre-forward: 67 apps. 26 goals.
Born: Watford, 11 July 1892.
Died: Abbots Langley, 27 February 1959.
Career: Watford (amateur 1909), Ferencvaros Torna (Hungary), Watford (season 1912-13), Sunderland (July 1913), Blackpool (November 1913), BLUES (£3,600, March 1920), Millwall (August 1922), Barcelona (coach, September 1924), Watford Printing Works FC (season 1935-36).
Club honours: Blues: Division Two champions 1921
Representative honours: Football Combination XI(1924)
A printer by trade, 'Joe' Lane started playing football seriously during a two-year attachment to a printing works in Budapest. On his return to England he quickly graduated to League football and became a quality marksman. Blues surprised everyone when they paid a record fee for his services from Blackpool but he immediately proved to be the perfect foil to Harry Hampton, helping the club win promotion from the Second Division. A real sharp-shooter, he was still scoring goals for Watford Printing Works FC when well into his 40s. Lane, who served in the Hertfordshire Yeomanry during WW2, was a very wealthy man (his father owned a printing company), and he tended to flaunt it, boasting that he never wore the same shirt twice and allowing his team-mates to have his cast offs.

LANE, John Geoffrey
Forward: 50 apps. 14 goals
Born: Selly Oak, Birmingham 10 November 1931.
Career: Selly Oak Old Blacks, Boldmere St Michael's, BLUES (professional, September 1949), Notts County (July 1956), Hinckley Athletic (August 1959), Kidderminster Harriers, Evesham United (June 1961).
Club honours: Blues: Division Two champions 1955.
Jackie Lane was a big, strong, sturdily built attacker who was the club's first long-throw expert and who proved a capable understudy for all forward positions but who enjoyed himself most when given an inside berth. He played in contact lenses, which came as a surprise to Notts County's manager who learnt of the fact only when Lane put them in to sign his contract with the Magpies. He went on to score 19 goals in 57 League games for County. His early years were spent as a boxer.

LANE, Moses Alexander Edmund
Centre-forward: 15 apps. 4 goals
Born: Willenhall, 17 February 1895.
Died: Cannock, 14 July 1949
Career: Willenhall Pickwick, Willenhall Town (August

1920), Walsall (December 1920), Willenhall (May 1921), BLUES (April 1922), Derby County (July 1924), Wellington Town (May 1925), Worcester City (August 1926), Walsall (June 1927), Brierley Hill Alliance (July 1929), Netherton, Dudley. Retired in 1933.

'Mo' Lane served in France and Italy during WW1 when his gallantry earned him the Military Medal. He was a player noted for his speed rather than his general footballing ability. His best football was played with Walsall for whom he scored 51 goals in only 57 League games.

LANGAN, David Francis

Right-back: 102 apps. 3 goals
Born: Dublin, 15 February 1957
Career: Bath Rangers, Cherry Orchard FC, Derby County (apprentice, June 1974, professional February 1975), BLUES (for a record fee of £350,000, July 1980) Oxford United (free transfer, August 1984), Leicester City (on loan, October 1987), AFC Bournemouth (on loan, November 1987, signed permanently December 1987), Peterborough United (July 1988), Ramsey Town, Holbeach United, Rothwell Town, Mirlees Blackstone FC (season 1990-91). Retired fully in 1992 with back injury - later employed in the security business.
Club honours: Oxford: Division Two champions 1985, League Cup winners 1986.
Representative honours: Republic of Ireland (25 full caps, Youth & Schoolboy caps).

David Langan was a very influential attacking right-back who was signed by Blues' manager Jim Smith for a record fee, having previously made 155 senior appearances for the Rams. Langan said he wanted to be with a more successful club (Derby's fortunes were dipping) and after leaving the Baseball Ground he became a firm favourite with the St Andrew's supporters. Alas, a series of knee injuries disrupted his run in the first team and he was eventually given a free transfer by Ron Saunders in 1984. Langan subsequently rejoined his former boss Jim Smith at Oxford where he regained some of his earlier form before injuries caught up with him again. He was forced to withdraw from major competition in 1989-90 after totting up in excess of 500 appearances, including games in all four Divisions.

LANGLEY, Kevin James

Midfielder: 86+2 apps. 2 goals
Born: St Helens, 24 May 1964
Career: Wigan Athletic (apprentice June 1980, professional May 1982), Everton (£100,000, July 1986), Manchester City (£150,000, March 1987), Chester City (on loan, January 1988), BLUES (£100,000, March 1988), Wigan Athletic (£50,000, September 1990), Halifax Town (August 1994), Bangor City.
Club honours: Wigan: Freight Rover Trophy runners-up 1986; Everton: FA Charity Shield winners 1986; Bangor

City: League of Wales champions 1995.

Kevin Langley was a tall, elegant ball-playing midfielder who earned a high reputation as a youngster with Wigan before his abortive flirtation with First Division football. On his arrival at St Andrew's he was touted as the vital cog in Blues' engine room, and the man to provide the chances that would take the team back into the First Division. Unfortunately, he never looked comfortable with the Blues' style of play although he later showed flashes of his old form after returning to Springfield Park.

LAPPIN, Hubert Henry

Outside-left: 12 apps. 2 goals
Born: Manchester, 1879,
Died: Liverpool, May 1925
Career: Springfield FC, Oldham Athletic (October 1900) Newton Heath (April 1901), Grimsby Town (August 1903), Rossendale United (August 1904), Clapton Orient (August 1906), Chester (1907), BLUES (August 1909), Chirk (1910), Hurst, Macclesfield.
Club honour: Chester: Welsh Cup runners up 1909

Hubert Lappin showed great skill on both wings - Blues and Grimsby used him on the left whilst Newton Heath and Orient played him on the right. He was rarely mentioned in reports of Blues matches, so it appears that he did not have a great impact on the team's overall play.

LARKIN, Bernard Patrick

Inside-forward/wing-half: 92 apps. 29 goals
Born: Digbeth, Birmingham, 11 January 1936
Career: Lea Hall Youth Club, Rockwood Albion, BLUES (amateur July 1952, professional July 1954), Norwich City (£10,000, March 1960), Doncaster Rovers (£5,000, September 1961), Watford (£4,000, June 1962), Lincoln City (November 1964), Wisbech Town (July 1966), Nuneaton Borough, King's Lynn, Stevenage Athletic, Attleborough Town (coach, 1975). He later settled in Norwich where he worked for Lyons, selling cakes.

'Bunny' Larkin was a cheerful, fair-haired player who, in 1958, was converted from an average wing-half into an exciting forward. He repaid the club's faith in him by netting 23 goals in 1958-59 before a loss of form cost him his place in the side. He was nicknamed 'Rip Van Winkle' after oversleeping and missing the coach on the way to a vital European match.

LATCHFORD, David Barry

Goalkeeper: 239 apps
Born: King's Heath, Birmingham, 9 April 1949
Career: Brandwood Secondary Modern School, South Birmingham Schools, BLUES (apprentice June 1964, professional May 1966), Motherwell (July 1977), Bury (March 1979), Barnsley (non-contract 1980), Redditch United (1981), Cheltenham Town (1983), East Worle (1985), later Solihull Borough (coach, 1992 to 1995).
Club honours: Blues: Division Two promotion 1972, FA

Youth Cup runners up 1967.

He is the eldest of a trio of brothers who all starred in Midlands football in the 1970s, he and Bob (q.v) played for Blues while Peter (also a goalkeeper) served with West Bromwich Albion. Dave Latchford showed great promise as a youngster and was called up into the England Youth squad but failed to gain a place due to the brilliance of Peter Shilton. He followed his brother (Bob) into the Blues' first team at the end of the 1968-69 season and made an immediate impression. Despite his bulky appearance, he was surprisingly agile and was also a clean handler of the ball, possessing the ability to make the occasional impossible save, although he conceded eight goals in his own testimonial match. After some years as a funeral director, he became a superintendent of cemeteries for Solihull whilst his son, Oliver, played for Solihull Borough and the West Midlands Police team.

LATCHFORD, Robert Dennis

Centre-forward: 190+4 apps. 84 goals
Born: King's Heath, Birmingham 18 January 1951
Career: Brandwood Secondary School, South Birmingham & Warwickshire County Schools, BLUES (apprentice, May 1967, professional August 1968), Everton (£350,000, February 1974 in deal involving Howard Kendall & Archie Styles), Swansea City (£125,000, July 1981), NAC Breda/Holland (February 1984), Coventry City (June 1984), Lincoln City (July 1985), Newport County (on loan, January-May 1986), Merthyr Tydfil (August 1986). Later Director of Alvechurch FC and also returned to work with Blues' Commercial Department in the mid-1990s, securing a coaching position at St Andrew's in 1999-2000.
Club honours: Blues: FA Youth Cup runners-up 1967, Division Two promotion 1972; Everton: Football League Cup runners-up 1977; Swansea: Welsh Cup winners 1982 & 1983; Merthyr: Welsh Cup winners 1987.
Representative honours: England (12 full caps, 6 Under-23 caps, 4 Youth Caps): Football League XI (1)
Brandwood School has produced several quality players over the years, but few if any better than Bob Latchford, a bearded, swashbuckling target man, who, like his elder brother Dave (q.v) was highly-rated as a youngster. Latchford who made his League bow for Blues during an injury crises, quickly figured on the scoresheet, but during the next year or so he found it hard to adapt to the top-class game. However, he battled on and eventually came good in season 1970-71 when he began a terrific strike-force with Trevor Francis and Phil Summerill. The arrival of Bob Hatton strengthened the attack even further and in 1971-72 Latchford took full advantage of this to net 30 goals in a season for the first time (and in doing so emulated winger Alex Govan's feat of 1956-57). Tall, well built, good in the air and with a thumping shot (mainly right-footed), his power and aggression inside the box made him a handful for any

defence. Eventually, with Blues facing another relegation battle, his transfer request was granted and he moved to Everton for what was then a League record fee. At Goodison Park he was an instant success, scoring seven times in his first 13 outings. In 1977-78 he was presented with a cheque for £10,000 by a national newspaper when he became the first player to register 30 goals in Division One since 1972. He stayed with Everton for seven years, during which time he scored 138 goals in 288 games.

LAYTON, George

Left-half/forward: 17 apps, 3 goals
Born: Stourbridge, 1865. Now deceased
Career: Stourbridge Royal, Cradley St Luke's (1896), Smethwick Wesleyan Rovers (season 1897-98), BLUES (September, 1898), Dudley Town (1901), Soho Villa (1903-04).
George Layton was a long striding half-back who was picked up from local non-League soccer. He had a taste for joining in the attack and possessed a cracking good shot, often delivered from well outside the penalty area. He dropped out of the Blues side when Walter Wigmore was switched to defence.

LAZARIDIS, Stanley

Winger: 97+37 apps*. 4 goals*
Born: Perth, Australia, 16 August 1972
Career: West Adelaide FC (Australia), West Ham United (£300,000, September 1995), BLUES (£1.6 million, July 1999).
Club honours: Blues: League Cup runners-up 2001, Division One promotion 2002.
Representative honours: Australia (55 full, 8 U-23 & Youth caps)
When on song Stan Lazaridis is a very dangerous customer who loves to take on defenders, race to the bye-line and whip over a cross (left-footed). Technically a wide-midfielder, he has excellent ball control and packs a fair shot when he chooses to deliver.

LEA, George Isaac

Right-half: 28 apps. one goal
Born: Donnington Wood, Shropshire 17 February 1911.
Died: Dawley, Shropshire 24 October 1972
Career: Oakengates Town, BLUES (September 1932), Millwall (May 1937 to May 1943 when he retired). Guested for Wrexham and Wellington Town during World War 2.
Club honours: Millwall: Division Three (South) champions 1938, Division Three (South) Cup winners 1937.
George Lea was originally quite a spindly youngster but after joining Blues he put on stones in weight and developed into a powerful half-back with prodigious shot. His first team opportunities were always going to be limited with Lew Stoker already established at right-

half, but the durable Lea remained as a patient and understanding deputy for a number of years. He was a breeder of pigeons and one of his customers was the champion flat race jockey Sir Gordon Richards.

LEAKE, Alexander

Defender: 221 apps. 23 goals
Born: Small Heath, Birmingham 11 July 1871.
Died Birmingham, 29 March 1938
Career: Jenkins Street & Green Lane Schools (Bordesley Green), Hoskins & Sewell FC, Kings Heath Albion, Saltley Gas Works FC, Singers FC, Hopkins & Sewell FC (again), Old Hill Wanderers (July 1892), BLUES (July 1894), Aston Villa (June 1902), Burnley (December 1907), Wednesbury Old Athletic (July 1910). Retired as player in June 1912 and became Crystal Palace trainer a month later, holding office until May 1915; Merthyr Town (trainer from October 1919 to July 1920), Walsall's (first team trainer from September 1932 to May 1933). He later coached at schools and colleges around the UK for six years.
Club honours: Aston Villa: FA Cup winners 1905.
Representative honours: England (5 full caps).
Football League XI (1).
'With Alex Leake, football is a pleasure. He will crack a joke with an opponent while he robs him of the ball' so said *Rover* in 1906. A genuine 'Brummagem Button', Leake was a good tempered, honest worker, whose stamina was unsurpassed. He never played to the crowd, but always battled well for his team. He was as safe as houses, never overdoing to fancy stuff, and was always hard to beat in 50-50 situations. A fine tackler, superb at intercepting long passes, his unfamiliar humour made him a great favourite with the fans. He skippered Blues for six years immediately prior to leaving, and during a fine career amassed 464 senior appearances for his three major clubs, including 140 for Villa. Leake was chosen as reserve for England at the age of 41. An excellent swimmer (he could dive to the bottom of the brine baths at Droitwich to retrieve a coin) he was also a fine all-round athletic, specialising in the 400 yards and hurdles events. A keen gardener and a blacksmith by trade, he was cousin of Blues' Jimmy Windridge (q.v.).

LEATHERBARROW, Charles Arnold

Inside-right: 5 apps. 3 goals
Born: Liverpool 1869. Now deceased
Career: Northwich Victoria, Rotherham Town, Walsall Town Swifts, (December (1893), BLUES (September 1894), Millwall (April 1895), Chatham (Sep 1896).
Club honours: Millwall: Southern League Title 1896
Stocky and very quick off the mark, Charlie 'Ginger' Leatherbarrow was a regular goalscorer wherever he went. Although he struggled at Blues he later had several highly successful years in the Southern League.

LEE, John Sebastian

Forward: 7 apps. 3 goals

Born: Walsall Wood, 1869. Now deceased
Career: Walsall Unity, BLUES (September 1893), Old Hill Wanderers (January 1895), Bilston United (1897), Darlaston (for two seasons 1899-1901).
Jack Lee, a diminutive sharpshooter, had a short spell in the first team and did well and it was only due to the ability of Billy Walton that he found himself out in the cold for long periods. He remained in his native Midlands rather than join another League club.

LEEK, Kenneth

Centre/inside-forward: 120 apps. 61 goals
Born: Ynysybwl near Pontypridd, South Wales 26 July 1935
Career: Pontypridd Youth Club, Ynysybwl Boys FC, Northampton Town (professional August 1952), Leicester City (May 1958), Newcastle United (£25,000, June 1961), BLUES (£23,000, November 1961), Northampton Town (£9,000, December 1964), Bradford City (£10,000, November 1965), Rhyl Town (August 1968), Ton Pentre (February 1970). Retired in June 1970. Later worked for the Ford Motor Company at Dagenham for many years after ending his career.
Club honours: Blues: Football League Cup winners 1963
Representative honours: Wales (13 full caps, one Under-23 cap)
Ken Leek was born next door to Don Dearson in the same Welsh village but did not play any sort of soccer until he was 14 years of age, having attended two rugby-playing schools prior to that. However, he quickly developed into a fine marksman who went on to total 147 goals in 397 League games during a very useful career. Leek who had a benefit match with Northampton, was in dispute with Leicester and as a result was sensationally dropped by his manager Matt Gillies on the morning of the 1961 FA Cup Final (v. Spurs) having scored in all the previous rounds. This inevitably led to his transfer to Newcastle a month later, but he failed to settle on Tyneside and soon joined Blues, where his goal touch returned to the team's advantage. His strikes were particularly important during the 1962-63 League Cup run and he crowned his career at St Andrew's with two goals in the Final against Aston Villa. From then on his playing days moved in a downward spiral.

LEES, Terence

Full back/defender: 18+1 apps.
Born: Stoke-on-Trent, 30 June 1952
Career: Stoke City (apprentice June 1968, professional July 1969), Crewe Alexandra (on loan, March-April 1975), San Jose Earthquakes/NASL (on loan, 1975), Port Vale (August 1975), Sparta Rotterdam/Holland (1976), Roda JC/Holland (1977-78), BLUES (July

1979), Newport County (August 1981), Altrincham, Morning Star FC/Hong Kong, DS79 Dordrecht/Holland, Stafford Rangers (1982-83), Scunthorpe United (non-contract, September 1984 to May 1985), Macclesfield Town, Kidsgrove Athletic, Hanley Town, Meir KA/Staffs County (coach).

A versatile defender - used initially by Blues as a sweeper - Terry Lees was virtually a permanent understudy during his time at St Andrew's. A useful club cricketer, he later became a sports centre manager in his native Potteries.

LEGG, Andrew

Midfielder/defender: 35+14 apps. 5 goals
Born: Neath, South Wales, 28 July 1966
Career: Briton Ferry FC, Swansea City (August 1988), Notts County (£275,000, July 1993), BLUES (February 1996), Ipswich Town (on loan, November 1997), Reading (£75,000, February 1998), Peterborough United (on loan, October 1998), Cardiff City (free transfer, December 1998).
Club honours: Swansea: Welsh Cup winners 1989, 1991; Notts County: Anglo-Italian Cup winners 1995; Cardiff: Division Three promotion 2002
Representative honours: Wales (6 full caps)

A long-throw expert in his younger days, Andy Legg, initially a left-sided midfielder, had good pace and smart footwork. He spent two useful seasons at St Andrew's and later, as full-back, became captain of Cardiff City, leading them into the Second Division. In 2002 he reached the milestone of 550 appearances (68 goals).

LEGGATT. Graham

Forward: 17+ 3 apps. 3 goals
Born: Aberdeen, 20 June 1934
Career: Torry Former Pupils FC, Banks O'Dee FC, Aberdeen (1953), Fulham (£16,000, August 1958), BLUES (£15,000, January 1967), Rotherham United (July 1968), Aston Villa (assistant trainer-coach, July 1969), Bromsgrove Rovers (as a player, March 1970), Toronto Star/NASL (manager, 1971-72). Remained in Canada after retiring from football.
Club honours: Aberdeen; Scottish League champions 1955, Scottish FA Cup runners-up 1954, Scottish League Cup winners 1956. Fulham Division Two promotion 1959.
Representative honours: Scotland (18 full caps, 1 Under-23 cap, Youth International): Scottish League XI & Football League XI appearances with Aberdeen (5) & Fulham (1) respectively

In his heyday, Graham Leggatt was a goalscoring forward, fast and decisive, usually found at outside-right. After a successful career in Scotland he moved to Fulham and in his first season at the Cottage played a vital part in helping the London club win promotion to Division One. He continued to score at a fair rate, averaging a goal every two games, until his move to Blues. By this time he had lost most of his speed and looked rather out of condition, but he remained a prolific marksman at Football Combination level. During his days with Blues he earned some extra money as a male model. Leggatt, who scored 127 goals in 254 League games whilst at Craven Cottage, is now a prominent sports commentator on Canadian television.

LEONARD, Arthur Ralph (Bamford)

Inside-right: 75 apps. 26 goals
Born: Leicester, 1874. Now deceased
Career: 17th Leicestershire Regiment, Leicester Fosse (1895), Rushden Town, Sheppey United, Glentoran, BLUES (£120, November 1901), Stoke (January 1904), St Bernard, Clapton Orient, Plymouth Argyle, Reading (1909-10).

This player appeared under a pseudonym for the latter half of his career, his real name being Arthur Leonard Bamford. He joined the club in bizarre circumstances: Blues saw him play with the Irish side Glentoran and were so impressed that they immediately signed him for £120. Leicester, however, were also represented at that match and recognised him as their absentee player, Arthur Bamford. After being accused of this, he disappeared for several days, sending a telegram to his wife saying that he had fled to America. He later resurfaced in Bristol and was persuaded to return to Birmingham to face the music. He admitted that he was, indeed, one Arthur Bamford and the case was settled when Blues paid Leicester a further £20 for his services. It proved to be money well spent for Leonard became a big hit with the Blues' supporters, a real bag of tricks, capable of scoring goals as well as making them for his colleagues. Indeed, he was regarded as the star forward in the side.

LEONARD, John

Outside-right; 9 apps. one goal
Born: Gloucester, 1876. Now deceased
Career: Bedminster, Bristol City (August 1899), BLUES (November 1899), Cheltenham Town (May 1900).

An intricate dribbler, Jack Leonard had one fine season with Bedminster in the Southern League, but when they merged with the Bristol City club he fell from favour. His face never really fitted in at Blues either and he quickly moved back to the West Country.

LESLIE, Alexander James

Left-half: 143 apps
Born: Greenock, Scotland, April 1902.
Died: Greenock, 1974
Career: Greenock Wayfarers, Port Glasgow Juniors, St Mirren (1919-21), Houghton-le-Spring FC (from 1921), Morton (season 1923-24), St Mirren (season 1924-25), Torquay United (£100, August 1925), BLUES (£750, April 1927), Retired in May 1932.

Club Honour: Blues: FA Cup runners-up 1931.

Alec Leslie was primarily a defensive wing-half, solid in the tackle despite his relatively slight build (5ft 7ins tall & 10st 3lbs in weight). He scored only six goals during his career, five coming from the penalty-spot while playing for Torquay in the Southern and Western Leagues - the other was a well-struck 35-yarder which crept through the goalkeepers legs! Leslie had a great influence in midfield and was a player who loved to push-pass the ball through to his forwards, using the toe-end rather than the instep of his boot. He became a regular in the Blues side in season 1927-28 and after a niggling knee injury ended his career he became landlord of the Freemason's Arms in Hawkes Street (Birmingham) and later worked for the Inland Revenue before returning to his native Scotland.

LESTER, Frank

Full-back: 78 apps 0 goals.
Born: Wednesbury, 1870. Now deceased
Career: Walsall Unity, BLUES (1895), Walsall (1901)
A sturdy, reliable back, Frank Lester demonstrated more power than finesse in this play. His partnership with Billy Pratt was regarded as one of the finest in the League.

LEWIS, William Jasper

Outside-right: 3 apps. 2 goals
Born: Bordesley Green, Birmingham 1871. Now deceased
Career: Windsor Street Gas Depot FC, BLUES (February (1894), Hereford Town (1896), Stourbridge, Leicester Fosse (May 1902 to April 1903)
Bill Lewis was a winger with a goalscoring bent who was perhaps unlucky to have played so few games for Blues. He later resurfaced with Leicester as a centre-forward but managed only three goals in 31 appearances before drifting out of League football in 1903.

LEWIS, Wilson Arnold

Centre-forward: 21 apps. 7 goals
Born: Evesham, 1873. Now deceased
Career: Hereford Thistle (1895), BLUES (August 1897), Bromyard FC (May 1898)
Wilson Lewis swapped the chocolate and yellow of Thistle for the blue of Small Heath and although rather slow for a forward he did reasonably well during the first part of the 1897-98 season, but his form dropped off after Christmas and the arrival of Bob McRoberts left him surplus to requirements, so he moved back to Herefordshire.

LIDDELL, George M

Wing-half/full-back: 345 apps. 6 goals
Born: Durham, 14 July 1895. Died: Hampshire, circa 1970
Career: Johnston Grammar School, City of Leeds Training College, The Honourable Artillery Company XI, Duke of Wellington FC, the Army (played rugby),

Yorkshire Amateurs, South Shields (as an amateur, 1916), BLUES (professional, May 1920). Retired in April 1932 and became team manager at St Andrew's (June 1933 to May 1939) in succession to Leslie Knighton, who had moved to Chelsea.

Club honours: Blues: FA Cup runners-up 1931.

George Liddell was a dapper, moustachio'd defender, cool under pressure, a fine positional player who possessed a healthy kick and strong tackle and could always be relied upon to give a solid performance. He began his career as a wing-half where he prompted his forwards well and notched a few goals with his powerful long range shooting. He switched to full-back after the departure of Frank Womack, and his skills shone above the average player in that position, being a defender who preferred to pass the ball rather than lash it blindly downfield. In later years he combined his football with a career as a teacher with the result that he frequently missed midweek away matches. Not the most popular of players with his team-mates, it was a surprise when Liddell was elected as Blues' boss and there was considerable dressing room rancour throughout his managerial career (Liddell had always wanted to manage Blues and his wish was granted by the club's Chairman Harry Morris). He was later a teacher at Leigh Road School in Washwood Heath and also at Cotteridge Infants' School before becoming headmaster of Handsworth Secondary Modern School. He retired to Hampshire in 1960 at the age of 65.

LIMPAR, Anders Erik

Winger: 4+1 apps.
Born: Solna, Sweden, 24 September 1965.
Career: Cremonese (Italy), Arsenal (£1 million, August 1990), Everton (£1.6 million, March 1994), BLUES (£100,000, January 1997, contract cancelled, May 1997). He later became a football agent.
Club honours: Arsenal: League Division One champions 1991; Everton: FA Cup & Charity Shield winners 1995
Representative honours: Sweden (69 full caps)
Anders Limpar was a crowd-pleasing winger who was equally at home on either flank. He possessed great pace and a powerful shot, and in an attempt to open up the play, it was a bold decision by Blues' manager Trevor Francis to bring him to St Andrew's. Although he showed some signs of his former greatness, the move backfired somewhat when he had his contract cancelled by the club after failing to turn up for a reserve team game. Limpar made 116 senior appearances for the Gunners and 83 for Everton.

LINDON, Albert Edward

Goalkeeper; 7 apps
Born: Aston, Birmingham 24 January 1891.
Died: Dowlais, Wales, 1 October 1976
Career: Vaughan United, Delta Metal Works FC (1907),

Birmingham Fruiters FC, BLUES (June 1910), Aston Villa (August 1911), Barnsley (May 1912), Coventry City (£1,000, May 1919), Merthyr Town (August 1920, becoming player-manager, August 1924), Charlton Athletic (December 1927, then player-manager, January 1928, player/assistant-manager, June 1928). Retired as player in 1931 and became caretaker-manager at The Valley in December 1932, taking over as assistant-manager, May 1933 to March 1934; Arsenal (scout 1947 to December 1949), Cardiff City (scout, January 1950), Merthyr Tydfil (two spells as manager: firstly from June 1958 to May 1959 and then from August-November 1959), Swindon Town (scout, 1960-61), Newport County (scout, October 1961). Quit football in 1963. Club honours: Merthyr: Welsh Cup runners-up 1924; Charlton: Division Three (South) Champions 1928-29, Aston Villa: Birmingham Senior Cup & League medals. Albert Lindon's long career in football began as a youngster fresh from works soccer. A tall, well-built goalkeeper, he was unable to make his mark in his hometown, his best years coming probably with Charlton, a club he served in most capacities during his time at The Valley. He put on quite a bit of weight later on in life and at 16 stone was by far the heaviest man ever to play for Charlton. Lindon guested for several teams during WW1 including West Bromwich Albion,

LINES, Wilton

Forward: 7 apps. one goal
Born: Birmingham 1874. Now deceased
Career: BLUES (season 1898-99)
Will Lines was given a run out in most forward positions by Blues but proved unable to replace any of the regulars.

LINFORD, John Russell

Centre-forward: 1+1 apps.
Born: Norwich, 6 February 1957
Career: Gorleston, Ipswich Town (August 1981), Colchester United (on loan, January 1983). Southend United (on loan, March 1983), DS79 Dordrecht/Holland, FC Den Haag/Holland, Ipswich Town, BLUES (on loan, November 1984), NAC Breda/Holland, Fortuna Sittard/Holland (1985), FC Zurich/Switzerland (1988), FC Utrecht/Holland (1988), Bury Town (1989), Go Ahead Eagles/Holland (January 1990), Fortuna Sittard/Holland (July 1990), Wrexham, King's Lynn.
John Linford was a lanky striker whose brief spell with Blues was far from impressive, although he proved more successful on the continent and scored almost 80 goals in Dutch football alone.

LINLEY, Edward A

Outside-left: 118 apps.11 goals
Born: East Retford, 26 September 1894. Now deceased
Career: Worksop Town, BLUES (£800 plus Tom Pike,

December 1920), Nottingham Forest (1926-27), Sutton Town (1927-28), Mansfield Town (March 1928).
Club honours: Blues: Division Two champions 1920-21
Balding and knock-kneed, Ted Linley was not an obvious choice as a professional footballer. Appearances can be deceptive, however, and he showed himself a guileful performer for several years, fighting off the challenges of a host of players who were bought to replace him. He had only short spells at Forest and Mansfield.

LINNECOR, Albert Roy

Wing half/inside-forward: 18 apps.
Born: Nechells, Birmingham, 30 November 1933
Career: Lea Village School, Brookhill Juniors, BLUES (amateur, February 1950, professional May 1952), Lincoln City (in a part-exchange deal involving Dick Neal, April 1957), Boston FC (August 1964), Grantham Town (July 1967), Worksop Town (June 1969), Bourne Town (January 1970), Lincoln City (as youth coach, season 1973-74), Ruston Sports FC/Lincoln (manager, 1974-75).
A local youngster who had been a star in schoolboy football before joining Blues, Bert Linnecor made his debut for the club in the run-in to the 1955-56 FA Cup Final when he replaced the injured Roy Warhurst, but lost out in the scramble for wing-half position at Wembley (that went to Johnny Newman). He was used regularly as a forward and proved a good marksman, netting five goals for Boston in a game against Swindon in 1965. He had a successful period at Lincoln for whom he scored 52 goals in 264 League appearances before moving into non-League circles in 1964.

LINNEY, David William

Midfielder: 0+1 apps.
Born: Kings Heath, Birmingham 5 September 1961
Career: Schoolboy football, BLUES (apprentice June 1977, professional September 1979), Oxford United (August 1982), Yeovil, Basingstoke Town, Weymouth, Chard Town
David Linney showed a fair degree of versatility in Blues' reserves side but was not given a real chance to show his worth in the first team. Discarded by Ron Saunders in his first clear-out as manager, Linney teamed up again with his former boss, Jim Smith, at Oxford, spending one season at the Manor Ground.

LINTON, Ivor

Right-back/midfielder: 3+1 apps.
Born: West Bromwich 20 November 1959
Career: West Bromwich & District Schools, Staffordshire Boys, Aston Villa (on trial, April 1976, apprentice, May 1976, professional September 1977), Peterborough United (free transfer, July 1982), BLUES (on trial, December 1983 to February 1984), Bilston Town (May 1984), Kasko IK/Finland, IF Kraft Narpes/Finland.

Club honours: Aston Villa: FA Youth Cup runners-up 1978. Ivor Linton was highly rated as a midfielder with Aston Villa, but failed to make the breakthrough and moved to Peterborough after only 28 games (11 as a substitute) in six seasons at Villa Park. Released by 'Posh', he had an unsuccessful trial with Blues and played briefly for Bilston Town before going to Finland where he became a forward.

LITTLEFORD, Arthur George
Right-back; 3 apps
Born: Wellington, 1868. Now deceased
Career: South Yardley FC, BLUES (August 1893), Berwick Rangers/Worcester (1895).
Archie Littleford was a regular reserve full-back with Blues and although given plenty of outings in friendlies and County Cup matches he was rarely tried in League competition, and generally disappointed when he did play.

LODGE, Lewis Vaughan
Right-back: 1 apps
Born: Darlington, 21 December 1872.
Died: Buxton, 21 October 1916
Career: Durham School (played for the Rugby XV), Magdalene College at Cambridge, Casuals FC (season 1893-94), Corinthians (1894 to 1998), BLUES (season 1896-97), Newbury Town, Durham Town.
Club Honours: Casuals: FA Amateur Cup runners up 1894
Representative honours: England (5 full caps, 1894-96), Cambridge University Blue (3 times).
Blues appeared to have pulled off a coup when this great Corinthian, Lewis Lodge, agreed to play for them. Pressure of work, however, prevented him from being able to turn out on a regular basis. Employed as a master at Harris Hill School, Newbury, he was a powerfully built 'back' of the old school brigade and was reliable in his tackling and kicking. He also played in three cricket matches for Hampshire, scoring only six runs and taking 0-6. He died in mysterious circumstances, being found drowned in a pool.

LOGAN, John Theodore
Outside-left: one app.
Born: Edinburgh, 1871. Now deceased
Career: Edinburgh Emmett, Partick Thistle, BLUES (season 1896-97), Musselburgh (1897-98).
Jock Logan was a disappointing Scottish signing whose performances, whether in League or friendly games, rarely threatened the opposition.

LOUGHRAN, Joseph Lane
Wing-half: 34 apps. 2 goals
Born: Consett, County Durham, 12 August 1915
Career: Medomsley Juniors, Consett FC, BLUES (August 1933), Dudley Town (May 1937), Burnley (July

1939), Southend United (September 1949 to May 1953), Newhaven (as a permit player: 1953-54)
Joe Loughran was a short, energetic wing-half who was physical education student at college when he came to the notice of Blues. He was able to play equally as well on either side of the field. After retiring he was employed as the organiser of physical education for East Sussex Schools.

LOVESEY, James
Left-back: one app
Born: Smethwick, 1864. Now deceased
Career: Hockley Hill Transport FC, BLUES (August 1886), Birmingham Belmont (season 1887-88)
Jim Lovesey was employed in the jewellery trade in Birmingham. He was a regular at full-back for just half a season, making his last appearance on Christmas Day 1886 against Mitchell St George's.

LOWE, C Bernard
Inside-left: 16 apps. 3 goals
Born: Cradley Heath, 1885. Now deceased
Career: Lye Cross Parish Church FC, Harborne Lynwood FC, Halesowen, BLUES (September 1908), Darlaston (1911), Netherton (1913). Retired during WW1.
Bernard Lowe was a skilful forward, often asked to play wider than he liked, who was a star of Birmingham League football for several years. He was not a prolific goalscorer and it was stated that his greatest strength was the manoeuvring of the ball in midfield.

LOWE, Kenneth, BSc
Midfielder: 19+10 apps. 3 goals
Born: Sedgefield, 6 November 1961
Career: Hartlepool United (apprentice 1977, professional 1979), Billingham Town, Gateshead, Spearwood Dalmatic (Australia), Gateshead, Morecambe, Barrow, Scarborough United (free transfer, January 1988), Barrow, Barnet (£40,000, March 1991), Stoke City (free transfer, August 1993), BLUES (£75,000, December 1993), Carlisle United (on loan, September 1994), Hartlepool United (on loan, August 1995), Darlington (non-contract, March to May 1997), later Barrow (manager, 2000-02).
Club honours: Barrow: Northern Premier League champions 1986 &1989, FA Trophy winners 1990.
Kenny Lowe, who was quite tall for a midfield player at 6ft 1in, was a useful squad member at St Andrew's. He made 59 appearances for Hartlepool, four for Scarborough, 84 for Barnet and 13 for Stoke. He gained a BSc in engineering.

LUNTALA, Tresor
Midfielder: 10+6 apps.
Born: Freux, France, 31 May 1982
Career: Stade Rennais FC/France (August 1996), BLUES

(free transfer, August 1999 to May 2002). Had unsuccessful trials with Wolverhampton Wanderers, Notts County and Grimsby Town between 2000-02.
Club honours: Blues: Division One promotion 2002
After two seasons without a sniff of first team football, midfielder 'Tres' Luntala was finally given his chance by caretaker-managers Mick Mills and Jim Barron in October 2001. He did well enough, passing the ball well but faded from the scene after Steve Bruce took over the reins.

LYNEX, Stephen Charles
Winger: 45+21 apps. 13 goals
Born: West Bromwich, 23 January 1958
Career: All Saints Junior & Churchfields Comprehensive Schools (West Bromwich), West Bromwich Town Boys, Charlemont Farm Boys Club, Sandwell Rangers, Aston Villa (on trial), Wolverhampton Wanderers (on trial), West Bromwich Albion (apprentice, July 1974, professional January 1977), Sligo Rovers (on trial), Shamrock Rangers (free transfer, July 1977), Queen's Park Rangers (on trial), BLUES (April 1979), Leicester City (£60,000, February 1981), BLUES (on loan, October-December 1986), West Bromwich Albion (£5,000, March 1987), Cardiff City (free transfer, June 1988), Telford United (March 1990), Trafford Park FC ((March 1991). After retiring from competitive football (in 1990) he became a publican, first in Birmingham and then in West Bromwich (The Red Lion), also playing for Ansells FC (1992-93).
Club honours: WBA: FA Youth Cup winners 1976; Shamrock Rovers: FA of Ireland Cup winners 1978: Blues: Division Two promotion 1980: Leicester City: Division Two promotion 1983.
Representative honours: League of Ireland XI (1978).
Unable to gain a place in the Baggies' first team, Steve Lynex went to Ireland where he gained valuable experience including games in major European competitions, but was happy to return to England when the opportunity presented itself. He made his debut for Blues after the club had already been condemned to relegation (in a 3-1 defeat at Manchester City in May 1979, scoring to celebrate the occasion!) The following year he earned a semi-regular place in the side and scored some vital goals in the promotion campaign where he demonstrated a happy knack of being in the right place at the right time. Lynex proved a highly successful signing for Leicester, playing principally on the right wing but was less successful after leaving Filbert Street. In a useful career of League football he amassed well over 400 senior appearances and netted more than 70 goals, including a fair number of penalties.

LYNN, Stanley
Right-back: 148 apps. 30 goals
Born: Bolton, 18 June 1928. Died: Solihull, 28 April 2002.

Career: Whitecroft Road School, Whitworth's FC (April 1944), Accrington Stanley (amateur August 1945, professional July 1947), Aston Villa (£10,000, March 1950), BLUES (£2,000, October 1961), Stourbridge (free transfer, August 1966). Retired in May 1968, but assisted Aston Villa All Stars for 15 years (1970-85). A keen golfer and later a storeman with the Lucas Industries Group, he resided in Shirley until his death at the age of 73.
Club honours: Aston Villa: FA Cup winners 1957, FA Charity Shield runners-up 1957, Division Two champions 1960, Football League Cup winners 1961; Blues: Football League Cup winners 1963.
Stan Lynn was a well-built full-back who could kick like a mule, especially from dead-ball situations and he once scored a hat trick - two goals coming from the penalty spot - for Villa against Sunderland in January 1958 to become the first full-back to achieve this feat in Division One. Lynn had lost a lot of his speed and was considered to be 'over the hill' when he joined Blues but he still gave an excellent account of himself during his four-year spell at St Andrew's. He finished up as Blues' top-scorer in 1964-65 from the right back position. He appeared in 446 League games during his career (64 goals scored) and netted 38 times in 324 senior outings for Villa. His League Cup winners' prize with Blues was won against Villa, his old club, in 1963.

McCAFFERTY, William
Inside-forward: 4 apps.
Born: Rutherglen, 9 December 1882. Now deceased
Career: Rutherglen Glencairn, Celtic (March, 1902), Bolton Wanderers (on loan, November 1902), Stenhousemuir (November 1903), Bathgate (July 1905), Reading (November 1905), BLUES (£350, December 1906), Bathgate, Portsmouth (February 1908), Brentford (November 1909).
A forward of Scottish extraction who made his name at Reading, Bill McCafferty signed for Blues on a free transfer plus the gate receipts of a friendly. He scored in that friendly game but that was, in fact, his only goal for Blues as Benny Green kept him out of the side. He was not a great success with any of his later clubs either.

McCARRICK, Mark Bernard
Right-back: 15+5 apps
Born: Liverpool, 4 February 1962.
Career: Winsford Verdin Comprehensive School, West Bromwich Albion (apprentice 1977), Caroline Hill FC, Christchurch United, Witton Albion (1982), BLUES (professional, May 1983), Lincoln City (£4,000, July 1984), Crewe Alexandra (non-contract, February 1986), Kuopion Pallotoverit/Finland (April 1986), Runcorn (October 1986), Tranmere Rovers (£5,000, August 1987), Altrincham (March 1991), Northwich Victoria (August-September 1991), Marine. Moved to Spain in

January 1992 to run a café/bar in Magaluf, returning to play for Winsford United (October 1993) and Bangor City.
Club honours: Tranmere: Division Three promotion 1991, Leyland DAF Cup winners 1990.

Mark McCarrick was regarded as something of a lucky mascot as his appearances in the first team coincided with a lengthy unbeaten spell. However, his lack of pace was cruelly exposed by Watford's John Barnes in the 1984 FA Cup quarter-final and he found himself 'freed' at the end of the season. He did exceedingly well with Tranmere, though, scoring 14 goals in 125 League outings.

McCARTHY, Jonathon David

Right-winger: 123+19 apps. 8 goals
Born: Middlesbrough, 18 August 1970
Career: Hartlepool United (juniors, July 1986, professional November 1987), Shepshed Charterhouse (March 1989), York City (free transfer, March 1990), Port Vale (£450,000, August 1995), BLUES (£1.5 million, September 1997), Sheffield Wednesday (on loan, March 2002), Port Vale (free transfer, August 2002). Carlisle United (2002-03)
Club honours: Blues: League Cup runners-up 2001
Representative honours: Northern Ireland (18 full & 2 'B' caps)
A record signing by Blues from Port Vale in 1997, popular right-winger Jon McCarthy brought a breath of fresh air to St Andrew's with his all-action approach. Unfortunately he broke the same leg three times and never made a full recovery. Eventually lack of matches caught up with him and on his release he rejoined the Valiants.

McCLURE, Alexander

Centre-half: 198 apps. 4 goals
Born: Workington, 3 April 1892. Died: Birmingham, August 1973.
Career: Grangetown Juniors, BLUES (January 1912), Aston Villa (December 1923), Stoke (October 1924), Coventry City (September 1926), Walsall (March 1928), Luton Town (colts trainer, late 1927), Bromsgrove Rovers, Market Harborough Town, BLUES (colts manager, 1928-32, later assistant-manager, May 1932 to April 1934). After leaving football worked for Rudge Motor Cycles and later ran a successful haulage company in Small Heath.
Club honours: Blues: Division Two champions 1921.
Representative honours: Football League XI (2).
Possessor of a fine physique and excellent positional sense, Alec McClure was the fulcrum of the Blues' defence for 12 years, injuries permitting. Few forwards relished a run-in with the powerful northerner who delivered a terrific shoulder-charge but who also had a suspect temperament. He skippered Blues' reserve side to victory in three competitions before establishing himself in the first team. After returning to St Andrew's as colts'

manager he earned the reputation as a hard taskmaster. His brother Sam played for Blackburn Rovers and his nephew Joe for Everton, Brentford and Exeter City. His daughter now lives in Droitwich.

McCOURTY, William

Left-half: one app.
Born: Morpeth, 1884. Now deceased
Career: North Seaton, BLUES (May 1909), Ryton FC (1910).
A former miner from the North-East, Bill McCourty's career in League football was brief. He enjoyed an early debut due to an injury to Tommy Daykin, but had a poor game as Blues struggled against Glossop. He never got a second chance!

McDONAGH, James Martin

Goalkeeper: one app.
Born: Rotherham, 6 October 1962.
Career: Rotherham United (apprentice November 1968, professional October 1970), Bolton Wanderers (£10,000, August 1976), Everton (£25,000, July 1980), Bolton Wanderers (£90,000, August 1981 in a player-exchange deal), Notts County (£50,000, July 1983), BLUES (on loan, September 1984), Gillingham (on loan, March-April 1995), Sunderland (on loan, August-September 1985), Wichita Wings/NASL (October 1985), Scarborough (free transfer, November 1987), Huddersfield Town (on loan, February-March 1988), Charlton Athletic (free transfer, March 1988), Galway United (player-manager, 1988), Derry City (manager to May 1989), Spalding United (September 1989), Grantham Town (February 1990), Telford United (player/reserve-team manager, season 1990-91), Arnold Town (1993-94), Ilkeston Town Vets FC.
Club honours: Bolton: Division Two champions 1978
Representative honours: Republic of Ireland (24 full caps; England (Youth caps).
When he joined Blues in 1984 (following the departure of Tony Coton) burly goalkeeper 'Seamus' McDonagh was vastly experienced but surprisingly his career at St Andrew's was restricted to just one outing due to the fact that two more 'keepers - Mark Prudhoe and David Seaman - were also signed in rapid succession! Unusually capped for two countries, McDonagh made 270 appearances for Bolton and 135 for Rotherham. He now works in the Insurance business.

McDONNELL, Martin

Centre-half: 32 apps.
Born: Newton-le-Willows, 27 April 1924.
Died: Coventry, 13 April 1988.
Career: Everton (August 1942), Southport (August) 1946), BLUES (May 1947), Coventry City (October 1949), Derby County (July 1955), Crewe Alexandra (July 1958). Retired June 1961.

Club honours: Derby: Third Division (North) Champions 1957

Principally deputy to Ted Duckhouse, tough guy Martin McDonnell was an accomplished defender - not surprising for a former paratrooper! He was a great favourite of manager Harry Storer who signed him three times - for Blues, Coventry and Derby. McDonnell played in 250 games during his time at Highfield Road. He bred Alsatian dogs in his spare time.

McDONOUGH, Roy

Striker: 2 apps. one goal
Born: Solihull, 16 October 1958.
Career: Warwickshire Schools, Aston Villa Boys, BLUES (apprentice, October 1974, professional October 1976), Walsall (£15,000, September 1978), Chelsea (£15,000, October 1980), Colchester United (£15,000, February 1981), Southend United (£5,000, August 1983), Exeter City (£2,000, January 1984), Cambridge United (free transfer, October 1984), Southend United (free, August 1985), Colchester United (player-manager, 1990 to May 1994), Braintree Town (August 1994), Dagenham & Redbridge (October 1994 to 1996), Chelmsford City (season 1996-97).
Club honours: Southend: Division Four promotion 1990, Division Three promotion 1991; Colchester: GM Vauxhall Conference champions 1992.
A tall, long-haired youngster, Roy McDonough was given a run-out in Blues' first team at the end of the 1976-77 season. He did okay but spent the next term in the reserves before dropping down to a lower level. He was a good, honest competitor, always giving his all, no matter what the circumstances. He drew up a fine scoring record: 15 goals in 82 League games for Walsall, 24 in 93 for Colchester and 35 in 201 for Southend. McDonough was, in fact, occasionally used as a goalkeeper in Blues' youth side. He was sacked as manager of Colchester by his father-in-law, Chairman George Parker. His wife, Jackie, however, continued to work at Layer Road in the lottery department.

MacDOWELL, Duncan John

Centre-forward: 2 apps.
Born: Paddington, London, 18 December 1963
Career: BLUES (apprentice, June 1980, professional August 1981), Leatherhead (non-contract, 1982-83).
A series of promising games in the reserves led to Duncan MacDowell receiving an early call-up up into the first XI. A pacy, strong-running forward, he failed to make an impression at the higher level and left St Andrew's to join Willie Bell's touring Christian missionary football team, later returning to England to play at non-League level.

McGAVIN, Stephen James

Striker: 21+12 apps. 7 goals
Born: North Walsham, 24 January 1969

Career: Ipswich Town (trainee, June 1985, professional January 1987), Thetford Town (1988), Sudbury (free transfer, 1989), Colchester United (£10,000, March 1991), BLUES (£150,000, January 1994), Wycombe Wanderers (£140,000, March 1995), Southend United (free transfer, February 1999), Northampton Town (July 1999), Colchester United (free, October 1999), Dagenham & Redbridge (July 2001).
Club honours: Colchester: GM Vauxhall Conference winners 1992, FA Trophy winners 1992, Blues: Second Division champions 1995.
A skilful, workmanlike footballer, Steve McGavin scored 19 goals in 70 games for Colchester before joining Blues. Unfortunately he failed to hit the target as often he would have liked during his time at St Andrew's. He was converted into a midfielder at Wycombe for whom he netted 17 times in 140 outings before transferring to Southend. When he quit 'League' football in 2001, McGavin's record stood at 62 goals in 336 appearances.

McGURK, Francis Reynolds

Outside-right: 19 apps. 2 goals
Born: Hamilton, Scotland, 15 January 1909. Died: Birmingham, 2 March 1978.
Career: Blantyre Celtic (1927), Clyde (professional, August 1931), BLUES (June 1933), Bristol City (May 1935), Whittaker Ellis FC (season 1936-37).
Representative honours: Scotland (one full cap)
Frank McGurk came south with the reputation as a goalscorer, but sadly he never lived up to that billing at St Andrew's. His dribbling skills, however, created such a favourable impression that he was rapidly promoted to the Scottish national team after being a professional for only two years. Unfortunately his decline was just as rapid and inside three years he was playing in the Birmingham Works League.

McINTOSH, Alexander

Inside-forward: 23 apps. 4 goals
Born: Dunfermline, 14 April 1916
Career: Heart of Beath FC, Folkestone Town, Wolverhampton Wanderers (May 1937), BLUES (January 1947), Coventry City (February 1948), Kidderminster Harriers (1949), Hednesford Town (1950), Bilston Town (1951), retired in 1953.
Club honours: Wolves: FA Cup runners-up 1949; Wartime Cup winners 1942; Blues: Division Two runners-up 1948.
Alex McIntosh was a skilful, two-footed inside-forward with a powerful shot. He had been a regular in the Wolves' side before WW2 but during the hostilities spent some time in a Prisoner-of-War camp. It was not surprising therefore that when peacetime football returned he struggled to regain his form. During his time at St Andrew's he acted, in the main, as reserve to Harold Bodle and Neil Dougall.

McKAY, John
Forward: 21 apps. 2 goals
Born: Hebburn, County Durham, 1885. Now deceased
Career: Hebburn, BLUES (August 1910), Blyth
(August 1912).
A dribbling forward whose appearances were split
between inside and outside-left, Jack McKay opened his
Blues career with a debut goal but was primarily a
supplier of chances.

McKEE, Frank
Left-half: 24 apps
Born: Cowdenbeath, 25 January 1923.
Died: Birmingham 1988.
Career: Lochgelly Albert, Dundee United (October
1947), BLUES (February 1948), Gillingham (July 1952),
Gloucester City (August 1956), Kidderminster Harriers
(season 1957-58).
Frank McKee was a versatile Scotsman who was at home
in most midfield roles. At his best prompting his
forwards, he was rarely given much of run in the first-
team as Blues' tactics demanded a more defensive wing-
half. He worked for South Staffordshire Water Company
until his retirement.

McMILLAN, John Stewart
Inside-forward: 52 apps. 28 goals.
Born: Port Glasgow, 16 February 1871.
Died: Derby, 4 November 1941.
Career: Port Glasgow Athletic, St Bernard's, Derby
County (December 1890), Leicester Fosse (May 1896),
BLUES (January 1901), Bradford City (May 1903),
Glossop North End (May 1906), BLUES (trainer,
August 1909), Gillingham (manager 1919 to
August 1922).
A prodigy in Scottish junior football, appearing regularly
whilst only 14 years of age, Johnny McMillan
nevertheless had only a brief spell in Scottish League
football, leaving St Bernard's after a row about
professionalism. A classy left-footed forward who had the
knack of complementing every centre-forward he played
alongside, he shares the Blues' record of scoring most
goals in a game - five against Blackpool on 2 March
1901 - a feat he also achieved with Derby. In his later
days at Blues he was slowed down by injuries and it was
no great surprise when Bradford City took him on as
their captain during their first League season. His son
Stuart managed Derby County when they won the FA
Cup in 1946, beating Blues in the semi-final.

McMINN, Kevin Clifton
Winger: 22+ 4 apps.
Born: Castle Douglas, 28 September 1962.
Career: Glenafton Athletic (1980), Queen of the South
(January 1982), Glasgow Rangers (£50,000, October
1984), FC Sevilla/Spain (£225,000, January 1987),

Derby County (£300,000, February 1988), BLUES
(£115,000, July 1993), Burnley (on loan, February,
signed full-time, March 1994).
Club honours: Rangers: Scottish League Cup winners
1986; Burnley: Division Two promotion 1994.
Known affectionately as the 'Tinman', Ted McMinn was
a strong player, good on the ball who enjoyed occupying
a position wide on the right. He played well over 140
games in Scotland before trying his luck in Spain. At
Derby he proved an exciting player who often threatened
to turn the game his side's way.

McROBERTS, Robert
Centre-forward: 187 apps. 82 goals.
Born: Coatbridge, near Motherwell, Scotland, 12 July
1874. Died: Birkenhead, 27 February 1959.
Career: Coatbridge FC (1892), Airdrieonians, Albion
Rovers, Gainsborough Trinity (August 1896), BLUES
(£150, August 1898), Chelsea (£100, August 1905).
Retired in May 1909 and returned to BLUES as a team
manager in July 1910, holding the position for five years,
up to August 1915.
Club honours: Blues: Division Two champions 1901.
Bob McRoberts was an elegant, ball-juggling forward
who preferred to score his goals with finesse rather than
using hurly-burly tactics. He was signed by Blues after a
short spell at Gainsborough where he stood out in a poor
side. At Muntz Street he rapidly made a name for
himself, although he once declared that he didn't 'give a
tinker's cuss' what people thought of his play. After seven
seasons with Blues he moved to London and was
Chelsea's first-ever signing. He played for the Londoners
in their initial League game in September 1905, against
Stockport County, and whilst at Stamford Bridge was
used as both a centre-forward and a centre-half. On
retiring McRoberts became Blues' first full-time paid manager.

MADDEN, David John
Midfielder: 5 apps. one goal
Born: London, 6 January 1963.
Career: Southampton (apprentice 1979, professional
January 1981), AFC Bournemouth (on loan, January
1983), Arsenal (free transfer, August 1983), Charlton
Athletic (free transfer, June 1984), Los Angeles
Lazers/NASL (1985), Reading (November 1987), Crystal
Palace (August 1988), BLUES (on loan, January 1990),
Maidstone United (free transfer, July 1990, coach
January 1992 to 1993).
Club honours: Crystal Palace: FA Cup runners-up 1992.
David Madden was a stylish midfielder who had his fair
share of ups and downs before he moved to St Andrew's.
His brief spell with Blues was a microcosm of his career
as a whole. Voted 'Man of the Match' on his debut, he
gave a goal away in his second game with an awful back-
pass, only to bounce back in his next outing with a quite
brilliant strike. Manager Dave Mackay wanted to sign

him permanently, but the money was not available and three months later he appeared at Wembley in the FA Cup Final, only to be freed by Palace shortly afterwards! He returned from his honeymoon in 1992 suffering from malaria.

MADDEN, Owen

Inside/outside-left: 15 apps. 5 goals
Born: Cork, 5 December 1916. Died: Cork, 20 January 1991.
Career: Cork High School, Cork Southern Rovers, Cork Hibernians, Norwich City (May 1936), BLUES (£2,000, February 1938), Cork City (May 1939), Sligo Rovers (WW2 guest: 1939-44), Cork United, Cork Athletic (1948, as manager 1953).
Club honours: Cork Utd: League of Ireland champions 1941, 1942, 1943, 1945 & 1946, Irish Cup winners 1941, 1947, runners-up 1942, 1943; Cork Hibs: Irish Cup runners-up 1936.
Representative honours: Republic of Ireland (2 full caps).
Owen Madden was highly-rated in Ireland and there were accusations of 'poaching' when Norwich signed him. He was unable to gain a regular place with either of his English clubs, but his place in Blues' history is earned by virtue of his two goals against Everton in the 1939 FA Cup-tie, a game watched by St Andrew's record crowd. After his return to his native country he enjoyed a phenomenally successful career as a goalscorer.

MAIN, Walter Seymour

Inside-left: 41 apps. 14 goals.
Born: Motherwell, 1875. Now deceased
Career: Airdrieonians, BLUES (August 1899), St Bernard's FC (season 1901-02).
A Scottish ball artist who took over the second striker's role when Walter Wigmore switched to centre-half, Walter Main had two years in and out of the team before being replaced by Johnny McMillan.

MANGNALL, David

Centre-forward: 39 apps. 15 goals
Born: Wigan, 21 September 1907.
Died: Penzance, 10 April 1962.
Career: Maltby New Church FC, Maltby Colliery, Rotherham United (on trial), Huddersfield Town (on trial), Doncaster Rovers (as an amateur, August 1926), Leeds United (professional, November 1927), Huddersfield Town (£3,000, December 1929), BLUES (February 1934), West Ham United (£2,950, March 1935), Millwall (May 1936), Queen's Park Rangers (May 1939). Guested for Fulham, Millwall and Southend United during WW2. Appointed QPR manager in April 1944, retiring in May 1952.
Club honours: Millwall: Division Three South champions 1937, Division Three (South) Cup winners 1937.
In a career spanning some 25 years (first as a goalscorer

and then as a manager) Dave Mangnall set foot on practically every ground in the country. He scored 52 goals for Maltby New Church in one season and 35 for Maltby Colliery in another. And he also netted ten goals in a single reserve match for Leeds. Whilst at Huddersfield he had the unusual experience of scoring 42 goals in the 1931-32 campaign and then finding himself dropped the next campaign. His spell with Blues was blighted by injury problems but he soon found his touch again after his departure to West Ham. He gave up his job as a miner to turn professional with Leeds United. Mangnall hit 61 goals in only 79 League games for the Terriers, and all told scored more than 120 times in less than 200 appearances as a professional footballer. After leaving the game he went into business in Cornwall.

MARCELO, Cipriano Dos Santos

Striker: 53+38 apps. 26 goals
Born: Niteroi, Brazil, 11 October 1969
Career: Benfica, Deportivo Alaves, Sheffield United (£400,000, October 1997), BLUES (£500,000, October 1999), Walsall (free transfer, February 2002).
Club record: Blues: League Cup runners-up 2001, Division One promotion 2002
A strong, forceful striker, a tireless worker with an eye for goal, Marcelo did well with Blues but when manager Steve Bruce signed Stern John, out went Marcelo - to neighbouring Walsall. He has now scored over 50 goals in more than 150 games in 'English' football.

MARDON, Paul Jonathan

Defender: 54+9 apps.
Born: Bristol, 14 September 1969.
Career: Boco Juniors, Bristol City (YTS June 1985, professional September 1987), Doncaster Rovers (on loan, September 1990), BLUES (for a tribunal-set fee of £115,000, July 1991), Liverpool (on trial, January 1992), West Bromwich Albion (£450,000, November 1993), Oldham Athletic (on loan, January 1999), Plymouth Argyle (on loan, September 1999), Wrexham (on loan, October-November 2000). Retired in January 2001.
Representative honours: Wales (one full & one 'B' cap)
A strong, forceful defender, 6ft, 11st 10lb, Paul Mardon had the ability to judge a last-minute tackle to perfection. He joined Blues after failing to earn a regular place in the Bristol City team, and came from the same junior side as Adrian Bird and Julian Dicks. He did well at The Hawthorns (155 appearances) before being struck down by injury that led to him announcing his retirement early in 2001.

MARSDEN, Christopher

Midfielder: 58+1 apps. 6 goals
Born: Sheffield, 3 January 1969
Career: Sheffield United (apprentice June 1985, professional January 1987), Huddersfield Town (July

1988), Coventry City (on loan, November 1993), Wolverhampton Wanderers (£250,000, January 1994), Notts County (£250,000, November 1994), Stockport County (£70,000, January 1996), BLUES (£500,000, October 1995), Southampton (£800,000, February 1998). Midfielder Chris Marsden, with his shaven-head, is a no-nonsense competitor, the engine-room workhorse who reached the personal milestone of 400 senior appearances during 2002. Signed by his former Stockport boss Dave Jones for Southampton, Blues certainly did good business when transferring him to The Dell.

MARSH, Simon Thomas Peter
Full-back: 7+1 apps.
Born: Ealing, London, 29 January 1977
Career: Oxford United (trainee, June 1993, professional November 1994), BLUES (£250,000, December 1998), Brentford (on loan, September 2000). Contract cancelled by Blues in April 2001.
Representative honours: England: (one Under-21 cap)
After failing to settle down with Blues (having done very well at The Manor Ground, making 68 appearances as well as having a month's loan at Griffin Park) full-back Simon Marsh had his contract cancelled at St Andrew's by mutual consent.

MARTIN, Jae Andrew
Midfielder: 1+8 apps.
Born: Hampstead (London) 5 February 1976
Career: Southend United (trainee, June 1992, professional May 1995), Leyton Orient (on loan, September 1994), BLUES (free transfer, July 1995), Lincoln City (August 1996), Peterborough United (free transfer, July 1998), Welling United (on loan, February 2000), Woking (free transfer, June 2000).
Left-sided midfielder Jae Martin never really made an impact with any of his five League clubs, making in total of 95 senior appearances in eight years up to 2000.

MARTIN, Raymond Barry
Full-back: 364+10 apps. one goal
Born: Wolverhampton, 23 January 1945.
Career: South-East Staffs Boys, Aston Villa (junior, July 1960), BLUES (apprentice June 1961, professional May 1962), Portland Timbers/NASL (on loan, May 1975, full-time May 1976), Minnesota Kicks/NASL (1979). Retired in 1979 and was later soccer coach at Oregon State University (USA).
Club honours: Blues: Division Two promotion 1972.
Whilst a youngster at Villa Park, Ray Martin broke manager Joe Mercer's toe in a training session. Within a few weeks he was released, although the two incidents were probably not related! Carefully nurtured at St Andrew's before being given his League baptism shortly before his 19th birthday, he impressed sufficiently to retain his place for most of that season and was a regular

member of the first-team squad for the next 12 years. During this time, Martin was the victim of much abuse from the terraces but to his credit he persevered and eventually won over his critics to become a much-loved character. A player who always gave the impression of thoroughly enjoying his football, his trademark was his amazing slide-tackle. His only goal for Blues came against Hull City in a home Division Two game in April 1970. Voted Blues' Player of the Year in 1969-70 and 1970-71, he was given a deserved testimonial by the club in 1971.

MARTIN, Robert
Full-back: 74 apps.
Born: Glengarnock Village, Kilwinning, Scotland 16 May 1929.
Career: Glengarnock Schools, Kilwinning Rangers, BLUES (professional, March 1950), Derby County (March 1956), Chesterfield (July 1960), Burton Albion (July 1961), Long Eaton United (1963 to May 1965).
Club honours: Derby County: Division Three (North) champions 1957. 'Roy' Martin was a polished full-back who provided highly capable cover for the Hall-Green partnership and tended to be rather overshadowed because of this. In his entire League career he was only once regarded as an indisputable first choice and that was in Derby's Third Division (North) championship winning season under former Blues manager Harry Storer and alongside another former Blues player, Martin McDonnell. Martin, who suffered a broken leg during his time at the Baseball Ground, was employed as a butcher after retiring from the game.

MASSART, David Louis
Inside/centre-forward: 3 apps.
Born: Yardley, Birmingham, 2 November 1919.
Career: Yardley Methodists FC, Bells Athletic, BLUES (amateur 1938, professional February 1939), Walsall (June 1947), Bury (March 1948), Chesterfield (briefly in 1951), Weymouth (August 1951). Later worked as a hotelier in Weymouth.
Club honours: Blues: Football League (South) champions 1946.
Dave Massart was a bold, strong, determined, never-say-die goalscorer who grabbed a hat-trick in each of his first three home games for Walsall at the start of 1947-48 and ended up with 23 goals in 27 games for the Saddlers that season. He later netted 45 goals in 85 League matches for Chesterfield. A real old fashioned number-nine, Massart could not wrest a regular place in the Blues side from Cyril Trigg.

MATTHEWSON, Trevor
Central defender: 202+1 apps. 13 goals
Born: Sheffield, 12 February 1963.
Career: Pye Bank Junior School, Herries Comprehensive

School, Sheffield Wednesday (apprentice June 1979, professional February 1981), Newport County (October 1983), Stockport County (September 1985), Lincoln City (£13,000, August 1987), BLUES (£45,000, August 1989), Preston North End (September 1993), Bury (August 1994), Witton Albion (1995-96), Hereford United (October 1996 to May 1997).

Club honours: Lincoln: GM Vauxhall Conference champions 1988; Blues: Leyland DAF Cup winners 1991. Trevor Matthewson, a tall, well-built defender, skippered Lincoln back into the Football League in 1988 and, indeed, the Imps were somewhat put out when the tribunal valued him at only £45,000. He has played occasionally as a full-back where he showed a flair for overlapping. His uncle Reg played Sheffield United, Fulham and Chester.

MEACOCK, William Robert
Centre-half: 14 apps.
Born: Hoole, 26 July 1910.
Career: Hoole & Newton FC, Blackpool (May 1930), Torquay United (August 1931), Tranmere Rovers (July 1933), Lincoln City (May 1935), BLUES (June 1938), Bristol City (May 1939). Did not figure after WW2.
An experienced defender, Bill Meacock was amongst a group of new players signed by Blues to boost the club's flagging fortunes in 1938. Not the tallest of centre-halves, he was a solid tackler but he was not quite up to top-class football.

MEATES, William Percival
Goalkeeper: 17 apps.
Born: Bournemouth, 1871. Now deceased
Career: Eastbourne FC, BLUES (August 1895), Warmley FC (1897-98), Nottingham Forest (on trial season 1898-99). Bill Meates, a tall, long-legged 'keeper, battled with Jimmy Roach for two years for the green jersey. He left to join West Country Southern Leaguers Warmley.

MERRICK, Gilbert Harold
Goalkeeper: 551 apps.
Born: Sparkhill, Birmingham, 26 January 1922.
Career: Acocks Green School, Fenton Rovers, Olton Sports, Shirley Juniors, Solihull Town (July 1939), BLUES (amateur, August 1938, professional August 1939), Retired in 1960 and became manager of BLUES (June 1960 to April 1964). Bromsgrove Rovers (manager 1967 to 1970), Atherstone Town (manager, 1970 to 1972). Guested for several clubs during WW2, including Northampton Town, Nottingham Forest and West Bromwich Albion.
Club honours: Blues: Football League South champions 1946, Division Two champions 1948, 1955, FA Cup runners-up 1956; (as manager): Blues: Inner-Cities Fairs Cup runners-up 1961, Football League Cup winners 1963.
Representative honours: England (23 full caps); Football

League XI (11), Army 1946-47.
Probably the best goalkeeper in Britain during the early to mid-1950s, Gil Merrick was powerfully built with a dapper moustache and huge hands, one of the long line of great Blues 'keepers who modelled his style upon that of his predecessor, Harry Hibbs - although he was perhaps a touch more 'showier' than 'H H'. Superbly athletic, Merrick was a brilliant handler of the ball but had the misfortune to be England's 'last line of defence' for both of those thrashings by the Hungarians in 1953-54. He was nicknamed 'Mister thirteen' in Hungary after the return game in Budapest. He played in 170 games for Blues during WW2, making over 720 appearances for the club overall - a superb record. He now lives in retirement in Birmingham. His son Neil played briefly for Bournemouth & Worcester City.
* Merrick's father played for Nuneaton Borough for many years and Harry Clutterbuck, Birmingham's goalkeeper in the 1890s and later trainer at Moor Green, lived in the road street as Merrick - Fenton Road, Acocks Green.

METCALFE, John
Outside-left: 2 apps.
Born: Acocks Green, Birmingham 2 June 1935
Career: Yardley Boys, BLUES (amateur June 1951, professional October 1952), York City (June 1957), Walsall (July 1956 to May 1959).
A short, sturdily built winger whose entire professional career was virtually spent playing reserve team football. In fact, John Metcalfe made only seven appearances for his major clubs in eight years.

MILLARD, Albert Alexander
Centre-forward/centre-half: 33 apps. 15 goals
Born: West Bromwich, 1 October 1898.
Died: Birmingham circa 1970.
Career: Bratt Street & Walsall Street Schools (West Bromwich), Swan Village, Coseley FC, Cardiff City (1915), BLUES (August 1919), Coventry City (November 1920), Crystal Palace (July 1922), Charlton Athletic (October 1924), Leamington Town (September 1925), Retired in June 1926.
Bert Millard was a versatile player, equally adept in defence or attack. He was Blues' top-scorer in 1919-20 when he was playing at centre-forward. Then, following the arrival of Joe Lane and Harry Hampton, he switched to the half-back line where he played with great composure. As a Charlton player he scored a hat-trick in an FA Cup-tie against Windsor & Eton on a snow-covered pitch at The Valley in December 1925 - two days later he played at centre-half in League game at Bristol. He netted 31 goals in 166 games for the Addicks.

MILLARD, Arthur Arnold
Forward: 4 apps. 3 goals

Born: Birmingham, 1869. Now deceased
Career: Smethwick Centaur, BLUES (season 1891-92),
Lea Hall FC.
Archie Millard was a player with a fine scoring record
who certainly deserved more first team outings than he got.

MILLER, Alan John

Goalkeeper: 16 apps.
Born: Epping, 29 March 1970.
Career: Epping Forest School, FA School of Excellence,
Arsenal (YTS, June 1986, professional, May 1988),
Plymouth Argyle (on loan, November 1988), West
Bromwich Albion (on loan, August-September 1991),
BLUES (on loan, December 1991), Middlesbrough
(£500,000, August 1994). Grimsby Town (on loan,
January 1997), West Bromwich Albion (£400,000,
February 1997), Blackburn Rovers (£50,000, February
2000), Bristol City (on loan, August 2000), Coventry
City (on loan, November 2000), St Johnstone (on loan,
during season 2001-02).
Club honours: Arsenal: FA Youth Cup winners 1888;
European Cup-winners Cup winners 1994;
Middlesbrough: Division One champions 1995.
Representative honours: England: 4 Under-21 caps plus
Schoolboy & Youth caps).
An excellent shot-stopper, Alan Miller was limited to
only eight League outings during his long association
with Arsenal. He did, however, give excellent service to
the clubs he served on loan and made 110 appearances
for WBA. He was Bryan Robson's first signing when the
former Albion and Manchester United midfielder took
over as manager of Middlesbrough.

MILLER, Kevin

Goalkeeper: 30 apps
Born: Falmouth, 15 March 1969.
Career: Falmouth Town (1985), Newquay United, Exeter
City (free transfer, March 1989), BLUES (£250,000,
May 1993), Watford (£250,000, August 1994), Crystal
Palace (£1 million, July 1997), Barnsley (£250,000,
August 1999), Exeter City (September 2002).
Club honours: Exeter: Division Four champions 1990.
Kevin Miller - 6ft 1in tall and 13st in weight - was
brought in by his former boss Terry Cooper to replace
Andy Gosney in the Blues' goal. However, he spent only
one season at St Andrew's before new boss Barry Fry
replaced him with Ian Bennett. He made exactly 200
appearances for Exeter (first spell), 151 for Watford, 76
for Palace and over 130 for Barnsley before returning to
St James' Park, signed by ex-Blues player John Cornforth.

MILLINGTON, Charles J H

Outside-right: 87 apps. 13 goals.
Born: Lincoln, 25 April 1884. Died: Lincoln, 13 June1955.
Career: Grantham Town (1901), Ripley Athletic
(January 1905), Aston Villa (September 1905), Fulham

(£400, October 1907), BLUES (£600, August 1909),
Wellington Town (August 1912), Brierley Hill Alliance
(March 1913), Stourbridge (April 1914). Retired in
May 1920 and went to work as an iron-moulder in a
Lincoln factory.
Charlie Millington was quick and strong with plenty of
courage, a player who proved a revelation on the wing
for Blues. Never a great goalscorer, he had a turn of
speed second to none and spent 20 years in football.
Millington netted 14 goals in 38 games for the Villa,
and 21 in 63 for Fulham. He was also a very capable
cricketer on the Minor Counties circuit with
Lincolnshire. His cousin, Ben, played for Fulham and
his son, Charlie junior, was a Blues trialist.

MILLS, Bertie Reginald

Inside-forward: 13 apps. 3 goals
Born: Multan, India, 23 February 1900.
Career: Barton Town, Hull City (September 1920),
Notts County (£3,750, March 1926), BLUES (February
1929), Hull City (December 1929), Scunthorpe United
(1933), Gainsborough Trinity (1935-36).
'Paddy' Mills was a direct, strong, hard-working forward
who never knew the meaning of surrender. A prolific
marksman with his other clubs, he had difficulty settling
into Blues' style of play. He earned the nickname 'Paddy'
because of his fiery temper. After retiring he earned his
living as a security man at a Scunthorpe steelworks. His
brothers, Percy and Arthur, were also professional
footballers

MITCHELL, Frank Rollason

Left-back: 106 apps. 8 goals
Born: Goulborn, New South Wales, Australia, 3 June
1922. Died: Lapworth, Warwickshire, 2 April 1984.
Career: Coventry City (amateur), BLUES (professional,
September 1943), Chelsea (January 1949), Watford
(August 1952). Retired in May 1958. Guested for
Arsenal, Northampton Town & Portsmouth whilst
serving in the Royal Navy during WW2.
Club honours: Blues: Football League South champions
1946, Division Two champions 1948.
Representative honours: FA XI.
Although born in Australia, Frank Mitchell moved to
England whilst in his teens. He originally regarded
cricket his major sport and joined Warwickshire's ground
staff at the age of 15. He guested for Blues in 1942-43
and so impressed the club that he was signed as a full-
timer soon afterwards. He gained a regular place in the
side in 1945-46 and developed into a cool, classy wing-
half. His calm temperament led to him getting the job of
penalty-taker and his method of taking spot-kicks is well
chronicled: at the start of his run-up he would always
hitch up his shorts before striding forward and aiming a
low shot into the corner of the net. On the cricket field
he was a medium-pace bowler for Warwickshire. He

played in 17 matches between 1946-48, taking 22 wickets at an average of 38.9. He also had trials for Kent CCC and assisted Cornwall and Hertfordshire, as well as Knowle & Dorridge CC (Warwicks), becoming secretary of the latter club, for whom he scored a century at the age of 47. Mitchell was in charge of the sports grounds and coaching facilities at Kynoch's for many years after taking off his soccer and cricket boots.

MITTELL, James Lyons
Goalkeeper: 6 apps
Born: Merthyr Tydfil, 1908.
Career: Wigan Borough (1929), BLUES (August 1931), Luton Town (September 1933).
Jim Mittell was an experienced reserve 'keeper who joined Blues when the Wigan club folded. He was more spectacular than Harry Hibbs but had few chances to show off his skills at St Andrew's.

MOBLEY, Frank
Centre-half: 103 apps. 64 goals.
Born: Handsworth, Birmingham, 21 November 1868.
Died: 1940.
Career: Hockley Belmont, Cape Hill, Singers FC of Coventry (May 1886), BLUES (April 1892), Bury (May 1896), Warmley (Bristol), Coventry City (August 1900). Retired in April 1902 and returned to Birmingham where he went into business.
Club honours: Blues: Division Two champions 1893.
At only 5ft 8in, Frank Mobley was certainly on the small side for a centre-forward. Nevertheless, he never let his size bother him, for he was fast and fearless and possessed a terrific shot. A lot of his goals came about when he charged the 'keeper and the ball over the line together. In 1892, the Blues Directors sent a scout to watch Harry Edwards in action for Singers. He impressed with his skill and enthusiasm and was duly signed by the club, along with Mobley who impressed even more!

MOFFATT, Sidney Hugh
Outside-right: 17 apps. 3 goals
Born: Congleton, Cheshire, 16 September 1910.
Died: Macclesfield, 20 September 1981.
Career: Congleton Town (1930), BLUES (December 1933), Millwall (June 1936 to May 1937).
Son of England wing-half Hugh Moffatt (ex-Burnley and Oldham Athletic), Sid Moffatt was something of a sprinter with a good body-swerve and a liking for cutting inside his full-back and trying a shot at goal. He could not settle in at Millwall and played only twice for the Lions.

MOLES, James R
Wing-half: 33 apps.
Born: Leyton, London, 1885. Now deceased
Career: Leyton, BLUES (August 1909), Edmonton (September 1911).

Despite being an enthusiastic half-back, Jim Moles' aggressive instincts were sometimes regarded as a liability. He had been a prominent player in London non-League circles when Blues signed him to understudy Buckley. He spent most of his career playing in the left-half poition.

MONTGOMERY, James
Goalkeeper: 73 apps.
Born: Sunderland, 9 October 1943.
Career: St Hilda's School (Sunderland), Sunderland (amateur June 1958, professional October 1960), Southampton (on loan, October 1976), BLUES (February 1977), Nottingham Forest (August 1979), BLUES (temporary coach, July-August 1980), Sunderland (player-coach and reserve-team player, August 1980 to July 1982). Returned to Sunderland as a youth coach in 1993; now Director of Youth Coaching at The Stadium of Light.
Club honours: Sunderland: FA Cup winners 1973.
Representative honours: England (6 Under-23 caps, Youth international).
Jim Montgomery was a superb goalkeeper who starred in more than 700 League and Cup games during a career that spanned over 20 years. He made a record 537 League appearances for Sunderland and it was undoubtedly his terrific 'double-save' that helped see off Leeds United in the 1973 FA Cup Final. He went to Nottingham Forest as cover for Peter Shilton, and was surely kept out of the senior England side only by the great Gordon Banks. Montgomery proved to be an inspired signing by Blues and produced some quite marvellous saves during his spell at St Andrew's.

MOONEY, Thomas John
Midfielder: 34+5 apps. 15 goals
Born: Billingham, 11 August 1971
Career: Aston Villa (trainee, July 1987, professional November 1989), Scarborough (free transfer, August 1990), Southend United (£100,000, July 1993), Watford (March 1994), BLUES (free transfer, July 2001), Stoke City (on loan, September 2002), Sheffield United (on loan January 2003).
Club honours: Blues: Division One promotion 2002.
A hard-running, hard-working industrious midfielder, Tommy Mooney certainly added impetus and competitiveness to the Blues team but manager Steve Bruce didn't think he would be as effective in the Premiership and he was allowed to join Stoke City after barely a season at St Andrew's. Mooney failed to make a single first team appearance with Villa, but he did net 65 goals in 288 games for the Hornets.

MOORE, Ernest Walter
Left-back: one app.
Born: Birmingham, 1869. Now deceased
Career: Sparkhill Alliance, BLUES (March 1893),

Hockley Hill (July 1895).

Ernie Moore was given a try out in the United Counties League in 1893, a late-season competition designed to fill gaps in the fixture list. He played in two games and seemed to have a promising future, but when Blues signed 'Dowk' Oliver, Moore was pushed out. He made his Football League debut the following season when Oliver was injured on Boxing Day but that was the end of his career with Blues.

MOORE, George S

Inside-forward: 3 apps. one goal
Born: Coventry, 1884.
Career: Nuneaton Borough, BLUES (season 1908-09), Leamington Town (1909).
George 'Kid' Moore was a highly popular youngster when with Nuneaton but his transfer to Blues didn't go down too well with the fans. He failed to settle in League football and was soon back in Warwickshire junior soccer.

MORAN, Richard

Centre-forward: 2+7 apps. one goal
Born: Maidstone, 9 September 1963.
Career: Fareham Town, Gosport Borough (1987), FC Fujita/Japan (1988), BLUES (on trial, August 1990, signed on a full-time contract, September 1990), Kettering Town (on loan, March 1991), Waterlooville (September 1991 to 1993).
Richard 'Whoopie' Moran was a big, awkward-looking forward who was signed by Blues after his return from a two-year spell in Japan. He was a prolific scorer in non-League soccer and was on the verge of having trials with Leeds until injury intervened. He had the unusual distinction of being substituted at half-time during his initial first-team trial with Blues because he had to dash off to be best man at a friend's wedding that afternoon. He scored on his debut for Blues but failed to show that he was good enough for League competition. He got his nickname from the American film star Whoopie Goldberg (a look-alike).

MORELAND, Arthur Geoffrey

Centre-forward: 3 apps
Born: Wolverhampton, June 1912. Deceased.
Career: Prestwood Amateurs, Stafford Rangers, Swindon Town (1937), BLUES (May 1938), Port Vale (November 1938-39). Did not figure after WW2.
A tall, well-built target man, Geoff Moreland was a prominent figure in non-League football before his move to Swindon. His League career was transient as he switched clubs rapidly with little success.

MORFITT, John William

Centre-forward: one app
Born: Sheffield, 28 September 1908. Deceased.
Career: Sheffield Heeley, Mansfield Town, BLUES

(March 1928), Blackpool (1931), Bradford Park Avenue (March 1932). Retired in June 1936.
Jack Morfitt failed to make his mark with any of his clubs. A player who relied on speed rather than muscle power, consequently he was knocked off the ball far too easily.

MORGAN, John

Centre-half: one app.
Born: Penicuik, Scotland, 17 March 1900. Now deceased
Career: Edinburgh Emmett, BLUES (August 1924), Doncaster Rovers (June 1926), Bristol City (August 1930), Barrow (June 1931), Walsall (1933), Worcester City, (then briefly in Ireland), Atherstone Town (season 1938-39). Retired in 1940.
Jack Morgan was a strongly built player whose only game for Blues came when both Cringan and Hunter were injured. He was never selected again.

MORGAN, Thomas

Centre-half: 2 apps.
Born: Walsall, 1860. Now deceased
Career: Darlaston Road Council School, Walsall Town Swifts, BLUES (August 1882), Darlaston (June 1883 to 1885).
A youngster who alternated with the more experienced Sam Gessey throughout his one term at Muntz Street, Tom Morgan lost the struggle and had dropped out of contention by February, moving on to Darlaston at the end of the season.

MORGAN, Trevor James

Forward/defender: 1+1 apps.
Born: Forest Gate, London 30 September 1956.
Career: Tonbridge (July 1977), Sydney St George, Dartford, Leytonstone, AFC Bournemouth (September 1980), Mansfield Town (November 1981), AFC Bournemouth (March 1982), Bristol City (March 1984), Exeter City (November 1984), Bristol Rovers (September 1985), Bristol City (January 1987), Bolton Wanderers (June 1987), Colchester United (October 1989), Happy Valley FC/Hong Kong, Exeter City (November 1990), South China FC/Hong Kong, BLUES (assistant-manager, January 1993), Solihull Borough (December 1993), Exeter City (assistant-manager, February 1994 to 1996).
Trevor Morgan had a long and interesting career before joining Blues as assistant-manager to Terry Cooper. He had amassed well over 600 senior appearances (481 in the Football League) as a professional prior to his arrival at St Andrew's.

MORGAN, William Albert L

Outside-left: 68 apps. 13 goals.
Born: Old Hill, 3 November 1891. Now deceased
Career: Cradley St Luke's, BLUES (November 1912),

Coventry City (August 1920), Crystal Palace (July 1922), Cradley St Luke's (June 1925), Shrewsbury Town (1927). Rather on the plump side for a winger, Bill 'Mollie' Morgan was one of the 'bulldozer-type' players who moved to inside-forward after leaving Blues. He maintained a respectable strike-rate throughout his career.

MORLEY, William Anthony

Outside-left: 4 apps. 3 goals.
Born: Ormskirk, 26 August 1954.
Career: Ormskirk & Burscough Schools, Skelmersdale Boys, Preston North End (apprentice June 1970, professional September 1972), Burnley (for a record fee of £100,000, February 1976), Aston Villa (£200,000, June 1979), West Bromwich Albion (£75,000, December 1983), BLUES (on loan, November-December 1984), FC Seiko/Hong Kong (on loan, August 1985), FC Den Haag/Holland (£25,000, July 1986), Walsall (on trial, June 1987), Notts County (on trial, early July 1987), West Bromwich Albion (late July 1987), Burnley (on loan, October-November 1988), Tampa Bay Rowdies/NASL (March 1989), Hamrun Spartans/Malta (1990), New Zealand League football (season 1990-91), Sutton Coldfield Town (1993), Bromsgrove Rovers (assistant-manager 1993), Stratford Town (April 1995).
Club honours: Aston Villa: Division One champions 1981, European Cup winners 1982, European Super Cup winners 1983, World Club championship runners-up 1983: Den Haag: Dutch Cup runners-up 1987.
Representative honours: England (6 full caps, 1 'B' cap, 1 Under-23 cap, 7 Youth caps).
A top-class winger whilst with Burnley and Villa, Tony Morley was a player who hugged the touch-line, had pace, dribbling ability and a telling shot. He first came to Blues' notice when he scored a quite stunning goal against them when playing for Burnley. The club never made an offer and Morley moved to Villa instead. He was in the doldrums when he finally arrived at St Andrew's on loan in 1984 and he subsequently became only the second player ever to turn out for Blues, Villa and Albion in League football. Blues could not sign him simply because they had no money!

MORRALL, George Richard

Centre-half: 266 apps. 7 goals
Born: Smethwick, 4 October 1905. Died: Birmingham, 15 November 1955.
Career: Gorse Street Primitive Methodists, Chance's Glass Works FC, Littleton Harriers, Allen Everitt's Sports, West Bromwich Albion (on trial), BLUES (professional, March 1927), Swindon Town (June 1936). Retired in May 1940.
Club honours: Blues: FA Cup runners-up 1931.
George 'Lofty' Morrall was a tall, commanding figure in the heart of the Blues defence. He dominated in the air was reliable on the ground and possessed a ferocious

tackle. He gained a regular place in the side in 1928-29 and went on to put in some sterling performances for the club, being tipped at once stage for England honours. He was uncle to Terry Morrall (formerly of Aston Villa).

MORRIS, Arthur

Inside-left: 4 apps 2 goals
Born: Market Drayton 1882
Died: Shrewsbury Town, Blues 1906 Shrewsbury Town 1908. A ball playing midfielder scored on his debut against Mancester United.

MORRIS, David J.

Inside-left: 3 apps
Born: Walsall, 1888. Now deceased
Career: Walsall Conduits FC, Darlaston, BLUES (August 1910), Tipton Town (1912).
David Morris, an inexperienced forward from the Black Country, was given his chance by Blues in season 1911-12, after the team had got off to an atrocious start. He looked lost in League competition, however, and was soon on his way back to junior circles.

MORRIS, Harry

Wing-half/centre-forward: 69 apps. 4 goals.
Born: Birmingham, 11 April 1886. Died: Birmingham, June 1931.
Career: Small Heath Council School, BLUES (August 1883). Retired in May 1893.
Few men gave Blues better service than Harry Morris, who joined the club as a 17-year-old centre-forward at a time when he was also an apprentice plumber. He eventually became an accomplished right-half, skippering the side many times, and was indeed a grand leader, showing immense determination and sportsmanship. After retiring it was Harry Morris who 'found' the St Andrew's ground, having become a director of the club in 1903. His two sons (Harry junior & Len) followed him on to the board, with the former attaining directorship in 1929, and taking over as chairman in 1933. He was president in 1967, the year of his death. Harry senior died in 1931, having attended that season's FA Cup Final when Blues lost 2-1 to West Bromwich Albion, 45 years after he had played for Small Heath against the Baggies in the 1886 FA Cup semi-final at Aston. A shrewd businessman, Harry Morris was one of the first people in Birmingham to see the potential in talking pictures and at the time of his death he was on the board of several local cinemas in the district. His brother Charles played for Blues in their pre-League days.

MORRIS, Ronald

Outside-left: 5+10 apps 0 goals
Born: Birmingham, 25 September 1970.
Career: FA School of Excellence, BLUES (YTS June 1986, professional September 1988, contract cancelled

1989), Nuovo Pistoiese/Italy (Inter-Regional League), Redditch United (1990), Kings Norton Ex-Servicemen FC, Sandwell Borough, West Bromwich Albion (on trial), Shrewsbury Town (on trial, February-March 1994). One of the first in-take of youngsters from the School of Excellence, Ronnie Morris soon fell foul of the authorities for a series of misdemeanours. Undeterred by this, Blues took him on and he impressed in the youth team, showing good pace and aggression. At the end of 1987-88 he was given a run-out as substitute and looked a fair prospect. Sadly he had a problem with his attitude and after some training ground incidents, Blues sacked him. He played a few games in Italy before he was sent back to England when it was found that his signing was declared null and void, as it had occurred after the Italian transfer deadline. He has since had occasional forays into non-League football with limited success.

MORRIS, Seymour

Winger: 83 apps. 31 goals
Born: Ynyshir, South Wales, 15 February 1908. Died: South Wales, 1991
Career: Ynyshir School, Cathay's FC, Lovells Athletic, Aberaman, Huddersfield Town (March 1933), BLUES (March 1935). Retired in 1944.
Representative honours: Wales (5 full caps).
Fast and tricky but somewhat frail, Seymour Morris' career at Blues was blighted by injuries. At Huddersfield he had been regarded primarily as an inside-forward but had made only six appearances for them, scoring three goals, when Blues stepped in. he switched to the left-wing - his more natural position - but it took him two years to establish himself as a regular in the side at St Andrew's. Then injuries and international call-ups saw him absent. He was one of five Welsh internationals on Blues' books in 1938-39, although only four ever appeared on the international scene together. Morris lived in South Wales until his death in 1991.

MORRISON, Clinton Hubert

Striker: 19+3* apps. 4 goals*
Born: Wandsworth, London, 14 May 1979
Career: Crystal Palace (trainee, June 1995, professional March 1997), BLUES (£4.25 million, August 2002).
Representative honours: Republic of Ireland (7* full & two under-21 caps)
Clinton Morrison scored his first two Premiership goals at Anfield, enabling Blues to come back from 2-0 down to earn a point in September 2002 - and then he netted the opener in the long-awaited 3-0 home win over arch-rivals Aston Villa nine days later. After an excellent last season with Palace (24 goals in 49 games) Morrison - fast, sharp and alert - was signed by his former Selhurst Park boss Steve Bruce to partner Stern John in the Blues attack - and what a great start he made to his St Andrew's career...with more to come.

MORTIMER, Dennis George

Midfielder: 37 apps 6 goals.
Born: Liverpool, 5 April 1952.
Career: Kirby Boys, Coventry City (apprentice July 1967, professional September 1969), Aston Villa (£175,000 December 1975), Sheffield United (on loan, December 1984), Brighton & Hove Albion (August 1985), BLUES (August 1986), Kettering Town (non-contract, August 1987), Redditch United (player-manager, late 1987-October 1988), West Bromwich Albion (casual reserve team player & Community Officer, August 1989, Youth-team manager 1992, assistant-manager June 1993 to October 1994), Aston Villa (Academy/Youth team coach, late 1990s).
Club honours: Coventry City: FA Youth Cup runners-up 1970; Aston Villa: Football League Cup winners 1977, Division One champions 1981, European Cup winners 1982, European Super Cup winners 1983, World Club Championship runner-up 1982.
Representative honours: England (3 'B' caps, 6 Under-23 caps, Youth caps); also toured Australia with FA in 1971.
A driving force in midfield, Dennis Mortimer first rose to prominence with Coventry when his hair was so long that the fans called him 'Doris'. He moved to Villa Park and became an instant success, his hard-running style making him the archetypal 'Ron Saunders player', although his game contained much more than sheer athleticism. His career was coming to an end when he joined Blues and after a promising start at St Andrew's he fell out of favour with the fans and left after only one season. He played over 400 games for Villa and during his League career amassed a total of 590 appearances.

MORTON, Roy Steven

Midfielder: 6 apps. one goal.
Born: Birmingham, 29 October 1955.
Career: Warley Boys, Manchester United (apprentice June 1971, professional November 1972), BLUES (free transfer, September 1973), AP Leamington (June 1977 to 1979).
Representative honours: England (Youth and, Schoolboy caps).
Roy Morton was a star of Midlands schools football for whom big things were predicted, but he struggled at Old Trafford and was freed when it became obvious that he was not going to break through. A chunky midfield workhorse with a terrific shot, he was restricted to a few games as Howard Kendall's understudy at St Andrew's.

MOULDEN, Paul Anthony

Striker: 20+3 apps. 6 goals.
Born: Farnworth, 6 September 1967.
Career: Bolton Boys' Club (two years: 1980 to 1982), Manchester City (apprentice June 1984, professional, September 1984), AFC Bournemouth (£160,000, August 1989), Oldham Athletic (£225,000, March

1990), Brighton & Hove Albion (on loan, August 1992), BLUES (£150,000, March 1993), Huddersfield Town (free transfer, March 1995), Rochdale (August 1995 to May 1996).

Club honours: Manchester City: FA Youth Cup winners 1986; Oldham Athletic: Division Two champions 1991.

Representative honours: England (15 Youth caps, Schoolboy caps).

As a teenager with Bolton Boys' Club, Paul Moulden scored 289 goals in the 1981-82 season. He continued his good work with Manchester City's intermediate and reserve teams and also did well in the senior side, scoring 26 times in 79 games. Thereafter his form see-sawed and he struggled with injury during his first full season at St Andrew's. He is the son of Tony Moulden, the former Bury, Rochdale, Peterborough and Notts County player.

MOUNTENEY, Arthur

Inside-forward: 97 apps. 30 goals.

Born: Belgrave, Leicester, 11 February 1883.

Died: Leicester, 1 June 1933.

Career: Leicester Imperial, Leicester Fosse (November 1903), BLUES (April 1905), Preston North End ((April 1909), Grimsby Town (July 1911), Portsmouth (December 1912), Hinckley Athletic (September 1914 to 1915). Although he was a big, burly forward, Arthur 'Pecker' Mounteney was not the 'battering ram' that one might expect. Indeed, during his stay at Blues, he was frequently criticised for not using his weight enough. Surprisingly quick for his size, he preferred to beat opponents with a short, sharp passing manoeuvres. He also played cricket and was an attractive middle-order batsman, representing Leicestershire for 13 years, scoring 5,306 runs (six centuries) at an average of 20.8.

MUIR, Ian James

Inside-forward: 2+1 apps.

Born: Coventry, 5 May 1963.

Career: Caludon Castle School, Stockingford Scholars, Bedworth Juniors, QPR (apprentice, June 1979, professional September 1980), Burnley (on loan, November 1982), BLUES (free transfer, August 1983), Brighton & Hove Albion (free transfer February 1984), Swindon Town (on loan, January 1985), Tranmere Rovers (July 1985), BLUES (£125,000, June 1995 to May 1997), Darlington (on loan, September-October 1995).

Club honours: Tranmere Rovers: Leyland DAF Cup winners 1990, Division Three promotion 1991.

Representative honours: England (1 Youth and, Schoolboy caps).

Ian Muir was a goal-poaching striker whose abilities were misjudged by a string of managers until his profitable association with Tranmere where he went on to beat the club's all-time scoring record (142 League goals). Although a regular marksman in Blues' reserves, he was

never given the extended run in the first team that perhaps he deserved. He was 33 years of age when he returned to St Andrew's for a brief second spell with the club.

MULLETT, Joseph

Left-half/full-back: 3 apps.

Born: Blackheath, 2 October 1936. Died: Cradley Heath, 1995.

Career: Malt Mill United, BLUES (amateur, February 1955, professional July 1955), Norwich City (£2,000, February 1959), King's Lynn (August 1968), Lowestoft Town (July 1970), Yarmouth Town (October 1971 to 1972).

Club honours: Norwich City: League Cup winners 1962.

Joe Mullett was a powerfully built wing-half who was given a run in the Blues' first team shortly after returning from his National Service in the Far East. He was never assured of a senior place due to the consistency of Dick Neal. Converted to full-back at Norwich, he proved a great favourite with the Carrow Road fans. He later became a market trader, shopkeeper and finally a scrap-metal worker (with Brookes Ltd) in Old Hill, West Midlands.

MULRANEY, Ambrose

Outside-right/left: 41 apps. 16 goals.

Born: Wishaw, near Motherwell, 18 May 1916.

Died: Kinver, 2001

Career: Wishaw White Rose, Carluke Rovers, Hearts (on trial), Celtic (August 1933), Hamilton Academical (on trial), Sligo Orient (on trial), Dartford (1935), Ipswich Town (August 1936), BLUES (£3,750, October 1945), Shrewsbury Town (July 1947), Kidderminster Harriers (July 1948), Aston Villa (September 1948), Cradley Heath (player-manager, August 1949), Brierley Hill (manager, season 1952-53). Retired in May 1954. Assisted several clubs during WW2 whilst serving in the RAF, including BLUES (118 apps, 41 goals), Blackburn Rovers, Brentford, Charlton Athletic, Chelsea, Hibernian, Leicester City, Manchester City, Millwall, Third Lanark & Wolverhampton Wanderers.

Club honours: Ipswich: Southern League champions 1937; Blues: Football League (South) champions 1946.

Representative honours: Scotland (Schoolboy trialist); Scottish Alliance XI 1934.

A fast raiding Scottish winger who could occupy either flank, 'Jock' Mulraney joined Blues after demobilisation from five years' RAF service. He joined Celtic after turning down Hearts but failed to break into the first team at Parkhead. He scored Ipswich Town's first-ever Football League hat-trick against Bristol City in April 1939. Mulraney went into the RAF in March 1940 and he rose to the rank of flight-sargeant as a PT instructor. He suffered a heart attack in 1968, recovered after surgery and then underwent two eye operations while continuing to work right as an odd-job man around the

Kinver area until 1997, finally putting away his paint (and ladders) at the age of 81.

MUMFORD, Wayne Ernest

Right-back: 6+2 apps
Born: Rhymney, 3 November 1964.
Career: Coventry Boys, Manchester City (apprentice, 1980), BLUES (professional, September 1982), Worcester City (season 1984-85), Coventry Sporting (August 1985), Leamington Town (April 1986). Retired in May 1987.
Representative honours: Wales (Youth caps).
Welsh-born but brought up in Coventry, Wayne Mumford came to Blues when Manchester City decided not to offer him a professional contract. He proved a competent deputy without really doing enough to justify a regular first-team place and spent a few years playing in non-League football until a knee injury ended his career.

MUMFORD, William Richard

Right-back: 3 apps
Born: Stirchley, Birmingham 3 March 1894.
Died: Birmingham 1971.
Career: Bournville, BLUES (August 1920), Brighton & Hove Albion (April 1921), Redditch (September 1921).
Bill Mumford was picked up from Birmingham Combination football and given a trial run in the first team at the end of 1919-20. With the arrival of Jack Jones the next season, though, he found himself pushed down the queue for a first-team place and was released in the summer of 1921.

MURPHY, Peter

Inside-left: 278 apps. 127 goals
Born: West Hartlepool, 7 March 1922. Died: 7 April 1975.
Career: Dunlop FC, Coventry City (amateur), BLUES (amateur), Millwall (guest 1945-46), Coventry City (professional May 1946), Tottenham Hotspur (£18,500 June 1950), BLUES (£20,000, January 1952), Rugby Town. Retired in May 1961 and went into licensing trade.
Club honours: Spurs: Division Two champions 1951; Blues: Division Two champions 1955, FA Cup runners-up 1956.
Born in the North-East but moved to the Midlands with his family at the age of four, Peter 'Spud' Murphy had been on Blues' books as an amateur before Coventry City signed him as a professional. He was initially a schemer and it was as such that he joined Arthur Rowe's 'Push and Run' side at Spurs, and played as an inside-forward in their 1950-51 championship winning season, deputising for Les Bennett. With Bennett fit again, Murphy found himself playing out of position on the left wing and was grateful of a chance to move to St Andrew's. He switched to a more attacking role when Tommy Briggs left, and thereafter his career blossomed. His phenomenal left-foot shooting from anywhere within

30-40 yards took many goalkeepers by surprise and he topped the Blues' scoring lists four times. In 1959 he was given the job of coaching the youngsters but at the end of the season was called back into the first team as Blues struggled against relegation. He repaid Blues' faith in him with four vital goals in seven games as relegation was avoided. He is perhaps best remembered as the Blues player involved in the incident with Manchester City's goalkeeper, Bert Trautmann, in the 1956 FA Cup Final, when the German broke his neck. Murphy had boundless energy and was always in the thick of the action. A magnificent marksman he netted a total of 158 goals in 399 League appearances for his three clubs.

MURRAY, Albert George

Outside-right/right-back: 151+9 apps. 23 goals
Born: Shoreditch, near Hoxton, 22 September 1942.
Career: Chelsea (junior June 1958, professional May 1961), BLUES (£25,000, August 1966), Brighton & Hove Albion (February 1971), Peterborough United (September 1973). Retired in May 1977.
Club honours: Chelsea: Football League Cup winners 1965.
Representative honours: England (Youth caps, 6 Under-23 caps).
Bert 'Ruby' Murray turned out in just about every position whilst with Chelsea including emergency goalkeeper (a role he also performed at Blues). Lightly built and quick, Murray was originally a winger and it was in this role that he shone for Chelsea, being particularly adept at finding scoring positions. It was as a winger that Blues initially played him and he got off to a fine start, scoring two goals on his debut. In November 1966, Ray Martin was injured and Murray took over the right-back berth, doing such a fine job that he held the position for the next 18 months. In 1969 he was switched back to a forward role and impressed, holding down the slot as a striker wide on the right until he was ousted by a promising youngster by the name of Trevor Francis! Murray made 595 League appearances and scored 108 goals for his four major clubs.
He later became landlord of the White Horse in Market Deeping, Lincolnshire.

MURRAY, James Arthur

Inside-right: one app. one goal
Born: Benwhat, Scotland, February 1879.
Died: Glasgow, June 1933.
Career: St Augustine's FC, Ayr United (1897), Aston Villa (March 1901), BLUES (November 1901), Watford (1902), Kettering Town (May 1903), King's Heath Albion (season 1905-06).
Jim Murray had a brief and unsuccessful spell at Villa Park, but drew fulsome praise after a goalscoring debut for Blues (v. Sunderland in November 1901), one critic saying: "He is fairly fast, has capital command of the ball and can shoot excellently." Despite this, his only other first-team outings came in friendlies.

N

MYHRE, Thomas

Goalkeeper: 9 apps

Born: Sarpsborg, Norway, 16 October 1973

Career: FC Viking Stavanger/Norway, Everton (£800,000, November 1997), Glasgow Rangers (on loan, November 1999), BLUES (on loan, March-May 2000), Tranmere Rovers (on loan, November-December 2000), FC Copenhagen/Denmark (on loan, March 2001), Besiktas/Turkey (November 2001), Sunderland (season 2002-03).

Club honours: FC Copenhagen: League champions 2001

Representative honours: Norway (19 full, 3 Under-21 and Youth caps)

Impressive goalkeeper, who commands his area with authority, Thomas Myhre, 6ft 4ins tall and weighing almost 14 stones, joined Blues on loan after failing to dislodge Steve Gerrard in Everton's first XI. He made 82 appearances for the Merseysiders.

NDLOVU, Peter

Forward: 100+34 apps. 28 goals

Born: Bulawayo, Zimbabwe, 25 February 1973

Career: Highlanders FC/Zimbabwe (1989), Coventry City (£10,000, August 1991), BLUES (£1.6 million, July 1997), Huddersfield Town (on loan, December 2000), Sheffield United (free transfer, February 2001).

Representative honours: Zimbabwe (16 full caps)

Peter Ndlovu did very well at Highfield Road, scoring 41 goals 197 senior appearances before moving to St Andrew's in 1997. During his three years with Blues he enjoyed playing wide on the left (and even the right) and gave defenders plenty to think about with his electrifying pace, ball skills and work-rate. Unfortunately injuries interrupted his game over the last year or so but was still a vital member of the Blues and Zimbabwean national squads. When he left St Andrew's for Huddersfield he was signed by his former manager Lou Macari.

NEAL, Richard Marshall

Left-half: 197 apps. 18 goals

Born: Dinnington, 1 October 1933.

Career: Wath Wanderers (August 1948), Wolverhampton Wanderers (juniors, August 1949, professional, March 1951), Lincoln City (July 1954), BLUES (£18,000, plus Albert Linnecor, April 1957), Middlesbrough (October 1961), Lincoln City (August 1963), Rugby Town (July 1964), Hednesford Town (player-manager, May 1965), Brierley Hill Alliance (player-manager, December 1967), Blakenhall (player-manager, February 1968). Later became a publican, first in Birmingham and then mine host of the Horse & Jockey at Penkridge (Staffs).

Club honours: Blues: Inter Cities Fairs Cup runners-up 1960.

Representative honours: England (4 Under-23 caps); England Youth XI. Dick 'Ticker' Neal was effective in both defence and attack. Powerfully built he failed to make a first-team appearance with Wolves but developed quickly at Lincoln. Blues signed him for what was then a considerable fee and gave him the job of prompting his forwards. As befitted a man of over 6ft tall and weighting in excess of 12st, Neal was also a fearsome tackler. He lost his place to Terry Hennessey before moving to Ayresome Park. He totalled 415 League appearances in his career, and skippered Blues in 1960-61. His father, Richard Neal senior, played for Blackpool, Derby County, Southampton, Bristol City and Accrington Stanley before WW2.

NEALE, Keith Ivan

Inside-forward: 5 apps. one goal

Born: Yardley, Birmingham, 19 January 1935.

Career: Metropolitan FC, BLUES (amateur August 1953, professional February 1954), Lincoln City (November 1957-May 1959), Kettering Town (July 1959), Boston United (September 1960), Gainsborough (August 1963).

A cheerful, fair-haired forward who was plucked out of the Works League, Keith Neale was groomed in the juniors for three years before being given his League debut. Always regarded as a reserve, his chances were few and he fared little better at Lincoln before dropping out of the League. He went to live in the village of Chaddesley Corbett, Worcestershire.

NEEDHAM, Andrew Paul

Forward: 2+1 apps. one goal.

Born: Oldham, 13 September 1955.

Career: Harlow & Essex Boys, BLUES (apprentice June 1971, professional August 1973), Blackburn Rovers (July 1976), Aldershot (March 1977 to May 1980).

Andy Needham was a tall forward whose aggressive attitude made him look a good prospect in junior football. But when given his chance by Blues, he looked out of place and although he scored in his second game he was quickly discarded. It was very much the same story at Blackburn but he scored over 30 goals in more than 100 games for Aldershot.

NEEDHAM, John

Inside-forward: 20 apps. 5 goals

Born: Newstead near Nottingham, 1891. Now Deceased

Career: Mansfield Wesleyans, Mansfield Town (July 1907), BLUES (June 1909), Wolverhampton Wanderers (April 1910), Hull City (March 1920). Retired in May 1921. Jack Needham was a promising youngster with an eye for goal but was mysteriously allowed to leave Blues after a good first season. However, he made Blues pay dearly by scoring against them regularly in later years. Needham became known as 'Mr Consistency' at the Molineux where he formed a marvellous left-wing partnership with Sammy Brooks while scoring 61 goals in 206 games for the Wanderers.

NEIL, Peter W H
Outside-right: 5 apps.
Born: Methil, Fife, Scotland, 1898. Now Deceased
Career: East Fife, BLUES (April 1921), Heart of
Midlothian (September 1922).
Peter Neil had only a handful of games (as deputy for
Billy Harvey) before returning to Scotland.

NEILSON, Peter M
Outside-left: 3 apps. one goal
Born: Glasgow, summer 1890. Now Deceased
Career: Airdrieonians, BLUES (August 1913), Wallyford
(March 1914).
Another of the long line of Scottish ball players who
came south to try his luck in England, Peter Neilson had
a tendency to 'play the dribbling game', which met with
some criticism from the local Press. His one goal did earn
Blues a victory, though - over Bury at St Andrew's in
October 1913 (won 1-0).

NEWELL, Michael Colin
Striker: 15+5 apps. 3 goals
Born: Liverpool, 27 January 1965
Career: Liverpool Juniors, Crewe Alexandra (September
1983), Wigan Athletic (October 1983), Luton Town
(£100,000, January 1986), Leicester City (£350,000,
September 1987), Everton (£850,000, July 1989),
Blackburn Rovers (£1.1 million, November 1991),
BLUES (£775,000, July 1996), West Ham United (on
loan, December 1996), Bradford City (on loan, March
1997), Aberdeen (£160,000, July 1997), Crewe
Alexandra (March 1999), Doncaster Rovers (June 1999),
Blackpool (February 2000, retired July 2001). Hartlepool
Utd (manager, 2002-03).
Club honours: Wigan Athletic (AMC winners 1985),
Blackburn (Premier League champions 1995)
Representative honours: England (two 'B' & 4
Under-21 caps)
In his nomadic first-class career Mike Newell scored 166
goals in 655 senior appearances. Always a willing worker,
he initially partnered Paul Furlong up front, but asked
for transfer after just 10 weeks, citing difficulty in
settling in at St Andrew's. Unfortunately he had one of
his leanest scoring spells in his career with Blues.

NEWMAN, John Henry George
Half-back: 65 apps
Born: Hereford, 13 December 1933.
Career: Hereford United Juniors, Hereford Lads' Club,
BLUES, St Andrew's Athletic (July 1949), BLUES
(amateur 1950, professional March 1951), Leicester City
(£12,000, November 1957), Plymouth Argyle (January
1960), Exeter City (£8,000, plus a player, November
1967). In April 1969 he was appointed manager of
Exeter (after a spell as player-manager at St James' Park)
and held the position until December 1976; thereafter

Grimsby Town (manager, January 1977), Derby County
(assistant-manager, July 1979, manager January-
November 1982), Hereford United (manager, March
1983-July 1987), York City (assistant-manager, season
1987-88), Notts County (assistant-manager, July 1988),
Mansfield Town (Youth Development Officer/Chief
Scout, 1990-93), Burton Albion (assistant-manager,
1994 to 1996), Worcester City (coach).
Club honours: Blues: Division Two champions 1955, FA
Cup runners-up 1956.
Representative honours: Wales (Junior international).
John Newman attended a Welsh school hence his
incongruous international record. He was a boot boy at
non-League Hereford United when Blues signed him in
1949 (playing him in their junior side St Andrew's
Athletic) and he came through the ranks to develop into
a solid, no-nonsense defender, able to deputise in all
three half-back positions. He was surprisingly chosen to
play in the 1956 FA Cup Final ahead of far more
experienced team-mates, but eventually left the club
when it became obvious that he was never going to
become a regular in the first team, despite the departure
of Len Boyd and Roy Warhurst. He did remarkably well
after leaving Blues, altogether accumulating well over
600 senior appearances (in major League and Cup
competitions) during his 20 years in the professional
game. In November 1964 he gained note by passing a
penalty-kick a yard forward for his colleague Mike
Trebilcock to run on to and score from less than 12
yards range.

NEWTON, Edward John Ikem
Midfielder/forward: 4+5 apps.
Born: Hammersmith, London 13 December 1971
Career: Chelsea (trainee, June 1988, professional May
1990), Cardiff City (on loan, January 1992), BLUES
(free transfer, July 1999), Oxford United (free, March
2000), Barnet (free, August 2000), Singapore soccer
(from September 2000).
Club honours: Chelsea: FA Cup winners 1997, League
Cup winners and European Cup-winners Cup
winners 1998
Representative honours: England (2 Under-21 caps)
Unfortunately Eddie Newton had a very disappointing
time with Blues. Although very skilful, his style was
considered unsuitable for the rigorous midfield and after
suffering a shin injury he was eventually transferred to
Oxford. He scored 10 goals in 213 games for Chelsea.

NORTH, Marc Victor
Forward: 4+1 apps. one goal.
Born: Ware, Herts, 29 May 1966. Died: Southend-on-
Sea, 25 September 2001.
Career: Hertfordshire Boys, Luton Town (apprentice
June 1982, professional April 1984), Lincoln City (on
loan, March 1985), Scunthorpe United (on loan, January

1987), BLUES (on loan, March 1987), Grimsby Town (£40,000 August 1987), Leicester City (March 1989), Luton Town (monthly contract, July 1991), Grimsby Town (October 1991), Shepshed Albion, Walsall (on trial), Kettering Town (April 1992), St Andrew's Social Club, Corby Town, St Andrew's Social Club (again). Marc North was signed by Luton as a schoolboy goalkeeper but made his League bow for the Hatters as a central defender. By the time he arrived at St Andrew's he had completed the transformation and had become a forward. North showed a fair degree of skill during his short spell with Blues, although no attempt was made to sign him permanently. He played for Lincoln in the match when Bradford City's stand burned down. Sadly, North died at the age of 35.

OAKES, Alfred William
Inside-left: one app.
Born: Bewdley, Worcestershire, 22 July 1901.
Died: Bristol, 25 December 1967.
Career: RAF (Uxbridge), Chesham United (August 1922), Millwall (July 1923), Reading (May 1925), Rhyl Athletic (June 1926), Worcester City, BLUES (£300, February 1927), Rhyl Athletic (June 1928), New Brighton (August 1929), Wigan Borough (June 1931), Frickley Colliery FC (November 1931), Stalybridge Celtic (August 1932). Retired through injury May 1933. Alf Oakes was a tall, red-haired forward who was a regular scorer in non-League circles but proved a big disappointment at St Andrew's. He was Wigan's top marksman with four goals when they withdrew from the League in October 1931. His son Don Oakes played for Arsenal.

OAKES, Thomas Frank
Forward: 38 apps. 8 goals
Born: Cheltenham, 1874. Now Deceased
Career: Hereford Thistle, BLUES (August 1896), Gloucester City (1900).
The Birmingham Gazette reported that this talented striker had a promising debut and announced that he had scored at hat-trick. The former is true; the latter is false, as he failed to score at all. He played in three different forward positions for Blues but was perhaps best at inside-right. He slipped out of the first-team reckoning for two years before moving back to the non-League game.

O'CONNOR, Martin John
Midfielder: 216+7 apps. 19 goals
Born: Walsall, 10 December 1967
Career: Bromsgrove Rovers, Crystal Palace (£15,000, June 1992), Walsall (on loan, March 1993, signed permanently for £40,000, February 1994), Peterborough United (£350,000, July 1996), BLUES (£500,000+, November 1996), Walsall (free transfer, February 2002).

Club honours: Blues: League Cup runners-up 2001, Division One promotion 2002
Representative honours: Cayman Islands (2 full caps)
A true professional, full of aggression and willpower, Martin O'Connor gave Blues excellent service for five-and-a-half years before surprisingly being 'given away' by Steve Bruce who said he wanted a younger player in the engine-room. Totally committed, quick in the tackle, with great positional sense, he overcame several injury problems including a damaged knee and Achilles tendon trouble to play in well over 200 first-class matches for Blues

O'GRADY, Michael
Winger/midfielder: 2+1 apps.
Born: Leeds, 11 October 1942.
Career: Huddersfield Town (juniors, June 1958, professional November 1959), Leeds United (£30,000, October 1965), Wolverhampton Wanderers (£80,000, September 1969), BLUES (on loan, February 1972), Rotherham United (November 1972). Retired through injury May 1974. Later worked for Yorkshire TV (as a grip) before taking over as mine host of the Royal Oak Pub at Aberford near Wetherby. He still plays occasionally for the Leeds United Old Stars XI.
Club honours: Leeds: Fairs Cup runners-up 1967, winners 1968, Division One champions 1969.
Representative honours: England (two full & three Under-23 caps); Football League XI (3).
Originally a pacy left-winger, Mike O'Grady gained his first full cap when only 20 and, wishing to play at a higher grade of football, he joined Don Revie's great Leeds side of the 1960's where, despite frequent injuries, he played his part in their quest for honours. Further injuries disrupted his spell at Molineux and it was while recuperating from one of these knocks that he joined Blues, becoming the first loan player to make a League appearance for the club.

O'HARA, Edward Patrick
Outside-left: 6 apps.
Born: Dalkey near Dublin, 22 February 1927.
Died: 8 March 1987.
Career: Dundalk, BLUES (November 1949), Hereford United (1951), Sligo Rovers, Drumcondra, Lockheed Leamington, Hereford United.
Eddie O'Hara was rated higher than Jimmy Higgins when they were transferred together to Blues. Things proved otherwise as O'Hara's first-team opportunities were limited owing to the presence at St Andrew's of so many other good wingers.

OKENLA, Folorunso
Winger: 4+9 apps. one goal
Born: Ibadan, Nigeria, 9 October 1967.
Career: Leventis United/Nigeria, Julius Berger FC/Nigeria, Wimbledon (on trial), Brighton & Hove

Albion (on trial), Blackburn Rovers (on trial), Burnley (on trial), Exeter City, BLUES (non-contract, August 1991), Montreal Impact/NASL(1993), Kingstonian.
Representative honours: Nigeria (19 full caps); African Nations Cup runners-up 1988.
The most unusual of Blues' 1991 signings, fast and tricky winger 'Foley' Okenla had been over in Britain for two years, trying his luck with a number of clubs. He made a devastating entry into League soccer with a goal in his first game, which led to the most spectacular display of celebration ever witnessed at St Andrew's. He played under his first name in Nigeria.

OLIVER, John
Left-back: 62 apps.
Born: Southwick, 1867. Now Deceased
Career: Southwick, Sunderland (August 1887), Middlesbrough Ironopolis (June 1892), BLUES (April 1894), Durham (season 1896-97).
John 'Dowk' Oliver was a star of Sunderland's pre-League days but was soon discarded as Roker men began their golden era in the 1890's. He spent two years with the Ironopolis club, as they tried to bring professional football to Middlesbrough, and proved a settling influence to Blues' defence when they struggled to establish themselves in the First Division. He drew appreciative comments for the power of his kicking.

OLLIS, William
Right-half: 112 apps. 2 goals.
Born: Bordesley Green, Birmingham 12 August 1871.
Died: Birmingham, May 1940.
Career: Newall Juniors, Southfield FC, Warwick County, BLUES (April 1891), Hereford Thistle (February 1896). Retired through injury 1899.
Club honours: Blues: Division Two champions 1893.
Billy Ollis was a solid, hard-grafting player who came to Blues' attention in friendly matches against them, taking over the captaincy when Caesar Jenkyns was sacked. He held the job for only a short while, however, and moved on halfway through the season.

OLNEY, James Fulford
Centre-half: 3 apps.
Born: Greet, Birmingham, February 1910. Died: 1944, killed whilst serving with the Grenadier Guards in WW2.
Career: Tyseley Rangers, Newbridge Albion, Redditch United (1935), BLUES (May 1936), Swindon Town (December 1938). Retired in 1943.
Jim Olney was a very tall, slim centre-half who was the nephew of the Aston Villa and Derby County goalkeeper, Ben Olney. Extremely powerful in the air as might be expected from a man topping 6ft 3in, he was too similar in style to 'Tosher' Fillingham to be able to gain a regular first-team place. He sadly lost his life in WW2.

O'NEILL, Alan
Forward: 2+2 apps.
Born: Cork, 29 August 1973.
Career: Cork City (1990), Cobh Ramblers (August 1991), BLUES (£15,000, February 1992), Cobh Ramblers (January 1993 to 1994).
Representative honours: Republic of Ireland (18 Schoolboy caps).
Alan O'Neill stayed at St Andrew's for less than a year. Perhaps too much was expected of him after Irish football.

O'REILLY, Gary Miles
Centre-half: one app.
Born: Isleworth, Middlesex, 21 March 1961.
Career: Tottenham Hotspur (apprentice June 1977, professional September 1979), Brighton & Hove Albion (£45,000, August 1984), Crystal Palace (£40,000, January 1987), BLUES (on loan, March 1991), Brighton & Hove Albion (July 1991). Retired in May 1992. Now a Sky Sports TV presenter (soccer).
Club honours: Crystal Palace: FA Cup runners-up 1990.
Representative honours: Republic of Ireland (Youth & Schoolboy caps).
An experienced defender, Gary O'Reilly joined Blues as cover on the transfer deadline. He scored for Palace in the 1990 FA Cup Final (v. Manchester United) but the following season found it impossible to hold down a regular place in their line-up. Sadly he broke his nose early in the second half of his one and only game in Blues' colours and failed to recover from the injury before his loan period expired. O'Reilly was the national javelin champion in 1978.

ORRITT, Bryan
Inside-forward/wing-half: 119 apps. 27 goals.
Born: Caernarfon, North Wales, 22 February 1937.
Career: Caernarfon Grammar School (where he played both rugby & soccer), Llanfair PG FC, Bangor City (1955), BLUES (January 1956), Middlesbrough (March 1962), Johannesburg Rangers/South Africa (1966).
Club honours: Blues: Inter Cities Fairs Cup runners-up 1960,1961.
Representative honours: Wales (3 Under-23 caps).
Bryan 'Orrible' Orritt, an enterprising footballer, appeared in all 11 positions during his playing career. Primarily a winger or inside-forward whilst with Blues, his best spell in the first team came in 1957-58 when he replaced Noel Kinsey. He was not really the playmaker Blues were looking for and when Johnny Gordon was signed, Orritt was one of the few Welsh-speaking footballers in the League. Later became a prominent coach in South Africa, working with black youngsters in Soweto.
Orritt played for the Welsh non-League club Llanfairpwllgwyngyllgogerychwyrndrowlllantysiliogogogoch (shortened for obvious reasons to Llanfair PG FC).

OSBORNE, Ian Leonard
Right-back: 11 apps
Born: Leicester, 28 October 1952.
Career: Mid-Leicester Boys, BLUES (apprentice 1968, professional October 1970), Port Vale (June 1976), Hillingdon Borough (June 1977), Westfields FC.
A nippy, overlapping full-back, Ian Osborne showed considerable promise as a youngster, his spell in Blues' reserve side was rather longer than usual, however, and on stepping up to the first team he proved disappointing, his defensive skills not being as strong as his attacking ones. He made his League debut in his home-town (Leicester).

OTTEWELL, Sidney
Inside-forward: 5 apps. 2 goals
Born: Horsley, Derbyshire, 23 October 1919. Deceased.
Career: Holbrook Miners' Welfare, Chesterfield (November 1936), BLUES (June 1947), Luton Town (December 1947), Nottingham Forest (July 1948), Mansfield Town (January 1950), Scunthorpe United (March 1952), Spalding United Player-manager (1954), Lockheed Leamington (manager 1960 to January 1969).
After a successful spell with Chesterfield, Sid Ottewell was signed by Blues as a utility forward to help with the push for promotion. Although impressing with his purposeful shooting, he did not stay long at St Andrew's. He appeared in a total of 188 League games (52 goals) during his career. Guested for Chester, Spurs, Fulham, Blackpool and BLUES in WW2.

OTTO, Ricky Junior
Forward: 38+24 apps. 8 goals
Born: Hackney, London, 9 November 1967.
Career: Haringey Borough, Dartford, Leyton Orient (free transfer, November 1990), Southend United (£100,000, July 1993), BLUES (£800,000, December 1994), Charlton Athletic (on loan, September 1996), Peterborough United (on loan, February 1997), Notts County (on loan, September-October 1997). Retired in December 1997 after being released from his contract by Blues.
Club honours: Blues: Second Division champions 1995, Auto Windscreen Shield winners 1995.
A record signing for Blues, Ricky Otto had the dubious honour of scoring for both sides on his debut, in the 1-1 draw against Cambridge United at St Andrew's on 17 December 1994. A dread-locked winger, skilful, enterprising and a big favourite with the fans, he hit 15 goals in 68 games for Orient and 20 in 70 for Southend. He came into League football late after serving a prison sentence for armed robbery.

OVERSON, Vincent David
Central defender: 209+3 apps. 5 goals.
Born: Kettering, 15 May 1952.
Career: Exeter Primary School, Kingswood Grammar School, Kingswood Boys, Corby Town, Long Buckby FC, Burnley (apprentice June 1968, professional November 1979), BLUES (£235,000, June 1986), Stoke City (for a tribunal set fee of £55,000, August 1991), Burnley (free transfer, August 1996), Shrewsbury Town (on loan, September 1997), Halifax Town (free transfer, August 1998), Padiham FC (September 1998 to 2000).
Club honours: Burnley: Division Three champions 1982; Blues: Leyland DAF Cup winners 1991; Stoke: Autoglass Trophy winners 1992, Division Two champions 1993.
Representative honours: England (Youth cap).
Vince Overson was a powerfully built defender who was on the verge of joining the Army when Burnley took him under their wing. His wholehearted approach to the game made him a great favourite with the fans but his relations with the St Andrew's club were not always amicable. His wife failed to settle in the Midlands and eventually returned to Burnley. Overson twice went on the transfer list in the hope of moving back north and when his contract expired in 1991 he walked out on Blues and joined his former manager, Lou Macari, at Stoke. He made 247 appearances for Burnley before transferring to St Andrew's. And after leaving Blues he chalked up 216 for the Potters, while also adding 10 more to his Burnley tally. Overson's brother Richard, was also a professional footballer, turning out for Burnley and Hereford United.

OWEN, Sidney William
Centre-half: 5 apps.
Born: Birmingham, 29 February 1922.
Died: January 1999.
Career: Birmingham YMCA, BLUES (professional October 1945), Luton Town (player June 1947 to May 1959, manager at Kenilworth Road from April 1959 to April 1960), Leeds United (coach, May 1960), BLUES (assistant-manager, October 1975 to September 1977), Hull City (coach, December 1977 to February 1978), Manchester United (Youth-team coach, May 1978 to April 1981).
Club honours: Blues: Football League South champions 1945-46; Luton: FA Cup runners-up 1959.
Representative honours: England (3 full caps); Football League XI (2).
Sid Owen was a commanding defender, particularly strong in the air. His chances of success with Blues were baulked by the consistency of Ted Duckhouse but he proved to be an excellent signing for Luton, for whom he played over 400 games (388 in the League) during his 12 years at Kenilworth Road. He later made a name for himself as a coach, playing a major role in Leeds' success in the 1960s and 1970s. Owen appeared in five WW2 games for Blues. He was voted 'Footballer of the Year' in 1959 after leading Luton to the FA Cup Final, where they were beaten 2-1 by Nottingham Forest.

P

OWEN, William
Goalkeeper: 6 apps.
Born: Coventry, April 1903. Deceased.
Career: Nuneaton Borough, BLUES (April 1926), Fulham (August 1929), Coventry City (1930), Stourbridge (1931), Nuneaton Town (season 1934-35).
A spectacular goalkeeper who had a short period in the first team whilst Hibbs was injured. This run coincided with four Blues' defeats and when Hibbs was fit again, Bill Owen went back into the reserves.

PAGE, Malcolm Edward
Defender/wing-half: 382+9 apps 10 goals
Born: Knucklas, Radnorshire, mid-Wales, 5 February 1947.
Career: Radnorshire & District Boys, BLUES (apprentice July 1964, professional September 1964), Oxford United (February 1981). Retired in March 1982.
Club honours: Blues: Division Two promotion 1972.
Representative honours: Wales (28 full caps, 6 Under-23 caps, 4 Schoolboy caps).
Blues' most capped player (whilst with club), Malcolm Page spent 17 seasons at St Andrew's and during that time played in every position for the club except goal. He skippered both club and country and was perhaps best equipped as a full-back or defensive midfielder, although he did have a lengthy run in the side as a centre-half, but at 5ft 9in was a little small for this role. Not a great creative player, Page was more of a 'man marker' and he could also unleash a powerful shot, once booming in a terrific goal against Huddersfield in the FA Cup of 1972. A grand servant to the club, he never asked for a transfer during his long association at St Andrew's. On quitting football Page took employment in Birmingham with a large insurance company.

PARR, Harold
Right-half: one app
Born: Newcastle-upon-Tyne, 1914. Deceased.
Career: Wellington High School, Dawley Rovers, Wrockwardine Wood, Donnington Wood FC, GKN Sankey's FC, Wellington Town, BLUES (October 1937), Dawley Rovers (October 1939), Stafford Rangers (season 1939-40). Did not figure after WW2.
Harry Parr was a forceful player who did the tour of Shropshire junior clubs before arriving at St Andrew's. His brief spell in League football was cut short by WW2.

PARRIS, George Michael
Defender/midfielder: 49+3 apps. 2 goals
Born: Ilford, 11 September 1964.
Career: Redbridge Schools, West Ham United (apprentice, July 1981, professional September 1982), BLUES (£150,000, March 1983), Brentford (on loan, August 1994), Bristol City (on loan, December 1994), Brighton & Hove Albion (on loan, March 1995), Norrkoping FC/Sweden (close season, 1996), Brighton

& Hove Albion (September 1996), Southend United (non-contract, August 1997), St Leonard's FC Stancroft (September 1997 to May 1998).
Representative honours: England (Schoolboys).
George Parris proved a hardworking, consistent and competitive midfielder who could also play in defence. In more than ten years as a professional at Upton Park he appeared in almost 300 senior games for the Hammers, scoring 18 goals. He added bite to the Blues' engine-room before being loaned out in late 1994 after losing his place in the first team. He ended his senior career with over 450 appearances in his locker.

PARTRIDGE, Charles
Goalkeeper: 30 apps.
Born: Wednesbury, 1867. Now Deceased
Career: Park Street School, Wednesbury Old Athletic, BLUES (September 1890), Willenhall Town (1896), Sparkhill FC, Park Mills (1897), Redditch Town, Headless Cross (January 1898 to 1900).
Although signed from the prestigious Black Country club Wednesbury old Athletic (known affectionately as 'The Old Uns') Charlie Partridge quickly earned the reputation as an erratic performer, as likely to lose a game on his own as save his team. In only one of his five seasons with Blues was he allowed to give full vein to his talents, and in that campaign he earned the distinction as the goalkeeper who conceded nine goals in Blues' record defeat.

PASKIN, William John
Striker: 8+3 apps. 3 goals.
Born: Capetown, South Africa, 1 February 1962.
Career: Hellenic FC/South Africa (July 1980), Toronto Blizzard/NASL (May 1983), South China/Hong Kong (August 1984), FC Seiko/Hong Kong (August 1985), KV Kortrijk/Belgium (August 1986), Dundee United (on trial, July 1987) West Bromwich Albion (non-contract, March 1988, professional August 1988), Wolverhampton Wanderers (£75,000, June 1989), Stockport County (on loan, September 1991), BLUES (on loan, November 1991), Shrewsbury Town (on loan, February 1992) Wrexham (free transfer, February 1992), Bury (free transfer July 1994 to May 1996).
John Paskin was a tall striker, taken on loan by Blues at a time when a goalscorer was desperately required. He failed to make much impression but later scored 14 goals in 60 games for Wrexham. Indeed, he is one of the few players to have appeared in League matches for Blues, Albion & Wolves.

PEART, John George
Centre-forward: 3 apps
Born: South Shields, 3 October 1888. Died: Paddington, London, 3 September 1948.
Career: South Shields Adelaide FC (August 1905),

Sheffield United (May 1907), Stoke (July 1901), Newcastle United (£600, March 1912), Notts County (February 1913), Rochdale (WW1 guest), BLUES (November 1919), Derby County (January 1920), Ebbw Vale (as player-manager, August 1920), Port Vale (as a player, January 1922), Norwich City (July 1922), Rochdale (as player-manager, March 1923, retiring as a player in May 1924), Bradford City (manager, July 1930), Fulham (manager from May 1935 to his demise in 1948).
Club honours: Notts County: Division Two champions 1914.
Representative honours: Football League XI (1), Southern League XI (3).
One of the great travellers of football, Jack Peart was a fine opportunist goalscorer although this facet of his game was missing at St Andrew's. He had a reputation for being 'the most injured man in football'. He proved to be a reasonably successful manager, taking Fulham to an FA Cup semi-final.

PEER, Dean
Midfielder: 133+17 apps. 12 goals.
Born: Wordsley, Stourbridge, 8 August 1969.
Career: Ashwood Park & Buckpool Schools (Stourbridge), Lye Town, Stourbridge Falcons, BLUES (YTS July 1985, professional July 1987), Mansfield Town (on loan, December 1992), Walsall (on loan, then full transfer November 1993), Northampton Town (August 1995), Shrewsbury Town (January 2000), Moor Green (July 2001).
Club honours: Blues: Leyland DAF Cup winners 1991.
Dean Peer was a distinctive gangling figure - 6ft 2in tall and 12st 6lb in weight - who initially played wide on the right side of midfield. Not the fastest of players but a genuine trier, he was then moved into a central midfield position where he looked far more comfortable although he had to take his fair share of abuse from the St Andrew's terraces. He displayed a hitherto unsuspected scoring ability at Walsall, netting a hat-trick shortly after his move. He later made over 150 appearances for Northampton and 60 for the 'Shrews'.

PENDREY, Garry James Sidney
Full-back/defender: 337+23 apps. 5.goals
Born: Lozells, Birmingham, 9 February 1949.
Career: Lozells Junior School, Handsworth Technical College Birmingham, Aston Schools, Stanley Star, Harborne Lynwood, BLUES (apprentice, July 1965, professional, October 1966), West Bromwich Albion (£30,000, August 1979), Torquay United (August 1981), Bristol Rovers (December 1981), Walsall (player-coach, July 1982, later assistant-manager, May 1983 to August 1986), BLUES (manager from June 1987 to April 1989), Wolverhampton Wanderers (coach, July 1989 to March 1994), Coventry City (coach, February 1995, then assistant-manager November 1996), Southampton (assistant-manager, October 2001). Also played in over 150 games for WBA All Stars 1982-95 (105 goals scored).
Club honours: Blues: FA Youth Cup runners-up 1967, Division Two promotion 1972.
Garry Pendrey skippered the successful Blues youth side of 1967 and later captained both the reserve and senior teams. A player who always believed in leading by example, Pendrey was not the most naturally talented of footballers but he was a tenacious tackler and whole-hearted grafter. He was the youngest-ever Blues captain in 1969, at 20 years 6 months, the honour perhaps coming a little too early for him to appreciate it. He became a cult hero with the St Andrew's fans, known as 'Gazza' when a certain 'Geordie' was still a child. He was surprisingly sold to West Brom shortly after his testimonial game against the Baggies. After a promising start to his coaching career, he came back to Blues as manager but he was not a success, and the advent of the Kumar brothers proved to be the end of his managerial exploits, and he returned to his coaching duties. He was assistant-manager at Walsall (under former Blues player Alan Buckley) and later served as right-hand man to Gordon Strachan, first at first Highfield Road and then at Southampton.

PENTLAND, Frederick Beaconsfield
Inside-left: one app.
Born: Wolverhampton, 18 September 1883.
Died: Poole, Dorset 16 March 1962.
Career: Willenhall Swifts, Avondale Juniors, BLUES (August 1900), Blackpool (June 1903), Blackburn Rovers (October 1903), Brentford (May 1906), Queen's Park Rangers (May 1907), Middlesbrough (June 1908), Halifax Town (February 1913), Stoke (May 1913). Coached in Germany at outbreak of WW1 and was interned for the duration. Afterwards coached in France (season 1920-21), Athletic Bilbao/Spain (coach 1921-36), Brentford (coach 1936-37) and Barrow (as team manager from January 1938 to September 1939).
Club honours: Brentford: Southern League champions 1908.
Representative honours: England (5 full caps).
Fred Pentland's father, a former Lord Mayor of Birmingham, was such an admirer of Benjamin Disraeli, Earl of Beaconsfield, that he named his son accordingly. During his career at Blues, Pentland was regarded as a reserve wing-half but was called up for a game as an inside-forward due to an injury crisis. Later he developed into an international class winger, and subsequently became a respected coach. He seemed to be unlucky with choice of jobs, being in Germany at the outbreak of WW1 and in Spain when the Civil War started. In Germany he started a football League with fellow internees and England internationals Steve Bloomer and Sam Wolstenholme.

PEPLOW, William Watling

Outside-right: 17 apps. one goal

Born: Derby, 1885. Now Deceased

Career: Redditch, BLUES (April 1907), Bristol Rovers (August 1908 to May 1915).

Bill Peplow had a patchy season with Blues, during which time his speed was not always matched by the quality of his crosses. He blossomed at Bristol, though, and became a regular scorer for Rovers, his performances catching the eye of the England selectors although he failed to reproduce his best form in an international trial and full recognition never came.

PESCHISOLIDO, Paulo Pasquale

Striker: 47+10 apps. 18 goals

Born: Scarborough Ontario, Canada, 25 May 1971.

Career: Toronto Blizzard/NASL, Kansas City Comets/NASL (1990-91), Toronto Blizzard/NASL, BLUES (£25,000, November 1992), Stoke City (£400,000 in a player-exchange deal involving David Regis, August 1994), West Bromwich Albion (£600,000, July 1996), Fulham (£1.1 million, October 1997), Queen's Park Rangers (on loan, November 2000), Sheffield United (on loan, January 2001), Norwich City (on loan, March 2001), Sheffield United (signed for £150,000, July 2001).

Club honours: Fulham: Division Two champions 1999

Representative honours: Canada (45* full caps, 11 Under-23 caps, 9 Olympic Games appearances).

Canadian international Paul Peschisolido, an exciting, all-action, industrious utility forward, sharp inside the penalty area, certainly made a big impact at St Andrew's and then did likewise at Stoke (where he was reunited with his former manager Lou Macari) and later at West Bromwich Albion. In 1990 he was voted the USA Major Indoor Soccer League's 'Newcomer of the Year'. He is married to Blues' Managing-Director Karren Brady.

PHILLIPS, Cuthbert

Outside-right/centre-forward: 25 apps. 10 goals.

Born: Victoria, Monmouthshire June 1910.

Died: Lichfield, Staffs, 15 October 1969.

Career: Victoria Council School, Ebbw Vale (1925-26), Plymouth Argyle (on trial), Wolverhampton Wanderers (professional, August 1929), Aston Villa (£9,000, January 1936), BLUES (March 1938), Chelmsford City (May 1939). Retired during WW2.

Club honours: Wolverhampton Wanderers: Division Two champions 1932; Aston Villa: Division Two champions 1938.

Representative honours: Wales (13 full caps, 2 Schoolboy caps).

'Charlie' Phillips was something of a rough and tumble character but a clever ball-playing utility forward for all that. He was coming to the end of a fine career when he arrived at St Andrew's. He also had quite a temper and

was sent off twice as a professional. He scored 65 goals in 202 games for Wolves and five in 22 outings for Villa. He was also a useful cricketer, a fine tennis player, did well at golf and also participated at rugby union and on the athletics track as a young lad. After leaving football he became a licensee, first at the Butler's Arms at Bushbury in Wolverhampton, and later in Lichfield.

PHILLIPS, Leslie Michael

Midfielder: 45+9 apps. 4 goals

Born: Lambeth, London, 7 January 1963.

Career: London Schools, BLUES (apprentice June 1979, professional August 1980), Oxford United (March 1984), Northampton Town (August 1993), Marlow (July 1994 to May 1996).

Club honours: Oxford: Division Two promotion 1985, Milk Cup winners 1986.

Representative honours: England (3 Youth caps).

Les Phillips was a busy little player who had all the makings of a useful midfield linchpin, fearless in the tackle and a good passer of the ball. However, his style was not ideally suited to the role he was asked to do at St Andrew's and he was rarely given a decent run in the first team. Manager Jim Smith took him to Oxford where he proved more successful despite injuries and occasional bouts of indiscipline.

PHILLIPS, Steven Edward

Forward: 19+7 apps. one goal.

Born: Edmonton, London, 4 August 1954.

Career: BLUES (apprentice June 1970, professional August 1971), Torquay United (on loan, December 1974), Northampton Town (£40,000, August 1980), Southend United (March 1982), Torquay United (on loan, January 1986), Peterborough United (November 1986), Exeter City (on loan, September 1987), Chesterfield (on loan, January 1988), Stamford, British Timken Duston FC (as player-manager, 1990-91).

Representative honours: England (2 Youth caps).

A pint-size, long-haired forward Steve Phillips had a marvellous career in the lower Divisions of the Football League, scoring over 250 goals in more than 700 senior appearances (560 in the League) before moving into non-League soccer in 1988. He always looked out of his depth in the First Division, but Blues must have regretted selling him. Certainly one that got away! Phillips now works in the Peterborough area, selling double-glazing.

PHOENIX, Arthur Frederick

Inside-forward: 3 apps.

Born: Hadfield, 5 July 1897. Now Deceased

Career: Urmston & District Schools, Hadfield, Glossop (season 1922-23), BLUES (May 1923), Aston Villa (May 1924), Barnsley (May 1925), Exeter City (July 1926), Wigan Borough (July 1929), Bath City (June 1930),

Torquay United (November 1930), Mansfield Town (July 1931), Racing Club de Paris/France (August 1932), Sandbach Ramblers (October 1933), Dublin Shelbourne (January 1934), Brierley Hill Alliance (January 1935). Retired in May 1937.

Arthur 'Ginger' Phoenix was yet another soccer nomad who never really settled in one place, yet always gave a good account of himself on the field of play.

PICKERING, Frederick
Centre-forward: 88 apps. 32 goals
Born: Blackburn, 19 January 1941.
Career: Blackburn amateur football, Blackburn Rovers (junior August 1956, professional, January 1958), Everton (£85,000, March 1964), BLUES (£50,000, August 1967), Blackpool (June 1969), Blackburn Rovers (March 1971), Brighton & Hove Albion (on trial, February 1972). Quit top-line football in May 1973.
Club honours: Blackburn Rovers: FA Youth Cup winners 1959.
Representative honours: England (3 full caps, 3 Under-23 caps); Football League XI (1).
Originally a right-back, Fred Pickering developed into one of the country's leading strikers. Fast, skilful and brilliant in the air, he scored a hat-trick on his international debut for England (in a 10-0 win over the United States) and claimed over 30 goals in each of two successive seasons in the 1960s, but missed the 1966 FA Cup Final through injury. With the emergence at Goodison Park of Joe Royle, Pickering was deemed surplus to requirements and manager Stan Cullis brought him to St Andrew's, hoping that he would lead Blues back into the First Division. Indeed, the fans were treated to two seasons of classic centre-forward play but although Pickering and his fellow attackers scored plenty of goals, the defence was leaky and promotion was missed. He returned to Division One with Blackpool, and later went back to his first club, Blackburn. But he had a few disputes with Rovers manager Ken Furphy and was eventually sacked from Ewood Park. He later worked as a fork-lift truck driver and is now resident in Blackburn.

PIKE, Theophilus Enos
Outside-left: 17 apps. 4 goals
Born: Sunderland, 25 March 1907. Died: Bury St Edmunds, 26 October 1967.
Career: Sunderland Co-op Wednesday FC, Fulham (1925), Bournemouth & Boscombe Athletic (June 1927), BLUES (February 1928), Southend United (June 1930), Norwich City (June 1933), Bury Town (player-coach from 1935 to May 1937), Norfolk & Suffolk FA (coach, season 1938-39). Did not figure after WW2.
Theo 'Tot' Pike was a ball-juggling but somewhat frail forward whose career was hampered by a string of serious injuries, culminating in him missing the entire 1929-30 season prior to his release from St Andrew's. He later became a publican in East Anglia.

PIMBLEY, Douglas William
Outside-left: 2 apps.
Born: King's Norton, Birmingham 19 June 1917.
Career: King's Norton YMCA, Northfield, Stourbridge, Leicester City (as an amateur), BLUES (July 1946), Notts County (March 1948).
Doug Pimbley was a powerful forward who had served four-and-a-half years abroad in the Army prior to joining Blues. He was signed in anticipation that his strength would assist the rest of the front line, but it was not to be and he spent most of his time in the reserves.

PLATNAUER, Nicholas Robert
Full-back/midfielder: 31+5 apps 2 goals
Born: Leicester, 10 June 1961.
Career: Bedford Town (1979), Bristol Rovers (August 1981), Coventry City (£50,000, August 1983), BLUES (£55,000, December 1984), Reading (on loan, January-February 1986), Cardiff City (free transfer, September 1986), Notts County (£50,000, August 1989), Port Vale (on loan, January-April 1991), Leicester City (free transfer, July 1991), Kettering Town, Scunthorpe United (March 1993), Mansfield Town (August 1993), Lincoln City (February 1994), Bedworth United (August 1995).
Club honours: Cardiff: Welsh Cup winners 1988; Notts Co: Division Three promotion 1990, Division Two promotion 1991.
Nicky Platnauer was working as a bank clerk when Bedford Town unfolded him. He was then surprisingly signed by Bristol Rovers and indeed, so impressed that Bobby Gould took him to Coventry when he left the Pirates to become boss at Highfield Road. Platnauer, though, proved a disappointment in the First Division but Ron Saunders enticed him to Blues to play wide on the left in the promotion bid. After a promising start he dropped out of the reckoning but in later years did well at full-back.
He ended his senior career in the mid-1990s with 473 appearances under his belt.

POINTER, Ernest
Goalkeeper: 29 apps.
Born: Sparkbrook, Birmingham, 1872. Now Deceased
Career: Redditch Town, BLUES (1896), Berwick Rangers/Worcester (1898), BLUES (September 1900), Kidderminster Harriers (May 1901).
A very erratic goalkeeper but capable enough to keep Blues in the promotion race in 1896-97, Ernie Pointer's only season in the League side. He came back for a second spell with the club but failed to gain a regular place, even in the reserve side.

POINTON, Thomas Seth
Outside-left: 4 apps. one goal
Born: Coventry, 1890. Now Deceased
Career: Coventry City (amateur), Redditch Town, BLUES (as an amateur August 1913), Redditch Town

(April 1914), Walsall (June 1914), Nuneaton Town (1919), Coventry City (season 1920-21), Redditch, Tamworth Castle (season 1925-26).
Representative honours: England (Amateur international trialist)
Blues were so eager to sign promising winger Tommy Pointon that they were fined £5 for playing him in the reserves before the transfer was completed. He impressed in the second XI, earning an amateur international trial, but was not selected for his country. In League football he was thought to be a little slow 'to work out what he had to do when he had the ball'.

POLLOCK, Jamie
Midfielder: 4+1 apps
Born: Stockton-on-Tees, 16 February 1974
Career: Middlesbrough (trainee, June 1990, professional December 1991), Osasuna/Spain (free transfer, September 1996), Bolton Wanderers (£1.5 million, November 1996), Manchester City (£1 million, March 1998), Crystal Palace (£750,000, August 2000), BLUES (on loan, March-April 2001). Released by Palace June 2002.
Club honours: Middlesbrough' (Division One champions 1995), Bolton: Division 1 champions 1997
Representative honours: England (3 Under-21 & Youth caps)
A midfielder with bite and experience, Jamie Pollock joined Blues as they aimed to secure a place in the 2001 Play-offs. In his 10-year professional career he appeared in well over 350 competitive games.

POOLE, Gary John
Defender: 100+3 apps. 4 goals
Born: Stratford, London 11 September 1967.
Career: Tottenham Hotspur (junior, July 1983, professional July 1985), Cambridge United (free transfer, August 1987), Barnet (£3,000, March 1989), Plymouth Argyle (free transfer, June 1992), Southend United (£350,000, July 1993), BLUES (in a player-exchange deal, September 1994), Charlton Athletic (£250,000, November 1996). Retired through injury in 2000.
Club honours: Barnet: GMVC winners 1991; Blues: Second Division champions 1995, Auto-Windscreen Shield winners 1995.
Gary Poole, a solid, tough-tackling right-back, was with Barry Fry at Barnet and Southend before joining Blues. He had made around 200 senior appearances as a professional prior to his move to St Andrew's in the move where no fee changed hands but he and Jonathan Hunt came to Blues whilst Dave Regis and Roger Willis went to Southend.

POOLE, Kevin
Goalkeeper: 67 apps.
Born: Bromsgrove, 21 July 1963
Career: Aston Villa (apprentice, June 1979, professional

June 1981), Northampton Town (on loan, November 1984), Middlesbrough (August 1987), Hartlepool United (on loan, March 1991), Leicester City (£40,000, July 1991), BLUES (free transfer, August 1997), Bolton Wanderers (free, October 2001).
Club honours: Leicester (League Cup winners 1997)
Kevin Poole had already made 240 League appearances before he joined Blues (as cover for Ian Bennett) in 1997. Sound on crosses and a specialist penalty-saver (it is believed he has stopped well over a dozen spot kicks in open play) Poole kept nine clean sheets for Blues in 1998-99. He has now amassed more than 350 senior appearances at club level.

POTTER, Graham Stephen
Midfield/defender: 30+2 apps 2 goals
Born: Solihull, 20 May 1975.
Career: BLUES (YTS, June 1991, professional July 1992), Wycombe Wanderers (on loan, September 1993), Stoke City (£75,000, plus Kenny Lowe, December 1993), Southampton (£250,000, July 1996), West Bromwich Albion (£300,000, February 1997), Northampton Town (on loan, October 1997), Reading (on loan, December 1999), York City (free transfer, July 2000).
Representative honours: England (One Under-21 & Youth caps).
Graham Potter was predominantly a defender whose great strength was in overlapping. A shade naive at times, he had a tendency to get sucked inside from time to time, leaving his flank unprotected. All the same it was still a surprise when he was traded to Stoke in part-exchange for midfielder Kenny Lowe. Potter later made almost 50 senior appearances for WBA and reached the century mark with York City early in the 2002-03 season.

POWELL, Aubrey
Inside-forward: 15 apps. one goal.
Born: Cynlais near Swansea, 19 April 1918.
Career: Cwm Wanderers, Swansea Town (amateur), Leeds United (November 1935), Everton (£10,000, July 1948), BLUES (August 1950), Wellington Town (August 1951). Retired in May 1952.
Representative honours: Wales (8 full caps, 4 victory internationals).
Aubury Powell was a neat if somewhat fragile footballer who fought back after his career was written off by doctors following a broken leg in 1937. He missed an extra season but regained his place pre- WW2, during which he served in Belgium before returning to pick up the first of his eight Welsh caps. Further injuries curtailed his career, both at Everton and Blues. He hit 19 goals in 73 League games for Leeds and five in 35 for Everton. He later opened a confectioner's shop in Leeds (after refusing to join Wellington Town). He now lives in Leeds.

POWELL, Darryl Anthony
Defender: 6+8* apps.
Born: Lambeth, London, 15 November 1971
Career: Portsmouth (trainee, June 1987, professional,
December 1988), Derby County (£750,000, July 1995),
BLUES (September 2002). Sheffield Wednesday
(January 2003).
Representative honours: Jamaica (17 full caps).
An enthusiastic, very experienced defender, able to play
at full-back or in the centre-half position, Darryl Powell
can also man midfield if required. He appeared in 170
games for Pompey and over 225 for the Rams before
teaming up with Blues when Steve Bruce boosted his
defence for the club's first season in the top flight for 16
years and, indeed, their first taste of Premiership football.

POWELL, Herbert
Inside-forward: 5 apps. one goal
Born: Maidstone, Kent, 1880. Now Deceased
Career: Treharris, Nottingham Forest (August 1904),
Gresley Rovers (1905), Grantham Avenue (February
1906), Chesterfield (1906), Barnsley (February 1907);
Carlisle United (1907), New Brompton (1908),
Coventry City (1909), BLUES (December 1910),
Rotherham Town (1911), Portsmouth (1913),
Bournemouth & Boscombe Athletic (1914), Brentford
(1915), Worksop Town (1919), Grantham (March
1922), Retford (season 1922-23), Sutton Town (August
1923). Retired circa 1925
A hard shooting forward Bert Powell had 'been about a
bit' before joining Blues, He scored on his debut for the
club (in a 2-1 win over Leeds City in February 1911) but
quickly fell from favour and soon continued on his
travels around the country.

PRATT, William
Outside-left: 27 apps. one goal.
Born: Highgate, Birmingham, 1872. Now Deceased
Career: St John's FC (Deritend), BLUES (September
1889), Small Heath Unity (August 1892), Worcester
Rovers (1898-99).
Billy Pratt was a local winger whose talents were more
given to providing chances rather than taking them. A
grand dribbler and crosser of the ball he was nevertheless
somewhat on the slow side. He was frequently confused
with his namesake (below) who didn't join Blues until
two years after the first 'Billy Pratt' had left!

PRATT, William
Left-back: 139 apps.
Born: Birmingham, 1874. Now Deceased
Career: Hoskins & Sewell FC, BLUES (August 1894).
Retired in May 1902 through injury.
Billy Pratt joined Blues as a youngster fresh from
Birmingham Works League soccer. By the time he left
eight years later, he had earned the reputation as a
powerful, uncompromising full-back with a terrific kick

in both feet. He was solid all down the line, never
shirking a tackle, always totally committed and was a
grand stalwart for Blues until a leg injury ended his
career at the age of 28.

PREECE, David William
Midfielder: 7 apps
Born: Bridgnorth, 28 May 1963
Career: Walsall (apprentice June 1978, professional July
1980), Luton Town (£150,000, December 1984), Derby
County (free transfer, August 1995), BLUES (on loan,
November 1995), Swindon Town (on loan, March
1996), Cambridge United (free transfer, September
1996), Torquay United (free, October 2000, later
appointed assistant-manager at Plainmoor).
Club honours: Luton (League Cup winners 1988).
Representative honours: England (3 'B' caps).
David Preece, a Wolves supporter as a lad, developed into
a tenacious, hardworking midfielder whose playing career
spanned some 23 years during which time he amassed
more than 650 senior appearances including 395 for
the Hatters

PRESTON, Josiah
Right-back: 7 apps
Born: Derby, 1885. Now Deceased
Career: Derby Midland FC, Burton Wanderers, Burton
United (1905), BLUES (August 1908), Halesowen
(May 1910).
Joe Preston was a sturdy player who was one of a group
of backs who struggled to replace the ageing Stokes and
Corbett. Not such a classy performer as either of his
predecessors, he was a strong and solid reserve nevertheless.

PRICE, George
Right-back: one app. one goal
Born: Sparkbrook, Birmingham, 1863. Now Deceased
Career: Hockley Belmont (1883), Aston Villa (1884),
BLUES (August 1885), St Luke's FC (September 1888).
One of a cluster of players from the Belmont club, Jack
Price was a good prompting half-back who was a virtual
ever-present in his only season at Muntz Street. He left
after a poor performance in the Derby Charity Cup Final
when Blues lost 3-0 to Derby County.

PRICE, John Lester
Inside-right: one app.
Born: Lichfield, 1879. Now Deceased
Career: Shenstone BC, BLUES (August 1897), Watford
(1900), Doncaster Rovers (October 1901).
John Price was a young forward who gave sterling service
to the Birmingham League side for several years. He left
Blues under a cloud after being charged with assault
upon a ticket collector at Small Heath Railway Station.

PRICE, Ryan
Goalkeeper: one app.

Born: Coven near Wolverhampton, 13 March 1970.
Career: Bolton Wanderers (YTS season 1986-87), Stafford Rangers, BLUES (£20,000 August 1994), Macclesfield Town (£15,000, November 1995), Telford United (December 1999), Rushall Olympic (2002).
Club honours: Blues: Auto-Windscreen Shield winners 1995; Macclesfield: FA Trophy winners 1996, Vauxhall Conference champions 1997
Representative honours: England (6 semi-professional caps)
Ryan Price (6ft 5ins tall and 14st in weight) made his debut for Blues in the Auto-Windscreen Shield game at Peterborough in September 1994, conceding a goal in the first minute. He was, though, a good, reliable 'keeper with safe pair of hands who in later years gave excellent service to Macclesfield, for whom he made well over 150 senior appearances during his time at Moss Rose.

PRITCHARD, Tilson
Right-back: one app.
Born: Walsall Wood, 1872. Now Deceased
Career: Burntwood Swifts, BLUES (April 1894), Lichfield Town (August 1895).
Tilson Pritchard was given a try-out by Blues in the United Counties League at the end of 1893-94 when he had a poor game. He resurfaced in the next January when 'Dowk' Oliver was injured, but was totally out of his class as Blues crashed 9-1 to Blackburn.

PRUDHOE, Mark
Goalkeeper: 5 apps.
Born: Washington, County Durham, 8 November 1963.
Career: Washington Youths, Sunderland (apprentice June 1980, professional September 1981), Hartlepool United (on loan, November 1983), BLUES (£22,000, September 1984), Walsall (£22,000, February 1986), Doncaster Rovers (on loan, December 1986), Grimsby Town (on loan, March 1987), Hartlepool United (on loan, August 1987), Bristol City (on loan, November 1987), Carlisle United (£10,000, December 1987), Darlington (March 1989), Stoke City (June 1993), Peterborough United (on loan, October 1994), Liverpool (on loan, November-December 1994), York City (on loan, February 1997), Bradford City (£70,000, July 1997), Southend United (free transfer, November 1999), Carlisle United (on trial, October 2000). Retired as a player in May 2001, then appointed Bradford City reserve team coach.
Club honours: Darlington: GM Vauxhall Conference champions 1990, Division Four champions 1991.
Squarely built goalkeeper Mark Prudhoe was signed three days before 'Seamus' McDonagh and eleven days before David Seaman, to become the second of four Blues goalies in four games in September 1984. With Seaman eventually settling in as first choice, Prudhoe was restricted almost entirely to League Cup games. He travelled around a bit after leaving St Andrew's and when he finally pulled out of League soccer in 2001 he had amassed well over 400 competitive appearances while serving with 14 different clubs. He was a real footballing nomad.

PUMFREY, Bernard
Left-back: 13 apps. one goal.
Born: Stirchley, Birmingham, May 1873.
Died: Gainsborough, 18 July 1930.
Career: Birmingham St Mark's FC, BLUES (September 1892), Gainsborough Trinity (August 1894 to May 1896).
Bernie Pumfrey was a slim, clean-cut defender, nothing at all like your old-fashioned Victorian full-back. Although born in Birmingham he came from a well-known Upton-on-Severn family who had owned land in the town since the 15th century. On signing for Gainsborough he set up as a joiner, building up his trade until he had established a large company that still exists in the town. Although not a footballer, his brother, Harry, played a major part in Blues' history as the designer of the St Andrew's ground.

PURDON, Edward John
Centre-forward: 70 apps 30 goals.
Born: Johannesburg, South Africa, 1 March 1930.
Career: Maritz Brothers FC/South Africa, BLUES (professional August 1950), Sunderland (January 1954), Workington (March 1957), Barrow (March 1958), Bath City (August 1959), Bristol Rovers (August 1960), Toronto City/Canada (1961), Polish White Eagles of Toronto/Canada (season 1961-62).
A powerhouse, thrustful blond centre-back, Ted Purdon was never afraid to go in where it hurt and was by far the most successful of Blues' signings from South Africa. At 6ft tall and 13st in weight he possessed all the physical attributes necessary for a striker and his physique allied to a total lack of fear made him a handful for any centre-half. Purdon scored 87 goals in 228 League games with his five English clubs.
A useful cricketer, he was once selected as 12th man by Warwickshire.

PURSE, Darren John
Defender: 158+27* apps. 11 goals*
Born: Stepney, London 14 February 1977.
Career: Leyton Orient (junior 1992, professional February 1994), Oxford United (£100,000, July 1997), BLUES (£800,000, February 1998).
Club honours: League Cup runners-up 2001, Division One promotion 2002.
Representative honours: England (2 Under-21 caps)
A rock solid centre-half, positive in all aspects of defensive play, Darren Purse is strong, hard tackler, powerful header of the ball and played his part in helping Blues secure a Premiership place in 2001-02, making 36 League appearances that season.

Q - R

PURVES, William Michael
Right-back: 43 apps.
Born: Belfast, 1870. Now Deceased
Career: Glentoran (1890), BLUES (April 1893),
Glentoran (May 1897). Later served as trainer with
Glentoran (from 1900).
A hot-headed Irishman with a crunching tackle, Bill
Purves was surprisingly free from disciplinary problems
during his career, despite being the sort of player
opposition fans love to hate. He was one of the few
successes in Blues' first season in Division One.

QUINN, Stephen James
Striker: 1+3 apps.
Born: Coventry, 15 December 1974.
Career: Cardinal Wiseman School, BLUES (YTS, July
1991), Blackpool (professional, July 1993), Stockport
County (on loan, March 1994), Stockport County (on
loan, March 1994), West Bromwich Albion (£500,000,
February 1998), Notts County (on loan, November
2001), Bristol Rovers (on loan, March-May 2002),
Willem II/Holland (June 2002).
Representative honours: Northern Ireland (25* full, 2
'B', one Under-21 & Youth caps)
James Quinn proved a talented young forward who was a
prolific scorer in Blues' youth teams. He was given an
occasional run-out whilst still a registered YTS player and
great things were predicted for him. Surprisingly he
refused to sign a professional contract and moved after a
considerable wrangle to Blackpool where he considered
there was a greater chance of first-team action. Once
there, however, he had difficulty establishing himself in
their team. After his move to West Bromwich Albion his
form improved dramatically and he became a regular
performer in both the Baggies' and Northern Ireland
senior sides. He scored 10 goals in 123 games for Albion
before losing his place in the side following the arrival of
new boss, Gary Megson.

QUINTON, Walter
Left-back: 9 apps
Born: Anston near Rotherham, 3 December 1917.
Deceased.
Career: Dinnington Athletic (1934), Rotherham United
(July 1937), BLUES (July 1939), Brentford (April 1949),
Southend United (August 1952), Shrewsbury Town
(October 1952 to May 1954).
A short, squat defender, Wally Quinton was fated to be a
reserve throughout his career. He was at his best when
dogging wingers and denying them space. He joined
Brentford in a double-deal with Jackie Goodwin,
spending one year in their first team before dropping
back into the Football Combination. He later worked at
Bulpitts and was a keen singer.

RANDLE, Jack
Left-back: 116 apps. one goal.
Born: Bedworth, Warwickshire, 23 August 1902. Died:
Bournemouth, 1990.
Career: Exhall Colliery FC, Bedworth Boys' Club,
Coventry City (August 1922), BLUES (November
1927), Southend United (April 1933), Bournemouth &
Boscombe Athletic (June 1933), Guildford City (1934
to 1936).
Like so many pre-war full-backs Jack Randle was an ex-
miner. Not the fastest of players but very strong, burly
and confident in his own ability, in the latter part of his
Blues career he played principally in mid-week matches
when George Liddell's evening classes would not allow
him to appear. He later became head groundsman at
Newdegate Colliery, Nuneaton. Randle once scored a
hat-trick of own-goals during his Coventry days.

RANKIN, Isaiah
Forward: 11+2 apps 4 goals
Born: Edmonton, London 22 May 1978
Career: Arsenal (trainee June 1994, professional
September 1995), Colchester United (on loan,
September 1997), Bradford City (£1.3 million, August
1998), BLUES (on loan, January-February 2000), Bolton
Wanderers (on loan, August-September 2000), Barnsley
(£350,000, January 2001).
'Izzy' Rankin has never really established himself with
any of the clubs he has served, albeit three of them on
loan. An aggressive player, with a big heart, his best spell
so far has come at Bradford (six goals in 43 outings, over
half as a 'sub').

RANSON, Raymond
Right-back: 157+1 apps.
Born: St Helens, 12 June 1960.
Career: Sutton High School, St Helens Schoolboy
football and District Boys teams, Manchester City
(apprentice June 1976, professional June 1977), BLUES
(£15,000, November 1984), Newcastle United
(£175,000, December 1988), Manchester City (on loan,
January 1993), Reading (July 1993 to May 1994).
Club honours: Manchester City: FA Cup runners-up 1981.
Representative honours: England (11 Under-21 caps, 2
Youth caps, Schoolboy caps).
An attacking right-back with a good turn of speed and
the ability to hit pin-point crosses, Ray Ranson gained a
regular first-team place with Manchester City whilst still
in his teens and progressed quickly to the England
Under-21 side. He had a disagreement with the
management at Maine Road and with his career at a
crossroads, Blues stepped in to sign him. He proved an
immediate success at St Andrew's but then tended to
struggle towards the end of his spell when his defensive
shortcomings were more noticeable, especially when he
was up against a fast-raiding or tricky winger.

RATHBONE, Michael John
Right-back: 22+3 apps.
Born: Sheldon, Birmingham, 6 November 1958.
Career: Sir Wilfred Martineau School (Birmingham), Aston Villa Boys, BLUES (apprentice, December 1974, professional November 1976), Blackburn Rovers (on loan, February 1979, signing permanently for £40,000, March 1979), Preston North End (£20,000, August 1987 to May 1991), Darwen (Commercial Manager, August 1991), Halifax Town (physiotherapist 1992, then manager-physiotherapist, sacked in March 1995).
Representative honours: England (2 Youth caps).
Mike Rathbone was a steady player who was always keen to support his forwards when possible, sometimes to the detriment of his defensive duties. Never an automatic choice at Blues, he later did an excellent job with his two Lancashire clubs, making over 300 senior appearances for Blackburn Rovers during his eight-year stay at Ewood Park and more than 100 for Preston North End.

RAWSON, Albert Norman
Centre-forward: 19 apps. 9 goals
Born: West Melton, October 1900.
Died: Yorkshire circa 1980.
Career: Sheffield United, BLUES (February 1923), Barnsley (season 1924-25).
Signed to boost Blues' flagging fortunes after they had lost seven games in a row and were heading towards relegation. Albert Rawson's arrival certainly did the trick as he scored in each of his first five games and the club survived. He missed the start of the 1923-24 campaign and was unable to command a first-team place thereafter. In later years he went into business in Yorkshire, working for a mining concern.

REA, Simon
Defender: 1+2 apps
Born: Kenilworth, 20 September 1976
Career: BLUES (apprentice June 1992, professional January 1995), Peterborough United (free transfer, August 1999).
Never really given a chance by Blues, Simon Rea later made a reasonable impression as a left-sided central defender with 'Posh' for whom he took his appearance tally to near the 100 mark in 2002.

REED, Arthur
Inside-forward: 29 apps 13 goals
Born: Sheffield, 1883. Now Deceased
Career: Leadhill St Mary's, Doncaster Rovers, BLUES (April 1912). Retired in May 1917 through injury.
An unlikely looking footballer being 5ft 5in tall with a 'roly-poly' physique, he was nevertheless quite a useful forward and the local Press described him as 'quick, eager and never afraid to let fly'. His Doncaster career was limited to one reserve and one first-team game, a Cup Final in which Reed scored the winning goal, only for Doncaster to be disqualified as he was an unregistered player.

REES, Anthony Andrew
Forward: 88+23 apps 16 goals
Born: Merthyr Tydfil, 1 August 1964.
Career: Aston Villa (apprentice, August 1980, professional August 1982), BLUES (free transfer, July 1983), Peterborough United (on loan, October 1985), Shrewsbury Town (on loan, March 1986), Barnsley (March 1988), Grimsby Town (August 1989), West Bromwich Albion (£30,000, November 1994), Merthyr Town (August 1996 to May 1998).
Club honours: Aston Villa: FA Youth Cup winners 1980; Grimsby: Division Four promotion 1990, Division Three promotion 1991.
Representative honours: Wales (one full cap, one Under-21 cap, Youth caps, Schoolboy caps).
Tony Rees built up a considerable reputation in Villa's youth side until a broken leg halted his progress, causing him to miss a complete season. On recovering he chose to join Blues and stepped straight into the first team. He played initially wide on the right where he displayed an ability to take on defenders, but he also seemed a little lacking in stamina. His career stagnated for a while but after joining Alan Buckley at Grimsby his fortunes improved.

REGAN, Matthew John
Centre-forward: 7 apps 2 goals
Born: Worcester, 18 June 1944.
Career: Sacred Heart College (Worcester), Worcester Royal Grammar School, Claines FC, BLUES (amateur June 1959, professional, September 1961), Shrewsbury Town (October 1964), Brentford (March 1966), Crewe Alexandra (November 1966), Doncaster Rovers (September 1968).
Although he attended a rugby playing school, John Regan did enough with his junior club to impress Blues' scouts. Given an early first-team try out, he responded by scoring on his debut but with Jimmy Harris playing so well, first-team chances were always a premium. He left the club whilst still very young and plied his trade around the lower Divisions before dropping out of League football at the age of 27. He scored 53 League goals in 181 games after leaving Blues.

REGIS, David
Striker: 5+2 apps 2 goals
Born: Paddington, 3 March 1964.
Career: Dunstable, Fisher Athletic, Windsor & Eton, Barnet, Notts County (£25,000, September 1990), Plymouth Argyle (£200,000, November 1991), AFC Bournemouth (on loan, August 1992), Stoke City (£100,000, October 1992), BLUES (£200,000, plus one player, August 1994), Southend United (September 1994), Barnsley (February 1996), Peterborough United

(on loan, September 1996), Notts County (on loan, February 1997), Scunthorpe United (on loan, August 1997), Leyton Orient (non-contract, October 1997), Lincoln City (non-contract, December 1997), Scunthorpe United (non-contract, February 1998). Retired in March 1998.
Club honours: Barnet: Clubcall Cup winners 1989; Stoke City: Division Two champions 1993.
Dave Regis came from a sporting family, being the brother of former England centre-forward Cyrille Regis, the cousin of international sprinter John Regis and uncle to the West Brom forward Jason Roberts. He made his name as a prominent member of Barnet's Conference side and was signed along with Paul Harding by Notts County. He got off to a good start with Notts and his value spiralled upwards, increasing rapidly over a period of 14 months before Plymouth signed him. He struggled in Devon, however, and it wasn't until joining Stoke that he regained some of his form. Barry Fry battled hard to sign him, eventually allowing Paul Peschisolido to go in exchange. On arriving at Blues he struggled to find his touch but it was something of a surprise when Fry transferred him again so quickly. Regis broke his leg shortly after joining Southend. He recovered full fitness and went on to score a total of 64 goals in 259 League and Cup games before being forced to hang up his 'shooting' boots at the age of 34.

RENNIE, David
Defender/midfielder: 34+3 apps 4 goals
Born: Edinburgh, 29 August 1964.
Career: Leicester City (apprentice July 1980, professional May 1982), Leeds United (£50,000 January 1986), Bristol City (£175,000 July 1989), BLUES (£120,000, February 1992), Coventry City (£100,000, March 1993). Later became physiotherapist at Leicester City.
Representative honours: Scotland (Youth caps).
David Rennie, an experienced defender, was 28 years of age when he joined Blues, and had already made over 250 senior appearances. He added stability to the Blues rearguard.

REYNOLDS, William Thomas
Left-back: 13 apps
Born: Tewkesbury, 1870. Now Deceased
Career: St Luke's, BLUES (April 1893), Berwick Rangers/Worcester (1894-95).
Blues used six left-backs on their way to promotion in 1893-94 and this stocky defender was the most regular choice. But he was not considered good enough for First Division Football and was released at the end of the season.

RICHARDS, Carroll Lloyd
Centre-forward: 18+1 apps 2 goals
Born: St Mary's, Jamaica, 12 January 1960.
Career: Dulwich Hamlet, Enfield, AFC Bournemouth

(£10,000, July 1986), BLUES (£70,000, October 1988), Peterborough United (£37,000, July 1989), Blackpool (£60,000, January 1990), Enfield, Bromley (on loan, then full transfer, 1992).
Club honours: Enfield: Gola League champions 1986; Bournemouth: Division Three champions 1987.
Representative honours: England (one semi-professional cap).
Bournemouth fought off several other clubs to land this highly-rated non-League striker. 'Carl' Richards was an immediate success at Dean Court where he formed an effective partnership with Trevor Aylott as the 'Cherries' ran away with the Third Division title. Garry Pendrey paid a large amount of money to bring Richards to St Andrew's but he proved a great disappointment. Being unable to settle off the field, he took his troubles on to the pitch and after a series of poor performances the crowd got on his back, his morale suffered, and in the end was grateful to move to Peterborough.

RICHARDS, David Thomas
Left-half: 66 apps.2 goals
Born Abercanaid, South Wales 31 October 1906.
Died: Yardley, Birmingham 1 October 1969.
Career: Abercanaid Council School, Riverfield FC, Belingoed FC, Merthyr Town (August 1925), Wolverhampton Wanderers (£300, August 1927), Brentford (November 1935), BLUES (March 1937), Walsall (August 1939), Sedgley FC (season 1945-46).
Club honours: Wolves: Division Two champions 1932.
Representative honours: Wales (21 full caps).
An out-and-out goalscorer at school, 'Dai' Richards developed into a first-class, tactical wing-half, an effective passer of the ball and a good covering player with a strong tackle. He became a building contractor after retiring from the game. His brother Billy Richards also played for Wolves in the late 1920s.

RICHARDSON, Ernest William
Outside-right: 3 apps.
Born: Bishops Burton, 1910.
Career: Leven FC, BLUES (February 1936), Swansea Town (November 1938).
A short, lightweight, but very fast winger, Ernie Richardson was third choice behind Frank White and Dennis Jennings at St Andrew's. His spell with Swansea was not a great success either, lasting barely a season in which he appeared 18 times.

RILEY, Harold
Outside-right: one app
Born: Oldham, 22 November 1909.
Died: Lincoln, 12 April 1982.
Career: Altrincham (August 1927), Hunt, BLUES (April 1928), Ashton National (season 1929-30), Accrington Stanley (July 1930), Lincoln City (August 1931), Notts

County (April 1933), Cardiff City (July 1934), Northampton Town (July 1936), Exeter City (May 1938), Rushton Bucyrus FC (August 1945). Retired in June 1947.

Club honours: Lincoln City: Division Three North champions 1932.

Starting his Football League career on the last day of the 1928-29 season, Harry Riley was an odd choice for a right winger, being naturally left-footed and normally an inside-forward 'link-man'. He was described as 'small and clever' but was said to reserve his best performances 'until the retained list was under review'.

RICHARDSON, Ian George

Defender: 9+7 apps.
Born: Barking, Essex 22 October 1970
Career: Dagenham & Redbridge, BLUES (£60,000, August 1995), Notts County (£200,000, January 1996).
Club honours: Notts County: Division 3 champions 1998
Representative honours: England (one semi-professional cap)
After embarking on his professional career at St Andrew's - and doing well initially - Ian Richardson became 'Captain Courageous' at Notts County for whom he had made over 200 senior appearances when the curtain came down on the 2001-02 season.

RIOCH, Bruce David

Midfielder: 3 apps.
Born: Aldershot, 6 September 1947.
Career: Stapsley High School, Dynamoes Boys Club, Cambridge & District & London Borough Schools, Luton Town (apprentice, July 1963, professional September 1964, Aston Villa (£100,000, with brother Neil, July 1969), Derby County (£200,000, February 1974), Everton (£180,000, December 1976), Derby County (£150,000, November 1977), BLUES (on loan, December 1978), Sheffield United (on loan, March 1979), Seattle Sounders/NASL (March 1980) Torquay United (October 1980, player-manager July 1982 to January 1984); Seattle Sounders/NASL (coach, July 1985 to January 1986), Middlesborough (assistant-manager, February 1986, manager March 1986 to March 1990), Millwall (manager April 1990 to March 1992), Bolton Wanderers (manager May 1992 to May 1995), Arsenal (manager, June 1995 to August 1996), Queen's Park Rangers (assistant-manager/coach, September 1996 to May 1997), Norwich City (manager, June 1998 to April 2000), Wigan Athletic (manager, July 2000 to February 2001). Applied, unsuccessfully, for other managerial/coaching jobs afterwards.
Club honours: Luton: Division Four champions 1968; Villa: Division Two champions 1972, Football League Cup runners-up 1971; Derby Co: Division One champions 1975; Middlesborough: (as manager): Division Two promotion 1988; Bolton: (as manager): Division One promotion 1995.

Representative honours: Scotland: (24 full caps); toured with FA party in 1969.

The first English-born player to captain Scotland, Bruce Rioch, the son of a Scottish Army Sergeant-Major, was a grand attacking midfielder with cannonball shot and was one of the first English players to represent Scotland on a parental qualification. Rioch joined Aston Villa from Luton but had his best days at Derby from where Blues took him on loan in December 1978. He scored 160 goals in 530 League games before launching a successful career in management, steering Bolton to the Premiership via the Play-offs, following some memorable cup victories in the early 1990s. His father represented Great Britain at athletics, and his brother Daniel (Neil) also played for Luton and Villa, as well as York City, Northampton and Plymouth.

ROACH, James

Goalkeeper: 17 apps
Born: West Bromwich, 12 January 1864.
Died: Birmingham c.1955.
Career: Small Heath Royal, 2nd Dragoon Guards, Saltley Gas Works FC, Hereford Thistle, BLUES (August 1895), Hereford Town (1896), Eastville (Bristol Rovers (1897-98). Jim Roach was already an experienced goalkeeper when he arrived in Birmingham and had a nerve-racking season when Blues were relegated. He re-appeared in 1950, as an entrant in a Sports Argus 'oldest reader' competition. He lost. Roach's grandson, James, was a Blues junior & England Youth international.

ROBB, William R

Goalkeeper: 45 apps.
Born: Rutherglen near Glasgow, 20 March 1895.
Died: Aldershot, 18 February 1976.
Career: Rutherglen Welfare, Lanarkshire Boys' Club, Kirkintilloch Rob Roy, BLUES (professional, January 1914). Armadale (1915), Third Lanark (guest in season 1916-17), Glasgow Rangers (April 1920), Hibernian (June 1926), Aldershot (£100, June 1930), Guildford City (August 1937). Retired May 1939.
Club honours: Glasgow Rangers: Scottish Division One champions 1921, 1923, 1924, 1925, Scottish Cup runners-up 1921, 1922; Guildford: Southern League champions 1938.
Representative honours: Scotland (2 full caps): Scottish League XI (2).
Billy Robb was a fine Scottish goalkeeper who enjoyed 27 years in the game before retiring at the age of 44. Big and weighty, he played all his early football in Lanarkshire before moving to the Midlands. He returned to Scotland during WW1 and spent six years at Ibrox Park before trying his luck with Hibernian. He holds the record for the longest gap between Football League appearances: over 17 years, from 1915 (with Blues) to August 1932 (with Aldershot).

ROBERTS, Brian Leslie Ford

Full-back/defender: 206+7 Apps.

Born: Manchester, 6 November 1955.

Career: Coventry City (apprentice June 1972, professional May 1974), Hereford United (on loan, February 1975), BLUES (£10,000, March 1984), Wolverhampton Wanderers (free transfer, June 1990), Coventry City (scout and then reserve coach, July 1992 to date). Was also employed as a soccer coach at Knightlow School, Stretton-on-Dunsmore (near Coventry). Signed by Blues as a result of a 'Buy a Player Fund' amongst the fans, 'Harry' Roberts was a determined full-back who had made 215 League appearances for Coventry, in close on 12 years at Highfield Road. And when he scored his first goal, some supporters were so shocked that they had special badges made proclaiming: 'I saw Harry score a goal'. A cheerful, likeable chap with a great sense of humour, he had to work hard to overcome the boo-boys at St Andrew's but when he left for Molineux he had become a cult hero, and passed the 500-mark in first-team outings whilst with Wolves. He wrote a witty column in a local newspaper and also wrote a book (Harry's Game)

ROBERTS, Frederick

Inside-left: 32 apps 10 goals

Born: Greets Green, West Bromwich, 9 October 1909. Died: Luton, January 1979.

Career: Smethwick Highfield, Thomas Pigott's Works FC, BLUES (September 1933), Luton Town (December 1934), Kettering Town (August 1945). Retired May 1948. Spotted playing in the Birmingham Works League, Fred Roberts made an immediate impression at St Andrew's, earning his debut after only one month with Blues. He continued to hold down a regular place for most of the season as a scheming inside-forward, although he was occasionally tried in the centre. He struggled early on in 1934-35 and was quickly transferred to Luton where he proved an extremely popular player. His brother, Bill Roberts, played for Cardiff City.

ROBERTS, Harold

Outside-left: 38 apps 3 goals

Born: Liverpool, 12 January 1920.

Career: Harrowby Juniors, Chesterfield (September 1939), BLUES (£12,000, November 1948), Shrewsbury Town (June 1951), Scunthorpe United (July 1953), Gresley Rovers (season 1956-57).

A former Commando, Harry Roberts was a hard-working winger who provided plenty of support to his fellow forwards and supplied a series of good quality crosses. He tended to be a little injury-prone and so missed a large proportion of matches during his two-and-a-half year stay at St Andrew's. Altogether, though, he made over 200 appearances in the Football League with his four clubs (27 goals scored).

ROBERTS, John Griffith

Centre-half: 79 apps. one goal

Born: Abercynon, near Swansea, South Wales, 11 September 1946.

Career: Abercynon Town (August 1961), Swansea Town (apprentice, June 1963, professional July 1964), Northampton Town (November 1967), Arsenal (£35,000, May 1969), BLUES (£140,000, October 1972), Wrexham (August 1976), Hull City (August 1980), Oswestry Town (player-manager, July 1981). Retired in June 1983.

Club honours: Arsenal: Division One champions 1971; Wrexham: Division Three champions 1978, Welsh Cup winners 1978, runners-up 1979.

Representative honours: Wales (22 full caps, one Under-21 cap, five Under-23 caps).

John Roberts was employed as a railway fireman when he joined Swansea Town in 1963. At first no-one really knew his best position (not even himself) but after some keen coaching he eventually took to the centre-half berth and remained there practically throughout his career, scoring his fair share of goals for Northampton despite his defensive duties (many of them coming from set pieces). He spent close on four years with Blues after being signed by manager Freddie Goodwin. After retiring Roberts became a salesman for a North Wales-based stationery company and later earned a living as a driving instructor. During his playing days he amassed in excess of 400 League appearances (145 for Wrexham) and netted 38 goals.

ROBERTS, Josiah Edmund

Right-back: one app.

Born: West Smethwick, 1871. Now Deceased

Career: Mitchell St George's, BLUES (season 1892-93), Walsall Wood (season 1893-94).

Josiah Roberts played in just one senior game for Blues (in a 4-1 win at Bootle in November 1892) in the aftermath of Fred Spiller's broken leg, but he lacked the ability needed to succeed in League football.

ROBERTSON, George

Wing-half/inside-forward: 87 apps. 17 goals

Born: Glasgow 1883. Now Deceased

Career; Rutherglen Glencairn, Clyde (August 1901), Glasgow Rangers (early August 1902), Clyde (late August 1902), Blackburn Rovers (September 1902), Clyde (August 1903), BLUES (December 1910), Bloxwich Strollers (May 1914), Brierley Hill Alliance (season 1921-22).

George Robertson was a hard-working schemer whose first spell in England was short-lived. He was primarily a left-half until Blackburn moved him further forward in 1902. He took to his new role quickly and his strong shooting proved profitable to the club. Robertson disappeared from the local football scene in September

1914, but a few weeks later it transpired that he had signed up for the Army and served in WW1.

ROBERTSON, James
Inside-right: 7 apps. 2 goals
Born: Glasgow, 1880. Now Deceased
Career: Glasgow United, Crewe Alexandra (1901), BLUES (£25, April 1903), Chelsea (£50, August 1905), Glossop North End (1907-08), Leyton (season 1908-09), Patrick Thistle (season 1909-10), Ayr United (seasons 1910-12), Barrow (briefly in 1912), Leeds City (season 1912-13), Gateshead (seasons 1913-15). Retired in May 1915.
Jim Robertson was a slim goal poacher, highly rated at Crewe but took some time to settle into League football. One of three Blues players signed by Chelsea in the London club's first League season, he became a regular marksman during his two years at Stamford Bridge, as he did with his later teams. He was described as 'speedy with a deadly shot' and scored 21 goals for Chelsea and 28 for Glossop.

ROBERTSON, James E.
Centre-forward: 8 apps. 2 goals
Born: Dundee, 1910. Deceased.
Career: Lochee United, Logie Thistle, Dundee (£100, June 1928), BLUES (£1,250, December 1933), Kilmarnock (£1,000, July 1934). Retired in June 1938.
Representative honours: Scotland (2 full caps).
A prolific scorer north of the border, Jimmy Robertson had difficulty settling in the Midlands. His homesickness badly affected his play and Blues were only too glad to recoup most of the money paid for him. At Kilmarnock he was unpopular with the fans but still maintained a record of a goal every two games. The 'Killie' supporters criticised him for lacking 'thrust and initiative'.

ROBERTSON, William
Left-half/inside-right: 103 apps. 15 goals
Born: Pontypool, 1873. Now Deceased
Career: Abercorn FC (1894), BLUES (February 1896), Eastville Rovers (April 1899), BLUES (July 1902), Bristol Rovers (season 1903-04).
Bill Robertson was a two-footed grafter whose career was quite the opposite to namesake George. He joined Blues as an inside-forward but did not find his true metier until switching to wing-half. Unusually, he scored a hat-trick from left-half against Luton in 1898 but he was unable to break into the team during his second spell at Muntz Street.

ROBERTSON, William Harold
Goalkeeper: 3 apps.
Born: Crowthorne, 25 March 1923.
Career: Crowthorne Boys' Club, Camberley ATC, RAF Lossiemouth, Chelsea (October 1945), BLUES

(December 1948), Stoke City (£8,000, June 1952). Retired in May 1960.
Bill Robertson started off as a centre-forward in junior football in his native Crowthorne, and was top-scorer for Camberley ATC whom he helped win the Aldershot Minor League championship (his only medal during his entire playing career). At the age of 20 he turned to goalkeeping in the RAF and quickly developed into a capable last line of defence. He had difficulties, however, in establishing himself at Stamford Bridge, and after moving to St Andrew's his career came to a complete standstill when the brilliance of Gil Merrick restricted him to only three games in-three-and-a-half years. His move to Stoke, however, resurrected his flagging fortunes and he settled in to become one of the League's most consistent performers, appearing in 250 League and Cup games for the Potters. On retirement he took a newsagent's shop in Bucknell, Staffs, but in 1963 he moved back to the south of England.

ROBINSON, Arthur Charles
Goalkeeper: 306 apps
Born: Coventry, 28 February 1878. Died: Coventry, 15 May 1929.
Career: Allesley FC, Coventry Stars, Singers FC, BLUES (professional, August 1898), Chelsea (July 1908), Coventry City (May 1910). He retired to become a publican at the Red House Inn, Barrass Green in Coventry.
Club honours: Blues: Division Two promotion 1901, 1903.
Representative honours: England (2 international trials): Football League XI (2).
'Nat' Robinson always donned two jerseys when keeping goal, irrespective of the weather and it is said that he wore only two pairs of boots throughout his lengthy career. He often used to whistle when annoyed, and he also had a pet dog called 'Ninety' after the number of minutes in a game. Robinson, a real character, was described by a contemporary as being 'all arms and legs' due to the way he used to 'windmill' his arms round in 'Catherine Wheel style' to put off his opponents. Nevertheless he was a brilliant, if somewhat eccentric goalkeeper, who was one of the first practitioners of the art of rushing out of the penalty area to clear the ball.

ROBINSON, Colin Roy
Forward: 39+3 apps. 6 goals
Born: Birmingham, 15 May 1960.
Career: Mile Oak Rovers, Shrewsbury Town (professional, November 1982), BLUES (January 1988), Hereford United (August 1989), Worcester City (July 1991), Bridgnorth Town (March 1994), Halesowen Town (August 1994), Shifnal Town (season 1996-97).
Club honours: Shrewsbury: Welsh Cup winners 1984.
Colin Robinson was a swarthy, bearded striker who had been a regular if not prolific scorer at Gay Meadow for some years before Garry Pendrey recruited him to St

Andrew's to boost Blues' mediocre attack. He scored in his second full game for Blues but was injured the next week and missed the rest of the season. The following term he earned a regular place in the side but rarely looked likely to provide the goals the club desperately needed to halt their slide into Division Three.

ROBINSON, David

Central-defender: 125+ 2 apps. 4 goals
Born: Bartley Green, Birmingham, 14 July 1948.
Career: Woodgate Valley Junior & Bartley Green Senior Schools, Birmingham District Boy & Warwickshire Schools, England Schoolboy trialist, BLUES (apprentice June 1964, professional July 1966), Walsall (February 1973), Chelmsley Town (manager 1976), Tamworth (September 1978), Oldbury United (manager for two seasons: 1980 to 1982).
An England Schoolboy trialist and avid West Bromwich Albion fan as a youngster, Dave 'Sugar' Robinson came to Blues as an inside-forward and struck up a fine partnership with Phil Summerill in the youth side. He was then moved back into the defence and after a good run in the reserves was given his League debut against Aston Villa in September 1968. He always looked impressive, and was entrusted with the job of taking penalties. When he signed Robinson, Blues' manager Stan Cullis said: 'He's saved us £80,000.' After leaving Blues, Robinson added almost 200 more appearances to his tally with Walsall.

ROBINSON, Philip John

Midfielder: 12 apps
Born: Stafford, 6 January 1967.
Career: Stafford & District Schools, Aston Villa (apprentice June 1983, professional January 1985), Wolverhampton Wanderers (June 1987), Notts County (£67,500 August 1989), BLUES (on loan, March-May 1991), Huddersfield Town (September 1992), Northampton Town (on loan, August-October 1994), Chesterfield (December 1994), Notts County (on loan, August-September 1996), Stoke City (July 1998).
Retired from League football in May 2000 to join Hereford United as assistant-manager/coach to Graham Turner, later team manager at Edgar Street (May 2001), then Stafford Rangers (manager, from July 2002).
Club honours: Wolves: Division Four champions 1988, Division Three champions 1989, Sherpa Van Trophy winners 1988: Notts Co: Division Three Play-off winners 1990, promotion to Division One in 1991; Blues: Leyland DAF Cup winners 1991; Huddersfield: Autoglass Trophy runners-up 1994.
Aston Villa were undecided as to whether, Phil Robinson, a busy redhead, was better in defence or midfield, and his career with them suffered from constant changes of position. Manager Graham Turner took him to Wolves where he blossomed as a ball-winner

in their meteoric rise through Divisions, and a further transfer to Meadow Lane led him to the unusual feat of winning promotion four seasons running. Lou Macari would have liked to sign him permanently for Blues but the money was not available. Robinson ended his 'senior' career with well over 500 appearances in his locker including 90 for Wolves, 173 for Notts County and 72 for Northampton.

ROBINSON, Steven Eli

Midfielder: 63+32 apps 2 goals
Born: Nottingham, 17 January 1975.
Career: Nottingham Schoolboy football, BLUES (trainee June 1991, professional June 1993), Peterborough United (on loan, March 1996), Swindon Town (£50,000, February 2001).
Steve Robinson is an eager-beaver footballer, aggressive with a terrific engine. He did pretty well at St Andrew's once he had established himself in the first XI and justifiably earned himself the nickname of 'turbo'. He failed to score a League goal for Blues but quickly made his mark with Swindon, netting with two superb volleys in his opening few games for the Robins.

ROBINSON, Thomas Edward

Inside-left: 10 apps. one goal
Born: Coalville, Leicestershire, 11 February 1909.
Now Deceased
Career: Coalville YMCA, Gresley Rovers (1926), BLUES (November 1928), Blackpool (May 1933), Chesterfield (October 1933), Lincoln City (June 1934), Northampton Town (July 1935), Gillingham (May 1936), Walsall (1937), Tunbridge Wells Rovers, Nuneaton Borough. Retired during WW2
Tommy Robinson was an inside-forward of limited ability whose wanderings took him through all four Divisions of the Football League. He scored a total of 37 goals in his 121 League outings. He was a collier by trade.

RODGERSON, Ian

Right-back/midfielder: 116 apps. 16 goals
Born: Hereford, 9 April 1966.
Career: Aylestone School, Hereford United (on associate schoolboy forms 1981-82), Pegasus Juniors (1984), Hereford United (June 1985), Cardiff City (£7,000, August 1988), BLUES (on loan, December 1990, signed permanently January 1991), Sunderland (£140,000, July 1993), Cardiff City (free transfer, July 1997), Hereford United (1998).
Ian Rodgerson suffered an early setback when he was not taken on as an apprentice at Edgar Street because the club axed its youth team. But he was eventually given a second chance by Hereford and developed into a very useful midfielder, playing wide on the right, ever eager to support his forwards. He was unlucky to miss the 1991 Leyland DAF Cup Final triumph through injury. The

son of Alan Rodgerson, the former Middlesbrough inside-forward, he was injured in a car crash before the start of 1993-94 season, and took quite a while to regain full fitness.

ROE, Arthur
Inside-forward: 3 apps.
Born: Newcastle-on-Tyne, 1892. Now Deceased
Career: South Shields (season 1918-19), BLUES (season 1919-20), Gillingham (August 1920 to May 1922).
Archie Roe was one of a string of inside-forwards Blues tried out in the first post-war season of 1919-20, but who met with no success.

ROGERS, Darren John
Defender: 22+4 apps
Born: Birmingham, 9 April 1970.
Career: Bartley Green School, West Bromwich Albion (YTS June 1986, professional July 1988), BLUES (free transfer, July 1992), Kidderminster Harriers (on loan, March 1993), Lincoln City (on trial, July 1994), Wycombe Wanderers (on loan, November 1993), Walsall (free transfer, July 1994), Stevenage Borough (October 1997).
Darren Rogers, a utility defender, fast and mobile with a good strong tackle, struggled to hold down a first team place at St Andrew's but later in his career he did well with Walsall, for whom he appeared in 76 competitive games despite suffering a cruciate ligament injury in 1996.

ROGERS, Kevin Penry
Midfielder: 8+1 apps. one goal
Born: Merthyr Tydfil, 23 September 1963.
Career: Merthyr & District Schools, Aston Villa (apprentice, September 1979), professional September 1981), BLUES (free transfer, April 1983), Wrexham (July 1984), Rhyl Athletic (1985), Merthyr Tydfil (October 1986).
Club honours: Merthyr: Welsh Cup winners 1987.
Representative honours: Wales (Semi-professional caps, Youth caps, Schoolboy caps).
Kevin Rogers was primarily a 'grafter' who was a regular member of Blues' reserve side but who did little to impress during his rare first-team outings. He was a school colleague of Tony Rees.

RONSON, William
Midfielder: 2 apps.
Born: Fleetwood, 22 January 1957.
Career: Blackpool Boys, Blackpool (apprentice, June 1973, professional February 1974), Cardiff City (£125,000, July 1979), Wrexham (£100,000, October 1981), Barnsley (£50,000, August 1982), BLUES (on loan, November 1985), Blackpool (non-contract, January 1986), separate spells in the NASL with Baltimore Blast and Tampa Bay Rowdies in 1992, later participating

strongly in the respected American indoor Soccer League. Billy Ronson was a tigerish midfielder whose talents were highly rated by all his clubs. He came to Blues following a disagreement with Barnsley manager, Allan Clarke, which had left him out of favour at Oakwell. Ronson was one of the most successful performers on the American indoor circuit. In England he accumulated a total of 368 League appearances as a professional, scoring 20 goals.

ROTHERHAM, Walter
Inside-left: 2 apps.
Born: Stafford, 1859. Now Deceased
Career: Wolverhampton St Luke's FC, BLUES (September 1880), Leabrook FC (August 1883).
Work commitments prevented Wally Rotherham, an exceptionally useful goalscorer, from making many senior appearances.

ROULSON, Joseph
Right-half: 125 apps. 4 goals
Born: Sheffield, 1890. Now Deceased
Career: Cammel Laird FC (1910), BLUES (August 1912), Swansea Town (April 1923), Clapton Orient (December 1924 to May 1925).
Club honours: Blues: Division Two champions 1921.
Joe Roulson was a 'hard as nails' wing-half, similar in style to his partner, Percy Barton. A former steelworker, he was picked up from the Sheffield Works' League and after a decent spell with Swansea (over 50 games) and a brief flirtation with Orient (16 outings) he returned to work in the Yorkshire city.

ROWBOTHAM, Darren
Striker: 34+7 apps. 6 goals.
Born: Cardiff, 22 October 1966.
Career: St Cogan's School; Plymouth Argyle (junior, July 1983, professional November 1984), Exeter City (October 1987), Torquay United (£25,000, September 1991), BLUES (£20,000, January 1992), Mansfield Town (on loan, December 1992), Hereford United (on loan, March 1993), Crewe Alexandra (free transfer, July 1993), Shrewsbury Town (July 1995), Exeter City (October 1996), Leyton Orient (on loan, November 1999), Weymouth (June 2000).
Club honours: Exeter: Division Four champions 1990.
Representative honours: Wales (Youth cap).
Darren Rowbotham scored plenty of goals in the lower Divisions, always giving 100 per-cent effort and was dangerous both in the air and on the ground. His final goal tally (before he entered non-League soccer with Weymouth) was 124 (in 534 outings). His record with Exeter was 101 goals in 274 games - and he was voted the Grecian's 'Player of the Year' in 1997-98.

ROWETT, Gary
Defender: 103 apps. 11 goals
Born: Bromsgrove, 6 March 1974
Career: Cambridge United (junior 1989, professional
September 1991), Everton (£200,000, May 1994),
Blackpool (on loan, January 1995), Derby County
(£300,000, July 1995), BLUES (£1 million, August
1998), Leicester City (£3 million+ July 2000), Charlton
Athletic (£3.5 million, July 2002).
Named in the PFA Nationwide League Division One
side for 1999-2000, Gary Rowett was a sterling
performer for Blues throughout that campaign, having
previously made 120 appearances for the Rams. An
impressive tackler, he left St Andrew's for a club record
fee to enter the Premiership, but fell back down a peg
when Leicester were relegated, only to return to the top
flight with Charlton in the summer of 2002, signed by
ex-Blues midfielder Alan Curbishley.

ROWLEY, Kenneth Frank
Inside-forward: 42 apps. 20 goals
Born: Pelsall, 29 August 1926.
Career: Pelsall Juniors, Elkingtons FC, Wolverhampton
Wanderers (professional, October 1947), BLUES
(January 1951), Coventry City (November 1954). Quit
League football through injury in April 1957, but later
played for Bromsgrove Rovers for two seasons: 1957 to 1959.
Ken Rowley was a pint-sized forward with a tremendous
shot who signed for Blues after a lengthy spell in Wolves'
reserve side. He had a marvellous strike-rate until
suffering a serious injury in November 1952. Doctors
said he would never play again but he defied them and
turned out in another 14 games, scoring eight goals,
before he was transferred to Coventry where he had only
three more outings before he was forced to climb down
the footballing ladder at the age of 30. He played on
tentatively with Bromsgrove for another couple of years
before hanging up his boots for good.

RUDD, William Thomas
Forward: 26 apps. 4 goals.
Born: Manchester, 13 December 1941.
Career: Manchester Schools, Manchester United
(amateur, August 1956), Stalybridge Celtic (season 1958-
59), BLUES (professional, October 1959), New York All
Stars (on loan, summer 1961), York City (November
1961), Grimsby Town (July 1966), Rochdale (£1,500,
February 1968), Bury (£5,000, June 1970 to May 1977).
After leaving Blues, Billy Rudd certainly came good and
scored 68 goals in 574 League games for his next four
clubs, including 34 in 193 outings for York and 18 in
189 for Bury whom he served for seven years. A former
cabinet-maker he was never a popular player with the
fans at St Andrew's and failed to gain a regular place in
the side. His career with Blues was effectively over when
Bertie Auld arrived from Celtic. Rudd's uncle Jack,
played for Manchester City.

RUSHFELDT, Sigurd
Striker: 5+4 apps. one goal
Born: Tromso, Norway, 11 December 1972
Career: FC Tromso, BLUES (on loan, October to
November 1995); later Rosenborg/Norway (1999 to 2002).
'Siggy' Rushfeldt spent barely two months with Blues.
He had always wanted to taste English football but he
never adapted to the pace and left without really making
much of an impression.

RUSHTON, Brian William Eric
Right-back: 15 apps.
Born: Sedgley, 21 October 1943.
Career: Brierley Hill Schools, Dudley Boys, BLUES
(amateur 1959, professional October 1960), Notts
County (June 1967 to March 1968).
Brian Rushton captained the successful Brierley Hill
Schools team before linking up with Blues. Although a
fine player as a lad his coltish physique was hardly ideal
for the role of full-back and latterly efforts were made,
unsuccessfully, to convert him into a wing-half.

RUSSELL, Cecil John
Forward: 27 apps. 2 goals
Born: Northfield, 19 June 1904.
Career: Northfield, Bournville, Bromsgrove Rovers,
BLUES (February 1924), Bristol Rovers (June 1927),
Worcester City (June 1928), Bournemouth & Boscombe
Athletic (June 1930), Luton Town (May 1934), Norwich
City (October 1934), Worcester City (May 1936),
Shirley Town (August 1937), Solihull Town (August 1939).
Owing to injuries to key players, Blues gave promising
youngster Jack Russell his League debut at inside-right
versus Bolton Wanderers at St Andrew's in October
1924. The promise was largely unfulfilled and the
remainder of his career with Blues was spent as a utility
reserve. He later had a successful spell at Dean Court,
scoring four goals in a game on two separate occasions.

RUSSELL, Guy Robert
Centre-forward: 9+5 apps.
Born: Shirley, 28 September 1967.
Career: Knowle North Star, BLUES (YTS, June 1984,
professional May 1986), Carlisle United (on loan, March
1987), Kemin Palloseura/Finland (April 1989), Moor
Green (October 1989).
Guy Russell was a regular scorer for Blues at both youth
and reserve-team levels but looked out of his depth in
the senior side. His brief excursion in Finland ended with
'KePs' being relegated. He returned to England and
scored regularly in the Southern League.

RUSSELL, Martin Christopher
Midfielder: 4+2 apps
Born: Dublin, 27 April 1967.
Career: Belvedere Youth Club, Manchester United
(apprentice June 1973, professional May 1984), BLUES

(on loan, October 1986), Norwich City (on loan, January 1987), Leicester City (£25,000, March 1987), Scarborough (£105,000, February 1989), Middlesbrough (£175,000, March 1990), Portadown (August 1991).
Club honours: Portadown Gold Cup winners 1992, Budweiser Cup winners 1992, Mid-Ulster Cup winners 1992, 1993, 1994. Voted Northern Ireland PFA 'Player of the Year' in 1992.
Representative honours: Republic of Ireland (4 Under-21 caps, Youth caps).
Martin Russell was a skilful midfielder who was particularly adept at quick changes of direction and short passes. He did not seem to relish a hard fight, however, and had the tendency to disappear when the boots were flying. He did, though, possess a good shot when he decided to use it.

RUTHERFORD, Mark Robin
Winger: 1+4 apps.
Born: Birmingham, 25 March 1972.
Career: BLUES (YTS, June 1988, professional July 1990), Shelbourne (October 1991), Shrewsbury Town (on loan, February 1994).
Club honours: Shelbourne: Irish League champions 1992, Irish Cup winners 1993, Football League Cup runners-up 1994; Shrewsbury: Division Four champions 1994.
Mark Rutherford proved a fast, tricky player who graduated through the YTS scheme at St Andrew's. He enjoyed a good scoring record for Blues' third team, but his League career was arrested by series of niggling injuries. He did reasonably well in Ireland before returning to have 14 League games for Shrewsbury, helping them clinch the Fourth Division title.

SABIN, Alfred
Right-half: 2 apps
Born: Oldbury, 1904. Deceased.
Career: Accles & Pollocks Works FC, BLUES (March 1930), Oldbury United (August 1930), Leamington Town (1932).
Alf Sabin was an attacking wing-half who was given a trial by Blues at the end of the 1929-30 season, but was not offered a contract.

SADLER, Matthew
Defender: 4* apps.
Born: Birmingham: 26 February 1985
Career: Birmingham Schools; BLUES (YTS June 2001).
Representative honours: England (Youth caps)
Highly-rated defender Matthew Sadler was handed his first team debut by manager Steve Bruce in a 2nd round 3-2 Worthington Cup win at Leyton Orient on October 2002, replacing Darren Purse, when several changes were made to the line-up following a 2-0 Premiership defeat at the hands of Newcastle United a few days earlier.

SAHLIN, Dan
Striker: 0+1 app
Born: Falum, Sweden, 18 April 1967
Career: Hammarby IF/Sweden, BLUES (on loan, November-December 1995); then back to Swedish football.
A mystery man to most Blues fans, striker Dan Sahlin had just 20 minutes of first team action with the club, coming on as a 'sub' versus Leicester City.

SALE, Mark David
Striker: 16+11 apps 3 goals
Born: Rugeley, Staffs, 27 February 1972.
Career: Stoke City (July 1990), Yeovil Town (on loan, 1991), Cambridge United (July 1991), Stafford Rangers (on trial), Rocester (October 1991), BLUES (March 1992), Torquay United (March 1993), Preston North End (August 1994), Mansfield Town (July 1995), Colchester United (March 1997), Rushden & Diamonds (July 1999).
Mark Sale, a 6ft 5in striker, was a good squad player, often appearing on the substitutes' bench. He later scored over 40 goals playing at a lower level.

SAMSON, Ambrose Arthur
Goalkeeper: 2 apps.
Born: Measham, 1897. Now Deceased
Career: Measham Town, BLUES (season 1922-23), Burton Town (August 1923).
Arthur Samson was a tall, bulky goalkeeper, rather flashy at times, whose outings were restricted due to the form of Dan Tremelling.

SAMWAYS, Vincent
Midfielder: 12 apps.
Born: Bethnel Green, East London, 27 October 1968
Career: East London & London Schools, Tottenham Hotspur (apprentice April 1985, professional November 1985), Everton (£2.2 million, August 1994), Wolverhampton Wanderers (on loan, December 1995), BLUES (on loan, February and March 1996), Las Palmas/Spain (July 1996), FC Sevilla/Spain (August 2002).
Club honours: Spurs: FA Cup & Charity Shield winners 1991; Everton: FA Charity Shield winners 1995
Representative honours: England (5 Under-21 & Youth caps) 'Vinny' Samways played in more than 250 first team games for Spurs. A hard-working, enthusiastic midfielder, with stamina and skill, he came on for the injured Paul Gascoigne in the 1991 FA Cup Final. Unfortunately he gained a reputation for being the 'hard man' of Spanish soccer after leaving England!

SANSOME, Paul Eric
Goalkeeper: 2 apps
Born: New Addington, 6 October 1961
Career: Crystal Palace (juniors 1977, professional October 1978), Millwall (free transfer April 1980),

Southend United (£40,000, March 1988), BLUES (on loan, January 1996), Gravesend & Northfleet (on loan, March 1987). Later reserve team coach at Southend (April 1997 to May 1999).

Club honours: Millwall: League Trophy winners 1983

A very safe handler of the ball, a fine shot-stopper, Paul Sansome made well over 525 senior appearances during his career. He was 'signed' by Blues to cover for the injured Ian Bennett (before Bart Griemink took over).

SAVAGE, Robert William

Midfielder: 21 apps* 1 goal*

Born: Wrexham, 18 October 1974

Career: Manchester United (trainee 1980, professional July 1993), Crewe Alexandra (free transfer, July 1994), Leicester City (£400,000, July 1997), BLUES (£2.5 million, June 2002).

Club honours: Manchester United: FA Youth Cup winners 1992; Leicester: League Cup winners 2000.

Representative honours: Wales (28* full, 5 Under-21, Youth & Schoolboy caps)

Right-sided midfielder Robbie Savage was huge favourite at Filbert Street, his aggressive style, off-the-ball running and terrific engine making him a mangers' dream - hence his move to Blues as Steve Bruce was eager to bolster up his squad for the Premiership battle ahead. Savage, with his long blond hair, made over 200 appearances for the 'Foxes' and is an important member of Mark Hughes' improving Welsh team. He is now a star performer for Blues.

SAVILLE, Andrew Victor

Striker: 57+8 apps 18 goals.

Born: Hull, 12 December 1964.

Career: Malet Lambert School, Hull City Minors (1979); Hull City (professional September 1983), Walsall (£100,000, March 1989), Barnsley (£90,000, March 1990), Hartlepool United (£60,000, March 1992), BLUES (£155,000, March 1993), Burnley (on loan, December 1994), Preston North End (£100,000, July 1995), Wigan Athletic (£125,000, October 1996), Cardiff City (£75,000, October 1997), Hull City (on loan, September 1998), Scarborough (March 1999), Gainsborough Trinity (June 1999).

Club honours: PNE: Division Three champions 1996

The scoring record of Andy Saville, a strongly built, 6ft striker, was not all that impressive when Blues paid £155,000 for his services on the transfer deadline of 1993. He had managed only 65 goals in 303 outings in League and Cup competition, but repaid some of that money spent on him by having a pretty good first full season at St Andrew's, being joint leading scorer with Paul Peschisolido (ten goals). After that he faded but later netted 31 goals (in 66 games for PNE) and 14 in 41 outings for Cardiff. He entered non-League football in 1999, having claimed a total of 133 goals in 520 appearances at competitive level.

SBRAGIA, Richard

Defender: 15+2 apps. one goal

Born: Lennoxtown, Scotland, 26 May 1956.

Career: Glasgow Amateurs, BLUES (apprentice June 1972, professional May 1974), Morton (on loan), Walsall (£15,000, October 1978), Blackpool (£35,000, July 1980), York City (August 1982), Darlington (on loan, August-September 1985), York City (youth-team coach 1989 to May 1994), Sunderland (Youth coach and then reserve team manager, 1994 to 2002). Manchester United (researve team manager 2002-03).

Of Italian descent, hence his surname, 'Ricky' Sbragia was a tall, slimly built defender particularly strong in the air but a little ungainly on the ground. He made 275 League appearances after leaving Blues, including 77 for Walsall and 149 for York. He then became a very successful coach.

SCHOFIELD, John Reginald

Goalkeeper: 237 apps

Born: Atherstone, Warwickshire, 8 February 1931.

Career: Nuneaton Borough Reserves, BLUES (professional, February 1950), Wrexham (July 1966 to May 1968), Atherstone Town (player-manager, August 1968), Bromsgrove Rangers (season 1969-70), Tamworth (1970 to 1972), Atherstone Town (manager, July 1972 to 1974).

Club honours: Blues: Division Two champions 1955, Inter Cities Fair Cup runners-up 1960, 1961, Football League Cup winners 1963.

Big-hearted and brave, Johnny Schofield survived a pit explosion (at Baddesley Colliery, Warwickshire in November 1957) and a fractured skull (playing for Blues against Manchester United in 1960, when diving at Alex Dawson's feet) and still came up smiling. A dedicated footballer, he understudied Gil Merrick for quite a while before taking over the green jersey in 1960. In 1962 he broke some fingers but this was his last major injury and he then held his place until the combination of advancing years and the signing of Jim Herriot led to him leaving the club. After retiring he became the proprietor of a wines and spirits off-licence business in Atherstone as well as being a season-ticket holder at St Andrew's.

SCOTT, Geoffrey Samuel

Defender: 18+1 apps.

Born: Birmingham, 31 October 1956.

Career: Solihull Borough, Highgate United, Stoke City (professional April 1977), Leicester City (February 1980), BLUES (February 1982), Charlton Athletic (October 1982), Middlesbrough (June 1984), Northampton Town (September 1984), Cambridge United (May 1985), Solihull Borough (1986), Moor Green (January 1987), Highgate United (manager July 1988, resigning in August 1989).

Signed in the midst of an injury crisis, Geoff Scott's career at St Andrew's was characterised by a series of errors, hence his short spell in the first team. He is one of a select band of players (George Smith and William Wragg are the others) to sign for Blues immediately after scoring a goal for them (an own-goal). Scott spent his best years with Stoke for whom he played 78 League games.

SCOTT, Richard Paul
Defender/midfielder: 17+2 apps.
Born: Dudley, 29 September 1974.
Career: BLUES (YTS July 1991, professional May 1993), Shrewsbury (March 1995), Peterborough United (July 1998), Telford United (July 2001).
Initially a right-back, Richard Scott's senior debut for Blues was in that position against Derby County at St Andrew's in April 1993 before a 15,400 crowd. A steady defender, he was converted into a hard-working right-sided midfielder at Shrewsbury for whom he made almost 130 senior appearances, adding another 70 to his tally with 'Posh'.

SCRIVEN, Aubrey
Outside-left: 52 apps 9 goals.
Born: Cleobury Mortimer, Shropshire, 7 July 1904.
Now Deceased
Career: Highley Boys' Club, Denaby United, BLUES (December 1923), Bradford City (£400, May 1927), Bristol City (May 1932), Worcester City (July 1934), Brierley Hill Alliance (August 1935 to May 1940). Did not figure after WW2..
Club honours: Bradford City: Division Three North champions 1929; Worcester: Welsh Cup winners 1934.
Aubrey Scriven was a talented but inconsistent player, one of the men tried to solve the perennial left-wing problem. He proved more successful than most but still could not establish himself in the side. Later he had a useful five-year spell at Bradford.

SCRIVENS, Thomas
Inside-forward: 16 apps 9 goals
Born: Walsall, 1876. Now Deceased
Career: Walsall Star, Smethwick Rovers, BLUES (January 1897), Wellingborough (June 1898), BLUES (August 1898), Willenhall FC (August 1900).
Tommy Scrivens was a hard-shooting forward who was an effective partner for Bob McRoberts during his second spell with Blues. He was then mysteriously released in the summer of 1900.

SEALEY, Leslie Jesse
Goalkeeper: 15 apps.
Born: Bethnal Green, 29 September 1957.
Died: London, August 2001
Career: Leyton High School, Interwood; Bethnal Green Boys' Club, Coventry City (apprentice April 1974, professional March 1976), Luton Town (£100,000, August 1983), Plymouth Argyle (on loan, October 1984), Manchester United (on loan, December 1989, signed permanently in May 1990), Aston Villa (July 1991), Coventry City (on loan, March 1992), BLUES (on loan, October 1992), Manchester United (January 1993), Blackpool (June 1994), West Ham United (December 1994), Leyton Orient (non-contract, July 1996), West Ham United (non-contract, November 1996-May 1997). Retired and later coached at Upton Park until his sudden death (from a heart attack) in 2001.
Club honours: Manchester United: FA Cup winners 1990, European Cup-winners' Cup winners 1991, 1994; Luton: Full Members' Cup runners-up 1988, Football League Cup runners-up 1989.
Les Sealey, a vastly experienced goalkeeper, had already accumulated some 500 senior appearances prior to joining Blues for a three-month loan period in 1992. He later added further appearances to his tally and ended his career with a total of 578 under his belt - his last was for West Ham in the Premiership, against his former club Manchester United at Old Trafford in front of 55,249 fans in May 1997.

SEAMAN, David Andrew
Goalkeeper: 84 apps
Born: Rotherham, 19 September 1963.
Career: Leeds United (apprentice September 1979, professional September 1981), Peterborough United (£4,000, August 1982), BLUES (£100,000, October 1984), Queen's Park Rangers (£225,000, August 1986), Arsenal (£1.3 million, May 1990).
Club honours: Arsenal: League/Premiership champions 1991, 1998 & 2002, FA Cup winners 1993, 1998 & 2002, League Cup winners 1993, European Cup-winners Cup winners 1994, runners-up 1995; FA Charity Shield winners 1998, 2002.
Representative honours: England (78* full, 6 'B' and 10 Under-21 caps).
A brilliant goalkeeper, with fine reactions and safe pair of hands, David Seaman was rated one of best in the world in the mid-1990s. He was released by Leeds without ever appearing in their first team but proved a shrewd buy for Peterborough and it was something of a coup when Blues signed him in 1984. Indeed, he was one of the few successes in season 1985-86, during which he played a 'blinder' at Highbury. He later won honours galore with Arsenal but as he got older - and perhaps not wiser - he was suspect under pressure and made a few blunders whereby important goals were conceded, by club and country! So far during his 21 years as a professional Seaman, tall, commanding, a fine shot-stopper with terrific reflexes, has amassed well over 950 club and international appearances.

SELLMAN, Alfred

Centre-half: one app.

Born: Exeter, 1881. Now Deceased

Career: Exeter Schoolboy football, Bridgetown Amateurs (Totnes), BLUES (January 1904), Leyton (1905-06), Newton Abbot (1906-09).

Alf Sellman was a powerful player who made a big impression on his debut, one critic describing him as 'very strong and his tackling and feeding give promise of his being a class half-back in the near future'. Alas, he never lived up to that promise. A useful cricketer, he once had a trial with Kent as a wicketkeeper, and played regularly in the Devon League.

SHARP, Frank

Inside-left: 5 apps.

Born: Tintwistle, 1900. Now Deceased

Career: Barton-Under-Needwood Schools, Barton BSC, BLUES (season 1922-23), Chesterfield (1923-24).

Frank Sharp, a former steel worker, earned a few games as a replacement for Jack Whitehouse shortly after turning professional. Principally a playmaker, he did not fit in when asked to play a more attacking role.

SHARPLES, Brian

Centre-half: 71+1 apps 2 goals.

Born: Bradford, 6 September 1944.

Career: Henry Parkes Junior School, Woodlands Comprehensive School, BLUES (amateur September 1959, professional December 1961), Exeter City (December 1968). Retired in May 1971.

Brian Sharples was brought up in Coventry. An awkward looking defender, he was tried in most positions before finally settling down in the centre-half spot after he had acted as sweeper in manager Joe Mallett's controversial 'M' plan. Never really a first-team regular at Blues, he fell from favour when Stan Cullis took over but came back into the side when Winston Foster underwent a cartilage operation. A rather limited player, Sharples was somewhat cumbersome when the ball was on the ground. He came from a sporting family - his sister was a county netball player and his father a champion sprinter. He is also a distant relative of Sam Cowan (ex-Manchester City and England). Sharples now owns a chain of shoe shops in and around Bristol.

SHAW, John

Left-half: 11 apps

Born: Oldham, 2 October 1916. Died: 22 October 1973.

Career: South Shore Wesleyans, Lytham (December 1933), Oldham Athletic (March 1934), Mossley (July 1936), Grimsby Town (May 1937), BLUES (March 1939), Watford (October 1945). Retired in May 1948.

Jack Shaw was a tall, muscular player, more destructive than constructive, whose arrival at St Andrew's found him pitched into the vain struggle against relegation. He

had little chance to show his prowess with Blues owing to the outbreak of WW2. His uncle, George Tyson, played Rugby League football for Oldham.

SHAW, Raymond

Wing-half: 13 apps.

Born: Walsall, 18 May 1913. Died: 1980.

Career: Walsall (amateur), Streetly Works, Darlaston, BLUES (May 1937). Retired in May 1947 to become BLUES' coach; later Walsall (manager October 1964 to March 1968).

Ray Shaw, a constructive player, seldom shone, although he did appear in 111 first-team games for Blues during WW2. He became a top-class coach, though, a role he played at St Andrew's for many years before taking over as boss at Fellows Park.

SHAW, Thomas Frederick

Inside-forward: 5 apps.

Born: Hucknall, Nottinghamshire, 27 March 1909. Now Deceased

Career: Annesley Colliery FC, Darlaston, BLUES (amateur September 1932, professional October 1932), Notts County (December 1934), Mansfield Town (July 1937), Bournemouth & Boscombe Athletic (1938), Ollerton Colliery FC (1939). Retired in June 1943.

Fred Shaw was a shade on the small side for the role of 'target man' - a position he was often asked to play. A lightweight, highly mobile, with an eye for goal, he proved far more successful after moving back to his native Nottinghamshire. He scored 21 goals in 56 League games for Notts County.

SHEARER, Peter Andrew

Forward: 33+5 apps 13 goals.

Born: Birmingham, 4 February 1967.

Career: Coventry City (associate schoolboy forms, 1981), BLUES (apprentice June 1983, professional February 1985), Rochdale (July 1986), Nuneaton Borough (1987), Cheltenham Town (1988), AFC Bournemouth (February 1989), Coventry City (on trial, 1993), Dundee (on trial, 1993), BLUES (January 1994 to June 1995). Thereafter played in non-League football.

Club honours: Blues: Second Division champions 1995, Auto-Windscreen Shield winners 1995.

Representative honours: England (semi-professional caps).

As a youngster Peter Shearer tended to be a bit lazy off the ball. In his first spell at St Andrew's he was played chiefly as a forward or attacking midfielder in the first team but as a centre-half in the reserves. Released whilst still a teenager he failed to make the grade at Rochdale either but a spell in non-League football seemed to do him good and he was a much better player by the time Bournemouth signed him. Nevertheless it was still a surprise when Barry Fry brought him back to St Andrew's. Again he struggled to establish himself and he was soon placed on the open to transfer list. However, the 1994-95 season brought about an amazing transformation as he emerged as a star of the team. His tenacious tackling coupled with the ability to score priceless goals made him the most improved player in the club although his aggression sometimes brought him problems with referees. Unfortunately he suffered a serious Achilles tendon injury in April 1995 and he never really recovered full fitness and was released by Blues in the summer

SHERIDAN, John Joseph
Midfielder: 3+1 apps
Born: Stretford, Manchester, 1 October 1964
Career: Manchester City (juniors 1981-82), Leeds United (professional, March 1982), Nottingham Forest (£650,000, August 1989), Sheffield Wednesday (£500,000, November 1989), BLUES (on loan, February-March 1996), Bolton Wanderers (£180,000, November 1996), Doncaster Rovers (July 1998), Oldham Athletic (free transfer, October 1998, later appointed coach at Boundary Park: 2002)
Club honours: Sheffield Wednesday: League Cup winners 1991; Bolton: Division 1 champions 1997
Representative honours: Republic of Ireland (34 full, one 'B', 2 Under-23, 2 Under-21 & Youth caps)
One of the best passers of the ball during his playing days, John Sheridan made more than 700 competitive appearances and club and international level. Older brother of Darren (Barnsley & Wigan Athletic).

SHORT, Charles
Inside/centre-forward: 19 apps 12 goals.
Born: Birmingham, 1868.
Career: Birmingham Excelsior, BLUES (August 1889), Unity Gas Depot FC (1890), BLUES (October 1890), Bloxwich Strollers (August 1892 to May 1893).
Charlie Short was a fine goal-poacher who gained notoriety as the player and got Blues kicked out of the FA Cup. He had played for the club in 1889-90, but his registration had been allowed to lapse. He returned to Blues after a few games with Unity Gas, but no one had bothered to re-register him for the competition. He scored in a 2-0 win over Wednesbury Old Athletic, who protested that Blues had fielded an ineligible player. Blues were subsequently thrown out of the tournament.

SHORT, George Frederick
Utility: 30 apps 2 goals
Born: Birmingham 1866.
Career: Unity Gas Company FC, BLUES (September 1887), Oldbury Town (1895).
Club honours: Blues: Division Two champions 1893.
An elder brother of Charlie Short (q.v) George Short was the first genuine utility player the club ever had. He began as a winger, but worked his way through most

positions before settling down in the full-back berth. He was Fred Speller's replacement for two years.

SHORT, John
Inside-forward: 17 apps 10 goals
Born: Hucknall, Nottinghamshire, April 1896.
Career: Arnold St Mary's, South Notts Hussars Yeomanry, Lincoln City (1916-17), Notts County (August 1917), BLUES (October 1919), Watford (May 1920), Ilkeston United (May 1922), Norwich City (May 1923), Newark Town (September 1924 to May 1925), Grantham Town, Lewison FC (September 1927 to April 1928).
'James' Short was another fine goalscorer whose stay at St Andrew's was brief but explosive. He kept up his fine markmanship record throughout his career which was seriously affected by wounds received during WW1.

SHUFFLEBOTTOM, John
Centre-half: one app
Born: Macclesfield, February 1888. Died: Crewe, 1954.
Career: Loughborough Town (1903), Notts County (1904), Old Mill FC (1913), BLUES (March 1905), Oldham Athletic (August 1907), Portsmouth (May 1909), Southport Central (£150, July 1911). Retired in October 1914.
Jack Shufflebottom was a long striding, dark-haired defender with a strong kick, who was basically a reserve with most of his clubs. Oldham Athletic retained his registration from 1907 until 1914, when he played outside the Football League. He worked as a timber merchant's agent in the Birmingham area for a number of years either side of WW1.

SHUTT, Carl Steven
Striker: 21+8 apps 4 goals
Born: Sheffield, 10 October 1961.
Career: Sheffield Wednesday (associate schoolboy forms, April 1976), Spalding United (September 1982), Sheffield Wednesday (free transfer, May 1985), Bristol City (£55,000, October 1987), Leeds United (£50,000, March 1989), BLUES (£50,000, August 1993), Manchester City (on loan, January 1994, full transfer September 1994), Bradford City (August 1994), Darlington (March 1997 to May 1999), Kettering Town (June 1999).
Club honours: Leeds United: Division One champions 1992, Division Two champions 1990.
Carl Shutt had a useful record to his credit - 68 goals in 226 appearances - when he was transferred to Blues from Elland Road, but he never really settled down at St Andrew's, injuries plaguing him in 1994. He played in the same side as Chris Whyte at Leeds. When he quit top-line football in 1999 he had taken his goal-tally to almost 100 (in some 430 matches). He was also a very capable stand-in goalkeeper.

SIMMS, Charles
Centre-half: 14 apps.
Born: Birmingham, 12 February 1859.
Died: Birmingham, 20 July 1935.
Career: Calthorpe FC, Mitchell St George's, BLUES
(first as a player from August 1884 to May 1892, then as
first-team trainer until 1905 and thereafter as head
groundsman at St Andrew's until January 1914, when he
retired from football).
Charlie 'Bowie' Simms was a real heavyweight who
served Blues for close on 30 years. Weighing almost 14st,
with his bandy legs and walrus moustache, he looked the
very epitome of a Victorian footballer. He joined Blues at
the age of 25 and was a regular performer in defence for
eight years, from 1884 until 1892, although from time
to time he was dogged by injury. He made his League
debut when he was almost ready to quit the game as a
player, taking over from Caesar Jenkyns who missed the
train to Lincoln (January 1893). He also turned out in
goal a few times in various friendly matches. Simms was
a grand club man, in every sense of the word and on
retiring as a player he was immediately offered the job as
'spongeman', a position he held for more than a decade
before taking up his duties as groundsman. His brother,
Arnie, was on Blues' books in the pre-League era. Simms
played cricket for Small Heath Langley for many years
and scored runs regularly.

SINGER, Dennis James
Inside-forward: 31 apps 15 goals.
Born: Cefn Hengoed, 30 August 1937.
Career: Fleur de Lys FC, Hengoed FDL, Newport
County (amateur 1954, professional May 1956), BLUES
(September 1960), Bournemouth & Boscombe Athletic
(£7,000, September 1962), Newport County (July 1964).
Club honours: Blues: Fairs Cup runners-up 1961.
Jimmy Singer had an excellent strike record as a League
player - 62 goals in a total of 138 games - but was never
very popular with the fans, especially those at St
Andrew's, despite his happy knack of being in the right
place when chances appeared. He later owned a
restaurant in Caerleon.

SISSONS, John Graham
Centre-half/full-back: 106 apps.
Born: Chester-le-Street, County Durham, 20 May 1934.
Career: Kiveton Boys, Erdington Juniors, Country Girl
FC, BLUES (professional July 1954), Peterborough
United (December 1962), Walsall (November 1964 to
May 1968). A dark haired, swarthy and honest worker,
Graham Sissons joined Blues prior to his National
Service. After demob he settled into the reserve team as
deputy to Trevor Smith, before finally taking over in the
left-back position following George Allen's departure. A
capable defender, if limited in his distribution, he played
exactly 100 League games for Walsall and 68 for 'Posh'.
He was later a hospital worker in Erdington, Birmingham.

SLATER, Frederick
Centre-forward: 5 apps. one goal
Born: Burton-upon-Trent, 25 September 1925.
Career: Burton Albion, BLUES (professional November
1947), York City (June 1951), Corby Town (1952),
Nuneaton Borough (August 1954 to 1956).
Fred Slater was a 'rough and tumble' striker, spotted in
non-League football. After a year in the reserves he was
given his chance as Blues attempted to replace Cyril
Trigg. Sadly after only ten minutes of his debut (versus
Huddersfield Town, at home, in November 1948) Slater
was stretchered off with a broken leg. He recovered
before the end of the season but could not permanently
depose Jimmy Dailey and was eventually transferred to
York City.

SLATER, William
Centre-forward: 5 apps. 4 goals.
Born: Birmingham, 1858.
Career: Calthorpe, BLUES (September 1879), Brades
Heath (August 1884).
A goalscoring star of the early 1880s, Billy Slater claimed
Blues' first-ever competitive goal - in an FA Cup-tie
against Derby Town in 1879. He was also a very
competent cricketer, being a middle-order batsman and
star bowler for the Small Heath Alliance CC.

SLEEUWENHOEK, John Cornelius
Centre-half: 29+3 apps.
Born: Wednesfield, 26 February 1944.
Died: Birmingham, July 1989.
Career: Wood End County & Wansbridge Secondary
Schools, Aston Villa (juniors, June 1959, professional
February 1961), BLUES (£45,000, November 1967),
Torquay United (on loan, March 1971), Oldham
Athletic (July 1971 to May 1972). Retired with knee
injury in July 1974 after a brief spell in the Cheshire
County League. Played for Villa Old Stars (1970s) and
later worked for Aston Villa on the lottery department.
Club honours: Aston Villa: Football League Cup
runners-up 1963.
Representative honours: England (2 Under-23 caps,
Youth caps, Schoolboy caps); Football League XI (1).
Son of a Dutch parachute instructor, Johnny
Sleeuwenhoek (nicknamed 'Slogger' and 'Tulip') was fed
on cheese and stout as a lad to build him up, but late in
his career had to fight the flab. At his peak this blond
defender was a solid performer who played 260 times for
the Villa. Blues signed him in an attempt to boost their
promotion chances but a tedious knee injury curtailed
his career at St Andrew's. He wore spectacles off the field
and his son, Kris, was once a junior with both Wolves
and Derby County. His League Cup runners-up prize
came against Blues in the 1963 Final. He sadly died in
1989 at the age of 45.

SMALL, Bryan

Full-back: 3 apps.

Born: Birmingham, 15 November 1971.

Career: Hurley Colts Aston Villa (YTS July 1988, professional July 1990), BLUES (on loan, September 1994), Bolton Wanderers (free transfer, March 1996), Luton Town (on loan, September 1997), Bradford City (on loan, December 1997), Bury (free transfer, January 1999), Stoke City (free transfer, July 1998), Carlisle United (on trial), Brentford (on trial), Walsall (January 2001). Retired through injury in July 2001.

Representative honours: England (8 Youth caps, 12 Under-21 caps).

Bryan Small signed for Villa from the same junior club that produced Paul Tait and Matthew Fox. A highly rated youngster, he could not displace Earl Barratt or Steve Staunton at Villa Park and so was loaned out to Blues to give him some first-team action. After a useful debut he found it difficult to adjust to life in Division Two and by the end of his loan spell was out of the Blues team as well. He went on to make well over 100 senior appearances before retiring in 2001.

SMALL, Samuel John

Centre-forward: 6 apps

Born: Birmingham, 15 May 1912. Died: Birmingham, 19 December 1993.

Career: Bromsgrove Rovers, BLUES (March 1934), West Ham United (January 1937), Brighton & Hove Albion (March 1948 to June 1950).

Club honours: West Ham: League War Cup winners 1940.

An unselfish, hard working forward, Sam Small was never able to force his way into regular contention with Blues but he proved a shrewd signing for West Ham, scoring 40 goals in 107 League games despite having his career disrupted by WW2. He assumed a more creative role as his career wound down.

SMALLEY, Mark Anthony

Central-defender: 7 apps.

Born: Newark, Notts, 2 January 1965.

Career: Nottingham Forest (apprentice June 1981, professional January 1983), BLUES (on loan, March 1986), Bristol Rovers (on loan, August 1986), Leyton Orient (February 1987), Mansfield Town (on loan, November 1989, signed for £15,000 January 1990), Maidstone Town (May 1991), Ilkeston Town (August 1993). Kettering, Erith +Belvedere, Sutton Town, Ilkeston, Shepshed Charterhouse, Hucknall Town.

Representative honours: England (one Youth cap).

Mark Smalley was a constructive centre-half who looked promising during his short spell at St Andrew's, but there was never any question of Blues signing him permanently.

SMITH, Andrew Walter

Centre-forward: 59 apps. 34 goals

Born: Camberwell, London, April 1896. Died: March 1968.

Career: Camberwell & Southwark School, Langley Green Juniors, Crosswell's Brewery FC, BLUES (amateur August 1912, professional August 1914), Manchester City (guest during WW1), West Bromwich Albion (£100, July 1919), Stoke (£1,500, March 1923), Wigan Borough, Bournemouth & Boscombe Athletic. Retired in May 1925.

Club honours: WBA: Division One champions 1920, FA Charity Shield winners 1920. Andy Smith was a strong forward, well built, who could also perform well at centre-half. A good header of the ball, he became an even more effective force with the advent of Jack Hall. He was one of four Smiths on Blues' books in 1914, although no more than two ever played together in the same team. He scored 22 goals in 81 games for West Bromwich Albion (including two in their 1920 Charity Shield win).

SMITH, Arthur R

Outside-left: 52 apps. 4 goals

Born: Stourbridge, 1887. Now Deceased.

Career: Brierley Hill Alliance, Queen's Park Rangers (August 1911), BLUES (June 1912), Brierley Hill Alliance (September 1914). Later was secretary of Brierley Hill Alliance, retiring from office in May 1934. Arthur 'Nipper' Smith was a short, very fast winger who was a master of the early ball into the middle. He was a teacher at St Peter's College, Saltley, Birmingham, during his stay with Blues and later became a respected administrator in local non-League football.

SMITH, Austin

Centre-forward: 2 apps. 2 goals.

Born: Birmingham, 1865. Died: abroad.

Career: St Phillip's College, Saltley FC, Aston Unity FC, Walsall Town (1886), BLUES (August 1887), Bournville FC (May 1888).

Austin Smith was a prolific marksman with the knack of being able to score goals in two and threes rather than in singles. He hit over 30 in various matches during 1887-88 but was then surprisingly released by the club. He emigrated in late 1888 for business reasons.

SMITH, Bernard

Left-back: 12 apps

Born: Sileby, 1908. Deceased.

Career: Loughborough College, Loughborough Corinthians, Derby County (on trial, 1931), BLUES (February 1932), Coventry City (August 1935). Retired in October 1939.

Club honours: Coventry City: Division Three (South) champions 1936.

A well-built defender, Bernard Smith's appearances were restricted due to the continued good form of Ned Barkas. He was a little more than an average player with a solid tackle.

SMITH, David
Midfield/winger: 40+4 apps. 3 goals
Born: Stonehouse, Gloucestershire, 29 March 1968.
Career: Coventry City (YTS June 1984, professional July 1986), AFC Bournemouth (on loan, January 1993), Dundee United (on trial, February 1993), BLUES (March 1993), West Bromwich Albion (£90,000, January 1994), Grimsby Town (£200,000, January 1998).
Representative honours: England (10 Under-21 caps).
A good attacking midfielder, a hard and effective worker, who preferred to left flank, Dave 'Smudger' Smith scored 19 goals in 182 outings for Coventry with whom he won England Under-21 recognition. He later had 117 outings for WBA and up to 2002 had amassed 134 for the Mariners.

SMITH, George
Left-half: one app.
Born: Birmingham, 1868. Now Deceased
Career: BLUES (season 1890-91).
A relatively unknown wing-half, George Smith played only once in Blues' League side, at Sunderland in April 1891 when Ted Devey missed the train.

SMITH, George
Midfielder: 41+4 apps
Born: Newcastle upon Tyne, 7 October 1945.
Career: Newcastle United (apprentice June 1961, professional September 1963), Barrow (March 1965), Portsmouth (May 1967), Middlesbrough (January 1969), BLUES (March 1971), Cardiff City (June 1973), Swansea City (May 1975), Hartlepool United (October 1977). Later manager of Gateshead, making a short return to playing before becoming coach at Queen's Park Rangers and later assistant-manager of Doncaster Rovers (from September 1994).
Club honours: Blues: Division Two promotion 1972: Cardiff: Welsh Cup winners 1974.
George Smith was a stocky, blond-haired bulldozer-type midfielder, able to perform no matter what the conditions, as was demonstrated by his brilliant display against Norwich in March 1972 on one of the most atrocious playing surfaces ever seen at St Andrew's. A boyhood fan of Newcastle, it was his greatest regret that he never made the first team during his spell at St James' Park. He once scored for Blues whilst he was a Middlesbrough player, putting ball past his own 'keeper! In all, he accumulated a grand total of 487 League appearances during his 16-year career.

SMITH, Gilbert
Right-back: 14 apps
Born: Oldbury, 1869. Now Deceased
Career: Oldbury Broadway FC, Causeway Green Villa, BLUES (September 1893), Berwick Rangers/Worcester (August 1894 to May 1895).

The Oldbury area was certainly productive for Blues scouts in the Victorian era and Gilbert Smith, a rather cumbersome defender, was duly recommended to the club by his good friend Fred Wheldon. He was given an early chance to show his worth when Teddy Jolly was considered too slow to play at full-back. However, Smith was no better and quickly returned to the reserves.

SMITH, John
Inside-left: 6 apps. one goal
Born: Wednesfield, 1882.
Career: Cannock, Stafford Road, Wolverhampton Wanderers (August 1902), BLUES (April 1906), Bristol Rovers (season 1907-08), Norwich City (May 1908), Luton Town (July 1909), Millwall Athletic (March 1911), Coventry City (May 1912-13).
John Smith was a short, stocky Black Countryman who had been a useful player at Molineux before joining Blues, with whom he struggled, finding it difficult to replace Arthur Mounteney, whose greater bulk was more suited to Blues' style of play at the time.

SMITH, Joseph
Right-back: 50 apps.
Born: Darby End, Dudley 17 April 1890. Died: Royal Hospital, Wolverhampton, 9 June 1956.
Career: Halesowen Road Council School (Netherton), Netherton St Andrew's, Darby End Victoria, Cradley Heath St Luke's, West Bromwich Albion (professional May 1910), guested for Everton during WW1, BLUES (May 1926), Worcester City (player-manager, May 1929 to July 1932 when he retired).
Club honours: WBA: Division Two champions 1911, Division One champions 1920, FA Charity Shield winners 1920.
Representative honours: England (2 full caps, one Victory international, Junior international).
Right-back Joe Smith was a strategist, a strong kicker with excellent positional sense, who amassed 471 appearances during his 16 years with West Bromwich Albion (mainly as partner to the great Jesse Pennington) before switching to St Andrew's, as cover for Frank Womack and Jack Jones. Despite his declining powers Smith continued to fill in at right-back effectively for a further three years. After leaving football he became a publican, running the Red Lion (Darby End), and later worked at Lloyds Proving House, eventually becoming chief tester. A well-respected local figure in the Dudley area, he is Netherton's only international footballer.

SMITH, Joseph Enoch
Left-half: 8 apps
Born: Barnard Castle, County Durham, 1888. Now Deceased
Career: Hickleton Main Colliery, BLUES (September 1912), Richmond FC (1915).
Former miner Joe Smith is the least know of the Smiths

of 1914. He was apparently always at his best when defending, the press declaring that 'he held his opponents in check effectively but should show more discretion putting the ball forward.'

SMITH, Samuel James

Centre-forward: 33 apps. 13 goals
Born: Pelsall, 7 September 1909. Deceased.
Career: Pleck Old Boys FC, Walsall (on trial, 1927), Walsall LMS (1928), BLUES (December 1930), Chelsea (July 1934), Norwich City (May 1935), Walsall (January 1936), Stourbridge (August 1936 to May 1937).
A dashing, tearaway striker Sam Smith became an instant hit by scoring two goals on his League debut for Blues at Aston Villa. Unfortunately, he saw his career flounder after leaving the Midlands, failing to make a single appearance for Chelsea and playing only once for Norwich.

SMITH, Stephen John

Goalkeeper: 3 apps.
Born: Lydney, Gloucestershire, 12 June 1957.
Career: Gloucester Boys, Cardiff City (associate schoolboy 1971), BLUES (apprentice June 1973, professional July 1975), Bradford City (£5,000, March 1978), Crewe Alexandra (August 1982), Trowbridge Town (November 1983, manager January 1984-86).
Representative honours: England Youth international.
Steve Smith was a reserve goalkeeper at St Andrew's who, if he was inconsistent and made some embarrassingly awful mistakes, saved Kenny Dalglish's penalty in Blues' Centenary Match v. Celtic in 1975. He held Bradford City's club record for most clean sheets in a season and made 105 League appearances for the Bantams in his four-year spell at Valley Parade, following on with another 54 for Crewe.

SMITH, Trevor

Centre-half: 430 apps. 3goals
Born: Brierley Hill. 13 April 1936.
Career: Quarry Bank Secondary Modern School, Brierley Hill & Sedgley Schoolboys (English Schools Trophy), BLUES (amateur July 1951, professional April 1953), Walsall (£18,000, October 1964). Retired in February 1966. Later a permit player in the Lichfield Sunday League (1967-68) and was manager of Mile Oak Rovers in season 1970-71.
Club honours: Blues: Youth tournament winners (Switzerland) 1952, Division Two champions 1955, FA Cup runners-up 1960, Football League Cup winners 1963.
Representative honours: England (2 full caps, 2 'B' caps, 15 Under-23 caps, Youth caps, Schoolboy caps); Football League XI (2), Army (2).
Trevor Smith was a skinny defender when he played alongside the great Duncan Edwards in the Brierley Hill Schools side, but thereafter he developed into a muscular centre-half weighing 13st 7lbs. A commanding figure in

the number-five shirt, Smith skippered Blues many times and put in several fine performances at the heart of the defence. He made his Blues' debut at the age of 17 and conceded an own-goal in his first match. When Billy Wright retired in 1959 it was Smith who succeeded him in the England team. He broke down shortly after leaving St Andrew's for Walsall and there were rumours that Blues had 'cheated' their neighbours in allowing an injured player to join the ranks at Fellows Park. After leaving the game Smith became a licensee in Tamworth and thereafter was manager of Thresher's wine store in the Bull Ring Shopping Centre, Birmingham, before moving in the same line to Dagenham, Essex.

SMITH, Walter

Inside-forward: 26 apps. 6 goals.
Born: Bootle, 1885. Now Deceased
Career: Liverpool (on trial, 1902-03), Southend United, Chester, Bury (December 1911), BLUES (April 1914), Altrincham (season 1916-17).
Walter Smith was an experienced, ball playing inside-forward when signed by Blues in 1914. Brought in to create the chances for main strikers Andy Smith and Jack Hall, he eventually lost out to the more talented Jimmy Windridge for this role, and had to be content with reserve-team football with only an occasional first-team outing coming his way, mainly due to injuries received by other forwards.

SMITH, William Alfred

Inside-right: 17 apps. 5 goals.
Born: Bedworthll, April 1882. Now Deceased
Career: Old Hill Wanderers, West Bromwich Baptists, Worcester City, West Bromwich Albion (November 1902), Brierley Hill Alliance (May 1905), Tipton Excelsior (1906), Coventry City (1907), BLUES (season 1908-09), Coventry City (1909), Nuneaton Town (August 1912), Coventry City (September 1913), Tipton Excelsior (1914). Retired during WW1 and later became a football referee.
Billy Smith was another excellent maker of chances, but a player who was also capable of scoring his fair share of goals. He formed a useful wing partnership with Benny Green, but eventually lost his place in the first team when the skilful Jack Wilcox joined the ranks at St Andrew's.

SMITH, William Henry

Wing-half/inside-forward: 62 apps. 23 goals
Born: Plymouth, 7 September 1926.
Career: Royal Marines, Plymouth United (August 1944), Plymouth Argyle (August 1945), Reading (August 1947), Northampton Town (July 1948), BLUES (February 1950), Blackburn Rovers (December 1952), Accrington Stanley (player-coach, July 1960-62, caretaker-manager, December 1961 to March 1962).
Devon-born Billy Smith had a good career in the game,

totalling 237 League appearances and scoring 42 goals, before drifting out of the top grade in 1962 when Accrington Stanley lost their Football League status. He played Rugby Union at school but took up soccer seriously after WW2. He began as a utility forward but reverted to the wing-half berth after leaving St Andrew's.

SMITHIES, George Herbert
Centre-forward: one apps.
Born: Ribchester, 1907. Deceased.
Career: Bangor College, Northern Nomads, Preston North End (August 1929), BLUES (May 1931), Darley Dale FC (season 1932-33), Measham Motors.
Representative honours: England (Amateur caps).
George Smithies was a late arrival into League football after a successful amateur career whilst he was busy completing his teaching studies. Despite being somewhat undersized for a striker (5ft 8in) he met with early success at Deepdale with Preston North End, top-scoring in his debut season. Thereafter, however, his career went into decline, leading to an early return to non-League action.

SONNER, Daniel
Midfielder: 47+9 apps. 3 goals
Born: Wigan, 9 January 1972
Career: Wigan Athletic (trainee), Burnley (professional, August 1990), Bury (on loan, November 1992), FC Preussen Koln/Germany (July 1993), FC Erzgebirge/Germany (August 1995), Ipswich Town (free transfer, June 1996), Sheffield Wednesday (£75,000, October 1998), BLUES (free transfer, August 2000, released by manager Steve Bruce, June 2002), Wolverhampton Wanderers (on trial, August-September 2002), Walsall (October 2002).
Club honours: Blues: League Cup runners-up 2001, Division One promotion 2002
Representative honours: Northern Ireland (7 full & 4 'B' caps)
Danny Sonner suffered with a niggling heel injury during the 2001-02 season, playing in only18 first-class matches. Prior to that he had been a competent, hard-working midfielder with boundless energy. He took his tally of League appearances to 161 before leaving St Andrew's.

SOUTHALL, George
Outside-left: 14 apps.
Born: Cradley Heath, 1880. Now Deceased
Career: Quarry Bank Celtic, Halesowen Royal, Redditch Excelsior, Stourbridge, BLUES (December 1905), Halesowen (August 1907), Dudley Town, Lye Town.
The hero of Stourbridge fans and for several seasons, George 'Sconnie' Southall was certainly one of the stars in the Birmingham League. At local non-League level he looked quite brilliant, both as a chance-maker and goal-taker, but unfortunately, as so often happens (even today)

he was unable to reproduce this form in league football with Blues. After leaving St Andrew's, he again did well on the non-League scene, especially at Halesowen.

SOUTHAM, James Henry
Left-back: 3 apps
Born: Willenhall, 19 August 1917.
Died: Birmingham 1982.
Career: Stowheath Junior & Senior Schools, Shornhill Recreational Centre FC, West Bromwich Albion (amateur March 1939, professional November 1942), Newport County (£300, May 1946), BLUES (November 1946), Northampton Town (June 1949). Retired May 1955, to become assistant trainer with Walsall. Guested for Aberaman, Arsenal, Colchester United, Ipswich Town and Newport County during WW2.
A steady, reliable full-back Jim Southam was rarely given a look-in due to the consistency of the Ken Green-Dennis Jennings combination at St Andrew's. However, he later established himself at Northampton for whom he made 144 League appearances before hanging up his boots. He was denied a testimonial match with the Cobblers because they 'couldn't find time to fit one in'.

SPEEDIE, David Robert
Striker: 12 apps. 2 goals.
Born: Glenrothes, 20 February 1960.
Career: Adwick School, Barnsley (apprentice August 1977, professional October 1978), Darlington (£5,000, June 1980), Chelsea (£70,000, June 1982), Coventry City (£780,000, July 1987), Liverpool (£675,000, February 1991), Blackburn Rovers (£450,000, August 1991), Southampton (£400,000, July 1992), BLUES (on loan, October 1992), West Bromwich Albion (on loan, January 1993), West Ham United (on loan, March 1993), Leicester City (free transfer, July 1993). Forced to retire in January 1995 and joined coaching staff at Filbert Street. Later became a footballers' agent.
Club honours: Chelsea: Division Two champions 1984, Full Members Cup winners 1986; Blackburn Rovers: Division Two promotion 1992; Leicester City: Division One promotion 1994.
Representative honours: Scotland (10 full caps, one Under-21 cap).
David Speedie was one of the game's characters. A highly skilful, occasionally brilliant footballer, yet sometimes very fiery and often in trouble with referees! He had scored 175 goals in 611 senior games up to 1994 when injury caused him to miss out on Leicester's return to the top flight.

SPELLER, Frederick
Full-back: 93 apps.
Born: Marlow, 1864. Died: Birmingham, 1940.
Career: Great Marlow FC, BLUES (summer 1888).
Retired in May 1864.

Not the muscular type one associates with Victorian full-backs but a player who preferred to pass the ball to his half-backs, Fred Speller was the undisputed first-choice left-back until a broken leg sustained against Darwen in October 1892 effectively ended his career. He attempted a comeback in late 1893 but called it a day at the end of that season.

SPRAKE, Gareth

Goalkeeper: 22+2 apps.

Born: Swansea, 3 April 1945.

Career: Llansamlet School, Leeds United (apprentice June 1960, professional May 1962), BLUES (£100,000 October 1973). Retired through ill health, in May 1975.

Club honours: Leeds: Division Two champions 1964, Division One champions 1969, FA Cup runners-up 1965, 1970, Football League Cup winners 1968, 1971, runners-up 1967, FA Charity Shield winners 1969

Representative honours: Wales (37 full caps, 5 Under-23 caps, Schoolboy caps).

Gary Sprake was a well-built goalkeeper who made a big impression whilst still a youngster culminating in an international debut at the age of 18 years and seven months, the youngest Welsh goalkeeper ever. He continued to star for Leeds, winning domestic and European honours under Don Revie's shrewd managership. At his best Sprake was a spectacular, athletic 'keeper, capable of pulling off seemingly impossible saves, but a series of well publicised errors led to him becoming something of a joke among opposition fans. He had been dropped by Leeds and was going through a bad patch when Blues signed him and he soon showed his new club both aspects of his game, saving a penalty on his debut and 'scoring' an own-goal in the next match. Keeping behind the Blues defence in the mid-1970s was not the ideal way of rebuilding one's confidence and Sprake struggled before succumbing to a chest virus. After working as a 'rep' for a sports firm, he took employment in local government as a training officer, based in Solihull, responsible for placing business trainees and monitoring their progress. He now lives in Solihull.

* As a youngster, Sprake lived next door to the former Arsenal and Wales goalkeeper Jack Kelsey. He played rugby union at school (as a centre) only becoming a goalie at the age of 14. He left school in 1960 and immediately became a fitter, playing in goal for his works team.

SPRIGG, Charles

Outside-left: 16 apps.

Born: Smethwick, 1889. Now Deceased

Career: Smethwick Centaur, Bilston United, BLUES (November 1912), Redditch (1913), BLUES (season 1914-15), Moor Green (1915-17).

Charlie Sprigg had two spells with Blues but never really

looked the part, although he did reasonably well in the Birmingham League. He was the first active Blues player to enlist during WW1, joining the Royal Field Artillery in July 1915.

SPROSON, Philip Jesse

Centre-half: 16 apps. one goal.

Born: Trent Vale, Stoke-on-Trent, 13 October 1959.

Career: Port Vale (apprentice 1975, professional December 1977). Announced his retirement through injury in May 1989 but was persuaded to return to the game by BLUES, who signed him for £50,000 in August 1989. He retired again in September 1990, but later played at non-League level for Stafford Rangers and Northwich Victoria.

A member of a family that was involved with Port Vale for many years and for whom his uncle Roy Sproson holds the club appearance record, Phil Sproson was a solid, no-nonsense pivot. He wore the centre-half shirt (for Vale) for twelve years until injury ruined his career. Doctors advised him to retire but after a short respite he tried to get back into League soccer and Blues were ordered to pay Port Vale a pretty large fee for his services in lieu of insurance money. At St Andrew's he looked slow and overweight but remained in the team until further knee trouble struck him down again.

SPROSTON, Neil Robert

Centre-forward: 0+1 app.

Born: Dudley, 20 November 1970.

Career: BLUES (YTS, June 1986, professional July 1988), Alvechurch (August 1990), Armitage '90 FC (November 1990), Oldswinford FC (August 1991), Dudley Town (1992), Gornal Sports, Lye Town (1993-94).

In the absence of Andy Kennedy, Tony Rees and Steve Whitton, this powerfully built youngster was called up for his League debut a month before his 17th birthday. Perhaps not surprisingly Neil Sproston looked overawed by the occasion and things were not made easier when he received a head wound that required stitches. On his return to the Youth team he was shuffled around from attack to defence before settling into a midfield role, prior to his release.

SQUIRES, Barrie

Outside-left: one app.

Born: Sparkhill, Birmingham 29 July 1931.

Career: Golden Hillock Road School (Sparkbrook), BSA Air Training Cadets, Wycombe Wanderers, Lye Town, Wolverhampton Wanderers (amateur), Portsmouth (on trial, April 1952), Bristol City (on trial, July 1952), BLUES (professional, May 1953), Bradford City (June 1954), Yeovil Town (1955-57).

Barrie Squires, an ex-airman, eventually got his chance of League action with his fourth club. He never really had a look-in with Blues due to the consistency of Alex Govan and wasn't too successful either at Bradford, making only nine appearances for the Bantams.

STAINTON, Ronald George

Left-back: one app.

Born: Bournville, Birmingham, 1909. Deceased.

Career: Kings Norton Schools, Bournville, BLUES (August 1927), King's Heath FC, Worcester City (July 1932), Shirley Town (season 1934-35).

Representative honours: England (one Schoolboy cap).

A stocky full-back of great loyalty, 'Mick' Stainton spent five seasons playing in Blues' reserve team without ever looking likely to make the first XI on a permanent basis.

STANLEY, Alfred

Forward: 30 apps. 17 goals

Born: Edgbaston, Birmingham, 1860.

Died: Birmingham circa 1930.

Career: Calthorpe, BLUES (September 1881). Retired in May 1891 through injury.

A brilliant dribbler who was the idol of the Blues fans throughout his career, Stanley was capable of playing in all the forward positions but was most comfortable at inside-right. He was frequently referred to as 'Eddy' Stanley in team lists.

STANLEY, Wilson

Outside-right: one app.

Born: Hockley, Birmingham, 1863. Now Deceased

Career: Hockley Belmont, BLUES (September 1886), Oldbury Broadwell (August 1887), Warwick County FC (seasons 1888-90).

The younger brother of 'Eddy' Stanley (q.v), Wilson Stanley was a capable winger, fast and tricky with a good scoring record. He had to share that position with Arthur Jones, but although near the end of his career, was still good enough to hold down the place.

STANTON, Arthur

Right-back: 6 apps.

Born: Bloxwich, 1892. Now Deceased

Career: Bloxwich Strollers, BLUES (April 1913), Oldbury (season 1918-19).

Arthur Stanton was a solid defender who understudied both full-back roles capably for two seasons. Although somewhat limited with a lack of pace, he had a powerful kick and a strong tackle.

STARBUCK, Philip Michael

Forward: 3 apps.

Born: 24 November 1968

Career: Nottingham Forest (apprentice June 1984, professional August 1986), BLUES (on loan, March 1988), Hereford United (on loan, February 1990), Blackburn Rovers (on loan, September 1990), Huddersfield Town (August 1991), Sheffield United (on loan, October 1994, full transfer January 1995), Bristol

City (on loan, September 1995), Oldham Athletic (free transfer, August 1997), Plymouth Argyle (March 1998), Cambridge City (June 1998).

Club honours: Huddersfield: Autoglass Trophy runners-up 1994. Phil Starbuck was one of several youngsters Forest allowed to be loaned out to gain experience. He signed for Blues when they were struggling in the lower reaches of Division Two and although impressing with his speed and ball control, he seemed to lack the killer touch in front of goal. When he dropped out of the Football League (in 1998) Starbuck's record in major competitions stood at 54 goals in 306 appearances.

STEEL, William Gilbert

Left-back: 91 apps.

Born: Blantyre, Scotland, 6 February 1908. Deceased.

Career: Bridgtown Waverley FC, St Johnstone (1926), Liverpool (August 1931), BLUES (£5,000, March 1935), Derby County (February 1939 to September 1940).

Retired during WW2, then Airdrieonians (trainer, April 1950, manager from April 1954), Third Lanark (manager, January 1963 to June 1964).

Billy Steel was a footballing full-back who received more than his fair share of criticism during his early days at St Andrew's for his reluctance to rely on the 'big boot'. He had, however, succeeded in winning over most of his hecklers by the time he left Blues. He moved to Derby but his career was curtailed by WW2. Steel later qualified as a masseur and assisted the Scottish national team in this capacity during the 1950s.

STEVENSON, William Byron

Defender: 85+6 apps. 3 goals.

Born: Llanelli, 7 September 1956.

Career: Leeds United (apprentice, April 1972, professional September 1973), BLUES (March 1982, in exchange for Frank Worthington), Bristol Rovers (July 1985), Garforth Minors Welfare FC (1988, later manager to 1990).

Representative honours: Wales (15 full caps, 3 Under-21 caps, Youth caps). Leeds United were grooming tall defender Byron Stevenson to take over from Norman Hunter, but circumstances meant that he found himself playing at left-back more often than not. He was never an automatic choice at Elland Road, although he was regularly called up for duty with Wales until he was sent-off for violent conduct, against Turkey in November 1979, and was banned from international football for four years. In 1982 he became Ron Saunders' first signing and fitted nicely into the heart of the Blues' defence, using his anticipatory skills to good effect. Stevenson later switched to midfield where his form became patchy, his lack of pace being sometimes exploited. He took charge of the Angel Hotel in Rothwell, Yorkshire after retiring from football, and later was mine host of the Golden Lion at Pudsey, West Yorkshire.

STEWART, John Gebbie
Outside-right: 218 apps. 55 goals
Born: Lochgelly, Fife, 4 September 1921.
Died: Scotland, 1990
Career: Lochgelly Welfare, Donibristle Youth Club, Raith Rovers (August 1939), BLUES (January 1948), Raith Rovers (February 1955). Later became trainer at Stark's Park, and remained in football until 1963 before going into business in Cowdenbeath.
Club honours: Blues: Division Two champions 1948.
Early in 1948 Blues manager Harry Storer announced that he was trying to sign a Scottish winger who would 'enable the team to gain promotion'. A week later he returned from Fife with all-action bag of tricks, Jackie Stewart. Fast, direct and a big favourite with the St Andrew's fans, Stewart was only 5ft 5in tall but he was tough and feared no one. A former miner, he possessed a terrific shot and once scored four goals in a match against Manchester City in September 1948. He returned to Scotland after suffering injury problems.

STOKER, Lewis
Right-half: 246 apps. 2 goals.
Born: Wheatley Hill, County Durham 31 March 1910.
Died: Birmingham, May 1979.
Career: Bearpark School, Brandon Juniors, Esh Winning Juniors, Bearpark FC, West Stanley, BLUES (on trial, June 1930, professional September 1930), Nottingham Forest (May 1938). Retired during WW2,
Representative honours: England (three full caps); Football League XI (1)
Lew Stoker was an excellent 'feeder of the attack'. A marvellously gifted and effective footballer, he loved to drive forward (given the chance) from centre-field and whenever possible tried a shot at goal, sometimes from fully 35-40 yards. After retiring from the game he worked as a charge-hand at Wimbush's bakery, just a short walk from St Andrew's. His younger brother Bob Stoker played for Bolton Wanderers and Huddersfield Town during the 1930s.

STOKES, Frank
Full-back: 213 apps. one goal
Born: Burlsem, Stoke-on-Trent, 7 June 1881. Died: 1945.
Career: Burslem Park Boys, Burslem Port Vale, Reading, BLUES (October 1903). Retired in August 1910, following a serious knee injury.
Representative honours: England (Trialist 1902, 1903, 1905 & 1906).
Frank Stokes was a magnificent full-back, all muscle, yet extremely mobile and safe under pressure. He and his partner John Glover were regarded as one of the best pair of full-backs ever to play for Blues. The reliable Stokes had the bitter experience of not being chosen for his own benefit match (he was playing in the second XI that same day). His only goal for Blues was a cracking 15-yarder,

fired in left-footed against Notts County in October 1906. He was easily recognisable on the pitch by the ungainly way he carried his arms.

STORER, Stuart John
Outside-right: 7+3 apps.
Born: Harborough Magna, 16 January 1967
Career: Rugby School, Wolverhampton Wanderers (on Associate Schoolboy forms 1982), Mansfield Town (YTS, August 1983), VS Rugby (March 1984), BLUES (apprentice June 1984, professional January 1985), Everton (£200,000, March 1987), Wigan Athletic (on loan, August 1987), Bolton Wanderers (on loan, December 1987, signed permanently, January 1988), Exeter City (£25,000, March 1993), Brighton & Hove Albion (£15,000, March 1995), Atherstone United (June 1999).
Club honours: Bolton: Sherpa Van Trophy winners 1989
Stuart Storer was a steady player during his stay at St Andrew's and showed himself capable of winning a game on his own, especially in the reserves, but rarely produced this sort of form in the first XI. His transfer to Everton (with striker Wayne Clarke) was highly controversial. The inflated valuation of Storer was looked upon by Wolves as a way of denying them money for Clarke (they were in effect entitled to 50% of any profit Blues made on him), However, Blues apparently decided that it was the only way of getting some of the money Wolves had not paid them for defender Joe Gallagher! Storer went on to score 39 in more than 540 competitive games including 15 in 165 outings for Bolton and 14 in 161 appearances for Brighton.

STUBBS, Robin Gregory
Centre-forward: 70 apps. 20 goals.
Born: Quinton, Birmingham, 22 April 1941.
Career: Castle Road Primary School, Oldbury Grammar School, Oldbury Boys, BLUES (amateur June 1956, professional April 1958), Torquay United (August 1963), Bristol Rovers (July 1969), Torquay United (February 1972). Retired in May 1974.
Robin Stubbs was a slim, fair-haired goalscorer who was tipped for great things at St Andrew's but never quite had the temperament to sustain his position. Nevertheless he was a player Blues should never have sold, for he went on to become a prolific scorer after leaving St Andrew's, netting 122 League goals in 238 games in his two spells with Torquay and 32 in 93 outings for Bristol Rovers. He made the national papers when his wife, Anthea Redfern, a television personality, left him to marry comedian Bruce Forsyth. He later worked as a salesman in Torquay where he still resides.

STURRIDGE, Simon Andrew
Forward: 161+25 apps. 38 goals
Born: Birmingham, 9 December 1969.

Career: William Cowper, Duddeston Manor & St George's Schools (Birmingham), BLUES (YTS, June 1985, professional July 1988), Stoke City (September 1993), Blackpool (on loan, March 1999), Northampton Town (August 1999), Shrewsbury Town (on loan, March-May 2000). Released by Northampton in June 2000.
Club honours: Blues: Leyland DAF Cup winners 1991.
A terrific marksman in the Birmingham Boys League, Simon 'Studger' Sturridge followed his elder brother, Michael, to St Andrew's. His goalscoring exploits continued at youth level, leading to an early call-up for the first team. His speed, ball-control and alertness in the box, combined to make him a firm favourite with the fans. Sturridge netted the vital goal at Brentford that sealed Blues' return to Wembley for the first time in 35 years, and he then scored the opening goal in that 1991 Leyland DAF Cup Final against Tranmere. When he left Northampton in 2000, Sturridge's record was pretty good - 58 goals in 314 appearances. His younger brother Dean has played for Derby County, Leicester City, Torquay United and Wolverhampton Wanderers.

SUTTON, Stephen John
Goalkeeper: 6 apps
Born: Hartington, 16 April 1961.
Career: Nottingham Forest (apprentice, June 1977, professional April 1979), Mansfield Town (on loan, March 1981), Derby County (January 1985), Coventry City (on loan, February 1991), Luton Town (on loan, November 1991), Derby County (£300,000, March 1992), Reading (on loan, January 1996), BLUES (free transfer, August 1996, released June 1997), Grantham (August 1998).
Club honours: Forest: League Cup winners 1989 & 1990, Simod Cup winners 1989.
Goalkeeper Steve Sutton made over 250 senior appearances for Forest and more than 80 for Derby before spending a season at St Andrew's, acting as cover for Ian Bennett. A fine shot-stopper, despite a slight eye defect, he bided his time at The City Ground before taking over between the posts from Peter Shilton.

STYLES, Arthur
Left-back: 79+3 apps, 4 goals.
Born: Liverpool, 3 September 1949.
Career: Liverpool Boys, Everton (apprentice August 1965, professional August 1967), BLUES (February 1974, in the deal involving striker Bob Latchford), Peterborough United (July 1978), Portsmouth (July 1979 to May 1980).
Representative honours: England (Youth caps, Schoolboy caps).
Archie Styles looked a good prospect at Goodison Park but his career stagnated as he was restricted to only 23 appearances in seven years with Everton. He came to Blues as a makeweight in the Latchford deal but had a few problems establishing himself in the side. His major asset was his speed off the mark and he was usually at his best when going forward, but was not very strong in the tackle.

SUMMERFIELD, Kevin
Forward: 4+4 apps. 2 goals
Born: Walsall, 7 January 1959.
Career: Alma Street & Joseph Leckie Schools (Walsall), Walsall Town Boys, West Bromwich Albion (apprentice, July 1975, professional January 1977), BLUES (free transfer, May 1982), Walsall (on loan, December 1982, signed permanently on free transfer, February 1983), Cardiff City (free transfer, July 1984), Plymouth Argyle (£5,000, December 1984), Exeter City (on loan, March 1990), Shrewsbury Town (October 1990, retired in May 1995 to become senior coach and assistant-manager at Gay Meadow), Plymouth Argyle (Youth team coach, 1997, caretaker-manager October 2000, then reserve team coach, assistant-manager/coach during season 2001-02)
Club honours: WBA: FA Youth Cup winners 1976; Shrewsbury: Division Three champions 1994.
Representative honours: England (Youth caps).
A reserve striker with West Bromwich Albion, Kevin Summerfield still achieved a respectable scoring record of five goals in 13 appearances when called into the first team. He came to Blues but failed to establish himself in the senior side and went on loan to Walsall. That was the signal for a fairy-tale: when the teams were drawn together in the FA Cup, Summerfield was recalled to St Andrew's and after coming on as a substitute he scored the winning goal. In later years he took up a midfield role and - after recovering from a broken leg suffered against Everton in January 1989 - he went on to amass an excellent career record of 89 goals in 460 League and Cup appearances before taking up coaching.

SUMMERILL, Philip Ernest
Forward: 118+13 apps. 52 goals.
Born: Erdington, 20 November 1947.
Career: King's Rise School, Aston Boys, BLUES (apprentice June 1963, professional December 1964), Huddersfield Town (January 1973), Millwall (November 1974), Wimbledon (September 1977 to May 1979), Highgate United (August 1979), Atherstone Town, Redditch United, then Highgate United again (1985-86).
Club honours: Blues: Division Two promotion 1972.
Representative honours: England (Youth caps).
Phil Summerill was a tall, spindly striker who started off as a winger and after moving into the centre became an instant success. He had three excellent seasons from 1968-71 at St Andrew's when he scored 52 goals in 118 games, some of his efforts being quite spectacular.
During a fine career he netted 81 goals in 289 appearances. After his second spell with Highgate United

he took up coaching at a youth centre in Sparkhill, Birmingham, which he did between working as a painter and decorator. In later years he worked for the City Council's Football Coaching Department, and is a regular visitor to St Andrew's.

SUMMERS, Lawrence A

Left-back/wing-half: 2 apps.
Born: Birmingham 1859. Died: Birmingham 1940.
Career: The Grove, BLUES (September 1880 to April 1882), Hockley Hill FC (for two seasons: 1882-84).
After an impressive display for Blues against Derby Town in the FA Cup in November 1881, Lawrie Summers held his place in the side, until injuries to the James brothers forced him to switch to the half-back line, a role which did not suit him. When the James men returned he found that the Gesseys had settled in at full-back and therefore he was allowed to leave the club.

SYKES, E Albert A

Left-half: one app.
Born: Shirebrook, Yorkshire 29 September 1900.
Died: Lincolnshire, 1994
Career: Maltby Victoria, Maltby Miners' Welfare, Maltby Victoria, Maltby Town, BLUES (August 1924), Brighton & Hove Albion (May 1926), Lincoln City (June 1928), Peterborough & Fletton United (August 1931), Luton Town (August 1932), Grantham Town (season 1933-34).
Albert Sykes was a chunky, former miner, whose play was in the Percy Barton mould and with Barton and Dickie Dale on the books at the same time he was regarded as surplus to requirements and was not given the chance to show off his talents.

SYKES, Ernest Alfred

Right-back: 10 apps
Born: Temple Normanton, 27 December 1912. Deceased
Career: Temple Normanton Old Boys, Sutton Town, BLUES (March 1936), Cardiff City (August 1939).
Retired in 1944.
Ernie Sykes was a tall, powerful defender who was a useful squad player. Frustrated by the lack of first-team action he moved to South Wales but after he had made only three appearances for Cardiff, his career was curtailed by WW2.

SYKES, John George

Left-back: 34 apps
Born: Wombwell, Yorkshire, 1915. Deceased.
Career: Wombwell FC, BLUES (August 1932), Millwall (May 1937 to September 1939). Did not figure in competitive League football after WW2.
Jack Sykes was a defensive half-back who spent three years in Blues' reserves before making his League debut. He was an immediate success with his strong-running and clever covering but a loss of form late in 1936 led to

him being dropped. He was rarely selected again and left at the end of the season. Later he was a licensee at the Park Tavern, Dudley Road, Birmingham, near the hospital.

TAIT, Paul Ronald

Forward/midfield: 169+43 apps. 18 goals
Born: Sutton Coldfield, 31 July 1971.
Career: Hodge Hill Junior and Byng Kendrick Senior Schools, Hurley Colts, BLUES (YTS June 1987, professional August 1988), Millwall (on loan, February 1994), Bolton Wanderers (on trial, July 1994), Northampton Town (on loan, December 1997), Oxford United (free transfer, January 1999 to May 2002), Bristol Rovers (August 2002).
Club honours: Blues: Second Division champions 1995, Auto-Windscreen Shield winners 1995.
Few people could look less like a professional footballer than the pale-faced, frail Paul Tait. Looks can deceive, however, and Tait possessed excellent ball skills and was a prolific scorer in Youth-team football. Later encouraged to play in midfield, he developed a telling pass and the ability to ghost past an opponent in the penalty area. A serious injury received against Leyton Orient in January 1991 led to him being fitted with a synthetic knee ligament and his career was in jeopardy, but he kept fighting back. In the Auto-windscreen Shield Final he came on as substitute and scored the winner, a feat marred by his controversial celebration of the goal, and a fortnight later, also as a substitute, scored Blues' second goal at Huddersfield that effectively sealed the Second Division championship. He had amassed well over 300 League and Cup appearances when he was released by Oxford at the end of the 2001-02 season.

TARANTINI, Alberto Cesar

Full-back/centre-half: 24 apps. one goal.
Born: Buenos Aires, Argentina, 3 December 1955.
Career: Boca Juniors/Argentina (August 1974), BLUES (£295,000, October 1978), FC Talleres Cordoba/Spain (May 1979), River Plate/Argentina (July 1980), Bastia/Corsica, Toulouse/France, Urania Geneva/Switzerland (May 1988), FC Platense/Argentina (for season 1989-90).
Representative honours: Argentina (59 full caps, World Cup winners 1978).
On 25 June 1978, Alberto Tarantini, a stylish, attacking full-back, proudly showed off his World Cup winners' medal after Argentina had beaten Holland in the Final in Buenos Aires. Four months later he made his Football League debut for Blues at Tottenham when he lined up opposite his Argentinian colleague Ossie Ardiles, with another fellow countryman, Ricardo Villa, watching from the stand. He took time to settle into the team and once even jumped into the crowd to deal with a heckler. After meeting with limited success in Europe he returned home when Urania were relegated into Swiss non-League

football in 1989. Tarantini now runs coaching schools for youngsters in Argentina.

TATTON, Joseph

Centre-half: one app.
Born: Handsworth, Birmingham, 1859.
Died: Birmingham, 1933.
Career: St Mark's FC, BLUES (September 1880 to May 1882), Nechells (1882-84), Aston Manor (1885-87). Later became a Director of BLUES in 1898.
Joe Tatton was a solid, no-nonsense pivot who was probably more successful as a committee man than he was a footballer. He helped mastermind the signing of Bob McRoberts and several other players around the turn of the century. He opened the batting for the Small Heath Alliance cricket team but his top score was only five runs. His brother Harry was also associated with Blues.

TAYLOR, Brian Joseph

Outside-left: 67 apps. 9 goals.
Born: Walsall, 24 March 1937.
Career: Walsall (amateur July 1952, professional September 1954), BLUES (£10,000, plus Jimmy Cochrane, June 1958), Rotherham United (October 1961), Shrewsbury Town (August 1963), Port Vale (August 1965), Barnsley (June 1967), Kidderminster Harriers (July 1968), Bromsgrove Rovers (season 1970-71).
A sprightly winger with terrific pace and ability, Brian Taylor's career received a major setback when he fractured his leg playing against Union St Gilloise in the Fairs Cup semi-final. He returned to action a year later, but by then had lost a lot of the speed that had characterised his game prior to that. Altogether he scored 43 goals in 316 League appearances (19 in 75 for Walsall).

TAYLOR, Gordon, Bsc

Outside-right/left: 189+14 apps. 10 goals
Born: Ashton-under-Lyne, 28 December 1944.
Career: Mossley Road County Primary School, Ashton-under-Lyne Grammar School, Curzon Ashton FC (season 1959-60), Bolton Wanderers (amateur June 1960, professional, January 1962), BLUES (£18,000, December 1970), Blackburn Rovers (March 1976), Vancouver Whitecaps/NASL (on loan, June-August 1977), Bury (June 1978). Retired in May 1980 and became secretary of the PFA, having served on the committee while a player at Bury. Later upgraded to Chief Executive of the PFA.
Club honours: Blues: Division Two promotion 1972.
Gordon Taylor was an orthodox winger, quick, with good skills who was mainly used on the right flank. His direct, all-action style and his ability to deliver high quality crosses made him a favourite with the Blues fans. One of several graduates to play for Blues, Taylor possesses a BSc in Economics, gained through part-time studies at Bolton Technical College. He made 622

League appearances during a career that coincidently saw him serve with four different League clubs whose names all began with the letter 'B'. He is now Chief Executive of the Players' Union and one of the most influential men in football.

TAYLOR, Joseph

Left-back: 3 apps.
Born: Aston, Birmingham, 1857. Died: Sutton, 1950.
Career: Britannia Victoria FC, Aston Shakespeare, Witton White Star, Hockley Belmont (1880), BLUES (August 1881), Brookvale FC (1884-86).
Joe Taylor was a heavily built defender whose initial spell in the first team coincided with Elliman's move forward. He later linked up with Elliman to form a fine partnership.

TAYLOR, William

Utility: 4 apps. one goal.
Born: Smethwick, 1869. Now Deceased
Career: Langley Green Victoria, BLUES (September 1891), Quinton (season 1892-93).
Bill Taylor was another friend of Fred Wheldon who recommended him to Blues, but who the club didn't know where to play. He was tried on both wings, at right-back and in two half-back positions before he was released.

TAYLOR-SMITH, Dr Ian Lennox

(known also as Ian Smith)
Centre-forward: 0+2 apps.
Born: Edinburgh, 2 April 1952.
Career: Queen's Park (as an amateur, season 1969-70), Medical College, BLUES (semi-professional, March 1975), Heart of Midlothian (August 1977), Queen of the South (1979), Bromsgrove Rovers (1984-85). Played also for West Bromwich Albion All Stars (1982-87). Retired and became a qualified doctor of medicine.
A big, strong player who scored regularly for Blues in reserve team soccer and always looked a good prospect. Ian Smith, however, was unwilling to commit himself to being a full-time footballer as he always regarded a medical career as his chief priority. He spent some time working at the Queen Elizabeth Medical Centre in Birmingham, at the Worcester Royal infirmary and later at a maternity clinic in Barbados.

TEBBS, James T

Outside-left: 4 apps. one goal
Born: Melton Mowbray, May 1878. Now Deceased
Career: Loughborough Town, BLUES (September 1900), Leicester United (season 1902-03).
Jimmy Tebbs was Loughborough Town's top-scorer in their last season in the Football League (four goals out of 18 scored by the club) but with Sid Wharton showing outstanding form, he was forced to switch to the right to get a game with Blues. He failed to impress and his stay

with the club was restricted chiefly to Birmingham League action.

TEBILY, Olivier

Defender/Midfielder: 23* apps.
Born: Abidjan, Ivory Coast, 19 December 1975
Career: Chateauroux FC/France (1997), Sheffield United (£175,000, March 1999), Glasgow Celtic (£1.25 million, July 1999), BLUES (£700,000, March 2002).
Club honours: Celtic: League Cup winners 1999
Representative honours: Ivory Coast (4 caps), France (3 Under-21 caps).
Olivier Tebily, with strength and pace in abundance, surprisingly never really settled in at Parkhead and when the opportunity arose Steve Bruce signed him for a second time, having initially recruited him to Bramall Lane. He was sent-off in the Premiership derby v. WBA at The Hawthorns in October 2002.

TEWKESBURY, Kenneth Cyril, BSc

Goalkeeper: 5 apps.
Born: Brighton, 10 April 1909. Died: 20 November 1970.
Career: Birmingham University, BLUES (amateur, October 1929), Aston Villa (December 1931), Notts County (1932), Aston Villa (professional, January 1933), Bradford Park Avenue (July 1935), Walsall (May 1936). Retired in August 1939.
Representative honours: England (6 Amateur caps).
Ken Tewkesbury joined Blues whilst studying for his BSc at Birmingham University. A quiet, bespectacled man, he was not the obvious choice as a goalkeeper but at 6ft 3in and 12st he possessed the necessary physical attributes. Despite relatively poor eyesight, he still proved to be a capable 'keeper but resisted all efforts to sign professional until 1933. He married the daughter of Blues' Director, W H Bull and worked for many years in Birmingham's Jewellery Quarter.

TEYCHENNE, Victor

Half-back: 2 apps.
Born: Wednesbury, July 1859. Died: West Bromwich, 1934.
Career: Wednesbury Town, Wednesbury Old Athletic, BLUES (September 1880), Smethwick Centaur (season 1882-83), Wednesbury Swifts.
Vic Teychenne was a tough Black Countryman who usually played at centre-half although the club sometimes lined up with two half-backs and six forwards, and therefore his role was not always easy to define. He kept wicket with great success for Small Heath Alliance CC and once he took off his pads and took four wickets. He was also a sprinter for Small Heath AC, of which he was a founder member.

THIRLAWAY, William James

Outside-left: 23 apps. one goal
Born: New Washington, Co. Durham, 1 October 1896.

Died: Sunderland, 1983.
Career: Usworth Colliery (County Durham), West Ham United (1921), Southend United (June 1924), Luton Town (May 1925), South Shields (November 1925), BLUES (May 1926), Cardiff City (March 1927), Tunbridge Wells Rangers (1930), Washington Colliery (1932). Retired in May 1934.
Club honours: Cardiff: Welsh Cup winners 1928, runners-up 1929.
Bill Thirlaway, a former miner, had a rapid rise to fame with West Ham. However there followed a dramatic loss of form almost as quickly and for two years he was 'out in the cold' with the London club. He then travelled around the country, unable to settle down long enough to make an impact. At Blues it was the same story and after a reasonable start he faded badly. Only at Cardiff did he manage any sport of consistency and there he was unfortunate to miss the 1927 FA Cup Final (v. Arsenal) because he had been cup-tied playing for Blues. Hardly the ideal build for a winger, Thirlaway was short and stocky, yet on his day he was a great crowd-pleaser.

THOMAS, Martin Richard

Goalkeeper: 176 apps.
Born: Senghenydd, Wales 28 November 1959
Career: St Helen's & Cardinal Newman Schools, Bristol Rovers (apprentice June 1975, professional, September 1977), Cardiff City (on loan, July to September 1982), Southend United (on loan, February & March 1983), Newcastle United (on loan, March 1983, signed permanently for £35,000, July 1983), Middlesbrough (on loan, October 1984), Aston Villa (on loan, early October 1988), BLUES (£75,000, mid-October 1988), Crystal Palace (on loan, during season 1992-93), Cheltenham Town (August 1994); later becoming a specialised goalkeeping coach for Blues, Norwich City, Swindon Town, Newcastle United and also for the FA, based at Lilleshall.
Club honours: Blues: Leyland DAF Cup winners 1991.
Representative honours: Wales (one full cap, 2 Under-21 caps, Youth caps)
Martin Thomas was an erratic yet sometimes quite brilliant goalkeeper who always seemed more comfortable making reaction saves rather than taking crosses. His penalty saves against Swansea City in 1991 were a major factor in Blues' Leyland DAF Cup success. He was, however, responsible for one of the more unusual goals ever scored at St Andrew's. Playing against Shrewsbury Town in March 1989, Thomas caught a high cross, but then, to the crowd's, his colleagues and manager's disbelief, surprisingly stepped back over his own line with the ball still in his hands. The 'Shrews' won the game 2-1. Thomas made over 400 senior appearances as a professional, appearing for five different clubs during 1982-83.

THOMPSON, Horace
Outside-left: one app
Born: Birmingham, 1900.
Career: BLUES (August 1922 to May 1923).
Horace Thompson was a little known winger who made only one League appearance for Blues, lining up on the left flank against Oldham Athletic on 3 February 1923. In some reports he is mistaken for Len Thompson, the former Blues, Swansea, Arsenal and Crystal Palace player (q.v.). Described as 'a youngster who has been doing well in the reserves' he was freed by the club at the end of the season.

THOMPSON, Leonard
Outside-left: 2 apps.
Born: Sheffield, 18 February 1901.
Career: Shire Green Primitive Methodists, Norfolk Amateurs, Hallam FC, Barnsley (amateur 1917), Hallam FC, BLUES (August 1918), Swansea Town (July 1922), Arsenal (March 1928), Crystal Palace (June 1933). Retired in May 1936. Later re-instated as an amateur and assisted Islington Corinthians. Also had a spell as Tottenham Hotspur's reserve-team manager.
Yorkshireman Len Thompson did well as a winger during the latter part of WW1 but met with greater success when he switched inside. He earned a reputation as a penalty-taker, but later in his career he was dogged by injuries. Thompson scored 89 goals in 188 League appearances for Swansea.

THOMPSON, Thomas
Outside-left: one app.
Born: Smethwick, 1879. Died: Birmingham 1939.
Career: Nettlefolds FC, BLUES (season 1902-03), Oldbury Town (1903-04).
With Sid Wharton nearing the end of his career, Blues were desperate for a new left-winger and they went for Tommy Thompson, a speedy performer who had been playing for the team of a well-known local factory. The local press were far from impressed, however, claiming that Thompson would be lucky ever to play in the League. They were almost right. He was released by the club after just one first team game.

THOMSON, Robert Anthony
Full-back: 69 apps.
Born: Smethwick, 5 December 1943.
Career: Lyndon High School, Wolverhampton Wanderers (apprentice, June 1959, professional July 1961), BLUES (£40,000, March 1969), Walsall (on loan, November-December 1971), Luton Town (July 1972), Harford Bicentennials/NASL (April 1976), Port Vale (October 1976), Connecticut Bicentennials/NASL (as player-coach, April 1977), Memphis Rogues/NASL (March 1979), Stafford Rangers (player-manager, August 1979); then brief spells with Brewood, Solihull Borough

and Tipton Town. Retired in May 1987. Later ran a sports shop in Sedgley, near Dudley, for many years, and occasionally turned out in local charity matches up to 1990, mainly for the ex-Wolves and WBA All Stars teams. He now lives in Sedgley.
Club honours: Wolves: FA Youth Cup runners-up 1962. Representative honours: England (8 full caps, 15 Under-23 caps): Football League XI (4).
All the local Midland clubs tried to sign Bobby Thomson, an elegant, speedy full-back who had starred in schoolboy football. Wolves won the chase for his signature and 'Thommo' quickly developed into an international player, gaining all his caps before he was 22 years of age, after which he suffered a loss of form and was omitted from the England squad. During a splendid career, though, he amassed a total of 477 Football League games for his five different clubs. He made close on 300 appearances for Wolves and added another 100 or so outings to his tally with the Hatters.

THOMSON, Robert Gillies McKenzie
Inside-forward/wing-half: 125+4 apps. 25 goals
Born: Dundee, 21 March 1937.
Career: Dundee & Dunblane Schools, Albion Rovers (amateur, August 1951), Airdrieonians (amateur, August 1952), Wolverhampton Wanderers (on trial, season 1953-54, then professional August 1954), Aston Villa (June 1959), BLUES (September 1963), Stockport County (December 1967), Bromsgrove Rovers (May 1968). Retired in 1970.
Club honours: Aston Villa: Division Two champions 1960, Football League Cup winners 1961, runners-up 1963.
Bobby Thomson was a chunky, wavy-haired Scot, with an aggressive approach. Tired of waiting for his chance at Molineux - he made only one League appearance in his five years there - he chose to leave Wolves for Villa Park where he became an instant hit with the fans. He was top scorer in Villa's promotion-winning season of 1959-60 and went on to net 70 goals in 171 games for Blues' arch rivals before moving to St Andrew's just four months after playing against City in his second League Cup Final, when he scored against his future club. He gave Blues excellent service early on and proved a fine and valuable replacement for Ron Wylie when his fellow countryman suffered a broken leg in 1966. Thomson now lives in Birmingham and keeps himself fit by regularly playing squash and tennis.

THOROGOOD, Jack
Outside-left: 24 apps. 2 goals
Born: Dinnington, Yorkshire 4 April 1911.
Died: Bridlington, November 1970.
Career: Owston Park Rangers, Frickley Colliery, Manchester City (on trial, 1929-30), BLUES (November 1930), Millwall (June 1934), Doncaster Rovers. Guested for several clubs during WW2.

Jack Thorogood looked very promising when he first arrived at St Andrew's, but although highly praised for both his speed and the quality of his crosses, he was never able to establish himself in the first team. His move to London brought him more regular League football and he scored his fair share of goals.

THRELFALL, Wilfred
Outside-left: 5 apps.
Born: Morecambe, 1901.
Career: Morecambe FC, Sunderland, BLUES (July 1927), Bournemouth & Boscombe Athletic (June 1928 to May 1929), Morecambe, Lancaster Town (season 1932-33).
Wilf Threlfall was an inexperienced winger who had failed to make a League appearance for Sunderland. Nevertheless, he started as first choice for Blues in 1927-28 but quickly dropped from favour. He made only three appearances for Bournemouth.

THWAITES, Dennis
Outside-left: 91+4 apps. 21 goals
Born: Stockton-on-Tees, 14 December 1944.
Career: Stockton Council School, BLUES (amateur June 1960, professional May 1962). Retired in 1972, but later played for Rover FC (Solihull) in the Birmingham Works League.
Representative honours: England (Youth Schoolboy caps).
Dennis Thwaites was something of a teenage prodigy who broke into the Blues' first team as a 17-year old in 1962. However, he spent ten seasons as a professional at St Andrew's without ever holding down a regular first-team place. Thwaites suffered badly from nerves, which materially affected his play. He later worked as a hospital porter in Blackpool. He is the uncle of Steve Lilwall, the ex-Kidderminster Harriers & West Bromwich Albion left-back.

TICKLE, Charles Howard
Inside-forward: 91 apps. 15 goals.
Born: Northfield, Birmingham, 1884. Now Deceased
Career: Selly Oak St Mary's, Bournbrook, BLUES (January 1904), Coventry City (August 1908), Bristol Rovers (August 1911), Worcester City (free transfer, June 1913), Birmingham Trams, Redditch Town, Birmingham Trams. Later became Birmingham City Trams FC secretary.
Described as 'fast, clever in footwork and able to centre accurately', Charlie Tickle was unfortunately a rather inconsistent player who struggled to make an impact during his six years with Blues. It was quite a surprise, though, when he was released just after enjoying his best-ever season. He netted 25 goals in 125 games for Coventry.

TILER, Carl
Defender: one app. 0 goals
Born: Sheffield, 11 February 1970.

Career: Barnsley (YTS June 1986, professional February 1988), Nottingham Forest (£1.4 million, May 1991), Swindon Town (on loan, November 1994), Aston Villa (£750,000, October 1995), Sheffield United (£650,000, March 1997), Everton (£500,000, November 1997), Charlton Athletic (£700,000, September 1998), BLUES (on loan, February 2001), Portsmouth (£250,000, March 2001).
Representative honours: England (13 Under-21 caps)
A strong, tall, dominant defender, Carl Tiler had already made almost 300 senior appearances (at club and international level) before having the briefest of spells at St Andrew's.

TINKLER, Alfred Arthur
Centre-half: 103 apps. 3 goals.
Born: Manchester, 1887. Died: Croydon, 1950.
Career: Ilkeston Town (amateur 1907), Derby County (January 1909), Heanor United, Ilkeston Town (May 1911), BLUES (December 1911), Burton United (1915). Retired in 1917.
Alf Tinkler was a teacher who arrived at St Andrew's with the reputation as a trouble-maker, having previously walked out on Derby County. Fortunately this side of his character was never in evidence during his spell with Blues and his robust style made him very popular with the fans. One report stated that he 'tackles with sureness and assists his forwards well'.

TODD, Colin
Defender: 107+1 apps.
Born: Chester-le-Street, County Durham, 12 December 1948.
Career: Chester-le-Street Boys, Sunderland (apprentice July 1964, professional December 1966), Derby County (£180,000, February 1971), Everton (£333,000, September 1978), BLUES (£300,000, September 1979), Nottingham Forest (£70,000, August 1982), Oxford United (February 1984), Vancouver Whitecaps/NASL (May 1984), Luton Town (October 1984). Retired in May 1985 and became manager of Whitley Bay, moving to Middlesbrough (as Youth team coach in May 1986, then became assistant-manager to Bruce Rioch at Ayresome Park in May 1986, taking over as manager in March 1990 and retaining his position until to June 1991), Bradford City (assistant-manager, January 1992), Bolton Wanderers (assistant-manager, May 1992, joint-manager, January 1995 with Roy McFarland, then manager, November 1996). He left The Reebok Stadium in 1999 and was out of the game for a short while, up to April 2000, when he became manager of relegated Swindon Town, briefly moving back into the hot-seat at Derby County (August-December, 2001). Thereafter did some local scouting for a handful of clubs.
Club honours: Sunderland: FA Youth Cup winners 1967; Derby County: Division Once champions 1972, 1975,

Texaco Cup winners 1972; Blues: Division Two promotion 1980. Voted the PFA 'Footballer of the Year' in 1975. (as manager) Bolton: promotion from Division One 1997.

Representative honours: England (27 full caps, 14 Under-23 caps, Youth caps); Football League XI (3).

Colin Todd was one of the finest defenders in the Football League during the 1970s, always elegant, poised, scrupulously fair and a brilliant reader of the game. Indeed, that was what inspired Brian Clough to pay what was then a record fee for a defender when he signed Todd for Derby. Todd always looked comfortable on the ball and in an exceptionally fine career he made over 800 senior appearances, chalking up his 500th game in the Football League (out of a total of 641) for Blues against Swansea City in October 1979. As manager he took Bolton up to and down from the Premiership. Todd is the oldest player ever to appear in a League game for Oxford United - aged 35 years, four months (in 1984).

TOMLINSON, Paul

Goalkeeper: 11 apps.
Born: Brierley Hill, 22 February 1964.
Career: Middlewood Rangers, Sheffield United (as a professional, June 1983), BLUES (on loan, March-April 1987), Bradford City (£47,500, June 1987 to May 1995); then non-League football for three years.

Paul Tomlinson was a tall, athletic goalkeeper whose spell with Blues coincided with troubled times, when he had to play behind a rather uneasy and leaky defence, but still produced some excellent performances. When he quit top-class football in 1995 (at the age of 31) Tomlinson (nicknamed 'Thommo') had accumulated in excess of 400 senior appearances, exactly 350 for Bradford (293 in the League) and he also kept 71 clean-sheets for the Yorkshire club.

TOWERS, Mark Anthony

Midfielder/defender: 100+3 apps. 4 goals
Born: Manchester, 13 April 1952.
Career: Manchester City (apprentice July 1967, professional April 1969), Sunderland (£100,000, plus Mick Horswill, March 1974), BLUES (£140,000, July 1977), Montreal Manic/NASL (March 1981), Tampa Bay Rowdies/NASL, Vancouver Whitecaps/NASL (August 1984), Rochdale (non-contract player, February-May 1985). Retired in May 1986.
Representative honours: England (3 full caps, 8 Under-23 caps, Youth caps, Schoolboy caps).

Tony Towers proved a huge disappointment at Blues after having built up a fine reputation as a midfielder with his two previous clubs. In his day he displayed fine ball skills, good passing ability and was very consistent, but his better performances were at the tail-end of his spell at St Andrew's when he was acting as a sweeper. In his 17-year professional career he amassed 324 League appearances (scoring 32 goals).

TRAVERS, James Edward

Centre-forward: 2 apps.
Born: Newtown, Birmingham, 4 November 1888.
Died: Smethwick, 31 August 1946.
Career: Birchfield Road School (Aston), Newtown Abbey FC (1903), Bilston United (1904), Rowley United (1905), Wolverhampton Wanderers (July 1906), BLUES (August 1907), Aston Villa (December 1908, in an exchange deal involving 'Jack' Wilcox), Queen's Park Rangers (May 1909), Leicester Fosse (August 1910), Barnsley (January 1911), Manchester United (February 1914), Swindon Town (1919), Millwall (June 1920), Norwich City (October 1920), Gillingham (July 1921), Nuneaton Town (September 1921), Cradley St Luke's (November 1922), Bilston United (1929). Retired in May 1931.
Club honours: Barnsley: FA Cup winners 1912.

'George' Travers was a real footballing 'wanderer' who after leaving school, served with no fewer than 17 different clubs (at various levels) over a period of 28 years (1903-31), scoring for virtually every single one of them in either first or second team matches, including a hat-trick on his debut for Aston Villa against Bury on Boxing Day 1908. Powerfully built, he was a grand header of the ball and packed a ferocious right-foot shot, but sadly he never really fitted in at St Andrew's or indeed at Villa Park, despite that sensational debut. His career realised a total of 164 League appearances.

TREMELLING, Richard Daniel

Goalkeeper: 395 apps.
Born: Mansfield Woodhouse, Nottinghamshire, 12 November 1897. Died: Birmingham, 15 August 1978.
Career: Langwith Junction Wagon Works FC (initially as a full-back), Shirebrook Juniors Lincoln City (professional, August 1918), BLUES (May 1919), Bury (May 1932), BLUES (assistant-trainer, from June 1936 to September 1941).
Club honours: Blues: Division Two champions 1921.
Representative honours: England (one full cap); Football League XI (3).

Affectionately known as the 'India Rubber Man' (apparently because he 'bounced' around on his line) Dan Tremelling joined Blues on the 13th of the month and left also on the 13th; he spent exactly 13 years at St Andrew's and played in 13 FA Cup-ties - but 13 was not an unlucky number for this utterly reliable, sometimes absolutely brilliant goalkeeper, who was a great catcher of the ball. He took up goalkeeping by accident after being placed there during an injury crisis at Langwith. After retiring he became landlord of the Old Lodge pub near St Andrew's. William, his brother, played for Blackpool and Preston North End.

TREWICK, John
Midfielder/left-back: 39+3 apps.
Born: Stakeford near Bedlington, Northumberland,
3 June 1957.
Career: Bedlington Grammar School, Northumberland
Boys, West Bromwich Albion (apprentice July 1972,
professional July 1974), Newcastle United (£234,567,
December 1980), Oxford United (on loan, January
1984, signing permanently in July 1984), BLUES
(£30,000, September 1987 to June 1989), Bromsgrove
Rovers (August-October 1989), Hartlepool United
(October 1989), Bromsgrove Rovers, Gateshead
(October 1990), Tamworth. He also coached the
Birmingham Festival League side Martini International
in 1979-80; West Bromwich Albion (Youth team coach
1993, later reserve team coach, also caretaker-manager at
The Hawthorns), Derby County (assistant-
manager/coach, 2001),* Cradley Town (manager 2002-03)
Club honours: WBA: Division Two promotion 1976;
Oxford: Division Two champions 1985, Milk Cup
winner 1986.
Representative honours: England (Youth Schoolboy caps).
John 'Tucker' Trewick was a determined midfield grafter
whose arrival at St Andrew's coincided with Blues'
heaviest home defeat for 27 years (6-0 against Crystal
Palace on 5 September 1987). Not the most naturally
gifted of players, he was the target of persistent heckling
from the fans throughout his days at Blues, probably
because of his preference for the short pass rather than
anything more ambitious. In later years he performed
well at left-back and amassed some 350 senior
appearances before entering non-League football in 1990.

TRIGG, Cyril
Centre-forward/right-back: 291 apps. 72 goals
Born: Measham, Leicestershire, 8 April 1917.
Died: Birmingham, 9 April 1993.
Career: Leicester & District Schools, Binley Welfare,
Coventry City (on trial), Bedworth Town, BLUES
(junior, August 1935, professional November 1935),
Stourbridge United (as player-coach, May 1954). Retired
in May 1957. Guested for Blackpool and Nottingham
Forest during WW2, also serving with the RAF in India
& Burma (where he played football for various units).
Club honours: Blues: Football League South champions
1946, Division Two champions 1948.
Cyril Trigg played through three generations of Blues'
teams, witnessing relegation, promotion, success and
failure. He saw many changes at the club, played under
four different managers, occupied several positions yet
still came up trumps, especially when he was at his peak,
scoring goals from the centre-forward berth. A dedicated
club-man, 'Triggy' (as his team-mates called him) was at
one stage simultaneously the best full-back and best
centre-forward inside St Andrew's. During WW2 he
appeared in 95 games for Blues, rattling in no fewer than

88 goals to bring his overall 'first team' record for the
club to 386 outings and 160 goals - par excellence.

TURNER, Arthur Samuel
Inside-right: one app.
Born: Birmingham, 1867. Now Deceased
Career: Aston Villa (1888), BLUES (September 1890 -
April 1891).
Arthur Turner was released by Aston Villa without
making a first-team appearance, and although given a
trial by Blues he was not taken on as a full-time player.
His only first team game was against Darwen in
November 1890 (Football Alliance).

TURNER, Arthur Owen
Centre-half: 53 apps.
Born: Chesterton, Staffs, 1 April 1909.
Died: Sheffield, 12 January 1994.
Career: Downing Tileries FC, Woolstanton PSA FC,
West Bromwich Albion (amateur, August 1929), Stoke
City (professional, November 1930), BLUES (£6,000,
January 1939), Southport (February 1948), Crewe
Alexandra (player-manager, October 1948, retired as a
player in May 1949, remained as team manager until
December 1951), Stoke City (assistant-manager, January
1952 to November 1954), BLUES (manager, November
1954 to September 1958), Oxford United (manager,
January 1959 to February 1969, then general manager
until 1972), Rotherham United (Chief Scout, mid-
1970s), Sheffield United (Chief Scout, August 1980 to
July 1981). Played cricket regularly for Silvendale CC for
whom he scored five centuries.
Club honours: Stoke: Division Two champions 1933;
Blues: Football League South champions 1946; as
(manager), Blues: Division Two champions 1955, FA
Cup runners-up 1956; Oxford: Division Four promotion
1965, Division Three champions 1968.
Arthur Turner served Blues for 13 years, in two excellent
spells with the club, first as a player and then as manager.
A resolute, no-nonsense defender, he was good in the air,
strong on the ground, never shirked a tackle and was
always totally committed. Unfortunately his career was
badly affected by WW2 yet he still appeared in 186
games for Blues during the hostilities, having made 312
appearances for Stoke City prior to his transfer to St
Andrew's. Turner was manager of Oxford when they
gained entry into the Football League in 1962.

TWELL, Terence Keith
Goalkeeper: 2 apps.
Born: Doncaster, 21 February 1947.
Career: Bourne Town, BLUES (professional, October
1964), Stamford Town (for two seasons: August 1968 to
May 1970).
Great things were expected of acrobatic goalkeeper Terry
Twell and, in fact, a series of excellent displays in the

reserves led to his first team debut in October 1967, in attempt to 'help' the defence which, up to then, had given away a number of 'bad' goals. However, on his first appearance for the seniors (v. Portsmouth at home) Twell was beaten by a 30-yard lob and in the next game he could do nothing when Norwich City went on the rampage, striking four goals past him. He returned to second team duties and was subsequently released at the end of the season, but not before he had played at centre-forward for Blues' Youth team!

VAESEN, Nico Jos-Theodor
Goalkeeper: 51+1* apps
Born: Hasselt near Ghent, Belgium, 28 September 1969
Career: Cercle Brugge (1991), FC Tongeren/Belgium (part-time professional, 1992), Aalst FC/Belgium (briefly), FC Brugge/Belgium (1993-95), SC Eendracht Aalst/Belgium (1995-98), Huddersfield Town (£80,000, July 1998), BLUES (£800,000, June 2001).
Club honours: Blues: Division One promotion 2002.
Nico Vaesen joined Blues with over 200 first-class appearances under his belt. A brave, 6ft in 'keeper, with good reflexes, he lost his place in the side due to a poisoned elbow - this after making a competent start to his St Andrew's career. He saved a penalty on his return in a vital game at Norwich and then has the promotion pace boiled up he pulled off a string of fine saves to help Blues reach the Premiership. Vaesen has a University degree in marketing.

VAN MIERLO, Antonius Wilhelmus Matthias Theodore
Outside-left: 47 apps 4 goals
Born: Soarandonk, Netherlands, 24 August 1957.
Career: Initially in Holland with FC Kraanvogals, SV Eindhoven (1976) and SV Willem II (1979); then BLUES (June 1981); back to Holland with SV Willem II (1982), later serving Racing White Daring Molenbeek/Belgium (1983), MVV Maastricht (1985), AA Gent/Belgium (1986), Racing Club Harelbeke (1988), VVV Venlo (on loan, 1989), SV Willem II (Youth team trainer, season 1990-01).
Club honours: Molenbeek: Belgium Division Two champions 1985.
Representative honours: Holland (3 full caps).
Tony Van Mierlo first sprang to the attention of Blues' fans with a brilliant display for Willem II in a pre-season friendly at St Andrew's in 1980. He had electrifying pace but found it difficult to cope with the physical demands of the English game. He was used to playing in the centre of the attack, and perhaps his talents could have been better utilised there, rather than on the left wing which is where Blues played him. He later worked behind the scenes at Willem II.

VICKERS, Stephen
Defender: 21+1* apps. one* goal
Born: Bishop Auckland, 13 October 1967
Career: Spennymoor United (1983), Tranmere Rovers (professional, September 1985), Middlesbrough (£700,000, December 1993), Crystal Palace (on loan, September 2001), BLUES (initially on loan, November 2001, signed for £400,000, December 2001).
Club honours: Tranmere Rovers: Leyland DAF Cup winners 1990, runners-up (v. Blues) 1991; Division Three promotion 1991; Middlesbro': Division 1 champions 1995; Blues: Division One promotion 2002.
Steve Vickers appeared in nearly 400 games for Tranmere and in over 300 for Middlesbrough. An experienced campaigner, he was signed by Blues' boss Steve Bruce who had been his manager at Selhurst Park. Unfortunately he missed the run-in towards Premiership football with a knee injury and, in fact, he was out of the first team for almost nine months (after undergoing an operation), returning for the Worthington Cup-tie at Leyton Orient in October 2002.

VINCENT, John Victor
Midfield: 190+4 apps. 44 goals
Born: West Bromwich, 8 February 1947.
Career: Brierley Hill Schools, BLUES (apprentice June 1962, professional February 1964), Middlesbrough (£40,000, March 1971), Cardiff City (£35,000, October 1972), Atherstone Town (August 1975), Connecticut Bicentennials/NASL (1977-78).
Representative honours: England (5 Youth caps).
Johnny Vincent played the old-fashioned game as he simply glided past challengers with style and grace. He triggered off many attacks and possessed a hard shot. Vincent was a star in schools and junior football and made his League debut shortly after his 17th birthday, gaining a regular place in the Blues first team in 1966. As his career progressed he showed a distinct dislike of the physical aspects of the game and Blues manager Freddie Goodwin eventually traded him for the more robust style of George Smith. Vincent later became a publican, first in Northfield, Birmingham (at The Travellers Rest) and thereafter in Oldbury and Warley.

VOWDEN, Geoffrey Alan
Forward: 245+8 apps. 94 goals
Born: Barnsley, 27 April 1941.
Career: Jersey DM FC (August 1957), Nottingham Forest (as an amateur 1958, professional January 1960), BLUES (£25,000, October 1964), Aston Villa (£12,500, March 1971), Kettering Town (player/assistant-manager, July 1974), New York Cosmos/NASL (May-August 1975). Coached in Saudi Arabia in mid to late 1970s as well as at local youth centres in the Nottingham area; appointed reserve-team coach at Sheffield United (season 1980-81).
Club honours: Villa: Division Three champions 1972.
Born in Yorkshire but brought up in the Channel

Islands, Geoff Vowden developed into a fine goalscorer who found the net over 150 times in more than 450 competitive matches between 1960 and 1974. He notched 40 goals in 90 League outings for Forest and on 7 September 1968, he wrote his name into the history books when he became the first substitute to score a hat-trick in a League game, in Division Two, for Blues against Huddersfield at St Andrew's. Vowden was a very positive player, always willing to go in where it hurt.

WADDELL, George Barr

Right-half: 2 apps.
Born: Lesmahagow, Lanarkshire, 13 July 1889.
Died: Sible Headingham, Essex, 17 September 1966.
Career: Dalziel Rovers (Motherwell), Burnbank Athletic, Larkhill United, Glasgow Rangers, Kilmarnock (on loan, season 1912-13), Bradford City (£1,000, June 1914), Preston North End (£1,750, September 1920), Oldham Athletic (£250, July 1922), BLUES (£325, October 1922), Hamilton Academical (July 1923), New Brighton (on a week's trial in November 1923), Wolverhampton Wanderers (November 1923), Aberaman Athletic (as player-coach, season 1924-25), Chorley (November 1925), Fraserburgh (as player-coach), Preston North End (assistant-trainer/reserve team coach, 1928-29), Dick Kerr's XI (women's team as trainer during season 1930-31), Ribble Motors FC (August 1931 to December 1933). George Waddell had a varied career and played in his last competitive game at the age of 43. A man of many clubs and principally a reserve with most of them, he was a heavily built midfielder with a powerful if not always accurate shot.

WALKER, William Baird

Centre-forward: 30 apps. 10 goals
Born: New Cummock, 5 MAY 1893. Now Deceased
Career: Lugar Boswell, Bradford City (August 1911), Lanemark (March 1913), BLUES (November 1919), Coventry City, Merthyr Town (1920), Bristol City (October 1922), Sheffield Wednesday (October 1923), Weymouth (player-manager, August 1924), Leamington Town (season 1925-26), Redditch Town.
Bill Walker suffered from homesickness during his first spell in England but Blues gave him a second chance and he repaid them with eight goals in 12 games in his first season at St Andrew's. He never found scoring quite so easy after that, but he did manage six hat-tricks in the reserves in 1914-15.

WALLACE, Alexander

Outside-left: 2 apps. one goal.
Born: Darwen, Lancashire, 1872.
Died: Bolton, 1950.
Career: Blackpool, Ardwick/Manchester City (June 1894), Baltimore/USA (October 1984), BLUES (November 1897), Hereford Thistle (January 1898).

Alex Wallace was suspended sine die after his departure to America in 1894, along with Manchester City's Tom Little and Mitchell Calvey. Little returned almost immediately and was pardoned by his former employees, but Wallace had to wait a shade longer before he was allowed back into the game. A talented ball player, his three years of inactivity showed after he joined Blues.

WALLACE, David Lloyd

Forward: 13+6 apps. 2 goals
Born: Greenwich, 21 January 1964.
Career: West Greenwich School, Southampton (apprentice June 1980, professional, January 1982), Manchester United (£1.2 million, September 1989), Millwall (on loan, March 1993), BLUES (£250,000, October 1993), Wycombe Wanderers (March 1995), Saudi Arabian football (season 1995-96).
Club honours: Manchester United: European Cup-winners' Cup winners 1991, FA Charity Shield winners 1990.
Representative honours: England (one full cap, 14 Under-21 caps, 9 Youth caps): UEFA Under-21 tournament winners 1984. 'Danny' Wallace enjoyed a tremendous career at The Dell - 79 goals in 321 appearances - where he played in the same team as his brothers, Ray and Rodney. A fast, skilful winger who also performed through the middle, Wallace joined Blues after losing his place at Old Trafford (he hit ten goals in 71 outings for the Reds). He had barely played for two years when he joined Blues and it was quickly obvious that he was still unfit during his spell at St Andrew's.

WALLINGTON, Sidney Percy

Left-half: 2 apps.
Born: Small Heath, Birmingham, 15 October 1908.
Died: Birmingham, 15 December 1989.
Career: Ada Road School, Birmingham Schools, Wolseley Sports FC, BLUES (April 1928), Bristol Rovers (October 1933), Guildford City (1935), Bristol Rovers (season 1936-37), Worcester City (1937), Cradley St Luke's (August 1939). Retired in May 1940.
Club honours: Bristol Rovers: Division Three South Cup winners 1935.
Representative honours: Birmingham Schools; English Schools FA Trophy runners-up 1923.
Sid Wallington spent four patient years in Blues' reserves before getting his chance in the senior side, but by then it was obvious that he had no future in the First Division. He switched to right-half with Bristol Rovers and did well in the lower Divisions. His son was on Blues' books in the 1950s.

WALTON, William Howard T

Inside-forward/wing-half: 200 apps. 63 goals
Born: Hockley Brook, Birmingham 6 August 1871.
Died: Dudley Road Hospital, Winson Green,

Birmingham, 10 February 1963.
Career: Hockley Belmont, BLUES (August 1888),
Dudley FC (May 1903).
Club honours: Blues: Division Two champions 1893,
Division Two runners-up 1894, 1901.
A clever ball-player with smart movement and strong
shot, Billy Walton served up some scintillating
entertainment for the spectators during his 15 years
service with Blues. Initially a dashing inside-forward, he
later switched to half-back where his encouragement of
the younger members of the team earned him the epithet
of 'Mother'. Walton watched Small Heath play in the
1886 FA Cup semi-final against West Bromwich Albion
after he had cleared snow off the pitch before kick-off; he
was present when St Andrew's was officially opened in
1905; and he attended the Wembley Cup Finals of 1931
and 1956. Indeed, he was a regular attender at St
Andrew's until shortly before his death at the age of 91.
Always a part-time footballer, he continued to work as a
silversmith in Hockley throughout his playing days.

WANT, Anthony George
Full-back/defender: 122+5 apps. 2 goals.
Born: Hackney, North London, 13 December 1948.
Career: Hackney Schools, London Borough Boys,
Tottenham Hotspur (apprentice June 1964, professional
December 1965), BLUES (£60,000, June 1972).
Contract cancelled by mutual consent, February 1978,
when he moved to the NASL, playing first with
Minnesota Kicks and later with Philadelphia Fury.
Representative honours: England (Youth caps).
Tony Want made over 50 appearances for Spurs before
signing for Blues as a full-back to strengthen their 1971-
72 promotion side. His best performances, however,
came after he had been successfully converted into a
central defender. He was hampered by injuries
throughout his career, and suffered a severe fracture of
his leg in a Texaco Cup-tie against Newcastle. But he
battled back to fitness and regained a first-team place.
After his NASL career had ended, he returned to
England in 1982 and became a warehouse manager for a
frozen food company in the Midlands while living locally
in Solihull. Want played in several charity games with
West Bromwich Albion All Stars during mid-1980s.

WARD, Mark William
Midfield: 81+1 apps. 8 goals
Born: Huyton, 10 October 1962.
Career: Everton (apprentice 1978, professional
September 1980), Northwich Victoria (free transfer
1981), Oldham Athletic (£10,000, July 1983), West
Ham United (£250,000, August 1985), Manchester City
(December 1989), Everton (£1.1 million, August 1991),
BLUES (on loan, March 1994, signed for £500,000,
August 1994, later player-coach), Huddersfield Town
(March 1996), Wigan Athletic (non-contract, September

1996). Quit League football in May 1997.
Club honours: Blues: Second Division champions 1995,
Auto-Windscreen Shield winners 1995.
Representative honours: England (semi-professional cap).
Midfielder Mark Ward returned to Goodison Park for
more than £1 million in 1991, ten years after Everton
had released him on a free transfer! He played 92 games
for Oldham, 209 for West Ham, 67 for Manchester City
and 94 for Everton (all in his second spell). Whilst on
loan to the Blues he was an inspirational figure in their
abortive effort to avoid relegation in 1994, so much so
that he was signed before the next season to orchestrate
the battle for promotion.

WARD, Walter
Goalkeeper: 5 apps.
Born: Birmingham 1869. Now Deceased
Career: BLUES (season 1890-91)
Walter Ward was a big, strong goalkeeper who
occasionally deputised for Chris Charsley when the
England man was absent from Blues' side.

WARDLE, William
Outside-left: 68 apps. 7 goals.
Born: Hetton-le-Hole, Co. Durham, 20 January 1918.
Died: January 1989.
Career: Fatfield Juniors, Houghton Colliery Welfare,
Southport (October 1936), Manchester City (£2,200,
October 1937), Grimsby Town (July 1939), Blackpool
(August 1948), BLUES (£8,000, September 1951),
Barnsley (November 1953), Skegness Town (1955).
Retired in June 1957.
A lightweight ball-playing winger with a reputation for
being one of the cleverest dribblers of his day, as is so
often the case with dribblers, Billy Wardle was frequently
criticised for a tendency to over-elaborate. Despite this,
his talents were much in demand throughout his career.
His brother, George Wardle, was also a 'wanderer'
playing for Middlesbrough, Cardiff City, Queen's Park
Rangers and Darlington.

WARHURST, Roy
Wing-half: 239 apps. 10 goals.
Born: Handsworth, Sheffield, 18 September 1926.
Career: Atlas & Norfolk FC, Huddersfield Town
(amateur 1943), Sheffield United (amateur, May 1944,
professional September 1944), BLUES (£8,000, March
1950), Manchester City (£10,000, June 1957), Crewe
Alexandra (March 1959), Oldham Athletic (August
1960), Banbury Spencer (August 1961). Retired in
May 1964.
Club honours: Blues: Division Two champions 1955.
Roy Warhurst was a stocky wing-half with a bone-
crunching tackle and it is hard to believe that such a fine
'destroying' player could have begun his career as a
winger. That, though, was the role he was asked to play

in his early days at St Andrew's. He lined up in the attack alongside Len Boyd, but it was not until these two fine players were switched to the respective wing-half positions that Blues' revival began. The hard-grafting style of Warhurst proved the ideal complement to the more artistic skills of Boyd. Warhurst missed the 1956 Cup Final through injury, and his absence was considered a crucial factor in the club's 3-1 defeat. Unpopular with opposition fans and in particular those at Maine Road, it was, indeed, a huge surprise when he eventually moved to Manchester City. He was appointed captain on his arrival at Oldham, after having amassed in excess of 300 League appearances prior to that, including 216 for Blues, 40 for Manchester City and 51 for Crewe. He rounded off his playing days with Banbury Spencer, a club that rejoiced in the nickname of the 'Gay Puritans'. Later he became a scrap metal dealer in Birmingham, while residing in Lichfield.

WARMINGTON, Peter
Inside-forward: 9 apps. 3 goals.
Born: Wythal near Birmingham, 8 April 1934.
Career: Redditch Boys' Club, Redditch Juniors, BLUES (junior August 1949, amateur December 1951, professional February 1952), Bromsgrove Rovers (June 1957), Redditch United, Droitwich Town.
Talented goalscorer Peter Warmington was a player who was unlucky with injuries throughout his career. He scored on his debut and found the net again two games later. Usually deputy for any of the regular inside trio, he occasionally filled in at half-back.

WASSALL, Darren Paul
Defender: 27+3 apps.
Born: Birmingham, 27 June 1968
Career: Nottingham Forest (apprentice, June 1984, professional June 1986), Hereford United (on loan, October 1987), Bury (on loan, March 1989), Derby County (£600,000, June 1992), Manchester City (on loan, September 1996), BLUES (£100,000, March 1997), Burton Albion (May 2000).
Club honours: Forest: Simod Cup winners 1992.
Shortly after joining Blues, strong, tough-tackling defender Darren Wassall was sidelined for 13 months (until December 1998). He underwent three Achilles tendon operations, having the heel of his right boot raised by 15mm in the process. He failed to regain full match fitness and eventually his League career ended in 2000 after he had made just over 225 senior appearances.

WASSALL, Harold
Left-back: 60 apps. one goal.
Born: Stourbridge, 21 September 1879. Died: Dudley, March 1951.
Career: Brierley Hill Alliance, BLUES (£75, January 1902), Bristol Rovers (August 1904).

Harry Wassall was a powerfully built defender with a terrific kick who often cleared the ball first time without taking time to get it under control.

WATKINS, Ernest Thomas
Inside-forward: 8 app. one goal.
Born: Finchley, 3 April 1898. Died: Finchley, London 10 October 1976.
Career: Army Football (during WW1), Barnet (August 1920), Finchley, BLUES (October 1922), Southend United (February 1924), Brentford (January 1926), Millwall (February 1930), Thames (June 1930), Fulham (August 1930), Gillingham (on trial, August 1931), Charlton Athletic (November 1931). Retired through injury in May 1932.
Blues were the odd stop in striker Ernie Watkins' much-travelled tour of the South-East. They were also the only club for whom he did not score regularly. A goal-poacher whose best work was done inside the area, his career was ended by a knee injury sustained in February 1932. He netted a total of 88 goals in his 202 League appearances.

WATSON, John Samuel
Right-back: 2 apps.
Born: Bulwell, Nottinghamshire, September 1892.
Died: Nottingham, 1957.
Career: Bulwell FC, Manchester City, Oldham Athletic (1916), Bloxwich Strollers (1918), BLUES (July 1919), Measham Town (1920).
Jack Watson was a tall, balding full-back who had tried his luck with two other League clubs before coming to Blues. He deputised in a couple of games for Ball but made very little impression and was quickly released.

WATSON, Thomas
Left-back/goalkeeper: 4 apps.
Born: Yardley Wood, Birmingham, 1870.
Died: Birmingham, April 1902.
Career: Yardley Victoria, BLUES (August 1893), Birmingham Police Force FC (June 1985)
Another of the group of policemen who have kept goal for the Blues as an amateur, Tom Watson was a fine all-round athlete and a prominent figure in organising athletics meetings in the Small Heath area. He joined the Birmingham Police Force in 1895, rose to the rank of sergeant in 'E' Division and could be seen policing Blues home games until his early death. Watson initially played as a full-back but was switched to 'keeper in the reserves due to an injury crisis. He did sufficiently well to play twice for the first team in this role.

WATTS, Ernest
Inside-right: 2 apps.
Born: Birmingham, 1875. Now Deceased
Career: BLUES (season 1899-90).
Ernie Watts was a local inside-forward who was given his

chance in the mass shake-up following Blues' 9-1 defeat at Sheffield Wednesday. The team's form did not improve and both games in which he appeared were lost. All the new men, Watts included, were then dropped.

WATTS, John William
Right-half: 248 apps. 3 goals.
Born: Vauxhall, Birmingham, 13 April 1931.
Career: Saltley Old Boys FC, BLUES (junior August 1948, professional August 1951), Nuneaton Borough (July 1963), Bromsgrove Rovers (August 1964). Retired 1969.
Club honours: Blues: Division Two champions 1955, Inter Cities Fairs Cup runners-up 1960.
Johnny Watts was a versatile wing-half who could also fill in at centre-half. A tireless worker who was totally reliable, he possessed a terrific sliding tackle which sometimes brought him into conflict with European referees during Blues' exploits in the Fairs Cup. He was spotted by Blues' Chief Scout Walter Taylor playing on Glebe Farm Recreation Ground and after returning from his National Service he quickly settled down at St Andrew's. With the retirement of Len Boyd, Watts gained a regular place in the side until Terry Hennessey appeared on the scene.

WEALANDS, Jeffrey Andrew
Goalkeeper: 118+1 apps.
Born: Darlington, 26 August 1951.
Career: Darlington Cleveland Bridge FC, Wolverhampton Wanderers (apprentice June 1968, professional October 1968), Northampton Town (on loan, February 1970), Darlington (July 1970), Hull City (£10,000, March 1972), BLUES (£30,000, July 1979), Manchester United (on loan, February 1983, signed later in year on full-time basis), Oldham Athletic (on loan, March 1984), Preston North End (on loan, December 1984), Altrincham (May 1985 to May 1987), Barrow (August 1987), Altrincham (1988-93, Director from March 1995), also goalkeeping coach with various clubs including Bury.
Club honours: Blues: Division Two promotion 1980.
A capable if unspectacular goalkeeper, Jeff Wealands was voted Blues' 'Player of the Year' in their promotion season of 1979-80, but fell into dispute with manager Ron Saunders in 1982 and found himself out of favour. He gained revenge on Saunders, however, when after bravely battling back from injury, he helped non-Leaguers Altrincham knock Blues out of the FA Cup in 1985. Wealands appeared in a total of 391 League games during a fine career, 240 coming at Hull and 102 with Blues. His days at Old Trafford were marred, however, by a recurring back injury, but he was still playing in the GM Vauxhall Conference at the age of 40. Wealands is now a successful property developer in Wilmslow, Cheshire.

WEBB, Isaac
Goalkeeper: 6 apps.
Born: Worcester, 1 October 1874. Died: Dudley Road Hospital, Winson Green, Birmingham, March 1950.
Career: Worcester Park School, St Clement's Rangers, Berwick Rangers/Worcester, Worcester Olympic, Evesham Town, Mansfield Town, Lincoln City, Mansfield Town, Wellington Town, BLUES (1898), West Bromwich Albion (May 1901), Sunderland (£250, December 1904), Queen's Park Rangers (1907). Retired in May 1910 and joined the West Yorkshire Regiment as a catering orderly. Made a comeback with WBA as a guest in August 1918, aged 43.
Club honours: WBA: Division Two champions 1902.
Ike Webb was employed as a salmon fisherman at Evesham before becoming a professional footballer. A big, burly goalkeeper with outstanding reflexes, he was quick off his line besides being spectacularly agile at times. He always wore a cap and at one stage in his eventful career he fractured his skull and played on for quite sometime afterwards before realising what had happened.

WEBB, Matthew Leslie
Winger: 0+one app.
Born: Bristol, 24 September 1976.
Career: BLUES (YTS July 1993, professional May 1995, released in 1997).
Regarded as a promising youngster, Matt Webb had an early call-up to first team after only one Pontins League match. A pacy player who delivered a useful cross when given the chance, his contract was cancelled by the club at the end of the 1996-97 season.

WEBB, Sidney
Inside-forward: 3 apps.
Born: Coventry, February 1884. Died: Leamington, 1956.
Career: St Saviour's FC, Stourbridge, Aston Villa (1908), Burton United, Wednesbury Old Athletic, BLUES (April 1911), Worcester City (August 1912).
Sid Webb was a rotund little schemer who had a very short League career but who was always regarded as one of the leading stars of the Birmingham League.

WESTON, Donald Patrick
Centre-forward: 25 apps. 3 goals.
Born: New Houghton, 6 March 1936.
Career: East Derbyshire Boys, 31st Training Regiment Royal Artillery, Wrexham (amateur July 1957, professional June 1959), BLUES (£5,000, January 1960), Rotherham United (£5,000, December 1960), Leeds United (£7,500, December 1962), Huddersfield Town (£3,500, October 1965), Wrexham (December 1966), Chester (August 1968), Altrincham, Bethesda FC (Wales).
Club honours: Rotherham United: Football League Cup runners-up 1961; Leeds United: Division Two

champions 1964; Blues: Fairs Cup runners-up 1960.
Fast, direct, incisive and likely striker Don Weston
acquired a useful record as a marksman. He netted a total
of 95 goals in his 275 League games for seven different
clubs. Although he had difficulty hitting the target for
Blues, he was top-scorer for Leeds in 1963-64. Weston
now lives in Mansfield, working as a senior salesman for
a Vauxhall car company, based at Wrexham.

WHARTON, Sidney Emmanuel

Outside-left: 167 apps. 25 goals
Born: Birmingham, June 1876. Died: Birmingham, 1951.
Career: Smethwick Wesleyan Rovers, BLUES (November
1897). Retired in May 1903, but remained with the club
for a short time acting as coach.
Club honours: Blues: Division Two runners-up 1901, 1903.
Representative honours: England (one unofficial
international cap); Football League XI.
A sprightly winger, rather rotund but with great speed,
good ball-control and fine shot, Sid Wharton was a
creator of chances rather than a taker, but he was forever
in the thick of the action, loved a battle, and was always
highly regarded. In later years he became a turf
accountant in Smethwick, the company surviving to this
day, and he was also an accomplished 'MC' especially in
the boxing ring.

WHATMORE, Neil

Forward: 25+2 apps. 7 goals
Born: Ellesmere Port, Cheshire, 17 May 1955.
Career: Bolton Wanderers (apprentice June 1971,
professional May 1973), BLUES (£350,000, August
1981), Bolton Wanderers (on loan, December 1982),
Oxford United (£25,000, February 1983), Bolton
Wanderers (on loan, March-April 1984), Burnley (in a
part-exchange deal involving Billy Hamilton, August
1984), Mansfield Town, (November 1984), Bolton
Wanderers (August 1987), Mansfield Town (player-
reserve team coach, October 1987), Worksop Town
(August 1988), Eastwood Town (1989) Manning
Rangers/South Africa (manager January 1990), Forest
Town Rangers (August 1990) Rainworth MV/ (manager-
coach, 1993-94).
Club honours: Bolton: Division Two champions 1978;
Mansfield: Freight Rover Trophy winners 1987.
A sharp, incisive striker, Neil Whatmore was top
marksman for Bolton in five of the previous six seasons
before joining Blues where he teamed up again with his
old team-mate from Burnden Park, Frank Worthington.
Alas, the pair could not reproduce the form they had
shown with the Trotters and Whatmore found himself
selected only spasmodically. When Ron Saunders arrived,
both players found themselves surplus to requirements,
although Whatmore remained at St Andrew's for a
further year but was rarely selected. Nowadays ex-
footballer Whatmore is a milkman in Mansfield.

WHEELER, William John

Goalkeeper: 13 apps.
Born: North Littleton, nr Evesham, 13 July 1919.
Career: Littleton Juniors, Evesham Early Closers FC,
Cheltenham Town, BLUES (professional, March 1938,
Huddersfield Town (August 1948), Kettering Town (July
1956), Evesham Town, Notts County (trainer June 1957,
caretaker-manager, September 1968 to November 1969).
Retired in May 1982.
Club honours: Huddersfield: Division Two runners-up 1953.
A goalkeeper who dominated his area, Jack Wheeler was
signed by Blues as the eventual successor to Harry Hibbs,
but with Gil Merrick emerging, he was sold to
Huddersfield after the war and following a brief spell in
the reserves at Leeds Road he went on to make over 165
League appearances for the Terriers up to 1956. When
they won promotion in 1952-53, Wheeler was part of a
six-man defence that played in every game.

WHELDON, George Frederick

Inside-left: 129 apps. 82 goals.
Born: Langley Green, Oldbury, 1 November 1869.
Died: Worcester, 13 January 1924.
Career: Chance's Infants School & Langley St Michael's
Senior Schools, Road End White Star, Langley Green
Victoria, West Bromwich Albion (on trial, 1888),
BLUES (February 1890), Aston Villa (£350, June 1896),
West Bromwich Albion (£100, August 1900), Queen's
Park Rangers (December 1901), Portsmouth (August
1902), Worcester City (July 1904). Retired in January
1907. Played county cricket for Worcestershire from
1899 to 1926, scoring 4,938 runs in 138 matches at an
average of 22.54. He hit three centuries, took 95 catches,
some as wicketkeeper and was a very occasional slow
right-arm spin bowler. He also played cricket for
Carmarthenshire and was later a publican in Worcester.
Club honours: Blues: Division Two champions 1893,
Division Two runners-up 1894; Aston Villa: Division
One champions 1897, 1899, 1900, FA Cup winners 1897.
Representative honours: England (4 full caps); Football
League XI (4).
The youngest in a family of ten, Fred 'Diamond'
Wheldon was a brilliant footballer, an exceptional talent,
a great goalscorer, who simply enjoyed playing the game.
His intricate footwork often bemused the best defenders
in the country and he developed the art of the 'daisy
cutter' shot. On the bumpy pitches of the 19th century
such a shot was a goalkeeper's nightmare and a high
proportion of Wheldon's goals were scored in this way.
He scored two goals on his debut for Blues - a game in
which the local press got his name wrong. He was also
the scorer of Blues' first-ever Football League goal in
1892. After leaving Blues, Wheldon was instrumental in
helping Villa achieve the League and Cup double and
when he joined Albion he became the first player ever to
represent the three big Midland clubs at senior level. He

was involved in an unusual incident early in his career when one of his shots struck the referee on the pocket where he kept his matches for his pipe. The matches set alight and the official's jacket went up in flames. Wheldon often played wearing a pair of golfing stockings and his brother, Sam, also served with West Brom.

WHITE, Frank Robert Harvey

Outside-right: 156 apps. 50 goals.
Born: Wilnecote, near Tamworth, 14 November 1911. Died: 1985.
Career: Stoneware Ltd FC (Tamworth), Tamworth (1930), BLUES (September 1931), Preston North End (December 1938), Redditch United (August 1946). Retired in May 1950, and later coached his former club, Tamworth. Guested for Aldershot, Mansfield Town, Sheffield United and Wrexham during WW2.
Frank White was a fine goalscoring outside-left, fast, a good dribbler with a telling shot, who was recommended to Blues by Harry Hibbs. He had been a prolific marksman in junior circles before moving to St Andrew's but surprisingly his early days with Blues were spent in the left wing berth. The management soon realised their mistake and thereafter he obliged with some sparkling performances and match-winning goals. He teamed up with Wilson Jones at Redditch after the war.

WHITE, Victor Thomas Wilson

Right-back: 15 apps.
Born: West Bromwich, September 1896. Died: Wednesbury, 1960.
Career: Notts County, BLUES (March 1918), Worksop Town (January 1921), Newport County (September 1922), Kidderminster Harriers (two seasons: August 1925 to May 1927).
Tom White was a slow, cumbersome defender who relied on the big clearance. Initially he understudied Billy Ball but then after winning his place in the side he lost out to Jack Whitehouse who had been converted from inside-forward.

WHITE, Vincent Harry

Left-half: 2 apps.
Born: Walsall, 22 October 1897. Died: 1972
Career: Erdington, Wednesbury Old Athletic, BLUES (May 1921), Ellesmere Port, Redditch Town (on loan, during 1922), Watford (1923), Ellesmere Port (1924), Oswestry Town (1925-26).
Harry White was a wing-half, whose greatest strength was in his tackling ability. His first team appearances were restricted due to the fine form of Percy Barton. He was also strong in his kicking.

WHITEHEAD, Alan James

Central defender: 5+1 apps.
Born: Bordesley Green, Birmingham, 3 September 1951.

Career: Erdington & Saltley Schools, BLUES (apprentice September 1967, professional August 1970), Kettering Town (free transfer, July 1974).
A promising winger when he joined Blues, Alan Whitehead appeared in almost every position before eventually settling at the back. He played some important games in Blues' run-in to promotion in 1972, when he replaced the injured Stan Harland, but appeared only once in the First Division. His brother Clive had a lengthy career, most notably with Bristol City, Portsmouth and West Bromwich Albion.

WHITEHEAD, James Gilbert

Inside-left: 2 apps.
Born: Birmingham, May 1858. Now Deceased
Career: King's Norton Boys' Club, BLUES (August 1881), Lea Hall (September 1882).
Jim Whitehead was a utility forward who was switched around all the inside positions with little success.

WHITEHOUSE, John Charles

Forward: 115 apps. 35 goals
Born: Smethwick, 4 March 1897. Died: Halesowen, 3 January 1948.
Career: Smethwick Hall, Blackheath Town, Redditch, BLUES (August 1916), Derby County (May 1923), Sheffield Wednesday (February 1929), Bournemouth & Boscombe Athletic (August 1930), Folkestone Town (May 1933), Worcester City (player-manager, 1934). Retired in August 1935, later scouted for Derby County.
Club honours: Blues: Division Two champions 1921.
Jackie Whitehouse rose to prominence as one of the local youngsters given their chance during WW1. A pugnacious forward with a reputation for being one of the game's hard men, he was never averse to 'mixing it' with a defender.

WHITTON, Stephen Paul

Striker: 117+2 apps. 35 goals.
Born: East Ham, London, 4 December 1960.
Career: Coventry City (apprentice June 1977, professional September 1978), West Ham United (£175,000, July 1983), BLUES (on loan, January 1986, signing permanently for £75,000, August 1986), Sheffield Wednesday (£275,000, March 1989), Halmstads BK/Sweden (on loan, 1990), Ipswich Town (£120,000, January 1991), Colchester United (as player-coach, March 1994, player/caretaker-manager, May 1994, retired as a player in May 1998, manager at Layer Toad from August 1999).
Club honours: (as manager) Colchester: Division 2 promotion 1999. Blues made a profit of £200,000 on Steve Whitton, which was very good business. Although a Londoner, he began his career in the Midlands where he developed into a strong, hard-running striker, with surprisingly delicate ball-control. He loved to run at

defenders before letting fly with a powerful right-foot shot. He was among the Swedish League's top scorers during his spell with Halmstads BK. Whitton retired in 1998 after suffering a tedious back injury, having scored 117 goals in 531 competitive games for his English clubs.

WHYTE, Christopher Anderson

Defender: 88+1 apps. one goal.
Born: Islington, 2 September 1961.
Career: Highbury Grove School, Highbury Hill & District Schools, Highbury Grove FC, Islington Boys and Inner London Schools, Arsenal (junior 1976, apprentice July 1977, professional December 1979), Crystal Palace (on loan, August 1984), New York Express /NASL, Los Angeles Lazers/NASL, Los Angeles Aztecs/NASL, West Bromwich Albion (free transfer, August 1988), Leeds United (for a tribunal set fee of £450,000, June 1990), BLUES (£250,000, August 1993), Coventry City (on loan, December 1995), Charlton Athletic (March 1996), West Ham United (on loan), Detroit Neon/USA Indoor League, Leyton Orient (as a non-contract player, January 1997), Oxford United (February 1997), Rushden & Diamonds (season 1997-98).
Club honours: Leeds United: Division One champions 1992, Blues: Second Division champions 1995.
Representative honours: England (4 Under-21 caps).
Chris Whyte came to St Andrew's with some 350 games under his belt and did an excellent job in Blues' defence. He was switched to left-back with great success by manager Barry Fry in 1994-95. Whyte amassed a grand total of 488 League and Cup appearances in English football (24 goals scored) and at one time it looked as if he might become a full England international, having won four caps at under 21 level. Sadly, that was not to be.

WIGLEY, Stephen

Winger: 98 apps. 5 goals.
Born: Ashton-under-Lyne, 15 October 1961.
Career: Curzon Ashton, Nottingham Forest (March 1981), Sheffield United (October 1985), BLUES (player-exchange deal involving Martin Kuhl, March 1987), Portsmouth (£350,000, March 1989), Exeter City (August 1993), Bognor Regis Town (1994), Aldershot Town (March 1995), Nottingham Forest (coach).
A speedy winger, good on the ball, Steve Wigley made over 100 appearances under Brian Clough before transferring to Bramall Lane. He teamed up at Fratton Park with former Blues player, Kevin Dillon. A good crosser of the ball, a lot of his work at St Andrew's went to waste because of the lack of a true centre-forward in the side. He did much better at Pompey with the likes of Guy Whittingham and Colin Clarke around.

WIGMORE, Walter

Inside-forward/centre-half: 355 apps. 25 goals.
Born: Chipping Sodbury, 25 February 1873.
Died: Worksop, 8 September 1931.
Career: Kiveton Park, Worksop (1889), Sheffield United (1895), Worksop Town (March 1896), Gainsborough Trinity (August 1896), BLUES (£180, March 1899), Brierley Hill Alliance (August 1912). Retired in May 1913.
Club honours: Blues: Division Two runners-up 1901, 1903.
Representative honours: Players Union XI (1); Football League XI (1).
Walter Wigmore was a powerful inside-forward who was signed by Blues to renew his partnership with Bob McRoberts, his former Gainsborough team-mate. Wigmore fulfilled these duties adequately until an injury to Alec Leake led to him being switched to centre-half where his form was a revelation, Leake being moved to wing-half on his recovery. Wigmore remained first-choice pivot for nine years, helping Blues to two promotions, before a series of injuries ended his League career. He was then tempted to Brierley Hill with the offer of a pub tenancy. Renowned throughout the footballing community as 'the man who would never head the ball', he always attempted to bring the ball to foot, no matter how high it was, and was therefore often in trouble with referees for 'dangerous play'. But most officials tended to be lenient with him, regarding his actions as clumsy rather than malicious.

WILCOX, Frederick Jeremiah

Inside-left: 84 apps. 32 goals.
Born: Bristol, 7 July 1880. Died: Bristol, 1954.
Career: Glendale FC (August 1899), Bristol Rovers (August 1901), BLUES (£125, March 1903, plus the proceeds from a friendly match against Rovers), Middlesbrough (March 1906). Retired in May 1910.
Representative honours: England (trialistl.)
Fred Wilcox was a dashing forward, regarded by some critics as the finest dribbler of his day, such was his ability that Middlesbrough saw him as the perfect foil for Steve Bloomer - and they were not at all disappointed as he managed 20 goals to Bloomer's 31 over the next two years. A damaged knee, suffered after colliding with a goal post, caused him to retire in 1910. He returned to Bristol where he set up his own business.

WILCOX, Harold Melbourne

Inside-forward: 17 apps. 3 goals.
Born: Hockley, Birmingham, 7 January 1878.
Died: Plymouth, 21 July 1937.
Career: King's Parish School (Bromsgrove), St David's YC, Selly Oak St Mary's, BLUES (September 1898), Watford (July 1900), Preston North End (1901), Plymouth Argyle (August 1905), Leicester Fosse (August 1906), West Bromwich Albion (November 1907), Plymouth Argyle (May 1908). Retired in May 1920.
Club honours: PNE: Division Two champions 1904; Plymouth: Southern League champions 1913.

Representative honours: Southern League XI (2).

A fine inside-forward, with a heavy moustache, Harry Wilcox amassed some 400 appearances during his lengthy career which finally ended when he was 42. He later switched to the centre-half position, albeit one with an attacking bent in those pre-stopper days. He scored 41 goals in 323 games in his two spells with Plymouth.

WILCOX, John Mitchell

Winger: 48 apps. 2 goals

Born: Stourbridge, January 1886. Died: Lichfield August 1940.

Career: Stourbridge Standard, Cradley St Luke's, Dudley, Halesowen, Aston Villa (July 1908), BLUES (player-exchange deal involving 'George' Travers, November 1908), Southampton (June 1911), Wellington Town (May 1912). Retired in 1916.

'Jack' was the most recent of the four unrelated players named Wilcox to perform for Blues before WW1. He was a winger of fitful brilliance who loved to take on defenders. He was never a great goalscorer but was a regular supplier of chances for his team-mates.

WILCOX, Leslie

Outside-left: 4 apps. 2 goals

Born: West Bromwich, 1865. Now Deceased

Career: West Bromwich Highfield, BLUES (September 1889 to April 1890).

Les Wilcox made his debut with Fred Wheldon and Jack Hallam as Blues tried a new-look forward-line in 1889-90. All three newcomers scored but whilst two went on to become stalwarts of the club, Wilcox found himself out in the cold. It is still quite a mystery as to why such a useful winger suddenly disappeared after only a few games.

WILKES, Frederick

Centre-forward: 5 apps. 4 goals.

Born: Handsworth, Birmingham, 1869. Now Deceased

Career: Grove Hill Council School (Handsworth), Handsworth Boys Club, BLUES (April 1891), Brownhills FC (September 1892).

Fred Wilkes played in several friendly matches for the Blues at the end of the 1890-91 season and looked a good acquisition but, despite Blues having a centre-forward problem during the next campaign, he was overlooked. He scored a hat-trick in his only FA Cup-tie, against Brierley Hill Alliance in 1891.

WILLETTS, Walter

Outside-left: one app

Born: Smethwick, 1860. Now Deceased

Career: Langley Victoria, BLUES (April 1884), Oldbury (1885).

Wally Willetts took quite sometime to bed into the first team but when he had settled down he proved to be a useful footballer, being quick and a fair provider of

chances. His finest game came against Excelsior in the Birmingham Senior Cup in November 1884, a match that had to be replayed when Excelsior claimed that the ball was 'insufficiently inflated during the last 25 minutes'.

WILLIAMS, Dean Paul

Goalkeeper: 5 apps.

Born: Lichfield, 5 January 1972.

Career: Hansbury Farm Junior & Glascote Comprehensive Schools, BLUES (YTS June 1988, professional January 1990), Cobh Ramblers (on loan, August 1991), Tamworth (March 1992), Newcastle United (on trial, July 1993), Brentford (August 1993), Doncaster Rovers (August 1994), Gateshead (December 1997).

Dean Williams, rather on the slim side for a goalkeeper, showed abundant talent in his first few senior outings with Blues, being a fine handler of high crosses. Unfortunately he could not gain a regular place in the side and left for pastures new in 1992. He went on to make almost 100 appearances for Doncaster, before falling out with Belle Vue boss Danny Bergara.

WILLIAMS, Harry

Left-back: One app.

Born: Aston, Birmingham, 1875. Now Deceased

Career: Aston Unity (1982), Aston Manor (1894), BLUES (April 1896), Nechells FC (season 1897-98).

Not much can be gleaned about this man's style of play. He came in for the indisposed Billy Pratt in a game at Blackpool in 1897 but the match itself was barely covered in the Birmingham press, and his contribution was not mentioned at all!

WILLIAMS, Jacques

Midfielder: 1+3 apps.

Born: Wallasey, 25 April 1981

Career: Bordeaux/France (1989), BLUES (free transfer, July 1999 to March 2002), Crewe Alexandra (on trial, July-August 2002).

Slightly built but competent midfielder whose Blues' career was disrupted by a hernia operation in December 2000, Jacques Williams never really regained full fitness and was released by the club in March 2002. In fact, he initially announced his retirement from the sport at the end of the 2001-02 season but was enticed back for trials by Crewe boss Dario Gradi.

WILLIAMS, James William

Inside-forward: 12 apps. 3 goals.

Born: Buckley, Flintshire, 1888. Died: France, 5 June 1916.

Career: Bury, Accrington Stanley (1907), BLUES (August 1908), Accrington (February 1909), Crystal Palace (June 1909), Millwall Athletic (February 1914).

Representative honours: Wales (2 full caps).

Jimmy 'Ginger' Williams was referred to in the press as a

'very smart forward, full of fire and dash'. He scored plenty of goals in junior football before joining Blues, but although he impressed in pre-season trials he had to wait for his debut. When he did get his chance, he failed to impress but later made a big impact with Palace. He was killed whilst serving with the Footballer's Battalion.
* Williams was known in the Buckley area of Flintshire as 'John Will Farm.'

WILLIAMS, Paul Anthony
Forward: 9+3 apps. one goal
Born: Stratford, London 16 August 1965.
Career: Aveley FC, Clapton, Woodford Town (1984), Charlton Athletic (£12,000, August 1986), Brentford (on loan, October-December 1987), Sheffield Wednesday (£700,000, August 1990), Crystal Palace (September 1992), Sunderland (on loan, January 1995), BLUES (on loan, March 1995), Charlton Athletic (free transfer, September 1995), Torquay United (on loan, March 1996), Southend United (free transfer, August 1996), Canvey Island (June 1998).
Club honours: Sheffield Wednesday: Football League Cup winners 1991: Crystal Palace: Division One champions 1994; Blues: Second Division champions 1995.
Representative honours: England (4 Under-21 and 'B' caps)
Paul Williams, a fast-raiding utility forward, had maintained a respectable strike record before finding himself 'out in the cold' at Selhurst Park after Palace's promotion. He joined Blues in time to make his debut against Orient in the Auto Windscreen Shield Area Final and marked his presence with a goal. At first he seemed a useful acquisition but later he struggled to show his best form. He went on to take his tally of League appearances to a respectable 299 (65 goals scored).

WILLIAMS, Thomas Andrew
Left-back/outside-left: 4* apps.
Born: Carshalton, 8 July 1980
Career: Walton & Hersham, West Ham United (£60,000, April 2000), Peterborough United (March 2001), BLUES (£1 million, March 2002), Queen's Park Rangers (on loan, August 2002).
A crowd-pleaser with Peterborough for whom he made 44 appearances, the versatile Tommy Williams was given his Blues' debut on the left-wing against Norwich City as the promotion race hotted up in March 2002. He later deputised for the suspended Martin Grainger at left-back.

WILLIAMS, Thomas Edward
Central-defender: 73+1 apps. 2 goals.
Born: Winchburgh, Scotland, 18 December 1957.
Career: Hazel Street School, Leicester Beavers (August 1972), Leicester City (apprentice, June 1974, professional December 1975), BLUES (free transfer July 1986), Grimsby Town (August 1988), Leicestershire County Police FC (from 1990).

Club honours: Leicester: Division Two champions 1980. Tommy Williams was a solid, no-nonsense defender, who played 241 League games for Leicester, initially as a full-back and latterly as a centre-half, before moving to St Andrew's. He overcame two broken legs during his stay at Filbert Street and put in some splendid performances for Blues, so it was something of a surprise when he was given a free transfer in 1988. Now a police officer, based in Leicestershire, he still plays occasionally for the force's football team.

WILLIS, Roger Christopher
Midfielder/striker: 12+8 apps. 5 goals
Born: Sheffield, 17 June 1967.
Career: Dunkirk FC (August 1987), Grimsby Town (professional, July 1989), Barnet (£10,000, August 1990), Watford (£175,000, October 1992), BLUES (£150,000, December 1993), Southend United (September 1994), Peterborough United (free transfer, August 1996), Chesterfield (£100,000, July 1987 to May 2002)
Club honours: Barnet: GMVC winners 1991.
Representative honours: England (semi-professional caps)
Attacking midfielder 'Harry' Willis did well at Barnet, scoring 17 goals in just over 50 games in their first season as a Football League club. Unfortunately he never settled at Watford or St Andrew's yet after leaving Blues, he went on to net almost 50 times in close on 250 appearances while serving with Southend, 'Posh' and Chesterfield.

WILSON, Alfred Richmond
Right-back: 2 apps.
Born: Sothall, Sheffield, 1895. Now Deceased
Career: Sheffield Wednesday (1915), BLUES (April 1919), Rotherham County (season 1920-21).
After failing to make the first team at Sheffield, Alf Wilson moved to Blues as cover for the regular full-back pairing, but alas he was restricted to only two outings on successive days over Christmas 1919. He did not break into Rotherham's team either.

WINDRIDGE, James Edwin
Inside-forward: 61 apps. 19 goals.
Born: Small Heath, 21 October 1882.
Died: Small Heath, 23 September 1939.
Career: Small Heath Alma, BLUES (junior 1899, professional 1901), Chelsea (£190, April 1905), Middlesbrough (November 1911), BLUES (April 1914). Retired in 1916.
Representative honours: England (8 full caps).
A highly effective but individualistic forward, Jimmy Windridge was certainly one of the best dribblers of his day. Although obviously skilful he seemed lazy during his first spell with Blues and was off-loaded to Chelsea with his colleague Robertson in time for the London club's

first-ever League season. The move south was perhaps the best thing he could have done, for he thrived in his new surroundings, gained England honours (scoring seven goals in eight internationals) and hit 58 goals in 152 games for the 'Pensioners' before going to Middlesbrough. He was well past his best when he returned to Blues but still managed to score five goals in a League game against Glossop in 1915. During WW1 he organised a scratch Blues team to play in local charity matches. A useful cricketer he had seven games for Warwickshire, scoring 161 runs at an average of 14.64. He also took one for 13 with the ball. Windridge was the cousin of Blues' defender Alec Leake (q.v).

WITHE, Peter

Centre-forward: 48 apps. 11 goals.
Born: Liverpool, 30 August 1951.
Career: All Hallows School (Speke), Smith Coggins FC (1966), Skelmersdale, Southport (August 1971), Barrow (December 1971), Port Elizabeth City/South Africa (1972) Arcadia Shepherds/South Africa (1973), Wolverhampton Wanderers (£13,500, November 1973), Portland Timbers/NASL (1975), BLUES (£50,000, August 1975), Nottingham Forest (£42,000, September 1976), Newcastle United (£200,000, August 1978), Aston Villa (for a record fee of £500,000, May 1980), Sheffield United (July 1985), BLUES (on loan, September-November 1987), Huddersfield Town (July 1988, initially as assistant-manager/player-coach), Aston Villa (assistant manager/senior coach to Josef Venglos, January 1991, then reserve-team coach under Ron Atkinson, July 1991), Wimbledon (manager, October 1991 to January 1992), Evesham United (player, February 1992), Community Liaison Officer for the West Midlands and for BLUES (1993), Aston Villa (Youth Development Officer, August 1994), Thailand (national coach/manager & football advisor, from September 2000).
Club honours: Nottingham Forest: Division One champions 1978, Football League Cup winners 1978, Anglo Scottish Cup winners 1977; Aston Villa: Division One champions 1981, European Cup winners, Super Cup winners 1982, FA Charity Shield winners 1981
Representative honours: England (11 full caps).
One of soccer's goalscoring nomads, Peter Withe (after leaving school) served with 16 different football clubs (at various levels) during his 20 years as a striker, during which time he chalked up a fine record: 232 goals in 640 games (all competitions). Big, strong and fearless, he never really established himself at St Andrew's where his power in the air seemed to be counter-balanced by his clumsiness on the ground. Under the guidance of Brian Clough he developed into a splendid target man, being a fine exponent of the chest pass. He played a major role in both Forest's and later Villa's glory years, netting the winning goal for the latter in the 1982 European Cup

Final. His brother, Chris, played for several League clubs, while his son, Jason, started off with West Brom and later served Burnley. Withe is now doing an excellent job as coach of the Thailand national soccer team.

WITHERS, Colin Charles

Goalkeeper: 116 apps.
Born: Erdington, Birmingham, 21 March 1940.
Career: Paget Road School, West Bromwich Albion (amateur 1956), BLUES (professional, May 1957), Aston Villa (£18,000, November 1964), Lincoln City (June 1969), Go-Ahead Eagles Deventer/Holland (1970), Atherstone Town (1972-73). Retired in May 1973.
Representative honours: England (Schoolboy cap).
Colin 'Tiny' Withers conceded six goals when making his League debut for Blues at White Hart Lane in November 1960. But after that heart-breaking baptism he settled down to give the club great service and later made 163 appearances for rivals Aston Villa. Standing 6ft 3in tall and weighing 13st, he was an imposing figure between the posts, often producing some sterling performances. After retiring, he ran a hotel in Blackpool and was later a publican in Bridgnorth.

WOLLASTON, Trevor John

Right-half: one app.
Born: Hall Green, Birmingham 1873. Died: King's Norton, December 1918.
Career: Yardley Vics, BLUES (April 1891), Stechford Royal Unity FC (August 1891).
Jack Wollaston was a local man whose career with Blues seemed to have been confined to just a month (April 1891) when he played in three friendlies and one Alliance match (a 6-2 defeat by Crewe Alexandra in April 1891). Normally a centre-half, he replaced Harry Morris at right-half in that Alliance fixture.

WOLSTENHOLME, John Trevor

Wing-half/inside-forward: 2 apps. one goal.
Born: Prestbury, near Manchester, 18 June 1943.
Career: Prestwick & Whitfield Boys, Chloride FC, BLUES (junior July 1959, professional September 1960), Torquay United (August 1963), York City (July 1966).
Trevor Wolstenholme made a dramatic entry into senior football when he replaced Welsh international Ken Leek for a League Cup-tie at Barrow, scoring Blues' goal in the 1-1 draw. He was switched to wing-half for the replay - and this turned out to be his last outing for the club. As a defender he played 82 League games for Torquay and 11 for York later in his career.

WOMACK, Francis

Full-back: 515 apps.
Born: Wortley, near Attercliffe, Sheffield, 16 September 1888. Died: Caistor-on-Sea, Lincolnshire, 8 October 1968.
Career: Rawmarsh FC, BLUES (professional July 1908),

Worcester City (player-manager, May 1928), Torquay United (manager July 1930), Grimsby Town (manager May 1932 to May 1936), Leicester City (manager, October 1936 to September 1939), Notts County (manager, July 1942 to March 1944), Oldham Athletic (manager, February 1945 to April 1947), Grimsby Town (caretaker-manager, January-May 1951).

Club honours: Blues: Division Two champions 1921.
Representative honours: England trialist (3); Football League XI (1).

Frank Womack skippered Blues for 17 consecutive seasons in a 20-year association with the St Andrew's club, subsequently becoming the first player-manager to be appointed in the Birmingham League (May 1928) and leading Worcester City to that championship in his very first season in charge at St George's Lane. According to fellow professionals, Womack was on par with West Brom's England international Jesse Pennington as being the best full-back in the Midlands in the five years leading up to WW1. He was involved in a bribery scandal in 1913, being offered 55 guineas to 'fix' the Blues v Grimsby match so that it would end in a draw. He reported the matter to the officials, a trap was set and the culprit duly arrested, charged and found guilty. One of Blues' greatest-ever players, Womack was obviously annoyed and very unhappy when he was released in 1928. At 39 years, 207 days old, he is the second oldest player ever to appear for Blues in a first-class match.

WOOD, Edmund Eli

Centre-half: one app.
Born: Shirley, Birmingham, 10 February 1903.
Now Deceased
Career: Redditch, Rhyl Athletic, Northampton Town (March 1923), BLUES (May 1925), Rhyl Athletic (1928), Newcastle United (£750, May 1928), Rhyl Athletic, Runcorn, Wellington Town (1930).
A powerful half-back, tall and well built, Eli Wood's career with Blues was restricted by the consistency of 'Lofty' Morrall. He seems to have had a great liking for the seaside town of Rhyl.

WOODHOUSE, Curtis

Midfielder: 41+14* apps. 2* goals
Born: Beverley, Yorkshire, 17 April 1980.
Career: Sheffield United (trainee, June 1996, professional December 1997), BLUES (£1 million, February 2001).
Club honours: Blues: Division One promotion 2002
International honours: England (4 Under-21 & Youth caps). A very combative midfielder with an excellent work-rate, Curtis Woodhouse did well initially before having to battle hard and long to gain a place in the first XI owing to the impressive form of Bryan Hughes and Darren Carter among others.

WORTHINGTON, Frank Stewart

Centre-forward: 84+4 apps. 33 goals
Born: Halifax, 23 November 1948.
Career: Huddersfield Town (apprentice July 1964, professional November 1966), Leicester City (£70,000, August 1972), Bolton Wanderers (£87,000, September 1977), Philadelphia Fury/NASL (on loan, April 1981), Leeds United (exchange for Byron Stevenson, March 1982), Southampton (£30,000, June 1983), Brighton & Hove Albion (May 1984), Tranmere Rovers (player-manager, July 1985), Preston North End (February 1987), Stockport County (on loan, November 1987, signed permanently, March 1988, Capetown Spurs/South Africa (April 1988), Chorley (October 1988), Stalybridge Celtic (December 1988), Galway United (February 1989), Weymouth, Radcliffe Borough, Guiseley, Hinckley Town (player-manager, September 1990 to May 1991), Halifax Town (part-time coach, October 1991).
Club honours: Huddersfield: Division Two champions 1970; Bolton: Division Two champions 1978; Blues: Division Two promotion 1980.
Representative honours: England (8 full caps, 2 Under-23 caps); Football League XI (1).

Anyone who saw Frank Worthington play will have their own thoughts and memories of this immensely skilful footballer. He had the ability to control the ball with one touch and always seemed casual in his approach, even arrogant at times, but he was a class player. Always a larger than life character, both on and off the field, his ill-concealed disdain of the regimented tactics employed during the 1970s probably cost him a hatful of caps. His cavalier approach earned him the nickname of 'swash-buckling hero', and as one of soccer's great nomads his lengthy League career saw him score 236 goals in a total of 757 appearances. His best period was with Leicester (72 goals in 210 games), but he also did well with Huddersfield, Bolton, Blues and Tranmere. His brothers - Dave and Bob - also played League football, while his nephew, Gary, carried on the family tradition with Wigan Athletic in 1991. Worthington was granted a benefit by the PFA in 1991, and a game was arranged for him at St Andrew's which attracted nearly 7,000 spectators. He is now living in Shelf (near Halifax) and is working as an after-dinner speaker.

Statistics don't always tell the story, but in Worthington's case they certainly do.
* He scored in League football in each of 22 consecutive seasons: 1966-67 to 1987-88 inclusive.
* In all competitions (League, FAC, LC, internationals, in America, etc) he netted close on 300 goals in 905 appearances - some record! And there is no doubt that he scored some real beauties - including that extra-special one at Bolton!

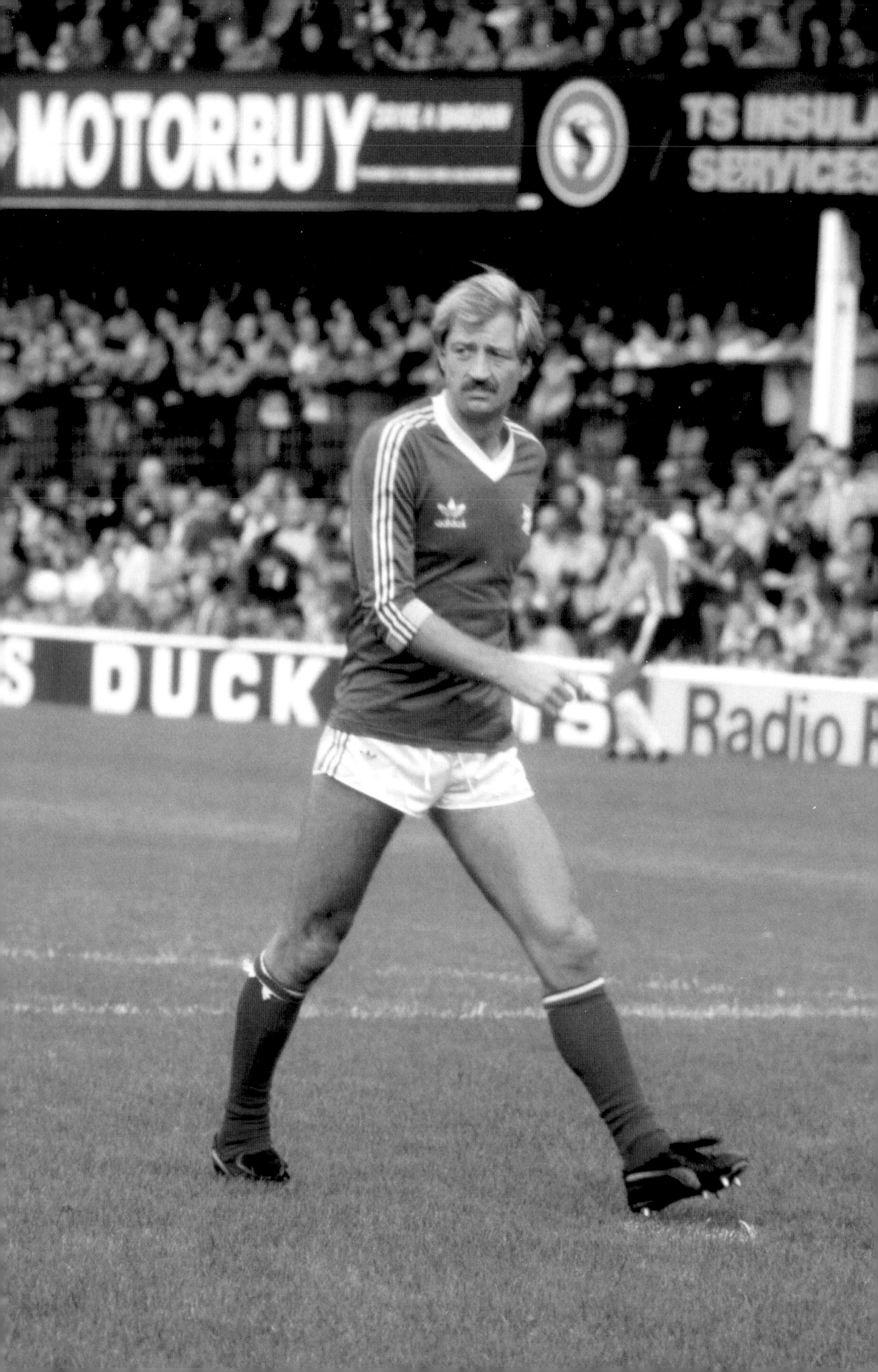
MOTORBUY
SERVICES
DUCK
Radio

WRAGG, William A

Full-back/left-half: one app.

Born: Knebworth, Leicestershire, 1877. Now Deceased
Career: Nottingham Forest (April 1896), Leicester Fosse (March 1899), BLUES (January 1901), Watford (August 1901), Hinckley Town (1902), Chesterfield (August 1903), Accrington Stanley (1904), Brighton & Hove Albion (September 1905 to May 1907).
Club honours: Nottingham Forest: FA Cup winners 1898.
Principally a constructive wing-half in his early days at Forest, Willie Wragg engineered their first goal in the 1898 Cup Final. He switched to full-back shortly before moving to Leicester and he was their free-kick expert. He was kept in reserve at Blues by the tigerish tackling of George Adey. Wragg was another player signed by Blues shortly after he had scored an own-goal for them.

WRATTEN, Adam Philip

Defender: 0+1 apps. 2 goals.

Born: Coventry, 30 November 1974.
Career: BLUES (YTS June 1991, professional May 1993), Yeovil Town (on loan, April 1995). Released from St Andrew's in May 1995.
Paul Wratten made a superb start to his Blues' career - scoring twice against Wolverhampton Wanderers at St Andrew's in the Anglo-Italian Cup in September 1993 after coming on as a substitute. Unfortunately he never figured again in the first XI.

WREH, Christopher

Striker: 6+1 app. one goal

Born: Liberia, 14 May 1975
Career: AS Monaco/France, FC Guingamp/France (1996), Arsenal (£300,000, August 1997), BLUES (on loan, October-December 1999), Al-Hilal/Saudi Arabia (December 1999).
Club honours: Arsenal: Premiership champions, FA Cup winners, Charity Shield winners 1998.
Representative honours: Liberia (13 caps)
An effective forward, with good pace and ability, Chris Wreh loved to run at defenders but perhaps found it tough in the Midlands! He scored five goals in his 46 outings for the Gunners.

WRIGHT, Patrick Daniel Joseph

Full-back: 3 apps.

Born: Oldbury, 17 November 1940.
Career: St Chad's School, Springfield Boys' Club, BLUES (professional November 1959), Shrewsbury Town (September 1962), Derby County (October 1967), Southend United (on loan, March 1970), Rotherham United (player-coach, September 1970), Waterlooville (player-manager, season 1971-72), Portsmouth (as reserve-team coach 1972, chief coach 1974), Zambia (national team coach, 1976), Saudi Arabia (national coach, 1978, Youth-team manager, early 1979), United

Arab Emirates (assistant-manager, mid-1979), Al Nasr of Dubai (Chief coach, for four seasons: 1980 to 1984).
Rarely called up by Blues, Pat Wright later developed into a useful full-back with the 'Shrews' for whom he made well over 200 appearances. He passed his preliminary coaching certificate in 1964 and thereafter coached in many different countries. He now runs his own company, organising coaching courses. He is also on the Planning Committee of the FA School of Excellence.

WRIGHT, William

Centre-half: 135+2 apps 14 goals

Born: Liverpool, 28 April 1958.
Career: Everton (apprentice June 1974, professional January 1977), BLUES (free transfer, June 1983), Chester City (on loan, February-March 1986), Carlisle United (August 1986), Morecambe (August 1988).
Club honours: Blues: Division Two promotion 1985.
Representative honours: England (2 'B' caps, 6 Under-21 caps).
A stocky performer and an ace penalty-taker, Billy Wright was an ever-present in Blues' promotion winning side of 1984-85. He had played in 198 games for Everton and overall accumulated more than 400 senior appearances whilst serving in all four Divisions of the Football League in a comparatively short period of time. Blues' skipper, he was very popular with the fans, and was released by the club after developing weight problems. His uncle, Tommy Wright, played right-back for Everton and England.

WYLIE, Ronald Maurice

Right-half/inside-forward: 146+3 apps. 2 goals.

Born: Glasgow, 6 August 1933.
Career: Clydesdale Juniors (1946-48), Notts County (amateur, April 1948, professional September 1950), Aston Villa (£9,250, November 1958), BLUES (July 1965). Retired in April 1970 and was briefly Public Relations Officer at St Andrew's, then Aston Villa (coach, June 1970 to May 1972), Coventry City (coach, July 1975, then assistant-manager 1978 to 1981), Cyprus FC (coach/football advisor), Bulova/Hong Kong (coach, early 1982), West Bromwich Albion (manager from July 1982 to February 1984), Aston Villa (reserve-team coach/manager, February 1984 to May 1987). Scouted for several clubs until becoming Football in the Community Officer at Villa Park in August 1990, later Community Liaison Officer with Villa from August 1995, then appointed the club's Academy coach.
Club honours: Aston Villa: Division Two champions 1960, Football League Cup winners 1961; Midlands 'Footballer of The Year' 1965.
Representative honours: Scotland (2 Schoolboy caps).
Ron Wylie was a talented midfielder who scored 77 goals in more than 700 games as a professional footballer, of which 51 came in 551 League appearances. Stylish,

cultured, skilful and very constructive, he was signed for Notts County by former Villa star and later manager, Eric Houghton. It was said that Wylie was well past his best when he joined Blues. No way - he proved everyone wrong by appearing in almost 150 games before announcing his retirement when almost 37 years of age. He later returned to Villa Park, and took his overall service record with that club to 25 years.

YATES, Mark Jason
Utility player: 48+17 apps. 7 goals.
Born: Birmingham, 24 January 1970.
Career: Heybridge School, Stourbridge & District Boys, Forest Falcons FC (1985), BLUES (YTS June 1986, professional July 1988), Colchester United (on loan, August 1990 to February 1991), Burnley (£40,000, August 1991), Lincoln City (on loan, February 1993), Doncaster Rovers (August 1993), Kidderminster Harriers (August 1994), Cheltenham Town (January 1999, joint-caretaker-manager January 2003).
Club honours: Blues: Leyland DAF Cup winners 1991; Kidderminster: FA Trophy runners-up 1995, Cheltenham: Nationwide Conference winners 1999, Division 3 promotion 2002.
Representative honours: England (2 semi-professional caps)
Mark Yates had a tough time with Blues - he was hampered by injury as well as him being asked to play in a number of positions, including that of targetman. Lack of inches prevented him from prospering up front, but he put in some sterling performances in midfield. In 2002 he passed the career milestone of 300 League and FA Cup appearances.

WARTIME GUESTS

During both the First & Second World Wars, Blues recruited several guest players, some of whom were established internationals or had already been playing competitive football for a number of years. Indeed, some had earlier played for the club or later joined the St Andrew's ranks. Here are details of some of those players who assisted the club during the hostilities. Those who were registered with the club outside the war years are listed elsewhere in the book

THE GREAT WAR (1915-19)

ANSTEY, Brendal (Aston Villa)
Goalkeeper Brendal Anstey also played for Bristol Rovers, Leicester City and Mid-Rhondda. He made three appearances for Blues.

BELL, John (Nottingham Forest)
An inside or centre-forward, Jack Bell also played for Reading, Plymouth Argyle, South Shields, Merthyr Town, Grimsby Town and Rotherham County. He scored eight goals in his 21 outings for Blues.

BOWSER, Sidney (West Bromwich Albion)
A strapping England international inside-forward (one cap gained) Sid Bowser also played as a centre-half for WBA, appearing in some 370 senior games and gaining a League championship medal in 1920. He also assisted Walsall and Belfast Distillery. He netted nine times in his 42 appearances for Blues.

BRELSFORD, William (Sheffield United)
Half-back Billy Brelsford made 277 League appearances for the Blades (1909-21).

BROOKS, Arthur (Wolverhampton Wanderers)
Right-back Arthur Brooks also played for Newport County in 1919-20.

BROOKS, Samuel Ernest (Wolverhampton Wanderers)
Black Country-born outside-left Sammy Brooks also served with Tottenham Hotspur, Southend United and Kidderminster Harriers. He scored 50 goals in 224 League games for Wolves (1910-21). He netted twice in nine outings for Blues.

BROWN, David (Dundee)
Centre-forward David Brown also played for Glasgow Rangers, Stoke, Notts County, Kilmarnock, Darlington, Crewe Alexandra and Barrow. He scored over 150 goals in almost 300 competitive games during his lengthy career (1905-28)

BUCHAN, Charles Murray (Sunderland)
Charlie Buchan, the famous England international forward (6 caps gained) netted 209 goals in 380 League games during his 14 years at Roker Park and after leaving in 1924 he netted 49 times in 102 First Division matches for Arsenal.

BUCKLEY, Christopher Sebastian (Arsenal)
Chris Buckley, the former Aston Villa centre-half, later became Chairman of that club. He made over 200 senior appearances during his career

COOPER, Arthur (Barnsley)
Goalkeeper Arthur Cooper was also associated with Oldham Athletic, and made over 100 appearances for the Tykes.

DOBSON, Harry (Coventry City)
An inside-forward, previously with North Shields, Harry Dobson also played for Newport County and Southend United.

EDGLEY, Harold (Aston Villa)
Harold Edgley, an outside-left, also played for Crewe Alexandra, QPR and Stockport County and was a Notts

County Director. He made well over 160 League appearances in total - but missed Villa's 1913 FA Cup Final triumph through injury. He played in seven wartime games for Blues.

FREEMAN, Bertram Clewley (Burnley)
Centre-forward Bert Freeman, capped five times by England, also played for Aston Villa, Arsenal, Everton, Wigan Borough and Kidderminster Harriers, scoring well over 200 goals in 320 League games.

HOWELL, Henry (Wolverhampton Wanderers)
Inside-forward 'Harry' Howell also served with Port Vale and Stoke (before Wolves) and Southampton afterwards.

HUNTER, George (Manchester United)
A resilient half-back, born in India, George Hunter also played for Aston Villa, Oldham Athletic, Chelsea and Portsmouth, making over 200 first-class appearances all told. He scored twice in 21 games for Blues.

JEPHCOTT, Claude (West Bromwich Albion)
Fast-raiding outside-right Claude Jephcott scored 15 goals in 174 First Division games for the Baggies, helping them win the 1920 League title. He was later a Director at The Hawthorns. He netted one goal in his 12 appearances for Blues.

JOHNSON, Harry (Coventry City)
Harry Johnson was serving in the British Army when he guested as a forward for Blues. He later played for both Southampton and QPR.

LEES, Joseph (Barnsley)
An inside-forward, Joe Lees joined Rotherham United after the war and later served with Lincoln City, Halifax Town, Scunthorpe & Lindsay United and Newport County.

MERCER, Alick (Bury)
Alick Mercer, a Tamworth-born forward, went on to score 16 goals in 102 League games for Coventry City (1919-22).

MIDDLEMISS, Herbert (Tottenham Hotspur)
A very useful player, Bert Middlemiss scored 50 goals in 243 League games for Spurs (1908-19). He also played for Stockport County and Queen's Park Rangers

MONTGOMERY, Harold (Glossop)
Outside-right Harry Montgomery played for Hyde United, Crewe Alexandra and Accrington Stanley after the hostilities. He scored seven goals in his 19 games for Blues.

PEERS, Edward (Wolverhampton Wanderers)
Welsh international goalkeeper Teddy Peers (12 caps gained) made 186 League appearances for Wolves (1911-20). He later played for Port Vale and Hednesford Town. He had 12 outings between the posts for Blues.

PENNINGTON, Jesse (West Bromwich Albion)
Jesse Pennington, a brilliant full-back and captain of Albion and England (25 caps), played in the 1912 FA Cup Final and gained a League championship medal in 1920. He made nearly 500 appearances for the Baggies and kept Blues' Frank Womack out of the England side.

RICHARDSON, Samuel (West Bromwich Albion)
Pennington's right-half team-mate at The Hawthorns, Sammy Richardson made over 200 appearances for Albion and later assisted Aldershot, Newport County and Kidderminster Harriers. He also gained a League championship medal in 1920.

SHEA, Daniel (Blackburn Rovers)
England international forward Danny Shea (2 caps gained) scored over 100 League goals in more than 300 League games while also playing for West Ham United, Fulham, Coventry City and Clapton Orient.

STEVENS, Samuel (Hull City)
Netherton-born centre-forward Sammy Stevens served with Notts County and Coventry City after the war. He scored 118 goals in a total of 231 League matches. He had a fine strike-record with Blues - netting 12 times in 15 games.

WALLACE, Charles (Aston Villa)
England international outside-left (3 caps won) Charlie Wallace played for Crystal Palace before making well over 300 competitive appearances for Villa, whom he helped win the League title and the FA Cup twice, although he did miss a penalty in their 1913 Cup Final success over Sunderland. He later played for Oldham Athletic.

WESTON, Thomas (Aston Villa)
Wallace's colleague in Villa's 1920 FA Cup Final triumph, Tommy Weston was a sturdy full-back who made 154 League appearances during his ten years at Villa Park (1911-21). He later played for Stoke.

WOOTTON, James (Walsall)
Outside-left Jimmy Wootton signed for Port Vale in 1919 and later played for Nelson.

WORLD WAR TWO (1939-46)

ACQUROFF, John (Norwich City)
Jack Acquroff was a prolific marksman, who also 'scored' League goals for Hull City and Bury. As well as Blues, he guested for WBA and Wolves during the war and was once on Spurs' books. He made 44 appearances for Blues in two seasons (1942-44) scoring 10 goals.

AINSLEY, George Edward (Leeds United)
Ex-Sunderland and Bolton Wanderers utility forward George Ainsley played for Bradford Park Avenue after leaving Elland Road in 1947.

ALLEN, James Phillips (Aston Villa)
England international half-back Jimmy Allen left Portsmouth for Villa Park in 1933. He made 282 League appearances all told.

BARTRAM, Samuel (Charlton Athletic)
Superb goalkeeper Sam Bartram made 582 League appearances for the London club between 1934-55. Was later manager of Luton Town. He missed a penalty playing for Charlton v. Blues at St Andrew's in 1945.

BRAY, John (Manchester City)
Jackie Bray, an England international left-half (6 caps won) scored 10 goals in 260 League games for Manchester City (from 1929).

BRIGHT, Richard (Local football)
A player who never ventured into League football, Dick Bright appeared in over 100 games during WW2 as a guest for Blues, Burnley and Preston North End. He scored 10 goals in 27 games for Blues in 1943-44. He died as recent as 2002.

BROOME, Frank Henry (Aston Villa)
Frank Broome was a splendid goalscorer who also played for Derby County, Notts County, Brentford and Crewe Alexandra, as well as gaining seven full caps for England. He later became Exeter City's manager. He netted 174 goals in a total of 392 League games and had seven wartime outings for Blues.

CUMMINGS, George (Aston Villa)
George Cummings, a great defender, made over 400 first team appearances for Villa (1935-49). A Scottish international (9 caps received) he also played for Partick Thistle and guested for Nottingham Forest among others during WW2. He made four appearances for Blues in the first wartime campaign.

DITCHBURN, Edward George Ted (Tottenham Hotspur)
England international goalkeeper Ted Ditchburn (6 caps won) played in 418 League games for Spurs (1946-58), gaining both First and Second Division championship medals. He appeared just once for Blues.

DOHERTY, Peter Dermont (Manchester City)
Brilliant Irish international inside-forward (recipient of 16 full caps) Peter Doherty also played for Glentoran, Blackpool, Derby County, Huddersfield Town and Doncaster Rovers, making over 400 League appearances

and scoring close on 200 goals. He helped Manchester City win the First Division title and Doncaster the Third Division (North) and was an FA Cup winner with Derby County and an Irish Cup winner with Glentoran. He also managed Northern Ireland and wore a Blues shirt on four occasions (one goal scored).

EASTHAM George Richard (Blackpool)
An inside-forward, capped once by England and, father of George junior (ex-Newcastle, Arsenal and Stoke City) George senior also played for Bolton Wanderers, Brentford, Swansea Town, Rochdale and Lincoln City, making over 250 League appearances (1932-49). He had six outings for Blues.

EDWARDS, George Robert (Aston Villa)
An inside or centre-forward, previously with Norwich City, George Edwards served Villa for 12 years (to 1950). He played in 10 games for Blues.

FINAN, Robert Joseph (Blackpool)
A utility forward, Bob Finan scored 99 goals in 235 League games during his career, which also saw him serve with Crewe Alexandra.

GOFFIN, William Charles (Aston Villa)
A lively winger, Billy Goffin spent seven years at Villa Park before moving to Walsall in 1954.

HAPGOOD, Edris (Arsenal)
A resolute full-back, Eddie Hapgood won 30 senior caps for England and made well over 400 appearances for Arsenal from (1927)

HARDWICK, George Francis Moutry (Middlesbrough)
Another splendid England full-back (13 caps gained) George Hardwick made 143 League appearances for Middlesbrough and 190 for Oldham Athletic before retiring in 1955. He also represented The Rest of Europe in 1947.

HAYWARD, Lionel Eric (Blackpool)
Centre-half Eric Hayward joined Blackpool in 1937 from Port Vale. He made 269 League appearances for the Seasiders (up to 1951).

HINSLEY, George (Bradford City)
A competitive half-back who also played for Barnsley and Halifax Town, George Hinsley made 155 League appearances either side of WW2.

IVERSON, Robert T (Aston Villa)
Ex-Spurs, Lincoln City and Wolves defender Bob Iverson served Villa for 11 years, making 135 League appearances (1936-47). He had seven outings with Blues.

JORDAN, Clarence (Doncaster Rovers)
Centre-forward 'Clarrie' Jordan also played for Sheffield Wednesday. He scored 83 goals in 152 League games between 1946-54.

McCORMICK, James (Tottenham Hotspur)
Jimmy McCormick was a dashing outside-right whose career also took him to Rotherham United, Chesterfield, Fulham, Lincoln City and Crystal Palace. He made over 250 League appearances in total and during the war scored five times in 28 games for Blues.

McEWAN, William (Queen's Park Rangers)
Scottish-born outside-right Billy McEwan also played for Leyton Orient (1949-50).

McPHERSON, Ian Buchanan (Glasgow Rangers)
Winger Ian McPherson also played for Notts County, Arsenal and Brentford. He scored 26 goals in just over 200 Football League games.

MARTIN, John Rowland (Aston Villa)
An inside-forward, signed by Villa from Hednesford, Jackie Martin quit League football in 1948.

MASSIE, Alexander (Aston Villa)
A Scottish international wing-half (18 caps won) Alex Massie also played for Ayr United, Bury and Hearts and later managed Villa.

METCALF, Walter Frederick (Coventry City)
Left-back, formerly of Scarborough, Sunderland and Brentford, Walter Metcalf made 77 League appearances for the Sky Blues.

MITCHESON, Francis John (Doncaster Rovers)
Inside-forward Frank Mitcheson later played for Crewe Alexandra and Rochdale. He made over 250 League appearances in his career.

MORGAN, Llewellyn David (Walsall)
Half-back 'Lol' Morgan played for Aberdare, Merthyr Town, Charlton Athletic, Bradford City and Aldershot before making 192 League appearances for the Saddlers from 1934.

MOSS, Frank (Aston Villa)
Frank Moss, the former Sheffield Wednesday centre-half, made more than 300 senior appearances for Villa (1938-54). He had just two outings for Blues. His father had earlier played for Villa.

O'DONNELL, Hugh (Blackpool)
An outside-left, formerly of Celtic and Preston North End, Hugh O'Donnell later played for Rochdale and Halifax Town and scored over 50 goals in more than 200 League and Cup games.

PEACOCK, Thomas (Nottingham Forest)
Tommy Peacock was an inside-forward with Chesterfield before going on to score 57 goals in 109 League games for Forest.

PEARSON, Thomas Usher (Newcastle United)
Scottish international (2 caps won) Tom Pearson netted 46 goals in 212 League games during his 14 years at St James' Park (1933-47).

POPE, Alfred (Heart of Midlothian)
Left-back Alf Pope also served with Leeds United and Halifax Town before moving to Tynecastle.

REDWOOD, Douglas James (Rochdale)
An outside-left, Doug Redwood was formerly with Cardiff City and Walsall.

REVELL, Charles (Charlton Athletic)
Wing-half Charlie Revell played for Derby County after leaving The Valley in 1951.

ROBINSON, George Henry (Charlton Athletic)
An inside-forward and team-mate of Revell's at The Valley, George Robinson also played for Sunderland and scored 42 goals in 238 League games for the London club from 1931.

SHELTON, John Benjamin Thomas (Walsall)
Competent full-back Jack Shelton was at Fellows Park for 12 years, making well over 100 senior appearances for the Saddlers.

SIBLEY, Eric Seymour (Blackpool)
A full-back, formerly with Spurs and Bournemouth, Eric Sibley later assisted Grimsby Town and Chester.

THAYNE, William (Walsall)
A colleague of Shelton's, half-back Billy Thayne also played for Crystal Palace, Hartlepool United, Luton Town and Northampton Town. He made almost 300 senior appearances during his career.

TRENTHAM, Douglas Harold (Everton)
Doug Trentham was an outside-left and brother of the West Bromwich Albion 1930s full-back, Bert.

TURNER, Herbert (Charlton Athletic)
Welsh international (8 full and 8 wartime caps won) Bert Turner made 196 senior appearances for Charlton as a full-back, scoring for both teams in the 1946 FA Cup Final (v. Derby County).

VAUSE, Peter Granville (Rochdale)
Outside-left Peter Vause also played for Blackburn Rovers, Blackpool and Darwen.

BLUES MANAGERS

Since entering the Football League in 1892, Blues have had 30 official team managers and/or secretary-managers. Nine of them have been former players of the club - Bob McRoberts, Billy Beer, Bill Harvey, George Liddell, Arthur Turner, Gil Merrick, Garry Pendrey, Trevor Francis and Steve Bruce.

Here are details of Blues' bosses over the last 110 years:

ALFRED JONES (July 1892 to June 1908)
Born: Birmingham, circa 1856. Now Deceased

Alf 'Inky' Jones assumed the role of team manager along with that of club secretary, a position he inherited from W H 'Billy' Edmunds. He held office for 16 years and during that time Blues won the Second Division Championship (1893) and finished runners-up the following season to gain promotion.

A manufacturer of scales, based in Birmingham, Jones was first engaged by Blues in 1885 - brought in to 'balance the club's books.' He was given the title of secretary soon afterwards and at the end of that first season Blues reached the semi-finals of the FA Cup (beaten 4-0 by West Bromwich Albion). He then took on the mantle of secretary-manager in 1892 when the team were elected to the Football League, having spent three seasons playing in the Football Alliance. Although the team went through a difficult period between 1896 and 1904, yo-yoing between Divisions, he battled on regardless. He recruited many fine players and generally did a wonderful job. He continued to work at the club as a part-time accountant (after being replaced by Alex Watson) and, in fact, Jones served Blues for almost 30 years, retiring at the outbreak of WW1.

ALEXANDER WATSON (July 1908 to June 1910)
Born: Birmingham, circa 1860. Now Deceased

Alex Watson, the son of a wealthy businessman who was working alongside his father within the context of the family company, had supported Blues since the formation of the club in 1875, but never actually played football himself, perhaps having the odd play-ground kick-about with his school pals. He was a strict person, however, who held the position of secretary-manager of the club for just two years during which time Blues finished 11th and 20th in Division Two, the latter being a particularly poor season when only eight out of 38 League matches were won and home attendances dropped alarmingly to an average of 8,921 - the lowest since 1900-01. He was not involved in football again, although he did attend matches at St Andrew's on a regular basis.

BOB McROBERTS (July 1910 - May 1915)
Until July 1910, the Blues team had been selected by a committee, usually comprising five club members, including the captain, secretary/manager and treasurer. The then chairman, Walter Hart, suggested that a full-time manager should be appointed and former goalscorer Bob McRoberts had the honour of being the first holder of the post of team manager at St Andrew's. He was in office for five years (see: elsewhere as player).

FRANK RICHARDS (May 1915-May 1923 & August 1927-July 1928)
Born: Birmingham circa 1880. Died: Birmingham circa 1963

Career: Hockley Schools, worked in Birmingham's jewellery quarter for two years (1904-06), joined the St Andrew's office staff in 1906, became secretary of club for season 1911-12, appointed Blues' secretary-manager (first time) in May 1915. Reverted back to club secretary for the 1924-25 season and then served with Preston North End as secretary-manager from May 1925 to July 1927 when he returned to Blues for a second spell in charge. He was later secretary-manager of Boscombe Athletic: July 1928 to June 1930

Although he acted as secretary-manager at St Andrew's in two spells, Frank Richards was generally regarded as an administration secretary of the club. He let his efficient trainers run the team on a day to day basis, not even discussing the signing or selling of players until the paperwork had to be completed - although he did have a say regarding team selection. Amazingly Richards forgot to enter the club into the draw for the 1920-21 FA Cup tournament and then dispatched his son, Sam, who was then assistant-secretary (and who was a long-serving member of the Blues board after WW2) to Lancaster Gate to plead for clemency, alas without success.

Honours with Blues: Second Division champions: 1921

BILLY BEER (May 1923 to March 1927)
Billy Beer played in 250 games for Blues as a wing-half before retiring. After a spell working in Australia and then as a licensee he took over as manager of Blues in 1923, acting as secretary-manager for the final two seasons (1925-27) of his four-year spell in charge (see elsewhere as player).

BILL HARVEY (March 1927 to May 1928)
One-time outside-right with the club, Bill Harvey spent only one full season looking after team affairs at St Andrew's (see elsewhere as player).

LESLIE KNIGHTON (July 1928 to August 1933)
Born: Church Gresley, Derbyshire near Burton upon Trent, 15 March 1884. Died: Bournemouth, 10 May 1959.

Career: local schoolboy football, Gresley Rovers (1900), Burton United (1901), Fazeley Swifts: Castleford Town (manager, 1904): Huddersfield Town (assistant-secretary/manager, 1909): Manchester City (assistant-secretary/manager, August 1912 to April 1919): Arsenal (manager, May 1919 to June 1925): Bournemouth & Boscombe Athletic (manager, July 1925 to July 1928), BLUES (manager, July 1928 to August 1933), Chelsea (manager, August 1933 to April 1939), Shrewsbury Town (manager, August 1945 to September 1948), thereafter golf club secretary in Bournemouth in 1950s, Portishead FC (manager, season 1952-53). Died after a short illness.

Leslie Knighton's playing days were cut short by injury, but then he joined a long and fairly successful managerial career, helping develop some fine youngsters at both Huddersfield Town and Manchester City. He struggled to keep Arsenal in the First Division, after being told by his chairman 'not to spend too much money.' Knighton did a reasonable job at St Andrew's and, indeed, his finest moment came with Birmingham when he took them to Wembley in 1931, where they were unfortunately beaten 2-1 by Midland rivals West Bromwich Albion in the FA Cup Final. He left St Andrew's for Chelsea after the London club had made him an offer he couldn't refuse.

GEORGE LIDDELL (August 1933 to September 1939)
George Liddell had long wanted to be a Football League manager and Blues obliged him in 1933 after he had made close of 350 appearances as wing-half and full-back for the club. He continued to attend matches at St Andrew's well into the 1950s (see elsewhere as player).

BILL CAMKIN (September 1939 to November 1944)
Born: Birmingham 1890. Died, Birmingham 1960. Throughout WW2, Bill Camkin was honorary Managing-Director of Birmingham (City). He looked after team affairs and took charge of running the club, allowing senior trainer George Blackburn, the former Aston Villa player, to organise training sessions and the match-to-match build-up. Camkin did an excellent job, steering Blues through a difficult period when St Andrew's was severely damaged by German bombs. In 1950 poor health forced his retirement as a Blues Director, but he continued to support the club until his death. His son, John Camkin junior, was a well-known sports journalist who later became a director of Coventry City.

TED GOODIER (November 1944 to May 1945)
Born: Farnworth, Lancashire. 15 October 1902. Died: Farnworth, 4 November 1967. Career: Brookhouse United (1919), Huddersfield Town (May 1922), Lancaster Town (August 1923): Oldham Athletic (June 1925), Queen's Park Rangers (November 1931), Watford (£1,000, June 1935), Crewe Alexandra (June 1936), Rochdale (June 1937, then a player-manager September 1938 to November 1944). Became BLUES (caretaker-manager in November 1944, then Rochdale manager (June 1945 to June 1952), Wigan Athletic (manager from June 1952 to May 1954) and finally Oldham Athletic manager (May 1954 to June 1958).
A fair-haired wing-half, 6ft 1in tall, Ted Goodier looked after Blues' team affairs for the second half of that transitional League season after WW2. In 1949 he guided Rochdale to victory in the Lancashire Cup Final over Blackpool.

HARRY STORER (June 1945 - November 1948)
Born: West Derby, Liverpool 2 February 1898. Died: Derby, 1 September 1967. Career: Heanor Secondary Modern School, then inside-forward with Heanor Wesleyans (1913), Marehay FC (1914), Codnor Park, Riddings St James FC (1916), Eastwood Bible Class FC, Ripley Town (1917): Eastwood Town, Notts County (amateur, 1918), Millwall (on trial), Grimsby Town (February 1919), Derby County (£2,500, March 1921), Burnley (£4.250,

February, 1929, retiring in May 1931), then Coventry City (manager, June 1931 to June 1945), BLUES (manager from June 1945), Coventry City (manager again, November 1948 to December 1953), Derby County (manager, June 1955 to May 1962), Everton (Scout mid-1960s). Also played cricket for Derbyshire: 1928-1936, scoring 13,513 runs including 18 centuries (average 27.63) and took more than 200 wickets, appearing in the County's championship-winning side of 1936. Harry Storer never won major honours as a player but he guided each club in managed to promotion, taking Coventry into Division Two in 1936, Blues into Division One in 1948 and Derby into Division Two in 1957. He also guided Blues to the Football League South championship and the FA Cup semi-finals in 1946. Unfortunately, after a replay, they lost to his former club, Derby County in the Cup semi-final..
A forthright character, he was the personification of traditional qualities of disciplined, economy, directness and commonsense. He came from a sporting family - his father kept goal for Arsenal and Liverpool and played cricket for Derbyshire while his uncle was a Derby County footballer and also played cricket for Derbyshire and for England.
Storer scored 63 goals in 274 appearances for Burnley and as a manager he signed one player, centre-half Martin O'Donnell, on three separate occasions - for Coventry, then Blues and finally Derby. Storer was a sharp-tongued football man with a heart of gold.

BOB BROCKLEBANK (January 1949 - October 1954)
Born: Finchley, 23 May 1908.
Died: Brixham, 3 September, 1981
Career: inside-forward with Finchley Boys, Finchley August (1925), Aston Villa (May 1929), Burnley (March 1936 to August 1945, retired as player), Chesterfield (manager, September 1945 to January 1949), BLUES (appointed in January 1949), West Bromwich Albion (coach & Scout, October 1954 to March 1955), Hull City (manager, March 1955 to May 1961), Bradford City (manager, May 1961 to October 1964 when he retired to Brixham).
One of eight brothers, Bob Brocklebank was one of Finchley's most famous players before moving into the Football League. He scored 110 goals in some 300 games for Burnley, including WW2 football, and took Blues to the FA Cup semi-finals in 1951, but also saw them relegated from First Division. Although he did not have the greatest of times as manager at St Andrew's, he did introduce some fine youngsters, including Trevor Smith, Johnny Schofield and Jeff Hall and he also secured the services of Eddie Brown, Tommy Briggs, Noel Kinsey, Roy Warhurst, Len Boyd, Gordon Astall, and Alex Govan, many of whom formed the basis of Blues great sides of the mid-1950s. He took Hull to promotion from Division Three in 1959.

ARTHUR TURNER (November 1954 to September 1958)
Arthur Turner spent 13 years with Blues, nine as a player and four as manager. He played over 300 games for Stoke before joining Blues and took the St Andrew's club back to the First Division in 1955 and to Wembley for

the FA Cup Final 12 months later. Malcolm Beard, Winston Foster, Terry Hennessey and Colin Withers were amongst his best introductions for Blues, while City's top signings included Dick Neal, Harry Hooper, Mike Hellawell and Bryan Orritt. For the last six months of his managerial career at St Andrew's, Turner was accompanied by Pat Beasley, who acted as joint-manager, an appointment that annoyed Turner because he was told, via the press and not by the club, that Beasley had been taken on. He threatened to resign but chose to stay on for the time being. After leaving Blues he took charge of Oxford United, and during his time at The Manor Ground he signed the Atkinson brothers, Graham and Ron, and he also guided the 'U's into the Football League in 1962 in place of Accrington Stanley. He then saw Oxford climb through the Divisions before quitting in 1969 after 10 years' service. He handed over the hot seat to Ron Saunders, who later became manager of Birmingham City (see elsewhere as player).

ALBERT 'PAT' BEASLEY (February 1958 to May 1960)
Born: Stourbridge, 17 July 1913. Died: Taunton, 27 February 1986.
Career: Brierley Hill & Brockmoor Schools, Cookley FC, Stourbridge, Arsenal (signed for £550 as a professional, May 1931), Huddersfield Town (May 1936), Fulham (December 1945), Arsenal (WW2 guest, season 1945-46), Bristol City (as player-manager, July 1950 to January 1958, retiring as a player in May 1952), BLUES (joint-manager in February 1958), Fulham (Scout, season 1960-61), Dover (manager, June 1961 to April 1964). Retired to live in Chard, Somerset
As a player 'Pat' Beasley represented England in one full international (v. Scotland in April 1939), won two Football League championship medals with Arsenal (1934 & 1935), collected an FA Cup runners-up with Huddersfield (1938) and gained a Second Division championship medal with Fulham (1950). As a manager, he guided Bristol City to the Division Three (South) championship in 1955.
Pat Beasley was a small, slightly built outside-left or wing-half who was reserve to Joe Hulme and Cliff Bastin at Highbury. He scored well over 75 goals in almost 500 appearances in League and Cup football before going into management. When he first arrived at St Andrew's, Beasley thought he was to be at assistant to Arthur Turner but, in fact, was made joint-manager by Blues' chairman Harry Morris, taking over as acting-manager in September 1958 and team manager in January 1959. He resigned from his position at St Andrew's in May 1960 after taking Blues to the Fairs Cup Final.

GIL MERRICK (May 1960 to June 1964)
Gil Merrick joined Blues as a professional just on the outbreak of WW2 and continued to play for the club throughout the hostilities and afterwards before retiring to become team manager. He spent almost 25 years at St Andrew's making more than 720 appearances in goal for Blues (over 170 in wartime and 551 in senior competitions). He was also capped 23 times by England after modelling himself on his childhood hero, the former Blues and England goalkeeper Harry Hibbs who

was still at St Andrew's when Merrick first signed for the club. Under Merrick, Blues' victory in the 1963 League Cup Final was the first major honour the club won (see elsewhere as player).

JOE MALLETT (July 1964 to December 1965)
Born: Gateshead, 8 January 1916.
Career: Dunston Colliery Welfare FC, Charlton Athletic (November 1935), Queen's Park Rangers (on loan, May 1937 to May 1938 - signed permanently for £800, February 1939), guested for both Fulham & West Ham United in season 1944-45, Southampton (£5,000, February 1947), Leyton Orient (July 1953), Nottingham Forest (coach, August 1954), BLUES (as coach, June 1964, team manager from July 1964, then assistant-manager until March 1970), Panionios/Greece (manager 1978 to 1973 and again from 1973 to July 1974), IF Appolon/Greece (as coach, in mid-1973 for six months), New York Cosmos/NASL (coach August 1975), Southampton (Scout, late 1970s), San Jose Earthquakes/NASL (coach 1982-83), Southampton (Scout again, based in the Midlands, mid-to-late 1980s).
Joe Mallett played as a wing-half until he was almost 40 years of age and although his career was disrupted by WW2, he still managed over 200 League appearances for Southampton. He made several useful signings for Blues but failed to get the right blend. He did well with the Athens-based Panionios club but when the military junta was overthrown in Greece, Mallett found himself under arrest for a short while.

STAN CULLIS (December 1965 to March 1970)
Born: Ellesmere Port, Cheshire 25 October 1915.
Died: Worcestershire, 27 February 2001.
Career: Ellesmere Port Council School, Bolton Wanderers (amateur, 1930), Ellesmere Port Wednesday FC, Wolverhampton Wanderers (February 1934, retiring as a player in May 1947 to become assistant-manager to Ted Vizard at Molineux). Appointed Wolves manager in June 1948, retaining that position until September 1964. Took over as manager of BLUES in December 1965 and after leaving St Andrew's in March 1970, he worked in a travel agency and later wrote a weekly column in the local Midlands sport paper, also occasionally appearing on commercial radio.
As a player, Cullis won 12 full caps for England and 20 more in Wartime football. He also played for the Football League on three occasions and skippered Wolves in the 1939 FA Cup Final. As a manager he guided Wolves to three League championships - in 1954, 1958 & 1959 - and to victory in the 1949 & 1960 FA Cup Finals. A hard-tackling, dominant defender, Cullis (who occupied the right-half and centre-half positions) played in almost 200 games for Wolves (170 in League & FA Cup) and as a manager at Molineux he bought or introduced some brilliant footballers to the club, players like Eddie Stuart, Eddie Clamp, Ron Flowers, Bill Slater, Peter Broadbent, Dennis Wilshaw, Roy Swinbourne, Norman Deeley, Ted Farmer, Jimmy Murray and Malcolm Finlayson, among others. He did remarkably well during his 16-year reign as boss of Wolves, and to a certain extent he achieved success at Blues, with semi-

final appearances in both the League Cup and FA Cup competitions in 1967 and 1968 respectively. In the mid-1950s, he brought the great European sides over to England to play under the Molineux floodlights - Honved, Spartak, Real Madrid and the likes - and it was Cullis who was certainly responsible for laying the foundation stones for Blues' 1972 promotion-winning side. He was an Army Physical Training Instructor during WW2, appearing in many representative matches at home and abroad. He was 50 years of age when he took over as manager at St Andrew's.

FREDDIE GOODWIN (May 1970 - September 1975)
Born: Heywood, Lancashire, 28 June 1933
Career: Chorlton County Secondary School, Manchester United (October 1953), Leeds United (March 1960), Scunthorpe United (player-manager, December 1964 to October 1967, retiring as a player in June 1966), New York Generals/NASL (coach, November 1967 to October 1968), Brighton & Hove Albion (manager, October 1968 to May 1970), appointed BLUES manager in May 1970, holding office for over five years. Later coach of the NASL side Minnesota Kicks (1976-79 and 1980-81). He also played cricket for Lancashire (11 matches, 27 wickets).
One of the Busby Babes, wing-half Freddie Goodwin was tall with a good technique. He came to the fore after the Munich air disaster in 1958 and played in that year's FA Cup Final defeat at hands of Bolton Wanderers. He discovered Ray Clemence when boss of Scunthorpe and held a unique post in America, coach of a team that did not exist (New York Generals), being given an air ticket to travel the world in an effort to assemble a side.
He gave a new meaning to training sessions at St Andrew's, bringing in a yoga expert, and it was Goodwin who introduced Trevor Francis to League football as a 16 year-old. In 1971-72 his leadership saw Blues regain their place back in the First Division (as runners-up). When he returned to America in 1976, he helped form that country's major at Indoor Soccer League, which is still flourishing today.

WILLIE BELL (September 1975 to September 1977)
Born: Johnston, Scotland, 3 September 1937
Career: Neilston Juniors, Queen's Park, Glasgow (1957), Leeds United (professional, July 1960), Leicester City (£40,000, September 1967), Brighton & Hove Albion (player-coach under Freddie Goodwin from July 1969, retired July 1970), BLUES (coach in August 1970, appointed manager in September 1975). Then Lincoln City (manager, December 1977 to October 1978) and Liberty Baptist College in Virginia/USA (as soccer coach 1978-80). He won two amateur caps with Queen's Park and two full Scottish international caps with Leeds United, also with Leeds he gained a Second Division championship medal in 1964, an FA Cup runners-up medal in 1965 and an Inter-Cities Fairs Cup runners-up medal in 1967.
Willie Bell, who was once a Clydeside apprentice engineer, turned down the chance to join Stoke City before going on to play in almost 300 League games as a left-back during his a very useful career (204 for Leeds).

He achieved nothing of note at St Andrew's and was sacked from his post in September 1977 after Blues' poor start to the season.
He left England to join a religious group in America.

SIR ALF RAMSEY (September 1977 to March 1978)
Born: Dagenham, Essex, 22 January 1920.
Died: Ipswich, 28 April 1999.
Career: Essex County & Beacontree High Schools, Five Elms FC (1937), Portsmouth (amateur, 1942), Southampton (amateur, 1943, professional August 1944), Tottenham Hotspur (£21,000, May 1949 - retired as player May 1955), Ipswich Town (manager, August 1955 to January 1963), England (manager, January 1963 to May 1974), BLUES (Director, January 1976, taking over as team manager in September 1977). He left the club seven months later.
A superb right-back, Ramsey won 32 full caps and one 'B' cap for England; he also made five appearances for Football League side,and gained a Football League championship medal with Spurs after winning a Second Division championship medal the season before. As a manager, he guided Ipswich Town to the League championship in 1962 after winning the Second Division title twelve months earlier in 1961 and Third Division South championship in 1957. And of course he guided England to World Cup glory in 1966.
Sir Alf Ramsey, whose name will always be associated with England winning the Jules Rimet Trophy, became the first Knight of the Realm to manage a Football League club when he took over at St Andrew's in 1977. He played over 100 games for Saints and 254 for Spurs before retiring to take over as team manager at Portman Road, bringing European football to Suffolk for the first time in that club's history. A shrewd football tactician (both as a player and manager) Ramsey was forced to quit his position as Blues boss due to poor health.

JIM SMITH (March 1978 to February 1982)
Born: Sheffield, 17 October 1940
Career: Sheffield schoolboy football, Sheffield United (amateur, July 1956, professional January 1959), Aldershot (July 1961), Halifax Town (July 1963): Lincoln City (March 1968), Boston United (player-manager 1968-72), Colchester United (player-manager, October 1972 to June 1975, retiring as a player in 1973), Blackburn Rovers (manager, June 1975 to March 1978), appointed BLUES manager in March 1978, Oxford United (manager, March 1982 to June 1995), Queen's Park Rangers (manager, June 1985 to December 1988), Newcastle United (manager, December 1988 to March 1991), Middlesbrough (coach, March to June 1981), Portsmouth (manager, June 1991 to February 1995), Derby County (manager, June 1995 to May 2001), Coventry City (assistant-manager/advisor/coach 2001-02) Portsmouth (assistant-manager 2002-03).
As a manager Jim 'Bald Eagle' Smith led Colchester to promotion from Division Four in 1974, Blues into the First Division in 1980 and Oxford to the Division Three championship and then the Division Two title in 1984 and 95 respectively, as well as seeing Queen's Park Rangers claim the runners-up prize in the League Cup

Final in 1986.

A typically hard-talking but cheerful Yorkshireman, very popular with the media, Smith played all his soccer in the Fourth Division as a no-nonsense half-back, amassing a total of 249 League appearances after failing to break into Sheffield United's first team. After retiring, he became a shrewd, intelligent manager, doing well with Boston and Colchester initially before reaching a higher standard. He bought many experienced players to St Andrew's, including Colin Todd, Frank Worthington, Don Givens, Archie Gemmill and Willie Johnston - and he also paid big fees for the Argentinian World Cup star Alberto Tarantini while also enlisting the Walsall striker Alan Buckley. Smith was sacked by chairman Keith Coombs to make way for Ron Saunders, himself a former manager of Oxford, which, ironically, was to be Smith's next club!

Smith then secured the services of John Aldridge for Oxford and later signed David Seaman from Blues when he was boss of Queen's Park Rangers. He had a tough time at both Blackburn and Newcastle, and whilst at Ayresome Park was coach under Colin Todd, a player he had signed earlier in his career when boss of Blues. Smith took Pompey to the FA Cup semi-final in 1992, seeing side lose in a penalty shoot-out to Liverpool. Smith was the first man to visit all 92 League grounds as a manager for competitive matches.

RON SAUNDERS (February 1982 to January 1986)

Born: Birkenhead, 6 November 1932.

Career: Birkenhead & Liverpool Schools, Everton (February 1951), Tonbridge (July 1956), Gillingham (£800, May 1957), Portsmouth (£8,000, September 1958), Watford (£10,000, September 1964), Charlton Athletic (August 1965), Yeovil Town (as general manager, May 1967 to late 1969), Oxford United (manager, March to June 1969), Norwich City (manager, July 1969 to November 1973), Manchester City (manager, November 1973 to April 1974), Aston Villa (manager, June 1974 to February 1982), appointed BLUES manager in February 1982; Later manager of West Bromwich Albion (February 1986 to September 1987). He came out of football on leaving The Hawthorns but returned later, albeit on a casual basis, working now as a soccer advisor as well as doing some general scouting in the Midlands area.

As a player Saunders gained England Youth international honours and as a manager, he guided Aston Villa to runners-up in Division Two and Football League championship in 1975 and 1981 respectively as well as leading them to League Cup glory in 1975 and 1977. Under his guidance, Norwich City also won the Second Division title in 1972 and finished runners-up in the 1973 League Cup Final, a similar fate suffered by his charges Manchester City in 1974 (beaten in the Final by Wolves). After relegation, he quickly guided Blues back into the top Division at the first attempt in 1985 (as runners-up) but then took West Brom down a year later! Saunders was a tough centre-forward who scored over 200 goals in almost 400 League appearances for his five major clubs, including 140 in 234 games for Pompey. He was the first person to manage three West Midlands-based Football League clubs in succession - Villa, Blues and Albion. He enjoyed great success at Villa Park, assembling a side good enough to win the European Cup in 1982 (after he had left), but thereafter never again reached the heights he had done earlier in his career both as a player and a manager. He briefly took over from former Blues man Arthur Turner at Oxford. He was a strict disciplinarian and there is no doubt that several players simply did not get on with him.

JOHN BOND (January 1986 - May 1987)

Born Colchester, 17 December 1932

Career: Colchester schoolboy football, Colchester Casuals (season 1946-47), Essex Army Cadets, West Ham United (amateur 1949, professional, March 1950), Torquay United (January 1966 to May 1969 when he retired), Gillingham (coach, season 1969-70), Bournemouth & Boscombe Athletic (manager, May 1970 to November 1973), Norwich City (manager, November 1973 to October 1980), Manchester City (manager, October 1980 to February 1983), Burnley (manager, June 1983 to August 1984), Swansea City (manager, December 1984 to December 1985), appointed BLUES manager in January 1986), Shrewsbury Town (assistant-manager, 1989, then team manager from January 1990), Shrewsbury Town (manager, January 1991 to May 1993). Represented Football League XI and toured South Africa with FA in 1956, won Second Division championship and FA Cup winners' medals with West Ham in 1958 and 1964 respectively. As manager he won promotion from Division Two and was a League Cup runner-up with Norwich City in 1975, gained promotion from Division Four (as runners-up) with Bournemouth in 1971 and saw Manchester City finish as FA Cup runners-up in 1981.

A solidly built, resourceful right-back, John Bond scored 35 goals in 428 League & Cup games for West Ham before moving to Plainmoor. He turned down a coaching job at Plymouth to manage Bournemouth, and when he left Dean Court (with his assistant Ken Brown) for Norwich, the Cherries got £10,000 in compensation. Bond seemed to have lost his touch when he joined Blues and never really settled in at St Andrew's. He quit Gay Meadow in 1993 after the 'Shrews' had failed to make the Play-offs in Division Three.

GARRY PENDREY (May 1987 to April 1989)

Garry Pendrey made more than 350 senior appearances in defence for Blues (1966-79) before leaving St Andrew's to play for West Brom - signed by Ron Atkinson immediately after his testimonial match against the Baggies! Eight years later he returned to his first football love (Blues) as manager and afterwards went into coaching with Wolverhampton Wanderers, and later Coventry and Southampton (see elsewhere as player).

DAVE MACKAY (April 1989 to January 1991)

Born: Edinburgh, 14 November 1934

Career: Edinburgh & District Schools: Slatford Athletic, Newtongrange Star FC, Heart of Midlothian (April 1952), Tottenham Hotspur (£32,000, March 1959), Derby County (£5,000, July, 1968), Swindon Town (player-manager, May 1971 to November 1972), Nottingham Forest (manager, November 1972 to October 1973, Derby County (manager, October 1973 to December 1976), Walsall (manager, March 1977 to May 1978), Al-Arabia Sporting Club/Kuwait (manager, August 1978 to 1984), Alba Shahbab/Dubai (manager, season 1986-87), Doncaster Rovers (manager, December 1987 to March 1989), appointed BLUES manager in April 1989, thereafter, FC Zamalek/Egypt, (coach, September 1991 to April 1992) - his last appointment in football.

Mackay won Scottish Schoolboy honours before going on to appear in 22 full internationals plus four at Under 23 level. He also represented a Scottish League XI on three occasions and the Football League side twice, and was named joint 'Footballer of the Year' in 1969 (with Tony Book). With Hearts Mackay twice won the Scottish League Cup, in 1955 and 1959, the Scottish Cup in 1956 and the Scottish League championship in 1958. With Spurs he gained a Football League championship medal in 1961 (the double year) and was again a League Championship winner as manager of Derby County in 1975. With Spurs he also collected three F A Cup winners' medals - 1961, 1962 & 1967 - and a Second Division championship medal with the Rams in 1969.

One of the great wing-halves of his era, Dave MacKay amassed well over 700 senior appearances as a professional, playing 416 games in the English League alone (268 for Spurs). After doing exceedingly well with Hearts and of course, Spurs, he then inspired Derby County. He succeeded Brian Clough as manager at The Baseball Ground and took the Rams to a second League title. Unfortunately he had a number of heated arguments with the owners of Blues and it was no surprise when he left St Andrew's after less than two years in office.

LOU MACARI (February 1991 to June 1991)
Born: Edinburgh, 7 June 1949
Career: St Michael's Academy, Kilwinning, Kilmarnock Amateurs, Kilwinning Rangers, Glasgow Celtic (June 1966), Manchester United (£200,000, January, 1973), Swindon Town (player-manager, July 1984 to July 1989, retiring as player in June 1986), West Ham in United (manager July 1989 to February 1990), appointed BLUES manager in February 1991). Thereafter, Stoke City (manager, May 1991 to November 1993), Glasgow Celtic (manager, November 1993 to June 1994), Stoke City (manager, October 1994 to May 1997), Sheffield United (Chief Scout, 1998), Huddersfield Town (manager, October 2000 to June 2002)

Lou Macari played for Scotland at Schoolboy and Youth team levels before gaining 24 full and two Under-23 caps. With Celtic he won two Scottish League championships in 1970 & 1972, two Scottish Cups in 1971 and 1972 and the Scottish League Cup twice, in 1972 & 1973. With Manchester United he won the Second Division championship in 1975 and the FA Cup in 1977, taking a runners-up in the later competition in 1976. As a manager Macari won the Fourth Division championship and then Third Division promotion with

Swindon in 1986 and 1987 respectively, after which he was a Leyland DAF Cup winner with Blues in 1991 and Stoke City in 1992 while also gaining promotion to Division One in 1993 with the Potters.

An all-action midfield player Macari scored his fair share of goals: 27 in 56 League games for Celtic, 78 in 329 for United and three in 36 for Swindon. In all games for United he netted 88 goals in 391 appearances and notched over 120 goals in more than 500 competitive matches in his career.

He was sacked by Swindon in 1985 after a row with Harry Gregg, but was reinstated within a week. When he took charge of West Ham he became only the sixth manager in the London club's history.

In 1990, the FA charged Macari, along with Swindon chairman Brian Hillier, of unauthorised betting on a match involving Swindon Town. He did exceptionally well when in charge at St Andrew's, leading Blues to Wembley for the first time since 1956 but resigned shortly afterwards saying that the club lacked ambition. In his first stint with Stoke he again visited Wembley but then had a rather disappointing stay with Celtic before returning to The Victoria Ground for a second spell, taking over from a fellow Scotsman, and former United colleague Joe Jordan. And when he took charge of Huddersfield he replaced Steve Bruce.

TERRY COOPER (August 1991 to December 1993)
Born: Castleford, Yorkshire, 12 July 1944.
Career: Brotherton School, Wath Wanderers, Ferrybridge Amateurs, Leeds United (apprentice, May 1961, professional July 1962), Middlesbrough (£150,000, March, 1975), Bristol City (£20,000, July 1978), Bristol Rovers (player-coach, August 1979, then player-manager, April 1980 to October 1981), Doncaster Rovers (player, November 1981 to May 1982), Bristol City (player-manager, May 1982 to March 1988, retiring as a player in May 1984; then Director of club: 1983-88), Exeter City (manager, May 1988 to August 1991), appointed BLUES manager in August 1991, also Director of club 1991-93), Exeter City (manager, January 1994-95).

An England international left-back, Terry Cooper won 20 full caps and played in the 1970 World Cup Finals. With Leeds United he was a First Division championship winner in 1969, an FA Cup runner-up in 1970, a League Cup winner in 1968, twice an Inter-Cities Fairs Cup winner in 1968 and 1971 and recipient of a runners-up medal in 1967. As a manager, he guided Exeter to the Fourth Division championship in 1990 and Blues to the Third Division runners-up spot in 1992, following up by Leading Bristol City to victory in the 1986 Freight Rover Trophy Final and then seeing the Robins claim the runners-up prize a year later.

Cooper was a fine attacking player who amassed some 350 appearances for Leeds before departing for Middlesbrough. He broke his leg at Stoke in April 1972 and it was thought that his career was over, but he fought back and was called up again by England in 1974. Under his managership, Bristol Rovers were unlucky - relegated to the Third Division in 1981 and seeing the main stand at Eastville burn down. At Bristol City, he became the first player-manager-Director of a Football League club since Vivian Woodward in the early 1900s. Blues were lucky not to be relegated in Cooper's first season at St Andrew's and following a takeover by David Sullivan, he duly quit the club after a disappointing start to the 1993-94 campaign.

BARRY FRY (December 1993 to May 1996)

Born: Bedford, 7 April 1945

Career: Bedford & District Schools, London Boys, Manchester United (professional, April 1962), Bolton Wanderers (May 1964), Luton Town (July 1965), Gravesend & Northfleet (1965-66), Leyton Orient (December, 1966), Romford (1968), Bedford Town (July 1969 to May 1972), Dunstable Town (manager, June 1973 to September 1976), Hillingdon Borough (manager, September 1976 to August 1977), Bedford Town (manager, April 1977 to August 1978), Barnet (manager, August 1978 to January 1985), Maidstone United (manager, January 1985 to July 1986), Barnet (manager again, July 1986 to April 1993), Southend United (manager, April to December 1993), appointed BLUES manager in December 1993. Became manager of Peterborough United on leaving St Andrew's in May 1996. An England Schoolboy international, Barry Fry didn't do too much as a player but as a manager he took Barnet to the GM Vauxhall Conference title in 1992, led Blues to victory in Auto-Windscreen Shield Final and to the Second Division championship in 1995.

A short and stocky inside-forward, Fry made a total of just 21 Football League appearances between 1964 and 1968, failing to make the first team at Old Trafford. He became something of a legend at Bedford Town for being too over elaborate with his free-kicks. Fry took Dunstable to runners-up spot in the Southern League (North) in 1975. And as a non-League boss he signed both Jeff Astle and George Best. He clashed several times with his Chairman at Barnet, Stan Flashman, but despite internal problems the team continued to do well. Fry had an eventful first 12 months at St Andrew's, signing and selling players galore, eventually suffering relegation from Division One but then everything went according to plan. And at the first attempt he guided Blues to promotion from the Second Division, as well as leading his team to victory at Wembley in the Auto-Windscreen Shield Final against Carlisle United.

The 1994-95 was a tension-packed from the word go. Like he had done in his first six months in charge, Fry bought several new players into the club while releasing very few in comparison...and his dealings proved to be justified at the end of the day. In fact, Fry used over 40 players in his first team in 1994-95, yet his transfer activities, his changes in style of play, his team formations, all worked out for the best. He had his differences with the club's owner, David Sullivan, and the Board of Directors, but at the end of the day he got his players to do the business where it matters most - out on the field.

TREVOR FRANCIS (May 1996 to October 2001)

Introduced to League football at the age of 16, Trevor Francis went on to have a superb playing career that spanned more than 20 years. He entered management initially 1988 with Queen's Park Rangers (whilst still an active player) and he returned to St Andrew's as boss in 1996 - some 27 years after signing for Blues as a junior straight out of his Plymouth School. Capped over 50 times by England (at senior level) Francis had the honour of scoring the winning goal in a European Cup Final (for Nottingham Forest) and he was also involved in several big-money transfers, being the first £1 million-rated footballer in Great Britain (1979). In all he scored more than 220 goals in over 750 appearances at first-class level. Unfortunately he simply couldn't win anything as a manager, especially with Blues - cursing his luck when the team lost three successive Play-off semi-finals (in 1999, 2000 & 2001) and also succumbed to Liverpool on penalties in the Worthington Cup Final of 2001. After five-and-a-half years in charge at St Andrew's he left the club on 15 October - soon to take over the reins of Crystal Palace (on 30 November), replacing Steve Bruce who, in turn was to move into his office at Blues (see elsewhere as player).

STEVE BRUCE (December 2001 to date)

Another ex-Blues player, Steve Bruce had hinted some years before that he would love to manage the club - and his wish was granted when he was handed an early Christmas present in 2001. And what a magnificent start he made (or should that be had) to his career at St Andrew's as Blues stormed through, via the Play-offs, to earn a place in the Premiership and so reclaim their top Divisional status after a break of 16 years. Vastly experienced in all aspects of the game, Bruce was a solid central defender who served, in turn, with Norwich City, Gillingham, Manchester United and Blues, amassing in excess of 900 first-class appearances and scoring 111 goals. He had brief spells as boss with Sheffield United, Huddersfield Town and at Selhurst Park before taking over the 'Blue' reins at St Andrew's (see elsewhere as player).

MANAGERIAL CHIT-CHAT

* Many assistant-managers have been employed by Blues over the years including (in A-Z order): Norman Bodell, Fred Davies (ex-Wolves goalkeeper), Don Dorman (briefly), Keith Leonard (ex-Aston Villa striker), Joe Mallett and Bill Shorthouse (ex-Wolves defender).
* Chief Scout Bill Coldwell was Blues' caretaker-manager for three months, prior to the appointment of Terry Cooper.
* Mick Mills and Jim Barron were joint caretaker-managers prior to Steve Bruce taking charge.
* Ex-Blues star Howard Kendall (with Everton in 1985) and former Blues boss Ron Saunders (twice with Aston Villa in 1975 and 1981) were both honoured with the 'Manager of the Year' award.
* Trevor Francis when boss of Queen's Park Rangers said: "I am not difficult to get on with. I'm just difficult to get to know."
* Barry Fry, when given the sack as Blues manager, left this message on his answerphone: 'Kristina (his wife) has gone shopping and I'm at the job centre looking for employment. Funny old game - isn't it.'
* Besides leading England to victory in the 1966 World Cup Final over West Germany, Sir Alf Ramsey took his

country to the quarter-final stage of that same competition (as holders) in 1970 and he also saw them gain third place in the European championships in 1968.
* Bob Brocklebank sold, transferred and/or released more than 40 players during his five years in charge at St Andrew's.
* In 1970, after manager Stan Cullis had left St Andrew's, Blues' first choice as his replacement was Brian Clough, followed by Don Revie and then Ronnie Allen. In the end they appointed Freddie Goodwin.
* If points had been awarded for performances (honours gained etc) by the team under a specific manager, then Arthur Turner (for his efforts in the 1950s) would have claimed a total of 40; Gil Merrick and Trevor Francis both 30; jovial Barry Fry 26; Harry Storer and Freddie Goodwin both 22.
* Included among Blues' players who went on to become major League club managers (other than at St Andrew's - and apart from those already mentioned/listed in the managers' section of this book) are: Ian Atkins, Bertie Auld, Noel Blake, Harold Bodle, Tommy Briggs, Kevan Broadhurst, Alan Buckley, Major Frank Buckley, Micky Bullock, John Cornforth, Alan Curbishley, Stan Davies, Neil Dougall, Greg Downs, Ronnie Fenton, Archie Gemmill, Jimmy Greenhoff, Mickey Halsall, Paul Hart, Harry Hibbs, Mike Kelly, Howard Kendall, Albert Lindon, Roy McDonough, Johnny McMillan, Dave Mangnall, Johnny Newman, Syd Owen, Jack Peart, Mick Rathbone, Bruce Rioch, Ray Shaw, Billy Steel, Colin Todd, Jack Wheeler, Peter Withe, Steve Whitton, Frank Womack, Frank Worthington and Ron Wylie. Several other ex-Blues players became managers of various non-League clubs after leaving the club.

NEW SIGNINGS....

Early in 2003 - after the transfer window was re-opened - Blues' manager Steve Bruce, besides signing the French international Christophe Dugarry (q.v), also recruited attacking right wing-back Fernando Coly, defender Matthews Upson, Polish World Cup star Piotr Swierczewski, the hard-working midfielder Stephen Clemence, left-wing-back Jamie Clapham. They all made their senior debuts for the club, along with Dugarry, in the home Premiership game against the champions Arsenal on 12 January. Unfortunately it was not a happy day for all concerned as the Gunners swept to a 4-0 victory in front of the 'live' TV cameras.
Earlier in the 2002-03 season Bruce gave a first team debut to youngster Craig Fagan.

CLAPHAM, James Richard
Left-wing-back/midfielder: 2 apps*
Born: Lincoln, 7 December 1975
Career: Tottenham Hotspur (trainee, June 1992, professional July 1994), Leyton Orient (on loan, January 1997), Bristol Rovers (on loan, March 1997), Ipswich Town (£300,000, January 1998), BLUES (January 2003).
Club honours: Ipswich: promotion to Premiership 2000.
A very important member of the first team squad at Portman Road, Jamie Clapham has a fine left-foot, loves to drive forward and enjoys shooting from distance. He made just five senior appearances for Spurs, six for

Orient, five for Bristol Rovers and well over 200 for Ipswich (14 goals scored) helping them Portman Road club reach the Premiership and play in the UEFA Cup Competitions of 2001-02 and 2002-03 before his transfer to St Andrew's.
* His father Graham Clapham, played for Shrewsbury Town and Chester.

CLEMENCE, Stephen Neal
Midfielder: one app*
Born: Liverpool, 31 March 1978
Career: Tottenham Hotspur (junior, June 1994, professional April 1995), BLUES (January 2003).
Club honours: Spurs: League Cup winners 1999
Representative honours: England (one Under-21, Schoolboy & Youth caps).
Son of the former Liverpool, Spurs and England goalkeeper, Ray Clemence, Stephen made more than 100 senior appearances during his time at White Hart Lane, helping Spurs win the League Cup at Wembley in 1999. Enthusiasm is one of his greatest assets and although plagued by injury during the 2001-02 season, having cemented himself in the London club's first team, he is now looking forward to a new challenge, that of serving Blues just as well as he did Spurs and keeping them in the Premiership.

COLY, Fernando
Right-back: one app*
Born: Dakar, 10 September 1973
Career: FC Poiters (July 1994), Chateauroux/France (August 1996), RC Lens/France (July 1999), BLUES (six-month loan spell from January 2003).
International honours: Senegal (22 full caps*)
A strong, hard-running, pony-tailed full-back who starred for Senegal in the 2002 World Cup Finals in Japan and South Korea, Ferdinand Coly was booked on his debut for Blues and later substituted. A positive footballer, he was a key member of the Lens team that finished runners-up in the French First Division in 2002 and played in four European Champions League matches before joining Blues halfway through the 2002-03 Premiership season. He scored four goals in 76 League games for Poiters, eight in 91 for Chateauroux and two in 74 for Lens.

FAGAN, Craig
Forward: 0+3 apps*
Born: Birmingham, 11 December 1982
Career: BLUES (trainee, April 1997, professional December 2000)
Promising youngster Craig Fagan was handed his senior debut by Blues as a substitute against Leyton Orient in the Worthington Cup in October 2002, later making similar appearances v. PNE (LC) and Fulham (FAC).

SWIERCZEWSKI, Piotr
Midfielder/forward: No apps*
Born: Nowy Sacz, Poland: 8 April 1972
Career: GKS Katowice (professional, April 1989), St Etienne, Olympique Marseille, BLUES (January 2003).
Club honours: Katowice: Polish League & Cup winners

1991 & 1993

Representative honours: Poland (64 full caps*)

A vastly experienced Polish international of eight years standing, Piotr Swierczewski was signed by Blues' boss Steve Bruce to strengthen the midfield department. Twice a double winner in his home country, he appeared in the 2002 World Cup Finals.

UPSON, Matthew James

Defender: one app*

Born: Stowmarket, 18 April 1979

Career: Luton Town (trainee, June 1995, professional April 1996), Arsenal (£1 million, May 1997), Nottingham Forest (on loan, December 2000), Crystal palace (on loan, March 2001), Reading (on loan November 2002), BLUES (£1 million, rising to £3 million, January 2003).

Club honours: Arsenal: Premiership winners 2002

Representative honours: England: Youth & 10 Under-21 caps.

Signed by Blues on a three-and-a-half year contract, central defender Matt Upson made 55 senior appearances for the Gunners but most of the time at Highbury he was acting as deputy to the likes of Tony Adams, Martin Keown and then Sol Campbell. A fractured fibia ruined his last season with the London club.

ROUND & ABOUT....

* In December 2002, Blues' boss Steve Bruce gave a trial to the Cameroon international Bill Tehato who was, at the time, registered with the French club, Montpellier.

* Steve Cooper, who was released by Blues back in 1984 without ever playing in the first team (at competitive level) announced his retirement from senior football in 2002 with more than 400 competitive appearances under his belt and 114 goals. He joined Blues from Moor Green in 1983 and prior to leaving St Andrew's assisted Halifax Town (on loan). He then served with Newport County, Plymouth Argyle, Barnsley, Tranmere Rovers, Peterborough United, Wigan Athletic, York City and Airdrieonians. One who got away!

* Stern John had the pleasure of scoring Blues' first goal in Premiership football - from the penalty spot against Everton at Goodison Park on 28 August 2002 (1-1 draw).

* Blues recorded their first win in the Premiership on 31 August 2002 when they defeated Leeds United 2-1 at St Andrew's in front of 27,164 fans. Paul Devlin (Blues' first at home) and Damien Johnson scored the goals.

* When Blues Beat Aston Villa 3-0 in a home Premiership game on 16 September 2002, Clinton Morrison scored the opening goal - Blues' first in the 'League' v. Villa since December 1987.

* Former Blues player Steve Whitton parted company with Colcheser in January 2003.

Nationwide
FOOTBALL LEAGUE
DIVISION 1 PLAY-OFF WINNERS 2002
BIRMINGHAM CITY F.C.